Electricity Deregulation

VOLUME IV IN THE BUSH SCHOOL SERIES IN THE ECONOMICS OF PUBLIC POLICY

Edited by James M. Griffin and Steven L. Puller

Corporate Sponsors of the Bush Advisory Board Members

Electricity Deregulation

Choices and Challenges

Edited by
James M. Griffin and Steven L. Puller

The University of Chicago Press
Chicago and London

JAMES M. GRIFFIN is the Bob Bullock Chair in Public Policy and Economics at the George Bush School of Government and Public Service at Texas A&M University. His books include *Energy, Economics, and Policy* and *OPEC Behavior and World Oil Prices.* STEVEN L. PULLER is assistant professor in the Department of Economics at Texas A&M University.

The University of Chicago Press, Chicago 60637
The University of Chicago Press, Ltd., London
© 2005 by The University of Chicago
All rights reserved. Published 2005
Printed in the United States of America

14 13 12 11 10 09 08 07 06 05   1 2 3 4 5
ISBN: 0-226-30856-1 (cloth)

Library of Congress Cataloging-in-Publication Data

Electricity deregulation : choices and challenges / edited by James M. Griffin and
    Steven L. Puller.
    p. cm. — (Bush School series in the economics of public policy ; v. 4)
    Includes bibliographical references and index.
    ISBN 0-226-30856-1 (cloth : alk. paper)
    1. Electric utilities—Deregulation—United States. I. Griffin, James M., 1941–
II. Puller, Steven L. III. Series.
    HD9685.U5E542 2005
    333.793'2'0973—dc22

                                                            2004015212

Contents

v

Introduction

A Primer on Electricity and the Economics of Deregulation

James M. Griffin and Steven L. Puller

Introduction

Until the onset of the California electricity crisis in summer 2000, all appearances were that electricity deregulation was proceeding satisfactorily and could soon be added to the list of industries successfully deregulated, including airlines, telecommunications, natural gas pipelines, trucking, and railroads. During summer 2000, the wholesale price of electricity in California shot from an average of about $30 a megawatt (MW) hour to over $150 a megawatt hour with prices in some hours reaching $750. Since the California debacle, the electricity deregulation movement has stalled. Further skepticism was fueled by the power outage in August 2003 that crippled much of the Northeast. Policymakers, consumers, producers, and academicians have been reassessing the question, "Electricity deregulation—where to from here?" This volume is intended to provide policymakers and interested citizenry with an answer to this question. It is the result of a Bush School conference on electricity deregulation in April 2003 at the George Bush Presidential Conference Center at Texas A&M University. The conference brought together the leading academic researchers, key policymakers, and influential leaders from industry.

    The contributors to this volume are to be applauded for writing very lucid, nontechnical explanations to some phenomena

1

that defy simple explanations. Even though most of the papers are by econo-mists, who by nature are enamored with mathematical equations, the contrib-utors have shown amazing restraint. But before proceeding to chapter 1, this introductory chapter provides a primer on electricity in order to explain how economists think about deregulation and to preview the contributed papers.

Electricity — A Natural Monopoly?

For over a decade, the electricity industry in the United States and elsewhere has undergone fundamental change. Markets have been created to trade wholesale power, enabling powerplant owners, energy traders, and consumers to buy and sell power on the open market. Now a company need not be a util-ity to enter the market, construct a powerplant, and sell power on the open market. In addition, many consumers are allowed to choose their own elec-tricity provider.

Today's markets for power stand in stark contrast to the structure of the industry just over a decade ago. Until quite recently, the electricity industry in the United States was typified by a number of vertically integrated compa-nies, while in Europe, state-owned enterprises were dominant. In the United States, the production, transmission, and distribution of electricity were con-solidated into vertically integrated firms that were highly regulated on the prices they could charge and investments that could be made. Both techno-logical and legal changes have contributed to restructuring of the industry.

Historically, the economic rationale for such a structure was that electric-ity production was a natural monopoly. A natural monopoly is simply the case where a single firm can produce the total market output at a lower cost than can a collection of individual competitive firms. Each sector of the industry— the generation at powerplants, the high-voltage transmission of power, and the local distribution and metering—has natural monopoly characteristics. Economies of scale in generation coupled with small localized pockets of de-mand and substantial line losses from long-distance transmission meant that generation plants were best located near individual market centers. Scale economies in transmission again supported building single high-voltage lines rather than multiple low-voltage lines. At the local distribution level, it clearly made sense to have only one local distribution grid rather than multiple lines strung about from competing generators. Thus single vertically integrated firms were ideally suited to serve the various isolated pockets of demand.

Even though a single firm may have been able to serve a market at lowest cost, there remained the problem that an unregulated monopolist would charge too high a price and produce too little, thereby sacrificing economic efficiency. Here, the standard economists' prescription—to grant single franchises and empower a regulatory commission to set prices—was widely adopted in the 1920s. While in principle there were a variety of pricing schemes a regulatory commission could employ, rate-of-return regulation often was adopted. Under rate-of-return regulation, the administered price was set so as to cover the firm's operating costs and reward its investors with a fair rate of return on the capital invested. In effect, prices were set roughly equal to average cost.

The growth in demand and technological advances presents a very different picture today. Particularly at the generation stage, there is no evidence of natural monopoly today. In 2000, U.S. per capita electricity consumption stood at 12,158 kilowatt hours per year as contrasted to only 609 per capita kilowatt hours in 1930. Besides the growth in the overall size of the market, technology has favored broader regional rather than local markets. The minimum efficient scale of new generators of several hundred megawatts or less fueled by natural gas is much smaller than the minimum efficient scale of the large thousand megawatt coal and nuclear units favored in the past. Advances in high-voltage transmission make it possible to transport electricity over a thousand miles. Sophisticated computer systems allow utilities to integrate their operations, which facilitates wholesale trading. These changes have increased the potential geographic scope of wholesale generation markets.

Several legal changes have made it possible for competition in the wholesale market of electricity generation to take off. Prior to the mid-1980s, independent power producers faced huge barriers to entry. Suppose there were a potential entrant who wanted to generate cheap power and sell it to either the local utility, another utility, or some retail customers. This potential entrant faced several problems. First, almost all end users were served by utilities who were under no obligation and had no incentives to purchase power from the entrant. Second, utilities owned the transmission network that the entrant needed to transport the power and did not have incentives to sell transmission services. A sequence of legislation and regulatory rules in the 1980s and 1990s effectively mitigated these problems and allowed both independent power producers and other utilities to compete in the merchant generation sector.[1] For this reason, when economists talk of "electricity deregulation," they are most likely talking about deregulation of the generation activity.

At the transmission stage, the case for natural monopoly and continued regulation remains relatively strong. The costs of acquiring long-distance transmission right-of-ways have been rising sharply because of increased environmental, health, and aesthetic concerns. Consequently, ownership of existing right-of-ways enjoy substantial first-mover advantages. Also, there are economies of scale in transporting electricity. The first 345-kilovolt line was built in 1953. By 2000, it was common to see lines with a rated capacity of 345 kilovolts with some as high as 750 kilovolts. Interconnected networks continue to grow and enable trading possibilities because transmission costs, while rising with distance, often only constitute a small fraction of the final retail price. Expansions of the transmission network involve substantial fixed costs that must be allocated among the many generation companies that benefit from them. And, finally, the physics of power flow create externalities and income transfers that make it problematic for the market to operate the existing transmission network or invest in new transmission assets.

At the local distribution stage, there is no opposition to the notion of natural monopoly. Imagine a local distribution network with ten different companies, each with their own distribution lines strung around on their own light poles. The fact that local distribution is a natural monopoly does not, however, preclude retail competition for consumers. Retail electricity providers can agree to supply local consumers and simply pay the local distribution company for use of the distribution grid. Likewise, retail providers can contract with generation companies, pay regulated tariffs for transmission and local distribution, and sell power to commercial, industrial, and residential end users.

Thus electricity generation and retailing would appear to be prime cases for deregulation where competitive markets could function quite satisfactorily. Deregulation could reduce operating costs of current generating plants, create incentives to invest in new efficient generating technology, and facilitate the adoption of new energy services by consumers. Thus, the standard economists' policy prescription would call for deregulation of electricity generation and retail distribution, leaving transmission and local distribution regulated.

This standard prescription is something one might hear in an undergraduate economics class. However, this prescription ignores many economic, legal, and political complications that are crucial to the success of deregulation. Deregulation does not consist of simply removing existing regulatory infrastructures. Rather, certain elements of existing regulation must be replaced with new institutions and rules designed to provide competitive and reliable electricity services. These complications and design decisions are the topics of this volume.

Design Choice for Deregulated Electricity Markets

Why is Electricity Special?

Electricity has special physical characteristics that make electricity markets different from most other commodity markets. Electrical energy is injected into the transmission grid by all generators and withdrawn by all end users. There is usually no way to identify the power generated by producer A to match with the power utilized by consumer B. One can think of the electricity grid as a big pond with producers putting water into the pond while consumers are simultaneously withdrawing water from the pond. However, the injection and withdrawal of energy must be carefully regulated. Electricity cannot be stored economically so the amount generated at every point in time must equal the amount consumed. The characteristics of the delivered power must be carefully maintained. In order to maintain the frequency within a certain narrow band of tolerance, the quantity injected must closely match the quantity withdrawn moment by moment. To extend the pond analogy, it is as if producers must fill the pond at the same rate consumers withdraw from it. The level of the pond must be nearly constant at every point in time for the system to operate properly.

Contrast this with a typical commodity market. In most markets, bilateral transactions between buyers and sellers coordinate the flow of goods, and no central coordinator is required. For example, the lettuce market has no need for central coordination. Lettuce farmers can independently contract with distributors and grocery stores to sell their produce. Adam Smith's "invisible hand" creates a decentralized coordination of supply and demand. It is true that lettuce has limited storage, so supply must roughly equal demand at each point in time. However, if too much lettuce is produced, excess supply can be freely disposed. If too little is produced, most consumers will get the lettuce they demand, but a few will substitute to other vegetables. But electricity doesn't work this way. In electricity, supply and demand imbalances cannot so easily be accommodated and could cause disruptions to the entire delivery system. A system operator must coordinate schedules of generation, load, and power flow, and balance deviations from expected supply or demand. In effect, Adam Smith's invisible hand is hardly invisible for electricity markets. As we discuss later, the central coordinator's job is complicated by the highly variable nature of electricity demand, which varies substantially from one hour to the next. Air conditioning in the summer and electric heating in the winter can cause demand or "load" to vary by well over 50 percent over a twenty-four-hour period in some parts of the United States. Anticipating the load requirements over a twenty-four-hour period is a nontrivial task given the variability in temperatures.

These characteristics have implications for both the type of markets that need to be organized and the competitiveness of those markets. The system operator must keep account of all trades *before they occur* to ensure that supply and demand will balance and create markets to adjust for contingencies such as a generating unit or transmission line going down. Restructured power systems require markets for reliability services such as generating units that can quickly increase or decrease power to adjust for unexpected demand shocks or outages. These reliability services are called ancillary services.

Restructured power systems will require the market to provide adequate reserve capacity and ensure that extra generating capacity is always available so that the lights stay on. Reserve capacity protects against risks posed by events such as unexpectedly hot summers, major plant outages, or dry years with low hydroelectric supply. Because blackouts can impose large externalities on the economy, the provision of reserve capacity has important public good characteristics. If there is no separate market for extra installed capacity, private generators are not likely to build sufficient capacity because the additional units would rarely be utilized and, when utilized, undercompensated by the market for energy. Because generating plants can take several years to build, special markets for installed reserve capacity may be necessary to incentivize the construction of generators that only operate during a limited number of critical hours each year. This problem is analyzed by Shmuel Oren in chapter 10.

The central coordinator can take an active or semipassive role in the market. At one extreme, the central coordinator can function as a market maker and serve as a central exchange for most transactions as in the initial U.K. and California markets. At the other extreme, as in Texas, the operator accepts schedules of generation and load from parties that negotiate trades bilaterally. In this more passive role, the central coordinator acts solely as a system operator to ensure that the system remains in balance. However, even in this semipassive role, the system operator conducts a real-time market for energy and ancillary services to ensure the system is balanced within operational parameters. These markets take the form of auctions. In these auctions, the system operator accepts the lowest-cost bids to ensure supply equals demand subject to constraints on the operating characteristics of the generators and the flow of power through the transmission grid.

This task of centrally coordinating the market is further complicated by the fact that trades are location specific. A local utility withdraws energy from the power grid at specific locations, and generators inject energy at specific locations. The "transportation system" for electricity is more complex than the

Figure 1. Supply and demand in a three-node world

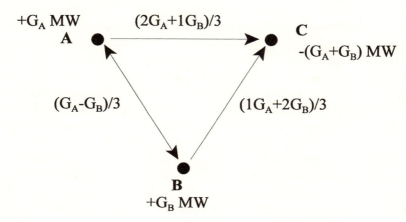

$+G_A$ MW
A $(2G_A+1G_B)/3$ C
$-(G_A+G_B)$ MW

$(G_A-G_B)/3$ $(1G_A+2G_B)/3$

B
$+G_B$ MW

transportation of other commodities. In particular, the physical laws of electricity known as Kirchhoff's laws govern how electrons flow in a transmission grid. These laws of electron flow imply that an injection or withdrawal of energy from any point in the network affects the system at every other point. These network externalities have important consequences for both the technical operation of the network and the efficiency of the market in promoting optimal incentives for the efficient operation and investment of generation and transmission assets.

To see a simple example of the flow of power on a transmission grid, consider the network depicted in figure 1. Suppose the transmission network has three nodes with generators (supply) at nodes A and B and load (demand) at node C. G_A MW are injected at node A, G_B MW are injected at node B, and load withdraws $(G_A + G_B)$ MW at node C. For simplicity, assume that each line is equal length and has the same electrical impedance (resistance).[2] Thus, for flows from node A to node C, the impedance along the direct path line AC is half the impedance along the indirect path of lines AB and BC. Kirchhoff's laws dictate that power flows inversely proportional to impedance. Therefore, if A injects 1 MW, 2/3 MW flows across line AC, while 1/3 MW flows across lines AB and BC due to differences in impedance. Similarly, if B injects 1 MW, 2/3 MW flows across BC and 1/3 MW flows across BA and AC. On net, the flows are 1 MW across line AC, 0 MW across line AB, and 1 MW across line BC.

If each transmission line has unlimited capacity, various combinations of generation by generator A and generator B can satisfy demand at node C. But because lines have finite capacity, the feasible combinations of generation are restricted. Suppose demand at node C is 10 MW. Additionally, suppose that the capacity of the line between nodes A and C is 4 MW. This transmission capacity will restrict the feasible sets of generation because $(2G_A + 1G_B)/3 \leq 4$. Generator A will be limited in its possible generation because feasible combinations of generation are only ones where demand equals supply $(G_A + G_B = 10)$ and the transmission constraint is not violated $([2G_A + 1G_B]/3 \leq 4)$. By solving the system of two equations and two unknowns, one can see that G_A cannot exceed 2, and G_B cannot be less than 8.

As a consequence, transmission constraints affect prices and the level of competition in auctions for power. Let both generators have enough generation capacity to supply the entire market (10 MW). Suppose generator A has a marginal cost of $20 and generator B has a marginal cost of $30. First, suppose that all transmission lines in the network have unlimited capacity. Assume the market is perfectly competitive, and both generators bid their marginal costs. Because it is the low bidder, generator A will produce all 10 MW, and the equilibrium price for power at node C is $20. Note that if there were demand for power at nodes A or B, the delivered price also would be $20.

Now assume the transmission capacity of line AC is 4 MW. Additionally, assume that both generators bid their marginal cost. The least-cost allocation of production that satisfies the transmission constraint is for generator A to produce 2 MW and generator B to produce 8 MW. Generator A would like to ship more across line AC, but the transmission capacity constraint generates scarcity rents. Generator A is willing to supply energy (at node A) for $20, yet the capacity constraint implies that some of generator B's $30 power must be purchased at node C. If line AC is congested, for one more MW to be delivered to node C, generator B must produce 2 more MW, and generator A must produce 1 less MW. Therefore, the price of power at node C is $2 \times \$30 - 1 \times \$20 = \$40$. However, the price is $20 at node A and $30 at node B. This form of pricing is called *nodal pricing* and leads to prices that vary by location when transmission constraints bind.

The story gets even more complicated if generators are not perfectly competitive and behave strategically. For example, generator B may recognize that its generation is necessary for load of 10 MW to be feasible and bid a price as high as is allowed. Thus, transmission constraints can create localized pockets of market power and, if generators own the transmission grid, will have no incentives to alleviate congestion.

This simple example illustrates several important points about the effect of the transmission grid or, more generally, the topology of the network on the operation of power markets. Power flows throughout the transmission grid rather than simply between two contracting parties. This is not the case for commodities that are transported by, say, trucks, where the transport of one firm's output often has no significant effect on the transport of another firm's output. The ability for a particular generator to send power through a transmission network is affected by both the amount of generation by other firms as well as by the capacity of transmission lines throughout the system. These bottlenecks affect the short-run efficiency of an auction market by creating local market power and impact the long-run incentives for investment.

Also, the amount of power that a generator can inject or a utility can withdraw at a given node varies over time in unpredictable ways if generators' outputs vary, plants suffer outages, or transmission lines are derated. As a result, prices at different locations are stochastic. The possibility that the price of electricity varies across location creates basis risk that parties on either the buy or sell side may wish to hedge against in a futures market. Hedging instruments need to be sufficiently sophisticated to allow for hedging at different locations on the transmission grid. One possibility is to establish tradeable property rights for use of the transmission grid. However, a system of transmission rights has complications. The definition of such rights is complicated because electricity flows according to Kirchhoff's laws (rather than how we tell it to). Also, if they are owned by a generating company that has local market power, the rights may exacerbate market power and create productive inefficiencies.[3]

The locational pricing of power and the design of transmission rights have important effects on investment in new generating plants. The technique of defining prices that vary by location in more complicated grid networks is both theoretically and practically challenging. If those prices are not defined in a way that provides the proper investment signals, the market may get new investment in the wrong locations while keeping old, inefficient plants that should be mothballed or abandoned. This lesson has been learned in several markets that have restructured. William Hogan discusses locational pricing and transmission rights in chapter 9.

Finally, the interaction between generation and transmission can hamper the ability of markets to yield the optimal level of investment. Generation and transmission assets can be both complements and substitutes. Additional transmission capacity can allow a generator to supply more power to the grid (e.g., in the preceding scenario, expanding the capacity of line AC allows generator A to produce more power). But additional transmission also can make a generator unnecessary if it allows power to be transported from a lower-cost generator. Generator A would have incentives to expand the transmission capacity if it owned the transmission network, but generator B would resist grid expansion if it owned the network. The externalities between generation and transmission are one reason that it is difficult for a market with vertically integrated firms in generation and transmission to align private and social incentives to invest optimally in new generation and transmission capacity.

Transaction Cost Considerations: The Case for Vertical Integration

The preceding discussion of how a market for power generation might function suggests that power-generating firms should operate independently of firms that own the transmission network. Otherwise, monopolistic abuses may arise with a vertically integrated firm having no incentive to eliminate transmission bottlenecks. But under regulation, virtually all power producers were vertically integrated. Was there a reason for this? Before embracing deregulation for generation and retailing and abandoning regulation with vertical integration, economists should not forget to ask whether transaction cost economics has anything to add to the dialogue.

The choice of deregulating electricity generation means that previously vertically integrated firms from generation through to local distribution will now be replaced by market transactions instead of intra-firm transfers. Transaction cost economics asks us to compare the efficiency of inter-firm transactions versus intra-firm transactions.

The writings of Oliver Williamson provide a clear framework for understanding how vertical integration among the three stages evolved.[4] In situations of long-lived, transaction-specific assets,[5] the market responds through long-term contracts or vertical integration to reduce transaction costs. Transaction-specific assets are those like a generation plant and an adjacent transmission line dedicated to moving the plant's output to the market. Both the plant and the transmission line are linked in a symbiotic relationship and would have little value without the other. Imagine separate owners of the generation plant and the transmission line. Both find themselves in a small numbers bargaining relationship and cannot simply walk away to another supplier. To avoid problems of holdup, they are likely to negotiate a long-term contract stipulating transmission charges, line flow rates, performance criteria, and other guarantees before embarking on such large investments. Obviously, if we assume costless enforcement, long-term contracts work fine as long as the two parties can enumerate the various situations they are likely to find themselves in and the obligations for each party. But as Williamson (1975) points out, economic agents have "bounded rationality," and contracts are not costless to enforce. In this situation, vertical integration may reduce transaction costs because within a firm, incentives are mutually aligned, and various sharing rules between the generation and transmission divisions can be resolved at lower costs.

Another feature of a vertically integrated firm is that it internalizes some of the externalities that would otherwise fall on third parties. To two parties engaged in a bilateral transaction, one party can take actions to avoid costs of x on himself and in turn impose costs of $x + y$ on the second party. In effect, the first party imposes an externality on the second party. While long-term contracts in principle also can avoid inefficient outcomes, vertical integration seems ideally suited for internalizing certain types of externalities. As previously described, we see that capacity constraints on the transmission network can impose substantial external costs or benefits on generating plants located elsewhere on the system.

Given the extreme amount of long-lived, transaction-specific assets in the electric utility industry, it is not at all surprising that regulated firms evolved as vertically integrated firms. It evolved exactly as Williamson's theory would suggest. The question now is what effect will deregulation have if market transactions between generation and transmission replace intra-firm transactions? To economists who downplay the importance of transaction costs, their answer is "none"—market transactions will have the same or better efficiency characteristics than transactions under vertical integration. Still others may argue that vertical integration was critical for the industry in its formative years, but now as a mature industry, market transactions between the generation/transmission nexus may well be adequate given the large existing infrastructure. In contrast, a skeptic about the wisdom of deregulation might argue that vertical integration economizes on transaction costs, and deregulation faces two serious problems. First, if deregulation is coupled with vertical disintegration, significant transaction cost inefficiencies will be lost. Second, if deregulation proceeds with generation companies continuing to own transmission facilities, their regulated transmission business can enable their generation facilities to exercise market power in specific locations.

Ultimately, the performance of a deregulated, vertically disintegrated market structure versus a regulated, vertically integrated structure hinges on which institutional framework provides the best coordination features in assuring adequate expansion of generation capacity and the transmission network at the lowest cost. Both structures must solve the coordination problem of efficiently locating new generating plants and transmission lines. The solutions provided by the two structures are likely to differ in terms of the location of the capacity expansion and the amount of new capacity added. Proponents of deregulation point to the existing transmission network as a Balkanized system tied to the service areas of the incumbent companies. To them, deregulation is likely to result in a more interconnected transmission network. In contrast, the skeptic would argue that it is not clear that deregulation will result in sufficient vertical disintegration to avoid market power problems, and it is not clear that the coordination problem will be solved efficiently by markets.

Susceptibility to Huge Price Volatility and Market Power

Price Volatility Is to Be Expected

Travelers to Europe are familiar with the high-season and low-season rates offered on hotels and airfares. Indeed seasonal variation in prices is quite common for commodities such as fruits and vegetables, gasoline, and heating oil. Price volatility in a deregulated electricity market (even a perfectly competitive one) will make the volatility in these other markets appear small by comparison. The explanation is simple. Demand during peak periods crosses the supply curve in the upward sloping section of the supply curve while off-peak demand crosses the supply curve in the highly elastic portion of the supply schedule, producing a much lower off-peak price. The extent of price variability depends on the following three factors: (1) the magnitude of the demand shift between peak and off-peak periods, (2) the price elasticity of demand, and (3) the elasticity of supply over the relevant range.

Figure 2 shows two demand schedules, a peak demand schedule and an off-peak demand schedule, and a single supply schedule for the Pennsylvania, New Jersey, and Maryland (PJM) market.[6] The supply schedule is the marginal cost of generating electricity from a variety of technologies. In a typical power system, these technologies may include generators fueled by nuclear, coal, natural gas, other petroleum products, hydroelectric, wind, and geothermal resources. The PJM system depicted in figure 2 shows the capacity of various generation technologies ranked from lowest marginal cost to highest. In PJM, there is a small amount of very low-cost hydroelectric capacity followed by nuclear and coal-fired capacity. The next units are efficient natural gas generators followed by less-efficient oil and gas peaking units. Each technology spins a turbine and generates mechanical energy by either burning a fuel that makes steam or a hot stream of gas or by using renewable resources such as falling water or wind. This mechanical energy is converted into electrical energy and injected into the transmission grid.

Figure 2 also depicts two hypothetical demand schedules. Both demand schedules are highly price inelastic because electricity does not have many short-run substitutes, and few consumers face the real-time wholesale price

Figure 2. Competitive supply and demand in Pennsylvania–New Jersey–Maryland (PJM)

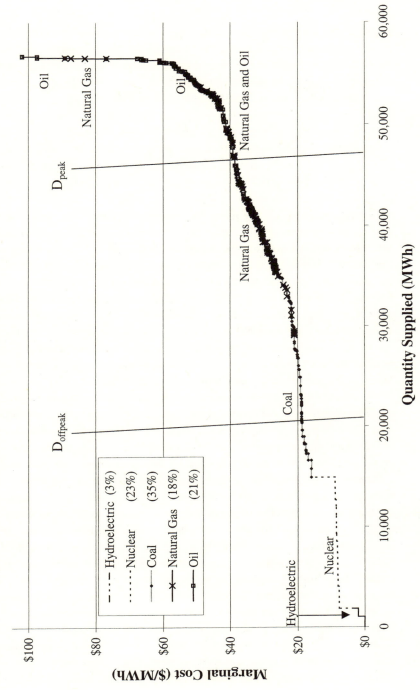

Source: Mansur (2001) and PJM data.

anyway. The peak demand schedule, D_{peak}, reflects demand on a hot summer afternoon when demand intersects the competitive supply curve at a price of about \$40/MW. In contrast, the off-peak demand period, $D_{offpeak}$, reflects demand in the middle of the night. Off-peak demand intersects competitive supply at a price of about \$20/MW. The reader can easily verify that the price variability between the off-peak price and the peak price increases for (1) greater displacements between peak and off-peak demand and (2) the less price elastic (in absolute value) are the supply and demand curves. As shown in figure 2, price volatility increases dramatically when the peak demand schedule crosses the supply curve near the vertical section or perfectly inelastic portion of the supply curve.

In a deregulated electricity market, the public should expect substantial price volatility because all of the conditions producing volatility are present in the case of electricity. First, peak and off-peak demand differ considerably. For example, in PJM in 2000, demand ranged from just above 18,000 MW to just below 50,000 MW. Air-conditioning in the summer and home electric heating in the winter produce a highly seasonal pattern of demand by residential and commercial users. Demand also follows distinct daily patterns. Because of the wide variability of demand, off-peak demand only requires the use of low-cost baseload supply. Off-peak customers operate in the highly price elastic range of the supply curve so that even if off-peak demand rises or falls by 10 percent, the effects on prices are minimal.

A second feature contributing to price volatility is the extremely price inelastic range of the supply curve during peak demand periods. At any point in time, the existing stock of generation equipment places a physical limitation on the ability to generate additional electricity. When demand approaches these constraints and it is necessary to start up high-cost generators, the resulting competitive price can be quite high. Prices must rise sufficiently high to compensate the less-efficient generators that only operate select hours of the year for their annual capital and maintenance costs. As noted earlier, a restructured market must provide the necessary capacity to meet these peaks in demand.

The third feature exacerbating the price volatility is the extreme short-run price inelasticity of demand. In the long run, when residential consumers have the ability to buy higher-efficiency appliances, the price elasticity of demand shows considerable responsiveness, ranging between 0.7 and 1.0.[7] But in the short run, it is a different story. In the short run, the stock of electricity-consuming equipment is fixed. The only question is what will be its usage rate, which in part depends on the price of electricity. Clearly, for many appliances, such as the microwave, electric oven, television, or computer, consumers are likely to be extremely price insensitive. For other uses, such as the thermostat setting on the air-conditioner or the time of day one operates the dishwasher, washing machine, or dryer, consumers can move demand out of the peak period into the off-peak period or perhaps choose to use less total electricity. Likewise, industrial users can move demand out of peak periods into off-peak periods by rescheduling downtimes and energy-intensive operations.

Yet another factor contributing to the extreme short-run price inelasticity of demand is that almost all retail consumers face a constant price of electricity that does not vary as cost varies. Under rate-of-return regulation, consumers pay the average cost of generation, which is typically flat over broad ranges of output. Indeed, regulators made little effort to distinguish between costs incurred during peak and off-peak periods. Figure 3 superimposes a hypothetical average cost curve on a marginal cost curve resembling the one in figure 2. Under rate of return regulation, consumers would pay a single price equal to average costs weighted over the year. Thus the price consumers pay, P_{AC}, which applies to both peak and off-peak periods, does not reflect the true social cost of power. There is no incentive to move consumption out of peak periods to off-peak periods and thereby conserve on peaking capacity. Many analysts advocate real-time pricing in which consumers pay prices tied to the hourly wholesale price. This would incentivize customers to move consumption out of peak to off-peak periods and thereby economize on system-wide capacity. Real-time pricing will send price signals that will evoke some price

Figure 3. Prices under average cost and marginal cost pricing

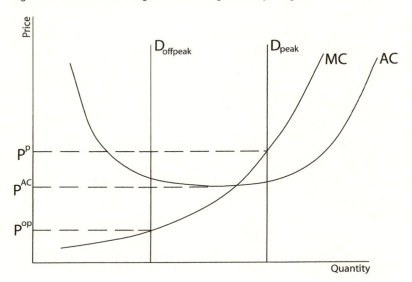

elasticity. Not all consumers will necessarily prefer real-time pricing because it is costly to monitor these prices and adjust consumption. For those who may benefit from real-time pricing, retail prices (on the margin) need to be as volatile as wholesale prices. However end-use customers can sign long-term contracts to hedge against variability in electricity bills, as Severin Borenstein explores in chapter 8.

Market Power and Price Volatility

The previous section explained that even in a perfectly competitive deregulated market, substantial wholesale price volatility is to be expected. Interestingly, these factors that naturally produce price volatility may also produce market power, which only exacerbates the price volatility. Market power is frequently measured by the ability to systematically charge a price in excess of the firm's marginal costs. Figure 4 illustrates how a generating company during peak demand periods is able to exercise market power. Total demand for electricity (D_{market}) is highly inelastic and would be perfectly inelastic if no consumers face the real-time wholesale price. Consider the decision of a par-

Figure 4. Exercising market power

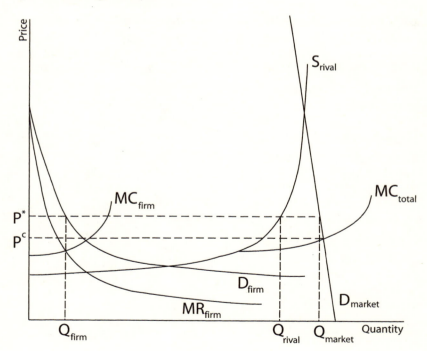

ticular firm choosing how much to bid. Suppose for simplicity that all other firms are perfectly competitive and supply according to their aggregate marginal cost (S_{rival}). Then the firm faces a individual demand function (D_{firm}) given by the difference between the total demand, D_{market}, and supply by rivals, S_{rival}. Notice that rivals can supply the entire market but only if the price is very high. If the firm wants to maximize profits in that particular hour, it will choose the price corresponding to the quantity where its marginal revenue (MR_{firm}) equals its marginal cost (MC_{firm}). This leads to an equilibrium price (P^*) above marginal cost. The market is not economically efficient because the firm has some low-cost capacity that is not utilized while higher-cost capacity is being utilized by the rivals. Alternatively, if the firm had behaved competitively, its marginal cost curve would be added to rivals' supply function, giving a total supply curve MC_{total} and a competitive equilibrium price of P_c—well below P^*.

This example can be generalized to multiple firms exercising market power. Economists use the Lerner index (L) to measure the degree of market power.

$$(1) \quad L = \frac{(P - MC)}{P},$$

where P is price and MC refers to marginal costs. The Lerner index shows the markup above marginal costs measured relative to the good's price. The Lerner index has the nice property of equaling zero when price equals marginal costs—indicating the absence of market power. Indeed, a value of zero implies a perfectly competitive market. At the other extreme, a monopoly with the ability to set price far in excess of marginal costs will have a Lerner index closer to one.

If an individual firm maximizes profit as depicted in the preceding, it turns out that the Lerner index varies inversely with the elasticity of demand (ε_i) facing the firm i.

$$(2) \quad L_i = \frac{1}{\varepsilon_i}$$

In turn, the firm's price elasticity of demand, (ε_i), depends on the (absolute value of) market elasticity of demand, (ε_d), the elasticity of supply from other firms, (ε_s), the firm's market share, (S_i), and the market share of other firms, (S_o), as follows:

$$(3) \quad \varepsilon_i = \left(\frac{1}{S_i}\right)\varepsilon_d + \left(\frac{S_o}{S_i}\right)\varepsilon_s$$

Applying a little arithmetic to equation (3) and then plugging into the firm's elasticity of demand in equation (2) leads to some very interesting observations about market power. For example, let us consider the value of the Lerner index for a market with a dominant firm who has a 10 percent market share. Normally, one would not think of a market with the dominant firm possessing a 10 percent market share as being able to exercise significant market power. That is surely the case when one applies demand and supply elasticities relevant for many commodity markets. Suppose the market demand elasticity is 1 and the supply elasticity from the other firms to be 2, the dominant firm's elasticity is 28, which translates into a Lerner index of 0.036. A Lerner index of 0.036 is so small as to be almost negligible and indistinguishable from 0— the Lerner index of a perfectly competitive firm. If the dominant firm were to withhold 10 percent of its output (1 percent of market output), the market price would rise by 0.36 of 1 percent! Withholding such output would not be profitable because it would lose the profit on the last 10 percent of output while getting only a slightly higher price on the first 90 percent of its output.[8]

But now consider demand and supply elasticities relevant in electricity markets, especially during high-demand hours. Suppose the demand elasticity is 0.1, indicating a very inelastic market demand response to higher prices. Also, assume the dominant firm finds itself operating in the very inelastic range of the supply curve ($\varepsilon_s = 0.1$) as shown in figure 4 when firms are operating near the engineering capacity limits. Now suddenly, the dominant firm's elasticity of demand becomes 1.9 (in contrast to 28), and the Lerner index shoots up to 0.53. In this case, a firm with a market share of 10 percent can withhold 10 percent of its production (1 percent of total production) and raise the market price by 5.7 percent! Even though the firm loses the incremental profit on the last 10 percent of its output, it earns a 5.7 percent higher price on the first 90 percent of its output. In this situation, withholding output is likely to be a profitable strategy.[9]

The preceding calculation reveals a very important fact about figure 4 and electricity markets. When electricity firms face very inelastic market demand schedules and find themselves operating near engineering capacity as during peak demand periods, even firms with a 10 percent or smaller market share will have strong incentives to withhold production. During peak demand periods, the price spike that would occur under perfect competition will be exacerbated by firms unilaterally withholding capacity. This is a very surprising result because most market structures with firms controlling 10 percent or less of the market are considered workably competitive markets, and mergers involving such firms are routinely approved.[10]

Economists who design restructured electricity markets have offered several policy prescriptions to mitigate these incentives to exercise market power. Two of the most popular can easily be illustrated in this context. They are real-time pricing and long-term contracts. As explained in Severin Borenstein's chapter, real-time pricing requires some fraction of consumers to face the real-time wholesale price of power. When prices spike, consumers are aware of such increases in real time and can respond by decreasing consumption or shifting consumption to off-peak periods. Although real-time metering equipment is relatively rare in the United States, Borenstein's chapter shows that the costs of installing these meters is low compared to the potential benefits. Adopting real-time pricing would make the elasticity of market demand ε_d larger (in absolute value), which would reduce the firm's market power as measured by the Lerner index.

As discussed by James Bushnell in chapter 6, economists suggest that electricity generating firms be required to sign long-term contracts—selling a substantial fraction of their power at a predetermined price instead of selling it all in the spot market. Suppose that half of a firm's output is sold under long-term contracts and half is sold on the spot market. When a firm considers withholding 10 percent of its output to raise the spot price, it will only earn the higher price on $90 - 50 = 40$ percent of its output rather than a full 90 percent of output. Substantial portions of production under long-term contract will dramatically reduce incentives to withhold.

One final issue that confronts regulatory agencies today is how to best respond to volatile prices. As one politician has noted, it is very difficult to sell electricity deregulation to constituents by offering to "subject voters to market prices." Highly volatile prices are likely to evoke a knee-jerk response by regulators to change market rules and reduce the volatility. Should market rules change dynamically as deregulation evolves? There exists a tradeoff in changing market rules. On one hand, there is much to be learned about the best way to design such markets and which rules are likely to make the market most competitive. This suggests that rules should evolve and regulators should have flexibility to adopt (presumably) better rules. On the other hand, uncertainty over the future rules of the game has its costs. Regulatory uncertainty can stymie investment, and better investment is the major theoretical upside of restructuring. Economists generally believe that uncertainty about the future competitive environment will dampen investment because choosing to make an investment is irreversible and forgoes the option value of making another decision later. However, the practical effect of regulatory uncertainty in electricity is not clear. One of the largest waves of new proposed powerplants occurred during the California crisis when prices were high but so was uncertainty about the future of restructuring.

There are a host of regulatory uncertainties that surround restructuring and affect investment. In the current context, a source of uncertainty that needs to be resolved is when prices should be allowed to go high. Consider two situations that could occur in a restructured market:

Situation 1: During periods when electricity demand is high and there are few additional supplies, generating firms exercise their potential for market power by bidding above the marginal cost of production.

Situation 2: Electricity demand is near the system capacity, yet firms utilize all available capacity at prices very close to marginal cost, and because expensive peaking units are called, the spot price is high.

These two situations call for very different regulatory responses. Regulators should mitigate attempts to exercise market power (situation 1) because it generates inefficiencies in production and leads to high prices for consumers. However, regulators should not interfere with the price-setting process in situation 2 because those prices signal scarce generation capacity and signal the value of new investment. Unfortunately, these two situations may be observationally equivalent to the regulator. The regulator sees high load and high prices but does not have sufficiently detailed information to determine if the prices reflect market power or true scarcity. And even if economic analysis can separate between the two situations, politics may not.

This complicated problem combined with the fact that the regulator may have no ability to commit to a set of rules for the foreseeable future generates a great deal of uncertainty to potential investors. Such regulatory uncertainty is one argument in favor of adopting a competition policy that mitigates market power by regulating the structure of the market (through divestiture or mandatory forward contracts) rather than regulating individual bidding behavior or instituting "good behavior" clauses.

The Political Economy of Electricity Deregulation

You are soon to embark on a tour through the various landscapes of electricity deregulation, but before doing so, it is important to remember that policy decisions may occur in a technical vacuum, yes, and even in an economic vacuum. But never do they occur in a political vacuum. The fact that the restructuring of electricity markets has been characterized as *deregulation* is in fact a misnomer. Because in recent years the word *regulation* conjures up many images of wasteful bureaucracies standing in the way of innovation, it is not surprising that proponents of restructuring electricity markets call it *deregu-*

lation. After you have finished the guided tour of this volume, it will be clear that as the restructured electricity industry makes greater use of markets, regulatory oversight will continue even for the deregulated generation and retail sectors. Transmission and local distribution will remain heavily regulated.

In assessing the success of electricity restructuring, the metric with which it is compared to matters greatly. Compared either to a model of perfectly competitive markets or to the model of omniscient regulators overseeing the market, it is clear that all examples of restructuring will fail. But this is the wrong comparison. The relevant comparison is the previous world left behind. But the world left behind is very different in Europe and Latin America than the various states within the United States. In the United Kingdom, as Richard Green's chapter explains, electricity generation was formerly a state-owned enterprise. In the United Kingdom, electricity deregulation was a transition from a public enterprise to private firms subject to loose regulation of prices. In contrast, electricity deregulation in the United States has not involved privatization but instead has involved releasing privately owned electricity generators from rate-of-return regulation and allowing them to earn market-based rates. To the extent that public enterprises were less efficient than their privately owned but regulated U.S. counterparts, the benefits of deregulation are likely to be much greater in Europe and Latin America than in the United States.

Another advantage to deregulation in Europe and Latin America is that by eliminating the public enterprises, policymakers are able to wipe the blackboard clean (or at least cleaner than in the United States). Public enterprises can be privatized and divided into pieces suitable for the promotion of competition. In the United States, the restructuring of the industry must work within the constraints of the existing private ownership of generation, transmission, and distribution assets. A classic example of vestiges from the past constraining the choices for deregulation in the United States arise from "stranded costs." Stranded costs are the costs of past investments in generation or contracts to buy power at high prices. For example, in the 1970s a number of utilities invested in nuclear plants with large cost overruns. These costs were primarily fixed costs that were embedded in regulated electricity rates that ended up being much higher than wholesale prices prevailing in the late 1990s. Because these investments were made in a regulated environment that assured investors a fair return on capital, these utilities demanded recovery of stranded costs as a condition for their acceptance of deregulation. In contrast, the legacy of past regulation was not as complicated in the United Kingdom—electricity assets were publicly owned and could be sold to private firms. But in the United States, the price of political support of the incumbent regulated utilities for deregulation depended critically on whether they could recover these stranded costs in future fees.

If the blackboard is already looking muddled for the U.S. deregulation experiment, we have yet another factor to add—consumer benefits. To rally consumer support for deregulation, there must be *immediate* evidence of consumer benefits in the form of lower prices. Obviously, policymakers have a problem. Utilities want recovery of stranded costs, which necessarily raises retail prices. Yet consumers want lower prices. Indeed, if utilities were not able to recover stranded costs, there would be a deregulation dividend for consumers. The problem becomes how to wring enough short-run efficiency gains out of a deregulated generation sector to pay stranded costs and at the same time provide consumers with rate reductions. This is a tall order, especially because any big cost savings are likely to be realized in the long run. In the long run, firms will invest in lower-cost generation technology and adopt lower-cost operating procedures, as Catherine Wolfram discusses in chapter 5. Also, if real-time pricing is implemented, demand can be shifted out of the peak periods and very high-cost peaking capacity can be reduced, enabling a much more efficient generation sector. But changes like this will take time, and consumer support for deregulation depends on immediate benefits.

Finally, U.S. restructuring is complicated by overlapping regulatory jurisdictions. Regulatory control is divided (sometimes not clearly) between federal, state, and local authorities, which can impair the coordination of markets and lead to power struggles. Two examples are noteworthy. Part of the blame for the California crisis can be attributed to the passing of the hot potato back and forth between the state of California and the Federal Energy Regulatory Commission (FERC). Frank Wolak discusses this example of regulatory failure in his chapter on the California crisis. As another example of divided authority, the pricing of power in wholesale markets lies largely in the purview of FERC, while retail pricing is governed by state public utility commissions. This can lead to problematic disconnects between the price signals sent by wholesale and retail markets. Interestingly, Texas does not have divided state and federal authority because the grid is not interconnected with the rest of the U.S. grid. It remains to be seen if Texas will overcome the potholes on the restructuring path more effectively than states with divided jurisdiction.

In sum, the political economy of electricity deregulation is far more complicated in the United States than elsewhere for a variety of reasons. First, unlike Europe's experience with public enterprises, it is less clear that the regulated, privately owned utilities in the United States were in need of fixing. Second, deregulation in the United States was constrained by existing patterns of vertical integration between distribution, transmission, and generation. The vestiges of that system cannot be erased. Third, both to avoid lawsuits and garner support for deregulation among incumbent utilities, stranded-cost recovery had to be an important component of any deregulation plan. Fourth, policymakers face the difficulty of producing immediate consumer benefits to obtain public support for deregulation and still paying the stranded-cost dividend to incumbent utilities. Paradoxically, to the extent that there are substantial benefits to consumers, these gains are likely to be realized in the long run. While the political economy of electricity deregulation is another whole monograph in itself, the reader can look forward to Paul Joskow's chapter, which enumerates many of these issues.

Outline of This Volume

In chapter 1, Paul Joskow highlights the critical policy questions in electricity deregulation. As discussed previously, electricity deregulation is not a hands-off process—it requires a substantial amount of design and regulatory oversight. There are many potential potholes on the road to an efficient deregulated market. Joskow provides a roadmap to the biggest challenges in transitioning from cost-of-service regulation to competition. Joskow, an economist at the Massachusetts Institute of Technology (MIT) and one of the most respected and prolific analysts of electricity markets, draws upon his many years of research experience in both the regulation and deregulation of the electricity industry. He reflects upon existing deregulation experiences to identify lessons learned about the performance of restructured electricity markets.

The next three chapters present case studies of specific markets that have been deregulated and discuss lessons that can be learned from those experiences. In chapter 2, Richard Green, a professor of economics at the University of Hull in England, analyzes the first major market to deregulate—England and Wales—which began restructuring in 1990. By perhaps the most important standard, U.K. electricity deregulation has enjoyed considerable success. The ultimate goal is to reduce prices, and U.K. prices have fallen substantially since initial deregulation in 1990. However, the market also has experienced some problems, including the exercise of market power. Green discusses how the England and Wales regulators anticipated and reacted to these problems, and he draws upon more than a decade of restructuring experience to illustrate lessons for other markets.

In chapter 3, Frank Wolak discusses the ill-fated California market. Policy analysts have widely divergent views on what caused the California market to collapse in 2000–2001. Most agree that the California crisis was some combination of rising input costs, poor market design and the exercise of market power, and failed market oversight by state and federal regulators. However, analysts differ on the weights to attach to each contributing factor. Wolak discusses each of these factors and argues that the California crisis was caused primarily by regulatory failure. Wolak, an economist at Stanford, is uniquely qualified to analyze the California market because he has served on the Market Surveillance Committee of the California Independent System Operator.

The final case study is the Texas market, which opened as a single market in 2001. Similar to England and Wales after reform, the Electric Reliability Council of Texas (ERCOT) is a "bilateral" market. Rather than serving as a market maker, the system operator takes the more passive role of collecting schedules of bilateral trades and only running a small residual market for balancing supply and demand in real-time. Texas has made other design choices that differ from other markets. For example, Texas developed policies to encourage new investment such as reducing the costs of connecting to the grid, but ERCOT has no market for installed capacity. Also, ERCOT allows generators to choose how to dispatch their generating units rather than dispatching units with an optimization algorithm run by the system operator. Ross Baldick and Hui Niu, electrical engineers at the University of Texas, take us on a tour of ERCOT's market design choices in chapter 4.

The second part of this volume discusses specific policies for the successful design of wholesale and retail markets. One of the themes that will recur is that electricity markets must be carefully designed to ensure that incentives are properly aligned and they operate efficiently. Otherwise, much can go wrong. These potential problems have led some policymakers and analysts to question whether we should go down the road of electricity deregulation. However, the focus on how to (and how not to) design such markets should not be taken as a prescription to halt deregulation. One of the difficulties in "selling deregulation" is the timing of the costs and benefits. The costs are likely to be front loaded, while the benefits are back loaded. Many of the costs are likely to come in the form of market design flaws as the industry transitions from costs-of-service regulation to competition. However, the benefits are likely to accrue in the medium and long run as generators find ways to shave off operating costs and invest in new generation technology. In chapter 5, Catherine Wolfram discusses the various channels through which deregulation can reduce costs of procuring electricity. Because many of the benefits will not show up in the short run, it is premature to make an overall assessment of the efficiency improvements. Wolfram provides some early estimates of cost reduction and lays out methodologies and data that can be used in the future to measure the benefits of deregulation.

After foreshadowing the current and predicted future benefits of deregulation, we turn to the downside risks. One of the biggest risks is that the markets will not be sufficiently competitive and electricity generators will be able to exercise market power. In chapter 6, James Bushnell evaluates tools to screen the potential competitiveness of restructured electricity markets. He reviews the screens that historically have been favored by U.S. antitrust authorities and the FERC. It turns out that these screens can fail spectacularly when applied to electricity markets. Bushnell illustrates techniques to detect potential market power that are better suited to electricity. These techniques draw upon oligopoly models in the economics literature to simulate what prices would be under various structural arrangements. Essentially, Bushnell assumes firms choose each period to produce the quantity that maximizes their individual profit taking their rivals' production as fixed (i.e., Cournot bidding). He simulates what prices would be under the ownership structure in California and finds that the simulated prices fit the data quite well.[11] This suggests it is reasonable to estimate what prices would be under various alternative ownership structures and use those simulations in deciding on whether divestiture is required or long-term contracts should be mandated. Bushnell's paper simulates other possible counterfactual ownership structures and finds that real-time pricing and reduced supplier concentration could have significantly reduced prices during the 2000 California electricity crisis. These techniques are useful screens that can be employed in other markets to determine ownership structures and contracts that will make prices competitive.

Market power mitigation can take several forms. While Bushnell describes the importance of market structure for obtaining competitive prices, Alvin Klevorick discusses the need for continual regulatory oversight of bidding. Klevorick, who teaches both law and economics at Yale, brings years of experience in regulatory oversight to market power concerns in electricity. In chapter 7, Klevorick explains why deregulated electricity markets must be constantly monitored to ensure they are competitive. He offers guidance on how market monitoring should be conducted at both the federal and local level. In addition, he compares the relative merits of different approaches to regulate prices including price caps and bid-adjustment procedures.

In chapter 8, Severin Borenstein discusses how electricity should be priced to retail consumers. Economic theory suggests that forcing consumers to face the real-time price of energy can reduce the amount of needed generating capacity as well as reduce prices and the overall cost of electricity. Despite the strong theoretical justifications for real-time pricing, few utilities in the United States have experimented with such programs. Two of the biggest obstacles to implementing real-time pricing are the costs of installing real-time metering equipment and the reluctance of customers (and their legislators) to face price risk. Borenstein argues that these obstacles are not difficult to overcome. Installing real-time meters for large customers easily passes the benefit-cost test. Also, cleverly designed pricing programs can protect consumers from substantial bill volatility yet still provide the proper price signals. Borenstein describes a variety of real-time pricing policies that yield the frequently cited benefits of demand response yet overcome some of the most common complaints of real-time pricing.

In chapter 9, William Hogan, professor of public policy and administration at the Kennedy School and research director of the Harvard Electricity Policy Group, discusses how use of the transmission grid should be priced to make the electricity market efficient. Ideally, prices should send signals about the optimal location of new generation and transmission investment on the grid. One means to ensure these signals exist is for wholesale electricity to have different prices at different points on the transmission grid reflecting scarcity of transmission capacity. But this leaves open the question of who will listen or who should listen to those price signals. Some analysts claim that "regulators" should decide on new transmission investments while others believe that new transmission investment should be left to merchant firms. Hogan analyzes these issues.

In chapter 10, Shmuel Oren, professor of industrial engineering and operations research at University of California, Berkeley, discusses how markets should be designed to ensure that adequate generation capacity is available to meet demand. Under the rate-of-return regulatory regime, utility planners in various agencies in conjunction with investor-owned utilities made investment decisions to ensure adequate generation capacity. In restructured markets, this planning process is "left to the market." It is possible that perfectly competitive markets for electricity will create the proper long-run incentives for investment. According to the theory, firms bid their marginal cost and earn scarcity rents during periods of high demand. Those scarcity rents exactly cover the capacity costs of generating units in long-run equilibrium. But this theory has complications in practice. In fact, Paul Joskow's chapter finds evidence of insufficient investment incentives from the energy-only market in New England. Some analysts recommend additional "capacity markets" where generators are paid for being available to generate, independent on the actual amount of energy generated. Oren discusses how such markets can be designed.

Finally, we want to ensure that our discussion does not occur in a political vacuum. So in chapter 11, we complement the academic analyses with perspectives from policymakers and stakeholders. The first perspective is from Pat Wood III, who is Chairman of the federal agency that regulates wholesale electricity markets—the FERC. Wood argues that electricity markets require certain structural elements to ensure they are efficient and function properly. Otherwise, these markets can fall victim to a variety of the textbook "market failures" of economics. He highlights eight elements of the FERC policy that should serve as core features of regulatory policy. Thomas R. Kuhn, president of Edison Electric Institute, offers his opinions on the best legislative and regulatory rule changes to ensure the continued growth of the electricity industry. In conclusion, U.S. Congressman Joe Barton, chairman of the House Subcommittee on Energy and Air Quality of the House Committee on Energy and Commerce, discusses his vision of future legislation to continue to push forward with competitive markets rather than return to regulated rates.

* * *

REFERENCES

Bergen, A. R., and V. Vittal. 2000. *Power Systems Analysis.* Englewood Cliffs, NJ: Prentice Hall.

Borenstein, S., J. Bushnell, and C. R. Knittel. 1999. Market power in electricity markets: Beyond concentration measures. *Energy Journal* 20:65–88.

Joskow, P. L. 2000. Deregulation and regulatory reform in the U.S. electric power sector. In *Deregulation of network industries: What's next?*, ed. S. Peltzman and C. Winston, 113–88. Washington, DC: Brookings Press.

———. 2002. Electricity sector restructuring and competition: A transactions-cost perspective. In *The economics of contracts: Theories and applications*, ed. Eric Brousseau and Jean-Michel Glachant, 503–30. Cambridge: Cambridge University Press.

Joskow, P. L., and J. Tirole. 2000. Transmission rights and market power on electric power networks. *RAND Journal of Economics* 31:450–87.

Mansur, E. T. 2001. Pricing behavior in the initial summer of the restructured PJM wholesale electricity market. POWER Working Paper no. 083. Berkeley, CA: Center for the Study of Energy Markets.

Puller, S. L. 2004. Pricing and firm conduct in California's deregulated electricity market. Texas A&M University, Department of Economics. Mimeograph.

Taylor, L. D. 1975. The demand for electricity: A survey. *The Bell Journal of Economics* 6:74–110.

Williamson, O. 1975. Markets and hierarchies: Analysis and antitrust implications. New York: Free Press.

NOTES

James M. Griffin holds the Bob Bullock Chair in Public Policy and Economics at the George Bush School of Government and Public Service at Texas A&M University. He serves as director of the Bush School's Program in the Economics of Public Policy. Steven L. Puller is assistant professor of economics at Texas A&M University.

We are grateful to Ross Baldick, Richard Green, and Cliff Hamal for helpful comments. They are not responsible for any of our conclusions. Joseph Wood contributed capable research assistance.

1. For a detailed discussion of the evolution of electricity restructuring, see Joskow (2000).

2. See Bergen and Vittal (2000) for a full description of power flows in various networks.

3. See Joskow and Tirole (2000).

4. See Williamson (1975) for a general discussion or Joskow (2002) for one specific to electricity.

5. Transaction-specific assets occur where the producer and buyer are tied together without easy access to alternative sources of demand and supply.

6. We thank Erin Mansur for providing us with the data underlying this graph. Further details of the PJM market can be found in Mansur (2001).

7. See Taylor (1975) as an example.

8. As long as the marginal cost was 3.3 percent or less below the initial price, it would not be profitable to withhold output.

9. In this case, withholding of output will always be profitable as long as marginal costs are 51 percent or less of the initial market price.

10. For a good analysis of the shortcomings of using concentration measures for inferring the competitiveness of electricity markets, see Borenstein, Bushnell, and Knittel (1999).

11. Puller (2004) uses another methodology and finds that producer behavior is fairly consistent with unilateral profit maximization.

PART 1

Experiences and Case Studies in Electricity Restructuring

1

The Difficult Transition to Competitive Electricity Markets in the United States

Paul L. Joskow

Introduction

Academic discussions about the opportunities and challenges associated with introducing wholesale and retail competition into the electric power sector have gone on for decades. However, serious considerations of comprehensive electricity sector restructuring and deregulation initiatives in the United States only began in the mid-1990s, following the first comprehensive privatization, restructuring, wholesale, and retail competition program undertaken in England and Wales in 1990. The first comprehensive U.S. programs did not go into operation until early 1998. Of course, wholesale power markets in which proximate vertically integrated utilities traded power on a daily and hourly basis subject to very limited regulation have existed in the United States for many years. In addition, during the 1980s the Public Utility Regulatory Policy Act (PURPA) of 1978 stimulated the development of a nonutility power sector selling electricity produced primarily from cogeneration facilities and renewable energy facilities to local utilities under long-term contracts (Joskow 1989). The Energy Policy Act of 1992 also removed important barriers to the broader development of unregulated nonutility generating facilities and expanded the Federal Energy Regulatory Commission's (FERC) authority to order utilities to provide transmission service to support wholesale power transactions. However, these developments largely reflected modest expansions of competition at the wholesale level built upon a basic model of regulated vertically integrated franchised monopolies.

The primary impetus for more fundamental restructuring and competition initiatives can be traced to electricity policy debates that began in California and a few states in the Northeast (Massachusetts, Rhode Island, New York, Pennsylvania, Maine, and New Jersey) in the mid-1990s, combined with supporting transmission and wholesale-market rules and regulations issued by the FERC (e.g., Orders 888 and 889) at about the same time (Joskow 2000a). These debates eventually led to regulatory decisions and state legislation in a number of states to embrace competitive electricity-market models. The first retail competition programs began operating in Massachusetts, Rhode Island, and California in early 1998 and spread to about a dozen states by the end of 2000. By that time about a dozen additional states had announced plans to introduce similar programs in the near future.

Since the year 2000, however, no additional states have announced plans to introduce competitive reforms of this type, and about nine states that had planned to implement reforms have delayed, cancelled, or significantly scaled back their electricity competition programs. Federal procompetition electricity legislation has also been stalled. The California electricity crisis of 2000–2001 (Joskow 2001), Enron's bankruptcy, the financial collapse of many merchant generating and trading companies, volatile wholesale-market prices, rising real retail prices in some states, phantom trading and fraudulent price reporting revelations, accounting abuses, a declining number of competitive retail supply options for residential and small commercial customers in many states, and continuing allegations of market power and market abuses in wholesale markets have all helped to take the glow off of electricity "deregulation" in many parts of the United States. As can be seen in figure 1.1, the average real retail price of electricity in the United States increased for the first time in fifteen years in 2000 for industrial customers and in 2001 for residential customers, though preliminary data indicate that real prices fell in 2002. The FERC has found itself at war with many states in the southeast and the west as they resist its efforts to expand institutions it believes are necessary to support efficient competitive wholesale markets in all regions of the country. In response to the resulting political pressure, in a white paper issued on April 28, 2003, the FERC indicated that it would provide states and regions with more time and flexibility to implement the wholesale-market reforms—the standard market design (SMD)—that it proposed in a Notice of Proposed Rulemaking (NOPR) issued in August 2002.

Figure 1.1. Real retail price of electricity ($1996): 1960–2001

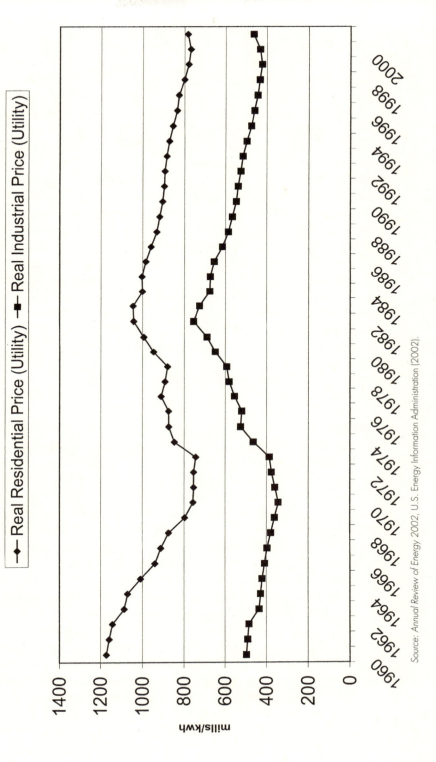

Source: *Annual Review of Energy 2002*, U.S. Energy Information Administration (2002).

At the very least, the pace of wholesale and retail competition and the supporting restructuring and regulatory reforms has slowed considerably since 2000. Many states have concluded that these types of electricity-sector reforms are not in the interest of consumers in their states or that it is prudent to wait to see if policymakers can figure out how to make competitive electricity markets work well and demonstrate that these reforms will bring long-term benefits for consumers. At the same time, most of the states in the Northeast, a few in the Midwest, Texas, and the FERC are committed to moving forward with the development of competitive wholesale and retail markets and to making them work well.

In this chapter, I discuss what has gone right, what has gone wrong, and the lessons learned from the experience with wholesale and retail electricity competition initiatives in the United States during the last five years. As events in California have attracted so much attention by industry analysts, the media, and policymakers, this paper will say little about California and focus instead on developments in the rest of the country.[1]

Why Wholesale and Retail Competition?

Background

Electricity sectors almost everywhere on earth evolved with (primarily) vertically integrated geographic monopolies that were either publicly owned or subject to public regulation of prices, service obligations, major investments, financing, and expansion into unregulated lines of business. That is, the primary components of electricity supply—generation, transmission, distribution, and retail supply—were integrated within individual electric utilities. These firms in turn had de facto exclusive franchises to supply residential, commercial, and industrial consumers within a defined geographic area. The performance of these regulated monopolies varied widely across countries and between utilities in the United States. While there is much to criticize about the institution of regulated monopoly, it is a mistake to assume that the performance of the U.S. electric-power industry during the twentieth century was extremely poor. The electric power sector in the United States had a very high rate of productivity growth from 1900 to 1970, and its performance compared very favorably to international norms regarding labor productivity, production costs, penetration rates, reliability, and prices. Serious problems began to emerge during the 1970s and 1980s as fossil fuel prices rose, inflation and interest rates rose, nuclear power plant costs exploded, and some states embraced the PURPA with excessive and costly enthusiasm (Joskow 1974, 1989).

As can be seen in figure 1.1, real retail electricity prices rose significantly in many states during the 1970s and early 1980s for the first time in the history of commercial electric power. Moreover, it became clear that there were significant variations in performance across utilities, but an industry structure that provided limited opportunities for more-efficient suppliers to expand and to place pressure on less-efficient suppliers to improve or contract.

On a national (average) level, real retail electricity prices began to fall once again after the mid-1980s, and continued to fall until 2000–2001, as fossil fuel prices and interest rates declined and inflation moderated significantly. Nevertheless, the legacy of costly nuclear investment and long-term contracting decisions made during the 1970s and 1980s continued to be reflected in regulated retail prices during the 1990s in those areas that had made major commitments to these resources (e.g., California, New York, New England). While on average real U.S. retail electricity prices fell after 1985, in the Northeast, California, and a few other states, real retail prices continued to rise into the late 1980s and early 1990s as legacy costs of nuclear plants and PURPA qualifying facility (QF) contracts, combined with excess generating capacity, continued to be reflected in regulated retail prices. Moreover, large disparities emerged between regulated retail electricity prices in different states and regions *and* between the embedded cost of electric generation services used to set regulated retail prices and the apparent market value of electric generation services in the regional wholesale-power markets. In the northeast, California, Illinois, and a few other states, a large gap appeared to exist between the regulated price of generation service and the wholesale-market value of these services. Industrial customers began to view regulated utilities as representing a barrier to obtaining lower-priced power available in wholesale markets. From the regulated utilities' perspective, the "gap" between regulated generation prices and wholesale-market values for generation services indicated the potentially "stranded costs" that utility investors would incur if generation service prices dropped from their regulated levels, reflecting historical capital costs of generating facilities and long-term contractual commitments to buy power from PURPA QFs, to reflect their current wholesale market values.

Three things are worth noting about this gap between the generation component of regulated retail prices and wholesale-market values. First, it largely (though not entirely) reflected sunk costs associated with historical investment and long-term contracting decisions. Second, the size of the gap varied widely from region to region and from utility to utility. In several areas of the country the gap was negative—that is, regulated generation prices were *below* their wholesale-market value. Third, wholesale-market prices observed in the early 1990s were a misleading indicator of what wholesale prices would be in the long run in an industry where generation services would be sold largely through market mechanisms rather than through vertical integration. The wholesale markets in the early 1990s were largely short-term "excess energy" markets in which utilities with capacity in excess of their retail customers' needs could sell it to neighboring utilities that had generating capacity with higher short-run marginal cost that could be displaced by lower-cost energy purchased in the wholesale market.

Initial interest in electricity-sector reform started in the states with the highest retail electricity prices and where the apparent gaps between wholesale and retail prices were the largest. They included California, Massachusetts, Rhode Island, New York, New Jersey, Maine, and Pennsylvania. As discussed elsewhere (White 1996; Joskow 2000a), the political pressures for reforms in these states, and in particular for retail competition, came from lobbying activities by industrial customers, independent power producers, and would-be electricity marketers with experience in the natural gas industry. Enron played a major role in stimulating interest in restructuring and competition in almost every one of these "pioneer" states. The primary selling point to state regulators, governors, and legislators was that by introducing competition, retail prices would fall significantly to reflect the lower-priced power available in the wholesale market. Incumbent utilities in these states initially opposed these retail competition proposals due to the potential for stranding sunk costs but ultimately negotiated settlements that provided for recovery of a significant fraction of these sunk costs. How retail prices could both fall dramatically to reflect lower wholesale prices *and* utilities could recover their stranded costs (roughly the difference between regulated generation prices and the expected wholesale price of electricity) was a bit of questionable arithmetic that was largely glossed over.

Public-Interest Goals

While the political debates at the state level focused on retail price reductions, stranded cost recovery, and the creation of opportunities for incumbents and hungry new entrants, the intellectual debates focused on a broader set of public-interest goals and implementation strategies. I think that there is fairly wide agreement about the goals that electricity-sector reforms should achieve—even on the basic architecture of the model for creating competitive wholesale and retail markets that will achieve these goals. It is less clear that there was broad understanding of what would have to be done to achieve these goals and how long it would take to achieve them.

The overriding reform goal is to create new governance arrangements for the electricity sector that will provide long-term benefits to consumers. These benefits will accrue by relying on competitive wholesale markets for power to provide better incentives for controlling capital and operating costs of new and existing generating capacity, to encourage innovation in power supply technologies, and to shift the risks of technology choice, construction cost, and operating "mistakes" to suppliers and away from consumers. Retail competition, or "customer choice," would allow consumers to choose the supplier offering the price/service quality combination that best met their needs, and competing retail suppliers would provide an enhanced array of retail service products, risk management, demand management, and new opportunities for service quality differentiation based on individual consumer preferences.

It is also widely recognized that significant portions of the total costs of electricity supply—distribution and transmission—will continue to be provided by regulated monopolies. Accordingly, reform of the traditional regulatory arrangements governing the distribution and transmission networks has generally been viewed as an important complement to the introduction of wholesale and retail competition to supply consumer electricity needs. This is the case for at least two reasons. First, regulatory mechanisms with good incentive properties would lead to lower distribution and transmission costs, and this in turn would help to reduce retail electricity prices. During the first decade of the electricity restructuring and competition program in England and Wales, as much as 35 percent of the reduction in real electricity prices was associated with cost reductions in distribution and transmission. Second, the efficiency of competitive wholesale electricity markets depends on a well-functioning supporting transmission network and its efficient operation by a system operator. Good operating and investments incentives are important for providing an efficient network platform upon which wholesale and retail competition would proceed.

In the long run, the promise was that these reforms would lead to lower costs and lower average retail price levels reflecting these cost savings *compared to regulated monopoly alternative*, while maintaining or enhancing system reliability and achieving environmental improvement goals. Anyway, this was the dream.

The Basic Model for Competitive Wholesale and Retail Markets

Whatever the political motivations, the basic architecture for transitioning to competitive electricity markets had already been developed in theory and applied in practice in other countries (e.g., England and Wales, Norway, Argentina). It involves several key components that are depicted in figure 1.2.

1. Vertical separation of competitive segments (e.g., generation, marketing, and retail supply) from regulated segments (distribution, transmission, system operations) either structurally (through divestiture) or functionally (with internal "Chinese" walls separating affiliates within the same corporation).

2. Horizontal integration of transmission and network operations to encompass the geographic expanse of "natural" wholesale markets and the designation of a single independent system operator to manage the operation of the network, to schedule generation to meet demand, and to maintain the physical parameters of the network (frequency, voltage, stability) so that the lights would stay on except under extremely rare conditions.

3. The creation of wholesale spot energy and operating reserve market institutions to support requirements for real time balancing, to respond quickly and effectively to unplanned outages of transmission or generating facilities consistent with the need to maintain network voltage, frequency and stability parameters within narrow limits, and to facilitate economical trading opportunities among suppliers and between buyers and sellers.

4. The creation of institutions to facilitate access to the transmission network by buyers and sellers of electric power to facilitate economical production and exchange, including mechanisms to efficiently allocate scarce transmission capacity.

5. Horizontal restructuring of the generation segment of the industry, forward contractual commitments and/or behavioral rules to mitigate regional and localized market power in wholesale markets.

6. Unbundling retail tariffs to separate the price for retail power supplies and associated support services to be supplied competitively from the prices for distribution and transmission services that will continue to be provided by regulated monopolies.

7. Permitting and encouraging retail consumers to purchase their power supplies from competing retail suppliers which in turn buy their power in wholesale markets, or own generating facilities to support their retail supply commitments, and deliver over the regulated transmission and distribution networks.

This is the basic architecture for promoting well-functioning competitive wholesale and retail electricity markets, but if we have learned anything in the last several years of U.S. and international experience, the devil is in the details of actual implementation in practice.

Figure 1.2. Comprehensive reform vision: Competitive wholesale and retail markets

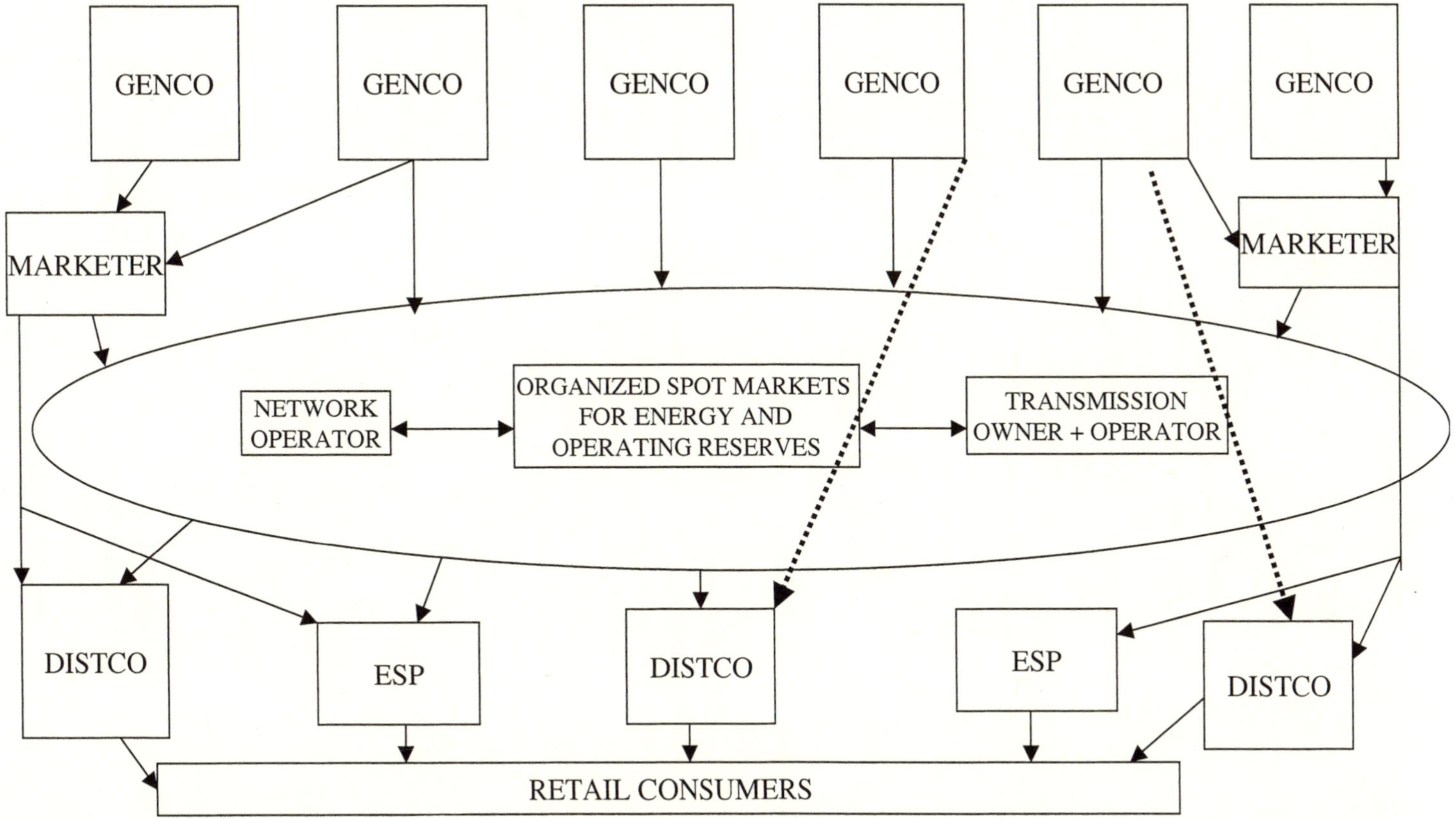

GENCO

GENCO

MARKETER

GENCO

GENCO

GENCO

GENCO

GENCO

MARKETER

TRANSMISSION OWNER + OPERATOR

ORGANIZED SPOT MARKETS FOR ENERGY AND OPERATING RESERVES

NETWORK OPERATOR

DISTCO

ESP

DISTCO

ESP

DISTCO

RETAIL CONSUMERS

Underestimating the Restructuring Challenge

In the United States, electricity-sector restructuring and competition initiatives got off on the wrong foot in many parts of the country at least in part because policymakers and many of their advisers underestimated the nature and magnitude of the technical and institutional challenges that must be overcome to introduce successfully competitive wholesale and retail markets for electricity and the uncertainties associated with how best to respond to these challenges. To some extent, the underestimation of the magnitude and extent of the challenge was strategic, reflecting efforts by some participants in the policy-making process to feather their own nests. However, it also reflected a combination of ignorance, political barriers, and true uncertainty about how best to restructure the industry to support competition and how to design effective wholesale- and retail-market transmission and system operations institutions. The experts did not, and in many areas still do not, agree on exactly how best to proceed with these structural and institutional reforms. This situation reinforced the natural inclination of policymakers to treat the details of the restructuring program as a political rather than a technical problem. This in turn resulted in numerous political compromises over restructuring and market design issues and the mixing and matching of pieces of alternative restructuring models that did not fit very well together.

Why is the transformation of a regulated monopoly electric power industry into one that relies on competition to supply power at the wholesale and retail levels so challenging? There are several sets of reasons. First, electricity has an unusual set of physical and economic attributes that significantly complicate the task of replacing hierarchies (vertical integration and multilateral agreements) with decentralized market mechanisms. These attributes include the following:

1. Electricity cannot be stored economically and demand must be cleared with just-in-time production from generating capacity available to the network at (almost) exactly the same time that the electricity is consumed.
2. Physical laws governing electricity network operations in real time to maintain frequency, voltage, and stability of the network, along with network congestion, interact with nonstorability to require that supply and demand be cleared continuously at every location on the network. Creating a set of complete markets that operate this quickly at so many locations and without creating market power problems is a significant challenge.
3. The short-run demand elasticity for electricity is very low, and supply gets very inelastic at high-demand levels as capacity constraints are approached. As a re-

sult, spot electricity prices are inherently very volatile and unusually susceptible to the creation of opportunities for suppliers to exercise market power
unilaterally.

4. Network congestion, combined with nonstorability, may limit significantly the
   geographic expanse of competition by constraining the ability of remote suppliers to compete, further enhancing market power problems.

5. Loop flow, resulting from the physics of power flows on alternating current
   (AC) networks, introduces additional complex interactions between generators
   at different points on the network, creating unusual opportunities for suppliers
   to take actions unilaterally to affect market prices, complicating the definition
   of property rights, and creating coordination and free-riding problems when,
   as in the Eastern and Western networks in the United States, there are multiple
   system operators responsible for interconnected portions of a single synchronized AC network.

6. Electricity demand varies widely from season to season, between day and
   night, with extreme temperatures, and between weekdays and weekends (and
   holidays). The difference between the peak demand and the lowest demand
   over the course of a year is a factor of about three. Because electricity cannot
   be stored and varies widely over the year, a significant amount of the generating capacity connected to the system operates for a relatively small number of
   hours during the year to meet peak demands. This means that the ability of
   generators that provide services for a small fraction of the year to recover their
   investment and fixed operating and maintenance costs is heavily dependent on
   the price-formation process during periods when demand (and prices) are at
   their highest levels.

7. The combination of nonstorability, real time variations in demand, low-
   demand elasticity, random real-time failures of generation and transmission
   equipment, the need to continuously clear supply and demand at every point
   on the network to meet the physical constraints on reliable network operations,
   and so on means that some source of real-time inventory is required to keep
   the system in balance. This inventory is generally provided by standby generators that can respond very quickly to changing supply and demand conditions,
   though demand-side responses can also theoretically provide equivalent services as well. Compatible market mechanisms for procuring and effectively
   operating these ancillary services are therefore necessary. Designing well-
   functioning integrated markets for electric energy to meet demand and for
   reserve generating capacity to stand ready to provide multiple ancillary services to maintain network reliability consistent with all of the other constraints
   and attributes enumerated just mentioned is very challenging.

8. The performance of competitive markets for electricity depends critically on

the way the regulated transmission network is operated, access to it is priced, and scarce transmission capacity is allocated. There are important complementarities between energy markets for electric power and efficient transmission network operations, especially congestion management and responses to emergencies. Integrating spot electric energy and ancillary services markets with the allocation of scarce transmission capacity is necessary for wholesale power markets to operate efficiently.

While there are many competitive industries that have one or perhaps two of these attributes, it is hard to think of any commodity market that has all of them.[2] Moreover, it is precisely these attributes of electricity that led to vertical integration between generation and transmission and either to extensive horizontal integration or to multilateral cooperative agreements between neighboring vertically integrated system operators. Ignoring these unusual attributes of electricity, and ignoring how and why historical governance arrangements evolved for dealing with them (Joskow 1997, 2002), is a very bad mistake. Replacing the traditional hierarchical governance arrangements with well-functioning decentralized market mechanisms is a very significant technical challenge, about which even the best experts have disagreements. Accordingly, it should not be surprising that electricity restructuring and competition programs have inevitably been a process that involves a lot of learning by doing and ongoing changes to market rules, regulatory arrangements, and governance institutions.

These technical challenges have been further complicated in the United States by a number of institutional, legacy investment, and political factors that many other countries have been able to avoid. First, the U.S. industry has been characterized by an unusually large number of *private* vertically integrated utilities of widely varying sizes that own and control generation, transmission, and distribution facilities in or near their distribution franchise areas. Many of these vertically integrated utilities are control area operators (about 140 in 1995) that were, and in many cases still are, responsible for operating portions of one of the three synchronized AC networks in the United States, subject to rules established by regional reliability councils and a variety of bilateral and multilateral operating agreements. Only in the Northeast did multiutility power pools emerge decades before interest in competition surfaced to centrally dispatch generation resources and integrate some operational aspects of the transmission facilities owned by the utilities who joined the power pools.

This legacy industry structure is not conducive to creating well-functioning competitive wholesale and retail electricity markets (Joskow and

Schmalensee 1983). Ideally, an industry restructuring program would have separated competitive generation and marketing functions from regulated transmission and distribution activities. Generation ownership would have been further decentralized if ownership concentration created significant additional market power problems. Horizontal integration of transmission assets would have taken place to create regional transmission companies to own and operate transmission networks spanning large geographic areas. This was the basic approach of the restructuring programs in England and Wales, Spain, Norway, Argentina, Australia, and Alberta.

Third, the electric power industry in the United States has historically been regulated primarily by the states. The states have divergent views about the desirability of transitioning to competitive wholesale and retail electricity markets and restructuring the utilities in their states to do so effectively. Unlike most other countries that have gone down this path, the United States has no clear and coherent national laws that adopt a competitive wholesale- and retail-market model as national policy and that give federal authorities the tools to do the necessary restructuring and market design work required to make it work. Congress has passed no legislation mandating the implementation of a comprehensive wholesale and retail competition model for the electricity sector. Instead, the United States has relied heavily on individual state initiatives and efforts by the FERC to use its existing but limited Federal Power Act authority to cajole and encourage the states and their utilities to create competitive wholesale markets and supporting transmission institutions. It is hard to force states to adopt policies they don't like, especially when the regulated utilities in these states don't like them either. It is also difficult to force private firms to divest assets and restructure vertically and horizontally without providing them with financial incentives to do so. In most other countries, the restructuring program was implemented in conjunction with the privatization of state-owned assets so that they did not have to confront issues associated with government takings of private property. As a result, to make progress, the FERC has had to rely on a variety of alternative regulatory and institutional arrangements and various regulatory carrots and sticks to provide incentives for cooperation in order to compensate for its inability to require the kind of restructuring program that can most effectively support wholesale and retail competition.

Fourth, the combination of many relatively small vertically integrated utilities, many operating small control areas, combined with state regulation, has had the effect historically of limiting investments in transmission capacity that provide strong linkages between generating facilities located over large geographic areas. So, for example, New England has only 1,500 MW of transmission capacity connecting this six-state region with the rest of the United States. The Pennsylvania, New Jersey, Maryland, Delaware, and Washington, D.C. area, where the major utilities have participated in a power pool (PJM) since the 1920s, has a strong internal transmission network, but only about 3,500 MW of firm simultaneous transmission capacity with neighboring states. Moreover, the configuration of the control areas' internal networks typically reflected a century of evolution of the utilities that began supplying electricity early in the twentieth century, with generating plants first located in or near load centers and then gradually expanding as more remote generating sites became necessary to accommodate larger generating stations. Interconnections with neighboring utilities were built primarily for reliability purposes rather to gain access to lower-cost power supplies located remotely from the local utility's franchise area. In addition, when the industry was composed of self-sufficient vertically integrated utilities, there was no need for these transmission investments to take account of the potential market power problems caused by transmission constraints. The legacy transmission networks therefore represent a potentially serious constraint on effective competition when wholesale power markets are deregulated due to the resulting limitations on the geographic expanse of wholesale power markets (Joskow and Schmalensee 1983).

These institutional, legacy investment, and political realities have significantly complicated the kind of industry restructuring that is necessary for effective implementation of what is already the very significant technical challenge of creating well-functioning competitive wholesale and retail markets for electricity. They continue to be a barrier to effective national reforms today.

Generation Restructuring and Merchant Generation Investment

The approaches to restructuring to support wholesale and retail competition have varied widely across the states. States that have implemented retail competition programs have also typically strongly encouraged or required the affected utilities to separate their regulated transmission and distribution (T&D) businesses from their wholesale generation and marketing activities. The first few states to implement retail competition programs also (effectively)[3] required their utilities to divest substantially all of their generating capacity through an auction process (e.g., California, Massachusetts, New York, Maine, Rhode Island). Other states that have implemented retail competition programs permitted the utilities under their jurisdiction to retain the bulk of

Table 1.1 Generating plant sales and transfers (MW)

Year	Divested	To unregulated affiliates	Total
1998	23,413	0	23,413
1999	50,962	4,108	55,070
2000	15,334	32,657	47,991
2001	8,135	20,051	28,186
2002	2,154	27,206	29,360

Source: Electric Power Monthly, U.S. Energy Information Administration (1998–2003, various issues).

their generating assets and to move them into separate unregulated wholesale power affiliates within a holding company structure (e.g., Pennsylvania, Illinois, Maryland, Ohio, Texas, New Jersey).[4] Whether the generating assets were divested or transferred to affiliates, the utilities affected typically retained some type of transition or "default service" obligation to continue to supply retail customers who had not chosen a competitive retail supplier at prices determined through some type of regulatory transition contract. The terms, conditions, and durations of these obligations vary widely from state to state and sometimes vary significantly among utilities in the same state (e.g., New York). I will discuss default service obligations further when I discuss the evolution of retail competition.

Table 1.1 displays the patterns of the migration of utility generating assets from regulated utility to unregulated "nonutility" status[5] through either divestiture to third parties or through transfers of generating assets to affiliates of the legacy regulated utility owners. It is evident from the data in table 1.1 that generation restructuring activity peaked in 1999–2000 and that the initial focus on divestiture of generating assets was replaced by generating asset transfers to affiliates of the regulated utilities within a holding-company structure. The latter holding companies still have common ownership of generation, marketing, retail supply, distribution, and transmission and from this perspective continue to be vertically integrated. However, the FERC and state regulations place some restrictions on communications between holding-company affiliates with regulated and unregulated assets and impose stringent cost separation requirements. Generation restructuring of either form (structural or functional separation) now appears to have largely been halted as a result of the hiatus in the implementation of additional state retail competition and restructuring programs following the California electricity crisis in 2000–2001.

During the last few years there has also been a significant amount of entry of new unregulated generating capacity seeking to supply power to both

Table 1.2 Generating capacity additions (MW)

Year	Generating capacity added
1997[a]	4,000
1998[b]	6,500
1999[c]	10,500
2000[d]	23,500
2001[e]	48,000
2002[f]	55,000

[a]*Inventory of Power Plants: 1997*, U.S. Energy Information Administration (1997).
[b]*Inventory of Power Plants: 1998*, U.S. Energy Information Administration (1998).
[c]*Electric Power Annual: 1999*, U.S. Energy Information Administration (1999).
[d]*Electric Power Annual: 2000*, U.S. Energy Information Administration (2000).
[e]U.S. Energy Information Administration website, http://www.eia.doe.gov/fuelelectric.html.
[f]*New Power Plant Spreadsheet*, Energy Argus, Inc. (2003).

unintegrated distribution companies and to vertically integrated utilities that have been encouraged or required by state regulators to meet their incremental generation needs through wholesale-market purchases. Table 1.2 displays the patterns of entry of new generating capacity between 1997 and 2002. About 80 percent of this new generating capacity is unregulated merchant or nonutility capacity built to make sales in competitive wholesale markets. Very little new generating capacity was added *anywhere* in the United States during the mid-1990s, reflecting the perception that there was excess generating capacity in most regions of the country and uncertainties about the direction of restructuring and competition policies at the state and federal levels. As the FERC issued new regulations governing transmission access and related wholesale-market rules, as a growing number of states adopted retail competition programs, and as wholesale power prices rose, a large number of merchant plants were announced, began to seek construction permits, began construction, and were ultimately completed. By 2002, the amount of generating capacity completed reached 55,000 MW per year, an order of magnitude greater than in 1997 and 1998, a total of nearly 140,000 MW of new generating capacity was completed between 1999 and 2002,[6] and about 50,000 MW of additional generating capacity is expected to enter service in 2003. Most of this capacity is gas fired and relies on clean and thermally efficient combined-cycle generating technology. Up to roughly the middle of 2001, investments in new merchant generating projects and trading power in wholesale markets was perceived to be a booming business with enormous profit opportunities and was pointed to as a notable success of policies aimed at stimulating competition in electricity.

Table 1.3 Nonutility power production (% of total electricity supplied)

Year	Nonutility (%)
1990	7.2
1991	8.0
1992	9.3
1993	9.8
1994	10.5
1995	10.8
1996	10.7
1997	10.6
1998	11.2
1999	14.3
2000	20.7
2001	30.0
2002	33.6

Source: Monthly Energy Review, U.S. Energy Information Administration (2003, 97).

As I shall discuss in more detail presently, however, the boom has now turned into a bust with abundant generating capacity in service in almost all regions of the country, merchant generating and wholesale electricity marketing sectors in difficult financial shape, and many planned new generating plants (even some under construction) being canceled or indefinitely postponed.

The combination of divestiture of existing generating plants by utilities, transfers of utility generating plants to unregulated utility affiliates, and entry of new merchant generating plants (a significant number of which are owned by utility affiliates), has led to a large increase in the fraction of electricity generating by unregulated nonutility generating plants. Table 1.3 displays the fraction of total electricity generated in the United States that has been accounted for by unregulated nonutility power suppliers between 1990 and 2002.[7] By 2002 unregulated generators were producing about 33 percent of the total electricity supplied in the United States. If we deduct generation supplied by municipal utilities, federal power projects, and cooperatives, unregulated private power generation now accounts for about 40 percent of the energy supplied by investor-owned companies. However, a significant fraction of this energy comes from generating plants held by affiliates of vertically integrated utilities and located in the same areas as their distribution and transmission facilities.

All things considered, there has been a very significant restructuring of the generating segment of the electric power industry in the last few years. How-

Table 1.4 Share prices of selected merchant generating and trading firms ($/share)

Company	May 2001 peak week	March 10, 2003	
		Share price	Standard & Poor's credit rating
AES	48.5	3.2	B+
AEP	50.4	21.2	BBB
Allegheny	53.8	5.1	BB–
Calpine	54.7	6.1	BB
Dynegy	57.0	2.2	B
Duke	46.1	12.2	BBB[a]
El Paso	64.9	4.4	B+
Mirant	45.4	1.4	BB
NRG	30.4	6.2	D
Reliant	33.8	3.7	B–
Williams	41.0	4.0	B+

Source: Yahoo Finance website, http://finance.yahoo.com/; S&P website, http://www2.standardandpoors .com/.
[a]Duke Energy Trading and Marketing.

ever, there are significant uncertainties about how quickly the pace of generation restructuring will be in the future. Since Texas, no additional states have
adopted and implemented retail competition and industry restructuring programs. There does not appear to be a lot of enthusiasm in the remaining states
to implement such reforms quickly or at all. These states are likely to continue
to require or provide incentives for their vertically integrated utilities to look
to the wholesale market for their incremental power supply needs, but there
is an emerging trend toward utilities again looking to build their own regulated generating plants to serve their native load customers. While the FERC
has continued to push reforms to wholesale-market and transmission institutions (more on this in the following), there has been growing resistance from
many states to procompetition policies.

The merchant generating sector is also now in terrible financial shape.
What had been an enormous boom has now turned into an enormous bust.
Table 1.4 displays the market values of a share of common stock for each of
eleven companies with major financial commitments to energy trading and
merchant generating capacity in May 2001 (peak week) and on March 10,
2003. The equity values of these companies has fallen dramatically in less than
two years and only two of these companies (both with large regulated utility
affiliates) now have investment-grade credit ratings. About 125,000 MW of
new power projects that had been announced prior to 2001 have now been
canceled or indefinitely suspended in the last two years. A significant amount

of additional capacity under construction or in the permitting process has been delayed.

The fact that many announced projects have now been canceled is not surprising. Many more generating projects were announced than could possibly have been absorbed profitably by the market. As new generating capacity was completed and demand slowed with the slowdown in the economy, wholesale-market prices softened, and it became clear that many regions would have capacity surpluses in the immediate future. The market responding to these price signals with reductions and delays in investment in new capacity is what we should expect in a competitive market. However, the slowdown appears to be more than simply an ordinary market response to changes in supply and demand conditions. The merchant generating and trading sector benefited from a financial bubble similar to the one supporting telecom and internet stocks, giving them easy access to cheap capital to finance new generating capacity without support from longer-term contracts as well as substantial credit lines to support large energy trading operations that expanded well beyond trading electricity produced from their own generating facilities into highly speculative physical trading and financial hedging activities.

The end of the stock market bubble, a better understanding by investors of the real economics and market risks associated with building merchant generating plants and trading commodity electricity, trading and accounting improprieties and uncertainties about the future direction of industry restructuring, wholesale market rules, and retail competition have led to credit-rating downgrades and refinancing difficulties that have decimated the merchant generating and trading sector. The companies in this sector in turn have slashed investment in new generated capacity and withdrawn from trading activity. The cost of capital for new generating plants has increased very significantly and liquidity in wholesale electricity markets has declined as well. Changes in capital market conditions and imperfections in wholesale-market institutions are likely to create barriers to stimulating efficient investment in new generating capacity and efficient retirement decisions of existing generating capacity in the near future.

Despite all of the restructuring that has taken place, overall the U.S. electric power industry continues with a substantial amount of vertical integration between competitive segments and regulated segments in the same geographic area. A majority of the states have decided against pushing forward with competitive market and restructuring initiatives, at least for the time being. In addition, transmission ownership and system operations continue to be very fragmented with ongoing barriers to the development of regional wholesale markets.

Wholesale Spot-Market Institutions

One of the most challenging things to explain to people who are not familiar with the unusual attributes of electricity is that wholesale electricity markets do not design themselves but must be designed as an integral central component of a successful electricity restructuring and competition program. Unlike England and Wales, Norway, Sweden, Spain, Australia, New Zealand, Argentina, and most other countries, the United States did not proceed with its wholesale and retail competition initiatives with a clear coherent blueprint for wholesale-market design, transmission institutions, or vertical and horizontal restructuring. Moreover, despite experience in other countries, the United States did not take adequate account of wholesale-market imperfections and the incentives and opportunities created by market imperfections for individual suppliers to engage in bidding, scheduling, and trading practices that could increase prices above competitive levels and harm consumers (the distinction that some have drawn between "market power" and "exploiting market inefficiencies" to the same end, is in my view, meaningless).

The FERC's efforts to reform wholesale-market institutions began with Orders 888 and 889 in 1996. These orders basically established rules under which jurisdictional transmission owners were required to provide access to their transmission systems to third parties and associated requirements to provide balancing and operating reserve services using formulas or procurement methods specified in the FERC-regulated transmission tariffs, to make information about the availability of transmission service, purchasing, and scheduling transmission capacity easily available to all market participants. However, Order 888's basic regulatory framework presumed that the prevailing structure of the electric power industry would remain largely unchanged, followed traditional utility practices regarding the provision of transmission service to third parties. These practices were based on utility-specific "contract paths" that were often inconsistent with actual power flows and average "postage stamp" embedded cost transmission service price ceilings.[8] Order 888 also gave the incumbents first refusal on available transmission capacity (they had paid for it after all) and relied on administrative rationing, rather than economic rationing, to allocate transmission constraints. Order 888 did not require utilities to operate transparent organized day-ahead or real-time markets for energy or operating reserves but, rather, required transmission owners to provide balancing services and operating reserves as cost-based prices. The transmission owners administering the Order 888 tariffs generally owned generating capacity and used the same network to buy and sell wholesale power as did their would be competitors.

The three Northeastern power pools, California, Texas, and, most recently, several Midwestern states (Midwest ISO), took a more comprehensive approach to developing new wholesale-market institutions. They created independent system operators (ISOs) to schedule and dispatch generation and demand on transmission networks with multiple owners, to allocate scarce transmission capacity, to develop and apply fair interconnection procedures for new generators, to operate voluntary public real-time and (sometimes) day-ahead markets for energy and ancillary services, to coordinate planning for new transmission facilities, to monitor market performance in cooperation with independent-market monitors, and to implement mitigation measures and market reforms when performance problems emerged. The FERC's proposed standard market design rules (SMD) would extend what it views as the best practices drawn from the experience with these ISOs to the rest of the country. However, at the present time, the United States has a patchwork of different wholesale-market institutions operating in different regions of the country. Moving power between portions of the networks operated by different system operators is sometimes difficult or costly, and coordination imperfections between control area operators increase costs of energy, operating reserves, and congestion, especially during tight supply conditions.

The debates over the design of these wholesale-market institutions in California in 1996 and 1997 got the reforms off on the wrong foot. These debates were contentious and highly politicized, reflecting perceptions by various interest groups about how different wholesale-market institutions would advance or constrain their interests and, in my view, an inadequate amount of humility regarding uncertainties about the performance attributes of different institutional arrangements. The discussion of alternative institutions was polluted by an unfortunate overtone of ideological rhetoric that attempted to characterize the debate about wholesale-market institutions as one between "central planners" and "free market" advocates (Joskow 1996). The market design process in California in 1997 and 1998 also demonstrates how market design by committee, reflecting interest group compromises and mixing and matching pieces of different market models, can lead to a system with the worst attributes of all of them (Joskow 2001).

Lessons Learned

There have been a number of studies of the performance of the wholesale-market institutions performed by independent market monitors, consultants, and academics that have been completed over the last several years. We have learned a number of important lessons from the experience of the last several years.

1. All wholesale-market designs work reasonably well in the short run when demand is low or moderate, supply is very elastic and generating resource ownership not too highly concentrated, there is little congestion on the transmission network, and barriers to scheduling power by competing generators are removed with reasonable transmission access and energy balancing procedures and prices. The performance challenges for wholesale-market institutions arise during the relatively small number of hours each year when demand is high, supply is inelastic, and transmission congestion is significant and widely dispersed. The performance of wholesale-market institutions under these conditions is very important because this is when markets have to work hard to facilitate an efficient allocation of scarce resources. It is during these hours when competitive market prices *should* be high, when congestion is likely to lead to significantly different prices at different locations on the network, when a significant fraction of competitive market "rents" are produced to pay for the capital costs of investments in new generating capacity, and when demand-side decisions are most important for providing investors with accurate price signals reflecting consumer preferences for investment in "reserve capacity" and reliability and for signaling consumer demand for risk-hedging instruments to financial intermediaries.

Unfortunately, it is also under these "tight supply" conditions when market power problems are most serious, when system operator discretion is most important, and when nonprice rationing by the system operator to balance supply and demand to maintain the network's physical parameters within acceptable levels are most likely to be necessary because incomplete markets cannot respond fast enough to rapidly changing system conditions that threaten network reliability. Price formation during these relatively few hours each year works its way through the system to affect forward prices, incentives for investment in new generating capacity and retirement decisions about existing generating capacity, and overall system reliability. In the end, the performance of wholesale-market institutions should be judged primarily by how they function during these tight supply conditions.

2. The debate about whether wholesale markets should be organized around "bilateral contracts" or "centralized dispatch" that took place in California in 1996 and 1997 was an empty and unnecessarily confusing debate. Bilateral financial contracts and self-scheduling and dispatch of generators and load can and should be an important component of any wholesale-market design. Nevertheless, there is an important role for the single system operator

responsible for maintaining the necessary physical parameters of the network and facilitating economic decisions by buyers and sellers of electric energy and ancillary services. This role includes operating voluntary, consistent, and transparent real-time balancing and (ideally) day-ahead scheduling bid-based auction markets that are cleared by the system operator using a security-constrained dispatch algorithm that incorporates, as accurately as possible, the physical topology of the network (Hogan 1992, 1993). This process necessarily will yield shadow prices at each supply and demand node reflecting network constraints. The difference between the nodal prices at any point A and at any other point B on the network (ignoring losses) is a measure of the costs of congestion associated with an incremental injection of generation at location (node) A and an incremental increase in demand at location (node) B. At least in the real-time balancing market, these locational marginal prices (LMP) are the proper prices to be used for settlement purposes for net sales and purchases of energy (deviations from day-ahead schedules) and pricing of congestion.

3. The allocation of scarce transmission capacity day-ahead and in real-time should be fully integrated with the operation of day-ahead and real-time electric energy and ancillary services markets as previously discussed. Where this integration has not been achieved, as in California, New England, and Texas, congestion costs (or at least congestion rents) have increased beyond the efficient level.

4. The definition and allocation of transmission rights is an important aspect of wholesale-market design and has implications for the design and performance of wholesale-market institutions. In the short run, these rights serve as (imperfect) hedging instruments against (basis) differences between prices at different points on the network. While these hedging properties can in principle be replicated through combinations of forward contracts to buy and sell power at different locations, or by third parties' marketing contracts to hedge differences in locational prices, thin markets, and potential market power problems may limit the development of liquid forward and derivative markets to a much smaller number of hubs. *Long-term* transmission rights are also likely to be important for securing financing for investment in new transmission facilities that are built on a merchant basis. There has been substantial debate about whether such rights should be point-to-point financial rights in conjunction with nodal pricing or physical flowgate rights in conjunction with a zonal pricing system. In theory these alternatives may look very similar if there is little intrazonal congestion, though physical rights raise additional operational issues (Joskow and Tirole 2000). In practice, my view is that financial rights are much easier to implement, involve lower transactions

costs, and are more difficult to use to exercise market power than are physical rights on a meshed network. They are also easier to make compatible with real-time balancing actions and the associated real-time balancing prices. On radial lines and DC interconnectors, physical rights may be more attractive, especially if the projects are developed on an unregulated merchant basis.

5. Day-ahead and real-time markets for electric energy and ancillary services should be fully integrated and reflect the efficient optimization of energy supply and operating reserve resources that can both supply energy (or reduce demand) and stand in reserve to respond to short-run fluctuations in demand and unanticipated outages of generating or transmission facilities. Wholesale-market designs that separate electric energy and individual ancillary services markets have performed poorly and are subject to unilateral behavior that increases prices and reduces efficiency.

6. The unusual attributes of electricity discussed previously create unusual opportunities for suppliers to exercise market power unilaterally. Market power problems have been extensively documented in the United States and other countries (Wolfram 1999; Borenstein, Bushnell, and Wolak 2002; Joskow and Kahn 2002). The former simply enhances the latter. Because electricity demand is very inelastic in the short run and electricity cannot be stored, individual suppliers may be able to move prices significantly even in markets that are not very highly concentrated by traditional standards. This is most likely to be the case when capacity constraints are approached and a large fraction of demand is being served by spot-market purchases in day-ahead and real-time markets rather than pursuant to forward contracts that establish the transactions price in advance. The allocation of transmission rights may enhance market power in generation markets as well (Joskow and Tirole 2000). The incentive and ability to exercise market power is *enhanced* by poor wholesale-market design attributes that expand opportunities for suppliers to take actions that affect market prices. Accordingly, the arguments about whether market performance problems are due to poor market design *or* market power is an empty debate. As a result, market design, transmission rights allocation, mergers and acquisitions of generating facilities, and market monitoring institutions must be sensitive to the potential for serious market power problems to emerge in unregulated wholesale power markets.

7. Expanding significantly the requirement that, as the default, larger *retail* consumers be billed based on their real-time consumption and associated real-time prices for energy can help to improve wholesale-market performance in a number of dimensions. This will allow consumer preferences for reliability and market price volatility to be more accurately represented in the wholesale market, help to mitigate market power, flatten load duration curves

and reduce the need for capacity that operates for only a few hours each year, encourage risk-averse consumers to cover their demand with forward contracts, and reduce the need for market power mitigation regulations and resource adequacy rules (see the following). At least some of the benefits of real-time pricing are public goods that benefit all consumers. Accordingly, it would be worthwhile to provide financing to distribution companies to expand the default utilization of real-time meters.

8. While it is important to move price-sensitive consumers on to real-time pricing for their price-sensitive demand, it is also important to provide appropriate incentives for load-serving entities and consumers to rely more on forward contracting and less on spot-market purchases to reflect their preferences for risk and the costs and benefits of insurance against price volatility. This will help to mitigate market power by reducing supply incentives to withhold output from the spot market and drive up spot-market prices and provide better signals and financing support for investments in new generating capacity. The real-time pricing goal and the forward-contracting goal are not incompatible. If the default is real-time pricing, consumers who are risk averse will have a stronger incentive to go out into the market and enter into forward contracts for some or all of their demand. Consumers who are less risk averse or can adjust more easily to real-time price variations will leave more of their demand in the spot market to enable them to respond to short-term price signals and will cover less with forward contracts.

9. There are important linkages between wholesale-market institutions, retail procurement, and retail competition institutions. The infirmities of retail competition institutions in many of the states that have implemented retail competition programs (see the following) and the uncertainties about whether, when, and how retail competition will spread to other states has undermined incentives for distribution companies and other load-serving entities to enter into longer-term contracts for power and transmission service with potential investors in generating and transmission capacity. This situation will exacerbate the boom-bust cycle of the industry, undermine investment incentives, increase incentives for suppliers to exercise market power when supplies are tight, increase prices volatility, and ultimately increase political pressures for regulatory interventions when prices are high.

10. Fraudulent and misleading accounting practices; false reporting of trading information to private entities publishing price indices upon which suppliers, traders and consumers rely; and the general trend of the late 1990s to make as little information as possible available to the public have undermined the confidence of consumers, regulators, and their representatives in state legislatures and Congress in competitive electricity markets. It has also

led to financial disaster for many merchant generating and energy trading firms and destroyed liquidity in forward electricity markets. Well-functioning competitive electricity markets depend upon the existence of efficient liquid forward markets for energy and associated derivative financial instruments to allow consumers and generators to manage their risks efficiently. Restoring public and investor confidence in energy trading and creating liquid transparent markets for physical contracts and supporting financial instruments to meet the needs of the ultimate buyers and sellers of electricity in these markets is an important policy priority.

Many features of the FERC's SMD NOPR issued on July 31, 2002 reflect these considerations and for this reason provide a useful, though far from perfect, blueprint for wholesale-market design.[9]

Retail Competition

Most of the academic research and many of the public policy debates about competitive electricity markets have focused on the design and performance of wholesale-market and transmission institutions. However, from a political perspective, the primary selling point for competition in electricity among consumers and government officials has been the prospect for *retail competition* or retail "customer choice" to lead to lower *retail* electricity prices. Yet, there has been very little work assessing the performance of retail competition programs in the United States, and there is a growing perception that, at the very least, retail competition programs have had disappointing results, especially from the perspective of residential and small commercial customers. It is too early to provide a comprehensive assessment of retail competition programs, many of which have not been in operation for very long. Moreover, inadequate information, especially on prices and value added services, makes it difficult to perform a good assessment. Nevertheless, there are things to learn from the experience to date and the data that are available.

With a retail competition program, an electricity customer's bill is "unbundled" into regulated components with a price P_R (transmission, distribution, stranded cost recovery, retail service costs to support default services) and a competitive component with a price P_C (generation service, some retail service costs, and perhaps an additional "margin" to induce customers to shop). The customer continues to buy the regulated component from the local distribution company and is free to purchase the competitive component from competing retailers or retail electricity service providers (ESP).[10]

In most jurisdictions that have introduced retail competition programs, the incumbent distribution company is required to continue to provide "default service" of some kind to retail consumers who do not choose an ESP. The terms and conditions of default service vary across the states but typically have been calculated in the following way. The regulators start with the incumbent's prevailing regulated cost of generation service. A fraction of this regulated generation cost component is determined to be "stranded generation costs" that can be recovered from retail consumers over some time period and is included in P_R. The residual, reflecting an estimate of the competitive market value of generation services, plus some fraction of retail service costs (metering, billing, customer call centers) is then used to define the initial "default service" price P_C or the "price to beat" by ESPs seeking to attract customers from the regulated default service tariffs available from the incumbent utility.[11] The value of P_C is then typically fixed for several years (sometimes with adjustments for fuel prices) but is expected eventually to reflect the competitive market value of providing competitive retail services to consumers.

Where incumbents have significant stranded costs, which is the case in most of the states that have introduced retail competition to date, regulators have been able to capture a small fraction of this sum for customers by mandating an initial retail price reduction that is reflected in P_R, though in many cases this is simply a deferral of recovery of these costs to future years. Regulators in a number of states have consciously left some of the stranded costs in the default service price P_C so that it exceeds the wholesale-market value of the associated generation services in order to encourage customers to switch to competitive retailers, though in a number of cases the utility may ultimately be able to recover any associated losses in stranded costs in the future through surcharges included in P_R.

Things become more complicated when the incumbent utility has a prevailing regulated price whose regulated generation cost component is *below* the competitive wholesale-market value of the associated electricity. And there are many utilities around the country that have regulated generation cost components of their retail rates that are *below* the competitive wholesale-market value price of electricity (mostly in states that have decided against implementing retail competition programs and this is not a coincidence). In this case, the bundled price is also below the price that would prevail if a customer purchased regulated services at the regulated price and competitive services at their market values; the incumbent utility effectively has negative stranded costs. Regulators could handle negative stranded costs symmetrically with positive stranded costs by setting the price for competitive service P_C at its competitive market value and then providing a "stranded benefit" credit in the distribution charge P_R to settle up on the historical "regulatory bargain." However, this is not how regulators have handled prices for the few companies with negative stranded costs in states that have implemented retail competition programs. Instead they have just unbundled (more or less) the low prevailing regulated generation cost component of the regulated bundled rate and established that as the default service price. In these cases, ESPs that purchase power in competitive wholesale markets cannot compete with the default service price P_C as it reflects prevailing embedded costs of generation that are below the competitive market value of generation services.

In some states the default service prices were set at levels that were expected to exceed wholesale prices by a significant margin, but wholesale prices subsequently rose unexpectedly to levels that exceeded the default service price in 2000 and 2001 before falling as new generating capacity entered the market. In most states, customers are free to return to the default service tariff if the prices offered by competitive retailers are higher than the distribution company's default service prices, and this is exactly what has happened in some states. The structure has made it possible for retail customers to switch back and forth between regulated default service and unregulated service provided to ESPs.

Consumers can benefit in at least four ways from the introduction of retail competition. First, even if they do not switch to an ESP they may benefit from reductions in regulated prices that have typically accompanied the restructuring process as an outcome of the bargaining over stranded cost recovery and the terms and conditions under which the incumbents can move their regulated generating plants into unregulated affiliates. Second, consumers can benefit by receiving lower prices than the default service price P_C from an ESP that has competed successfully for their business. Third, ESPs may offer consumers a variety of value added services, including price-risk management, demand management, and energy efficiency services. Finally, competing ESPs may be able to provide "retailing" services more efficiently than can the incumbent. However, here we must recognize that retail service costs are a small fraction of a typical customer's bill, amounting to 0.3 to 0.4 cents/kWh or about $3–$7 per month for a typical residential customer (depending on assumptions about fixed vs. variable components of retail service costs [Joskow 2000b]). Since the incumbent monopolies did not have to incur marketing and advertising costs to attract customers, these are additional costs that are not now reflected in regulated retail prices but would have to be incurred by ESPs.

Retail Customer Switching Activity

Rational residential consumers will switch to an ESP if the price offered by competitive ESPs plus any transactions costs associated with switching suppliers is less than the incumbent utility's default service price P_C plus the value of any value added services that the ESP provides. There is reasonably good data available (with some effort) to measure the extent to which customers have switched to ESPs, and I will focus on that information first. Switching behavior by consumers reflects their revealed preference for default service or ESP service, though absent information on ESP prices and value added services we cannot disentangle switching costs, commodity price differences, and the value of any value added services provided to consumers. In tables 1.5 to 1.10 and figure 1.3, I have displayed the most recent data available for the fraction of residential, commercial, and industrial customers who have switched to ESPs in several representative states that have implemented retail competition programs. The states that have introduced retail competition provide different amounts of information regarding customer switching activity, so the information reflected in the tables and figures is not always comparable across states.

Let us start with Massachusetts (see table 1.5), which was the first state to make retail competition available to all customers in March 1998, so that retail customer choice has been available for almost five years. During that period of time, less than 3 percent of the residential customers and less than 9 percent of the small commercial and industrial customers have switched to ESPs. About 30 percent of the largest industrial customers have switched to ESPs. Within each customer class, the customers consuming more electricity are more likely to switch to an ESP. Overall, 3.4 percent of the retail customers and 22 percent of the retail demand is supplied by ESPs. The remaining customers are served on one of two default service tariffs (called "standard offer service" and "default service" in Massachusetts, with the latter tracking wholesale-market prices). During the period of time that retail choice has been available, the standard offer tariff has often provided electricity at a price below the wholesale-market price, making ESP supplies unprofitable. The default service price fluctuates with wholesale-market conditions, but leaves little if any margin for ESPs to recover their retailing costs. While all consumers have the right to choose their electricity supplier in Massachusetts, there are presently few ESPs competing to serve smaller customers.

Let us turn next to New York (see table 1.6), where retail competition became available between May 1998 and July 2001 depending on the utility service area and the type of customer. There has been somewhat more switching

Figure 1.3. Pennsylvania direct access load: A, Industrial (%); B, residential (%)

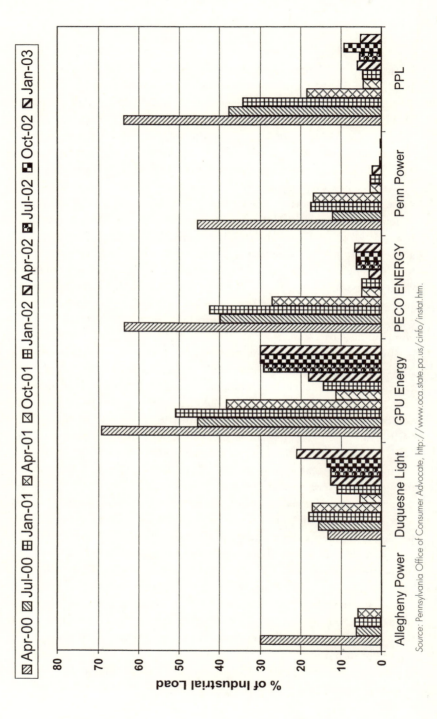

Source: Pennsylvania Office of Consumer Advocate, http://www.oca.state.pa.us/cinfo/instat.htm.

Figure 1.3. continued

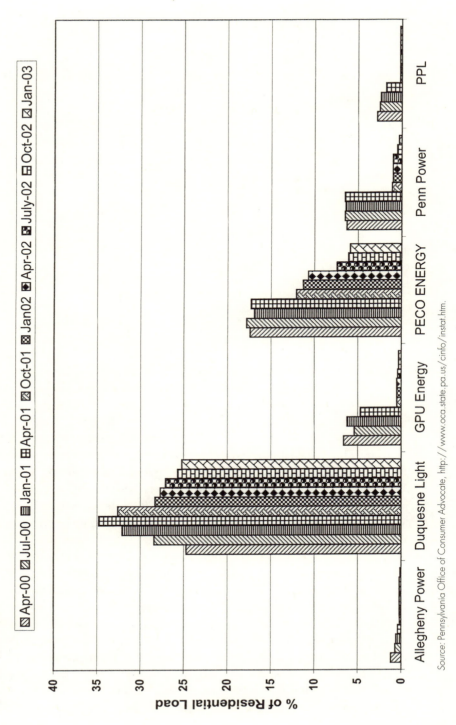

Source: Pennsylvania Office of Consumer Advocate, http://www.oca.state.pa.us/cinfo/instat.htm.

Table 1.5 Retail choice in Massachusetts, December 2002

Customers	% of customers served by ESPs	% of load served by ESPs
Residential	2.6	2.4
Small C/I	8.8	11.5
Medium C/I	11.1	17.3
Large C/I	29.2	46.2
Total	3.4	22.2

Source: http://www.state.ma.us/doer/pub_info/migrate.htm.
Notes: Retail choice began March 1998. C/I = commercial and industrial.

Table 1.6 Retail choice in New York as of December 2002

Customers	% of customers served by ESPs	% of load served by ESPs
Residential	5.0	5.6
Nonresidential	7.1	32.3

Source: http://www.dps.state.ny.us/Electric_RA_Migration.htm.
Note: Retail choice began May 1998–July 2001.

than in Massachusetts, but the basic patterns and economic incentives are very similar. In both Massachusetts and New York, there has been some switching back and forth between ESPs and default service tariffs as wholesale prices have fluctuated and ESPs have exited the market. In Maine (see table 1.7) as well, residential and small commercial customers have not switched to ESPs (or those who switched have now switched back to utility default service), though there has been more switching by larger industrial customers. We can compare Massachusetts, New York, and Maine to New Jersey (see table 1.8), where retail competition began in November 1999. After over three years of customer choice there are almost no customers of any kind who have chosen to be supplied by an ESP in New Jersey, largely because the regulated default service price has been below the comparable wholesale market price for electricity. The situation in New Jersey appears to have evolved into a wholesale competition model in which the incumbent distribution companies purchase wholesale generation services through a state-approved competitive auction process and then pass along the associated costs to retail customers. In summary, at the present time in New England, New York, and New Jersey, a residential or small commercial customer who wanted to be supplied by an ESP would find it hard to find one. Most of those that were active in this region when retail competition was first introduced have now exited the market or are not actively marketing services to residential and small commercial customers.

Table 1.7 Retail choice in Maine (Central Maine Power, January 2003)

Customers	% of load served by ESPs
Residential/small commercial	<1
Medium industrial	28
Large industrial	73
Total	33

Source: http://www.state.me.us/mpuc/electric%20restructuring/migrationrates.htm.
Note: Retail choice began March 2000.

Table 1.8 Retail choice in New Jersey as of December 2002

Customers	% of customers served by ESPs	% of load served by ESPs
Residential	0.06	
Nonresidential	0.14	
Retail		1.9

Source: http://www.bpu.state.nj.us/wwwroot/energy/elecswitchdata.htm.
Note: Retail choice began November 1999.

Pennsylvania provides an interesting example of the interactions between changing wholesale-market prices, default service prices, and the initial regulated utility cost conditions that had an impact on the level of these default service prices. Figure 1.3 displays the fraction of retail demand that has been served by ESPs at various points in time from April 2000 through January 2003 for each of six major Pennsylvania utilities. Panel A of figure 1.3 displays this information for residential customers. Except for Duquesne, all of these utilities are in PJM and buy and sell power out of the same wholesale market. Yet each of them has a different default service price, reflecting the different levels of their regulated retail prices (and stranded generation costs) prior to restructuring. Note first that there is a very large variation across utilities in the fraction of residential demand served by ESPs. Those with the highest switching rates (Philadelphia Electric Company [PECO] and Duquesne) serve Philadelphia and Pittsburgh, had high regulated retail prices and significant stranded costs prior to the implementation of the retail competition and restructuring program.[12] In their restructuring settlements, the value of P_C was set relatively high compared to then-prevailing wholesale-market prices, reflecting stranded cost allocations. The "price to beat" faced by ESPs was sufficiently high relative to then-prevailing wholesale-market prices to make it profitable, at least initially, for ESPs to make offers to customers that were sufficiently far below the default service price to get a significant number of customers quickly to switch to an ESP. The other utilities in Pennsylvania had relatively low regulated rates prior to restructuring and relatively low values for P_C. Because ESPs must buy power in the wholesale market at higher prices than the utility default price available to retail customers they have not been able to profitably offer attractive competitive alternatives to retail customers in these areas. Note as well that over time, the fraction of residential customers in Pennsylvania receiving service from an ESP has *declined* very significantly. This reflects the fact that as wholesale prices rose after the default prices were set and retailers realized how costly it actually is to serve residential customers, they raised their prices or withdrew from the market, and the residential customers they were serving found it advantageous or necessary to return to their utility's default service tariff. Based on the results of PECO's recent effort to auction off some of its small commercial default service customers to ESPs, there seems to be little interest among ESPs in providing service at a price significantly below PECO's default service price.[13]

Panel B of figure 1.3 displays the same data for industrial customers. A larger fraction of industrial customers initially switched to ESPs. Then many of them returned to default service when wholesale prices rose. Some now appear to be returning again to ESPs in a few utility service areas. This back and forth between utility default service and competitive ESP service is a consequence of the "safety net" provided by the regulated default service prices available from the incumbent utility supplier.

Ohio also provides an interesting example of how the interaction between regulation, default service terms, and wholesale-market prices affects consumer switching behavior. Retail competition began in Ohio in January 2001. Table 1.9 displays the fraction of customers served by ESPs in different utility service areas. In the areas served by subsidiaries of AEP and Dayton Power and Light, essentially no customers are served by ESPs. These are utilities that had very low regulated retail prices and the value of P_C established at the beginning of retail prices reflected these low regulated rates. The regulated default prices in these areas are lower than the wholesale-market price. However, in the areas served by First Energy's subsidiaries there has been very significant movement of retail customers to ESPs. Indeed, residential customers appear to have switched at the same rate or even at a greater rate than industrial customers. First Energy's subsidiaries had high regulated retail prices, the value of P_C was consciously set at a relatively high level to put recovery of some of the utilities' stranded costs at risk, and there were some other incentives related to stranded cost recovery that made it in First Energy's interest to migrate customers to ESPs. Moreover, the data for residential customers is misleading. Ohio has a municipal aggregation program that allows municipalities

Table 1.9 Retail choice in Ohio, September 30, 2002

	% of customers served by ESPs
AEP subsidiaries	
Columbus Southern	
Residential	0.00
Commercial	0.25
Industrial	0.00
Ohio Power	
Residential	0.00
Commercial	0.00
Industrial	0.00
First Energy subsidiaries	
Cleveland Electric	
Residential	55.05
Commercial	54.84
Industrial	27.69
Ohio Edison	
Residential	23.85
Commercial	23.51
Industrial	27.70
Dayton Power and Light	
Residential	0.00
Commercial	0.01
Industrial	0.16

Source: http://www.puco.ohio.gov/ohioutil/MarketMonitoring/ECC_Switch_Rates_Summary.
Note: Retail choice began January 1, 2001.

to purchase power on behalf of the customers within their municipal boundaries (customers have an opt-out option). About 90 percent of the residential customers listed as being served by ESPs are actually being served through municipal aggregation programs in which an ESP can effectively serve all of the customers located in that municipality. This is really a wholesale competition program rather than a retail competition program.

Finally, let's turn to Texas (see table 1.10). Retail competition began officially in Texas in January 2002, though there was a pilot program implemented before that, and customers who had switched before the official program began could stay with the ESPs they had chosen. By the end of 2002 between 4 percent and 10 percent of the residential customers had switched to ESPs, and the fraction continues to grow (rather than to decline as in Pennsylvania). For commercial customers, 10 percent to 15 percent had switched

Table 1.10 Retail choice in Texas, December 31, 2002

	% of customers and load served by ESPs	% of load served by ESPs
Residential	4–10	4–10
Secondary voltage	10–14	30–50
Primary/transmission voltage	20	55

Source: Public Utility Commission of Texas (2003).
Notes: Retail choice began January 1, 2002. Includes customers switching in 2001 pilot program. Reported numbers are the range for five Texas distribution companies except for primary/transmission voltage, which is the total for the state.

to ESPs by the end of 2002, while 20 percent of the largest customers, accounting for 50 percent of the revenues from large industrial customers, had switched to an ESP, and virtually all of the largest customers have negotiated competitive contracts either with the retailing affiliate of their incumbent utility or an unaffiliated ESP. So, in only a year, and despite some initial technical problems experienced with switching customers, Texas appears to be on a trend in which customers are migrating relatively quickly to ESPs. It is also the state that has the largest number of active ESPs competing to sell service to retail consumers.

We can compare the switching experience with that in England and Wales since 1990. In England and Wales, retail competition started with the largest industrial and commercial retail customers (greater than 1 MW initially) and was gradually expanded to industrial and commercial customer groups with smaller consumption levels (peak demand greater than 100 kW in 1994). By 2000, about 80 percent of industrial and commercial customers with peak demands above 1 MW and about 70 percent with peak demand below 1 MW (and greater than 100 kW) had switched to a competitive retail supplier other than the incumbent distribution company's ESP affiliate. These switching shares have increased monotonically over time (Department of Trade and Industry [DTI] 2000). In May 1999, retail competition was opened up to residential (domestic) customers. Initially, the prices that could be charged to residential customers by the incumbent electricity distributor-affiliated ESP were regulated with a price cap and the incumbent retail supplier had a continuing obligation to provide service to residential customers in their service areas at a price no higher than the regulated supply price. By the end of 2001, about 30 percent of the residential customers had switched to competing ESPs, and by mid-2002 this fraction had reached 34 percent (DTI 2003, 97). In April 2002, the default service price caps applicable to residential customers were lifted and retail supply prices were fully deregulated for all types of customers (Office of Gas and Electricity Markets [OFGEM] 2001; DTI 2003). The retail competition program in England and Wales has been much more successful in facilitating migration of retail customers from default service to nonincumbent ESPs than have the programs in the United States.

Retail Price and Value Added Service Effects

Unfortunately, there is very little information available to evaluate systematically the price effects of retail competition or even the level of retail prices charged by ESPs in the United States. Nor is there information about the diffusion of the value added services that many retailers argued would be made available to retail customers. The Energy Information Administration (EIA) has begun to collect retail price data separately for utility- and ESP-supplied retail service, but sufficient data are not yet available to do a proper comprehensive analysis. Moreover, the relevant comparison is not between what retail prices are today and what they were when retail competition began, but rather the difference between what they are with retail competition and what they would have been without it. This will be a difficult counterfactual analysis to undertake, requiring an incorporation of fuel price changes, other changes in operations and maintenance (O&M) costs, changes in the utilities' rate bases, cost of capital, and so on to measure what regulated prices would have been absent restructuring settlements.

Since so few customers have switched to competitive retailers in most states, it must be the case that the bulk of any savings that they have achieved are attributable to reductions in *regulated* prices implemented as a consequence of restructuring compared to what these regulated prices would have been absent restructuring. This is especially true for residential customers. The Texas Public Utility Commission (PUC) estimates that default service or so-called price-to-beat customers (residential, commercial, and industrial customers with peak demands below 1 MW) saved $902 million in 2002 if they simply stayed on the price-to-beat rates. This sum is composed of $262 million attributed to a mandated 6 percent retail price reduction included as part of the restructuring program and $677 million attributed to reduced fuel costs and the expiration of fuel surcharges.[14] Roughly 10 percent of these customers have switched to ESPs and, assuming (contrary to fact) that they all switched to the ESP offering the lowest price, this would imply another $64 million in savings directly attributable to retail competition for residential customers in 2002.[15] Comparisons between the price to beat for the major distribution utilities in Texas and the prices being offered to residential customers by competitive ESPs during 2002 indicate discounts as large as 8 percent (range of 5 percent to 8 percent, ignoring "green power" options) for residential customers consuming 1500 kWh/month.[16] Discounts of this magnitude are apparently sufficient to overcome transactions costs associated with switching by roughly 8 percent of the residential and smaller commercial customers during the first year that the retail competition program is in effect. However, so far it appears that the bulk of any retail price savings resulting directly from retail competition have accrued primarily to industrial customers in Texas and most other states that have implemented retail competition programs.

We can gain some further insights into the challenges associated with measuring the impact of retail competition on retail prices by comparing the patterns of retail prices charged to residential customers by utilities between states that have introduced retail competition and those that have not. Ninety percent or more of residential customers continue to take service from their local utility in most states that have introduced retail competition. If there were significantly more attractive prices offered by ESPs we would have seen much more switching by now, as in Texas. Figure 1.4 compares the percentage changes in average nominal residential prices for eight states with the most active retail competition programs, along with the average nominal residential price for the United States as a whole, for the period 1995 through 2002.[17] Note that except for Texas, in the mid-1990s all of these pioneer retail competition states had regulated retail prices that exceeded the national average, typically by a substantial amount.[18] Retail prices for residential customers in Texas in 1995 were just slightly below the national average. On average residential prices fell by 3.72 percent in these eight retail competition states between 1995 and 2002, compared to an average increase of 0.5 percent for the United States as a whole. The two states with the largest reduction in residential prices are New Jersey and Illinois. Both states have essentially no residential customers who have switched to an ESP, so any savings from restructuring are reflected entirely in changes in the prices of regulated default service. Since seven of the eight retail competition states had residential prices that were above the national average, it is also likely that the prices in these states would have fallen more than the average if regulation had continued, reflecting the declining rate bases associated with costly nuclear power plants, increased capacity utilization as demand increased, and the gradual end of high-priced QF contracts signed during the 1980s. Texas, the only state in the group that had residential prices below the national average in 1995, experienced the largest increase in prices by 2002. If retail competition per se has had any effect on residential prices in the United States it must be small. However, this is an area where a more comprehensive analysis of counter-

Figure 1.4. Percent change in residential retail price (1995–2002)

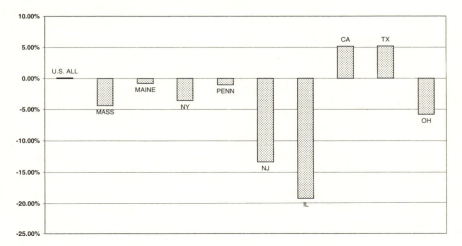

factual regulated prices and ESP prices would be valuable when and if the necessary data become available.

I think that it is fair to say that retail competition is still a work in progress in the United States and that retail competition has been a disappointment in many of the states that have implemented it. It should be no surprise that the remaining states, which typically have much lower regulated prices than did the retail competition pioneer states, would not find the performance to date to provide a particularly compelling case to introduce retail competition.

There are several factors that need to be recognized and issues that need to be addressed in reforming existing retail competition programs or designing new programs. If the primary selling point for introducing retail competition continues to be that it will result in significantly lower retail prices from those that prevail today, retail competition will be a very tough sell politically in many of the states that have not already embraced it. In the states that have introduced retail competition, few residential or small commercial customers have chosen to be served by ESPs, and the direct benefits of retail competition per se, in terms of lower prices, appear to be very small. Large industrial and commercial customers appear to have done much better in states that had relatively high regulated rates, at least based on revealed preference in the absence of publicly available retail price data for these customers. Many of the states that have not introduced retail competition have relatively low regulated retail prices, many with regulated prices for generation services that are below comparable wholesale market prices. Unless state regulators are willing to allow retail prices to rise to reflect the competitive market value of generation services, ESPs will not be able to compete against these low regulated generation prices if they are unbundled at their current or lower levels. Accordingly, it is not surprising that there is little interest in retail competition in those states that have low regulated retail prices.

If default service prices are set below the comparable wholesale-market price of power, ESPs will not be able to compete for retail customers. Moreover, allowing customers that choose to take service from an ESP to return to a regulated tariff when wholesale prices are high without being charged an appropriate price for this option seriously undermines the development of retail competition because it effectively provides a subsidized option for retail customers who switch back and forth and a very unstable customer base for ESPs.[19] This subsidized default service option also has adverse effects on wholesale markets by discouraging both utilities with default service obligations and ESPs from entering into long-term forward contracts because under the rules in place in most states, consumers are free to come and go from the regulated default tariff as they choose.

Even if the regulated default service price P_C is higher than the comparable competitive wholesale-market value of the power supplied, ESPs need an additional margin both to induce sticky retail customers to switch suppliers and to cover their retail supply costs. The retail supply costs for the mass market (residential and small commercial) are much higher than many retailers had anticipated. Billing, customer service, bad debt, advertising, and promotion costs add up quickly. Moreover, there are significant economies of scale associated with several components of these costs. Accordingly, P_C may have to be much higher than the comparable wholesale-market price to induce much customer switching. The evidence from England and Wales suggests that price reductions of 5 percent to 10 percent of the *total bill* are necessary to get significant customer switching for mass market (residential and commercial) customers. This is consistent with the limited experience in Texas as well. If the generation component of the retail price is 50 percent of the total bill, then price reductions of 10 percent to 20 percent on the generation component are necessary to get significant switching. To this must be added about another 5 percent to 10 percent for retail service costs. So, a margin of 15 percent to 30 percent between P_C and the comparable wholesale-market value of power may be necessary to induce significant switching by residential and small commercial customers. In many areas of the United States, this kind of margin is incompatible with reducing retail prices from their prevailing regulated levels.

It is far from obvious to me that residential and small commercial customers have or will benefit much, if at all, from retail competition compared to a regime where their local distribution company purchased power for their needs by putting together a portfolio of short-term forward contracts (from days to several years) acquired in wholesale markets (Joskow 2000a,b).[20] This is effectively what is happening in most of the states that have introduced retail competition anyway, except the wholesale contracts are largely short-term and the threat of draconian policy changes to "make retail competition work" lead both utilities and ESPs to be very reluctant to make longer-term commitments for power supplies of any kind. There is no evidence that residential and small commercial customers are getting any significant value added services that they find sufficiently attractive to shop and choose an ESP. For those states that have not introduced retail competition it would be worth considering introducing it first for larger customers and then expanding eligibility over time as the retail-market institutions develop.

If policymakers are committed to fostering retail competition for residential and small commercial customers, despite the possibility that retail prices will rise in the short run due to increased transactions costs, switching costs, and market power, the framework adopted by Texas, a framework with many similarities to what was adopted in England and Wales, is likely to be the most successful in stimulating retail shopping and the development of a viable retail supply sector. It has several components:

1. All retail supply functions of the incumbent regulated utility are shifted to a retail supply affiliate and, ideally, this retail supply affiliate should be separated through sale or flotation from the regulated delivery business. All of the associated retail supply costs are unbundled from the distribution and transmission charges and included in the default service price. ESPs then can compete with the incumbent's default service price P_C that includes all of the incumbent's retail supply costs. The retail supply affiliate has the obligation to provide regulated default service to retail customers for a defined period of time or until market conditions are sufficiently competitive to deregulated retail prices completely. The decision to fully deregulate should be sensitive to evidence that residential customers have high switching costs and that the incumbent may have significant market power for some period of time (Giulietti, Price, and Waterson 2003).

2. The default service price should reflect the competitive wholesale-market value of electricity over the period during which the default service prices are to be in effect plus retail service costs. The incumbent supplier should be free to cover these commitments with a portfolio of contracts and

ownership of generating assets and to try to reduce retail supply costs under a price cap and subject to quality-of-service criteria and penalties for failing to meet them. For utilities that have stranded costs, they can be recovered through a nonbypassable surcharge attached to distribution or transmission charges. Utilities whose regulated prices for generation service are below competitive market values should be treated symmetrically. A measure of the associated "stranded benefits" should be developed and accounted for as a *rebate* attached to regulated *distribution and transmission* prices. Thus, even in states with very low regulated prices, the unbundled generation component will reflect prevailing market values while consumers still capture their entitlement to the "cheap" power from generating plants they have paid for through regulated prices through lower delivery charges.

3. Once customers turn to an ESP they do not get to come back to the default service price. Instead they are served by a provider of last resort (POLR) at market-based prices determined through an auction of the POLR service responsibility.

4. When wholesale and retail markets are deemed to be sufficiently mature and competitive, retail generation prices are deregulated and the incumbent's retail supply affiliate has the opportunity to charge any remaining customers an unregulated price. This provides the incumbent retail supplier with a potentially valuable opportunity to supply the stickiest customers at unregulated prices *if* the competition in the retail market evolves sufficiently to trigger the deregulation brass ring. This potential business opportunity also makes it fair for the incumbent to be at risk for some of its retail service costs prior to full deregulation, many components of which are fixed in the short run and needed to serve the initially large default service customer base. Rather than being indifferent to whether retail customers switch to an ESP or not, which is the case in most states where retail competition has been implemented, the incumbent has an interest in encouraging enough of its customers to turn to competitive retail suppliers so that the competitive retail supply market will flourish.

Long-Term Resource Adequacy

Despite the substantial amount of new generating capacity that has been completed in the last few years, and what appears to be more than adequate capacity to meet peak demands in most regions of the country, there are growing concerns that wholesale energy and operating reserve markets will not provide adequate incentives to bring forth sufficient new generating capacity in the future to meet traditional reliability criteria. These concerns reflect a number of phenomena, including the financial collapse of the merchant generation and trading sector, the cancellation of many planned generating projects, tougher financial requirements and increased cost of capital to finance new merchant projects, very thin markets for medium- and long-term forward contracts for energy and operating reserves to help to support financing of new projects, proposals to terminate installed capacity (ICAP) obligations that now exist in the three Eastern ISOs, the effects of price caps and various bid mitigation rules that are applied to spot markets, and increasing pressures to close older existing plants as they face low wholesale prices and additional costs to meet new environmental requirements.

Questions about whether competitive wholesale and retail markets would produce adequate generation investment incentives to balance supply and demand so as to match consumer valuations of reliability have been raised since the transition to competitive electricity markets began. Until 2001, the system in England and Wales provided for additional capacity payments to be made to all generators scheduled to supply during hours when supply was unusually tight (high loss-of-load probability).[21] The wholesale markets created and managed by the Eastern ISOs during the late 1990s have continued their traditional policies of requiring distribution companies (or, more generally, "load-serving entities" (LSE) to encompass ESPs) to enter into contracts for capacity to meet their projected peak demand plus an administratively determined reserve margin. Similar requirements continue to be applied by utilities in those states that have not introduced retail competition and continue to rely primarily on vertically integrated utilities that may purchase some of their forecast capacity needs in the wholesale market. Argentina's competitive electricity market system also included capacity payments to stimulate investment in reserve capacity. In Chile, distribution utilities are required to enter into forward contracts to meet forecast demand plus a reserve margin. However, California's electricity market design did not impose capacity, reserve- or forward-contract obligations, nor does Texas.

Questions about whether wholesale markets will bring forth adequate investments in generating capacity arises from the unusual characteristics of electricity supply and demand discussed earlier: (1) large variations in demand over the course of a year; (2) nonstorability; (3) the need to physically balance supply and demand at every point on the network continuously to meet physical constraints on voltage, frequency, and stability; and (4) that even under the best of circumstances (i.e., with effective real-time pricing of energy and operating reserves) nonprice mechanisms will have to be relied upon from time to time to ration imbalances between supply and demand to meet physical operating reliability criteria because markets cannot clear fast enough to do so without unplanned outages. These attributes have a number of implications. First, a large amount of generating capacity that is available to meet peak demand plus the associated operating reserve requirements supplies relatively small amounts of energy during the year. For example, in New England in 2001, 93 percent of the energy was supplied by 55 percent of the installed generating capacity while the remaining 45 percent of the capacity supplied only about 7 percent of the energy.[22] Potential investors in new generating capacity must expect to cover their variable operating costs, their fixed operating and maintenance costs, and their capital costs from sales of energy and operating reserves over the life of generating capacity under consideration. The return of and on the associated capital investment in new generating capacity is the difference between the prices they receive for generation services (including capacity payment, if any) and their operating (primarily fuel) costs. The profitability of generating units that are likely to operate only for a relatively small number of hours in each year ("peaking capacity") are especially sensitive to the level of prices that are realized during the small number of high-demand hours in which they provide energy or operating reserves.

Second, the generating capacity available to supply energy at any point in time must always be greater than the demand for energy at that point in time as a result of the need to carry "inventory" in the form of generators providing frequency regulation and operating reserve services. That is, generating capacity (or, in principle, demand response) must be available that is either "spinning" or available to start up quickly to provide energy to balance supply and demand at each location on the network in response to real-time variations in demand and unplanned equipment outages. When these operating reserves fall below a certain level (e.g., 7 percent of demand), system operators begin to take actions to reduce demand administratively according to a prespecified hierarchy of "operating reserve conservation" actions. The final actions in this hierarchy are voltage reductions and nonprice rationing of demand (rolling blackouts).

Finally, there is an important but underappreciated linkage between the retail procurement environment and the performance of the wholesale market with regard to investments in generating capacity that runs infrequently to meet peak demands for energy and operating reserves. If we are in a world where regulated monopoly distribution companies (i.e., no retail competition) are required to purchase electricity for their retail customers to meet their forecast demand subject to a clearly defined reliability criterion (e.g., specified loss-of-load probability and associated capacity margin above expected peak demand), then wholesale-market prices (spot and forward) would rise, in one way or another, to clear the market at this reliability level. If, however, we are in a retail competition world, or in a world where distribution companies choose to have no predetermined reliability criterion but simply buy enough energy and operating reserves to meet demand at each point in time as it is realized, the implicit reliability and generating capacity level at which the wholesale market will clear will depend on exactly how consumer preferences for electricity with regard to price levels and price volatility are represented in the wholesale market, the associated ability of consumers to respond to real-time prices and to match their preferences for market-price risk with the costs of forward contracts.

A well-functioning perfectly competitive wholesale electricity market will (to oversimplify for this discussion) operate in one of two states of nature. Under typical operating conditions (State 1), market clearing prices for energy *and* operating reserves should equal the marginal (opportunity) cost of the last increment of generating capacity that just clears supply and demand at each point in time.[23] In the case of wholesale electric energy supply, this price is the marginal cost of producing a little more or a little less energy from the generating unit on the margin in the merit order. Figure 1.5 depicts the spot-market demand for electricity and the competitive supply curve for electricity under typical operating conditions (State 1). Inframarginal generating units earn net revenues to cover their fixed costs whenever the market clearing price exceeds their own marginal generation costs. In the case of operating reserves, the efficient price is (roughly) equal to the *difference* between the price of energy and the marginal cost of the next increment of generation that could supply energy profitably if the price of energy were slightly higher plus any direct costs incurred to provide operating reserves (e.g., costs associated with spinning). This price for operating reserves is equal to the marginal *opportunity cost* incurred by generators standing in reserve rather than supplying energy. Under typical operating conditions (State 1) the price of operating reserves will be very small—close to zero, and far below the price of energy.

The second wholesale-market state (State 2) is associated with a relatively small number of hours each year when there would be excess demand at a wholesale price that equals to the marginal supply cost of the last increment of generating capacity that can physically be made available on the network to supply energy or operating reserves. In this case, the market must be cleared "on the demand side." That is, consumers bidding to obtain energy would bid prices up to a (much) higher level reflecting the value (or value of lost energy or load) that consumers place on consuming less electricity as demand is re-

Figure 1.5. Perfectly competitive wholesale spot electricity market

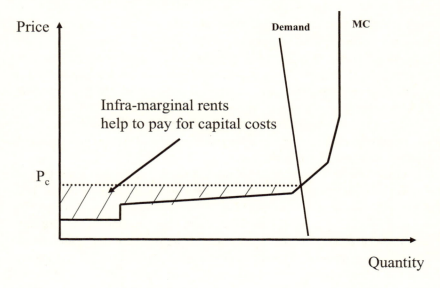

duced to match the limited supplies available to the market. This second state is depicted in figure 1.6. In what follows, I will refer to the conditions depicted in figure 1.6 as *competitive* "scarcity" conditions.[24]

Under competitive scarcity conditions (i.e., in the absence of seller-market power), the competitive market clearing price of energy will now generally be much higher than the marginal production cost of supplying the last available increment of energy from generating capacity available to the network, reflecting the high opportunity cost (value of lost energy or lost load) that consumers place on reducing consumption by a significant amount on short notice. Furthermore, while the price of operating reserves will continue to be equal to the marginal opportunity cost incurred by generators standing in reserve rather than supplying energy, the opportunity cost of standing in reserve rather than supplying energy will rise significantly as well in response to the higher "scarcity value" of energy. *All* generating units actually supplying energy and operating reserves in the spot market during scarcity conditions would earn substantial "scarcity rents."

These scarcity rents in turn help to cover their fixed capital and operating costs. For base-load and cycling units, the net revenues they earn during scarcity conditions may account for a significant fraction of the total net revenues they earn throughout the year. For peaking capacity that supplies energy or operating reserves primarily during such scarcity conditions, the net

Figure 1.6. Rationing scarce capacity

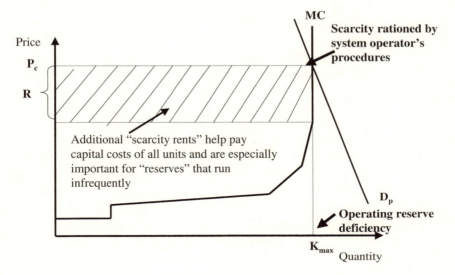

revenues they earn during these periods will account for substantially *all* of the net revenues available to cover their fixed costs (capital, maintenance, and operating). The number of hours in which "scarcity" conditions emerge depends upon the amount of generating capacity that has been installed and is physically available to operate relative to the tail of the distribution of aggregate demand realization during the year. This amount of generating capacity that is physically available to the network will then depend on investors in generating capacity balancing the costs of additional investments against the net revenues they expect to receive, including the "scarcity" rents produced when this state of nature emerges, from spot-market sales and through forward contracts. The prices for such forward contracts are necessarily linked to future expected spot-market prices and consumer and supplier preferences for market price risk.

Wholesale-Market Imperfections

If wholesale markets worked perfectly, prices during State 1 conditions and State 2 conditions would provide the appropriate price signals to link consumer preferences for reliability with the costs of supplying reliability with compatible investments in generating capacity. Moreover, with a set of liquid competitive forward markets for energy and for associated derivative instruments, consumer risk preferences and investor costs of bearing risk (and their cost of capital) could be matched through forward contracting and price-hedging actions. Unfortunately, there are a number of market imperfections that undermine the operation and performance of the idealized (and necessarily oversimplified) competitive wholesale market that I have just described. The most important market and institutional imperfections are discussed in the following:

1. Consumer demand for energy and reliability are not well represented in wholesale spot markets today. Due to metering costs, communications, and consumer response limitations and the slow diffusion of both, consumers do not "see" all relevant spot prices for energy and operating reserves and cannot respond effectively to variations in them. These imperfections severely limit the ability of market mechanisms to reflect properly consumer valuations for alternative levels of reliability and for investors on the supply and demand sides to respond efficiently to them.

2. The limited amount of real-time demand response in the wholesale market leads to spot-market demand that is extremely inelastic. Especially during high-demand periods as capacity constraints are approached, this creates significant opportunities for suppliers to exercise unilateral market power leading to supracompetitive prices even with a relatively unconcentrated distribution of suppliers.

3. Scarce generating capacity is not price rationed during true scarcity conditions. Reliance by system operators on "out-of-market" supply-side and demand-side resources to manage operating reserves deficiencies leads to spot prices for energy and operating reserves that may be too low during these conditions. The costs of these scarcity management tools are not reflected in spot-market prices and may be spread in charges to consumers over many nonreserve deficiency hours through some form of uplift charge. As system operators manage operating reserve deficiencies, the reliability of the system may deteriorate and "random" blackouts may be necessary. These reductions in effective service quality are generally "shared" across the network rather than allocated based on consumer valuations and the associated social costs are not accurately reflected in market prices. This creates incentives for free-riding, which in turn leads to underinvestment in generating capacity and demand-response programs. Immature, incomplete, and illiquid forward markets for risk-hedging/contracting arrangements undervalue rare events and make it difficult for consumers and suppliers to manage long-term risks efficiently. This in turn reduces the ability of investors in new generating capacity to hedge market risks and increases their financing costs above what they

would be if consumer and supplier risk preferences could be better matched. Ambiguities in retail procurement responsibilities, competitive retail market imperfections, and regulatory opportunism and uncertainty affects contracting incentives and behavior and leads to too much short-term forward contracting and too little long-term contracting. This undermines the development of liquid forward markets for energy and operating reserves, which in turn reduces the ability of investors in new generating capacity to hedge market risks and increases their financing costs above what they would be if consumer and supplier risk preferences could be better matched.

Institutional Imperfections

Whether it is too much or too little investment also depends in part on other institutional arrangements that affect spot-market prices and the structure, behavior, and performance of forward markets. The institutional arrangements of particular importance are the following:

1. *Market power mitigation mechanisms:* The FERC, along with the market monitors in the existing ISOs have imposed a variety of general and locational price mitigation measures to respond to potential market power problems in spot markets for energy and operating reserves. These mitigation measures include general bid caps (e.g., $1000/MWh) applicable to all prices, location-specific bid caps (e.g., marginal cost plus 10 percent), and other bid mitigation and supply obligation (must offer) measures.[25] Unfortunately, the supply and demand conditions that should lead to high spot-market prices in a well-functioning *competitive* wholesale market (i.e., when there is true *competitive* "scarcity") are also the conditions when *market power* problems are likely to be most severe (as capacity constraints are approached in the presence of inelastic demand, suppliers' unilateral incentives and ability to increase prices above competitive levels, perhaps by creating contrived scarcity, increase). Accordingly, even the best-designed mitigation measures will inevitably "clip" some high prices that truly reflect competitive supply scarcity and consumer valuations for energy and reliability as they endeavor to constrain high prices that reflect market power. They may also fail to mitigate fully supracompetitive prices during other hours. The FERC's SMD NOPR reflects the judgment that, on balance, these mitigation measures will lead to prices that are too low during extreme conditions (e.g., reserve deficiency conditions) to attract sufficient investment in peaking capacity and demand response capabilities available during very high demand contingencies to match consumer preferences for reliability, though it offers no empirical support for this conclusion.

2. *Discretionary behavior by ISOs/RTOs/ITPs during true scarcity conditions:* The level of prices for energy and operating reserves realized during scarcity conditions also depend critically on the ways in which system operators respond to reserve deficiencies and how these responses are reflected in spot-market prices for energy and operating reserves. Small changes in system operators' behavior can have large effects on the "scarcity rents" earned during these hours and, in turn, large effects on the profitability of investing in and making available the marginal capacity that has traditionally cleared the market under these conditions. There are three separate issues affecting investment incentives that emerge here. First, as I have already mentioned, to the extent the system operators manage reserve deficiencies (true competitive scarcity) using "out-of-market" measures that are not reflected in spot-market prices, spot-market prices will be too low. Second, bid mitigation mechanisms are likely to become binding constraints during reserve deficiency conditions and may also depress spot-market prices too much during these conditions. Third, the mere prospect that the discretionary behavior of system operators can have significant effects on the profitability of this marginal capacity raises classical opportunism problems. It is now widely recognized that opportunism problems lead to underinvestment and that credible long-term contracts or vertical integration are efficient institutional responses to opportunism problems (Tirole 1988; Joskow 1987).

In theory, these market and institutional imperfections could lead to too little *or* too much investment in generating capacity and associated operating reserves. Whether on balance, the incentives are for too much or too little generating capacity is an empirical question.

Empirical Evidence on Net Revenues during Scarcity Conditions

Exactly how these market and institutional imperfections balance out and affect investment incentives is ultimately an empirical question. This section presents a method to calculate the "scarcity rents" that are earned by the marginal generators that just clear the market when there is true competitive "scarcity." I then apply this method to measure the scarcity rents produced from spot energy and operating reserve markets operated by ISO-New England during the period 1999–2002. That is, the method measures scarcity rents under conditions where available generating capacity must be "rationed" to balance supply and demand and to maintain the network's frequency, voltage, and stability targets because available capacity to supply en-

ergy and the minimum level of operating reserves pursuant to bilateral contracts and the ISO's spot markets has been exhausted.

I focus on the *marginal generating capacity* that supplies electric energy and
operating reserves only during "scarcity conditions" and, as a result, have very
low capacity factors. Generating units that are expected to operate at very low
capacity factors typically have relatively low fixed costs and relatively high
marginal operating costs. Let C_K be the annualized fixed cost per MW-Year
(including the amortization of investments in this capacity where relevant—
see the following) and MC_E the marginal operating costs per MWh *of the last
(highest operating cost) generating unit in the merit order physically capable of providing energy or operating reserves*. Let P_s be the average market price of electricity during "scarcity hours" and H_s the expected number of scarcity hours
per year. The probability that "scarcity" conditions will exist is then given by
$H_s/8760$. The condition for investors in the marginal unit of capacity that
runs for H_s hours to just break even given any particular probability of scarcity
($H_s/8760$) is then given by[26]

(1) $C_K = (P_s - MC_E)H_s = R,$

where R equals the annual expected scarcity rents that are available to cover
the fixed costs of the "last unit of capacity" available to supply energy or operating reserves.

The "optimal" amount of generating capacity should reflect as well the
valuation that consumers place on reliability and (ultimately) on being curtailed during scarcity conditions. Let V be the average *hourly* opportunity
cost that the *marginal* consumer incurs by consuming a little less during
scarcity conditions, reflecting any associated reductions in network quality,
the increased likelihood of being curtailed, and actual curtailments.[27] Then
the efficient level of investment will be defined by equating the marginal cost
of the last unit of generating capacity to the marginal consumers' expected
cost of being in scarcity conditions:

(2) $C_K = H_s \cdot V$

If we know V and C_K, then we could derive the optimal H_s, the optimal probability of being in scarcity conditions ($H_s/8760$) and the optimal quantity of
generating capacity and demand response capability consistent with this
probability. The higher is V, the lower is the optimal H_s and the higher is the
optimal amount of reserve capacity (and vice versa).

I now estimate the values for R (and H_s) implied by hourly energy and operating reserve prices observed in ISO-New England's energy and ancillary services markets during the four-year period 1999–2002 (through November 27, 2002). The analysis assumes that a $1000/MWh price cap has been in effect during this entire period.[28] I compare these scarcity rents to alternative measures of C_K. The analysis shows that R has been much lower than C_K (defined in a number of different ways) in New England over the last four years.

Many simple discussions of competitive "scarcity conditions" implicitly assume that this is the level of supply/demand where the lights will go out if supply is reduced by 1 MW.[29] In fact, this is not an accurate characterization of how electric power networks are operated. "Scarcity conditions" are triggered when system operators find that they have an operating reserve deficiency that cannot be satisfied by buying more energy or operating reserves through ordinary organized spot-market mechanisms.[30] This in turn typically triggers the system operator's implementation of a set of "operating reserve conservation" actions to reduce demand or augment supply using out-of-market instruments. Only as a last resort—and very infrequently—has it been necessary to implement rolling blackouts with traditional reliability criteria and associated generating reserve margins. The calculations that I present here reflect this "operating reserve deficiency" protocol framework.

First, I identified all hours when ISO-New England declared an operating reserve deficiency. Operating reserve deficiencies trigger New England Power Pool (NEPOOL) Operating Procedure 4.[31] NEPOOL Operating Procedure 4 (Op-4) has sixteen action steps of increasing severity. For example, action 11 allows thirty-minute reserves to go to zero. Action 12 begins the implementation of voltage reductions. Op-4 (or at least some steps in Op-4) seems to me to be a reasonable definition of "scarcity" when we should expect competitive market prices to rise far above the marginal operating cost of the last generator physically capable of supplying energy and operating reserves.

During these scarcity conditions, marginal generators selling in the real-time energy and ancillary services markets can earn revenues in one of two ways.[32] They may be called to supply energy and are paid for the energy supplied. Or they may be providing operating reserves and are paid for the operating reserves they supply. *These payments are not cumulative at a given point in time.* A generator (or in theory demand) is paid for one or the other at any moment in time. As previously noted, for generators supplying energy, the "scarcity rent" is the difference between the price they are paid and their marginal supply costs. For generators supplying operating reserves, the "scarcity rent" is no higher than the payment they receive for operating reserves. As discussed previously, if energy and operating reserve markets are integrated efficiently, there is also a "textbook" relationship between the price of energy and the price of operating reserves during scarcity conditions. Specifically, the price of operating reserves should be roughly equal to the price of energy *minus* the marginal operating cost of the units providing operating reserves. That is, the price of operating reserves is equal to the "opportunity cost" incurred by generators supplying operating reserves rather than energy.

For all Op-4 hours during the period 1999 through November 27, 2002, I obtained the price of energy and the price of ten-minute operating reserves. When the price of energy exceeded $1000, I set it to the $1000 price cap that was implemented after May 2000.[33] When the price of ten-minute spinning reserves and ten-minute nonspinning reserves were different (as was often the case during Op-4 conditions, especially in 1999), I took the higher of the two prices. There was only one hour when the operating reserve price exceeded $1000 and the price was set to $1000 for that hour.[34] To calculate the "scarcity rents" associated with supplying energy during Op-4 conditions, I assumed that the short-run marginal cost of supplying energy from the marginal generator was either $50/MWh or $100/MWh (it doesn't matter much). This range should bracket the true marginal generating costs and any associated start-up, no-load, and ramping costs for these units given variations in gas prices during this time period. I took the operating reserve revenues without making an adjustment for any operating costs incurred to supply operating reserves and, as a result, my method probably slightly overestimates the scarcity rents accruing to suppliers of operating reserves during scarcity conditions. I then aggregate the data for each year to calculate values for the "scarcity rents" per MW-year available from supplying either energy or operating reserves (or any combination of the two) during scarcity conditions.

The results are reported in table 1.11. The average scarcity rents from supplying either energy or operating reserves during Op-4 conditions earned by marginal generators is about $10,000/MW-Year. The scarcity rents generated from selling energy and operating reserves during scarcity conditions (Op-4) are, on average, almost identical (as theory suggests they should be).[35] There is significant volatility from year to year in the rents earned, however. On average there are forty-six hours per year when Op-4 is in effect and thirty-two hours per year when Op-4 step 11 is in effect. There is significant volatility in the annual number of operating reserve deficiency hours as well. *On average there were only six hours per year when the price cap was binding, again with considerable year-to-year variation.*[36] This suggests that the $1000 price caps are unlikely to be the primary source of the revenue deficiencies (more on this in the following).[37] There are other factors, at least partially related to the reliance on out-of-market instruments to manage reserve deficiencies, that are depressing spot prices during reserve deficiency conditions associated

Table 1.11 Scarcity rents in ISO-New England

Year	Op-4 rents energy; MC = $50 ($/MW-year)	Op-4 rents energy; MC = $100 ($/MW-year)	Op-4 rents operating reserves ($/MW-year)	Op-4 hours all	Op-4 hours step 11	Price cap binding hours
2002	$5,070	$4,153	$4,723	21	21	3
2001	$15,818	$14,147	$11,411	41	37	15
2000[a]	$6,528	$4,241	$4,894	25	14	5
1999	$18,874	$14,741	$19,839	98	55	1
Average	$11,573	$9,574	$10,217	46	32	6

Note: Computation procedures are discussed in the text.

[a]There were *five hours* when energy prices exceeded the $1,000 price cap in May 2000 before the caps were imposed. For four of these hours the average price was $6,000/MWh. If we include the actual revenues earned during these five hours rather than capping them at $1,000, the values for 2000 $/MW/Yr would be $28,349 (MC = $50/MWh) and $27,362 (MC = 100). There was only one hour when operating reserve prices exceeded the $1000 price cap. The operating reserves revenues were $7,294/MW/Yr in 2000 without imposing the $1000/MWh cap.

with the mechanisms used by the system operators to manage reserve deficiencies.

The $10,000/MW-Year average value estimated for scarcity rents in New England during this period can be compared with the fixed costs (capital amortization and fixed O&M) of a new combustion turbine that might be built to provide the systems "reserve capacity." This cost would be roughly $60,000–$80,000/MW-Year in New England. Clearly, the scarcity rents are far below what would be necessary to attract combustion turbines (CT) to the market to be available to supply operating reserves and energy only during scarcity conditions.

One might argue that this is the wrong comparison, as there are many other hours when these generators can earn scarcity rents. If this were true then the $10,000/MW/Year value is an underestimate of the true quasi-rents available to cover capital costs. However, I have examined all hours when the market price for energy exceeded $100/MWh during this period and find that about 80 percent of the scarcity rents are earned during Op-4 conditions.

Another possible objection to this comparison would be that the total costs of a new CT is not the relevant benchmark for New England. Because New England has a lot of old conventional oil, gas, and coal-fueled steam-turbine generating capacity, the market clearing prices reflect their relatively high heat rates (say 11,000 Btu/kWh) during many hours of the year. The combined-cycle gas turbines (CCGTs) with much lower heat rates (say 7500

Btu/kWh) are attracted to the market and earn rents to cover their capital costs on the "spark spread" associated with the difference between their heat rates and the heat rates of the generators that clear the market, as well as from the scarcity rents I have identified. Under this scenario, CCGTs are infra-marginal, but push older conventional steam plants higher up in the merit order. These old plants then can provide operating reserves during tight supply situations. In this case, the scarcity rents identified must be high enough to cover the fixed-O&M costs of the existing generators that will provide this reserve capacity so that they find it profitable to stay open and available to provide operating reserves. I am told that the annual fixed O&Ms of older fossil steam units is in the range of $20,000 to $35,000/MW/Year.[38] The scarcity rents that I have measured for New England are not high enough to compensate for these annual fixed costs either and absent an additional source of revenues these plants would simply be mothballed or retired permanently.

A third objection could be that the system is too reliable and that the shortfall in spot-market revenues reflects excess capacity relative to consumer valuations of consuming more or less on the marginal during scarcity conditions. Resolving this question requires making assumptions about the appropriate value for V, a number that is very difficult to measure.[39] We can obtain some insight into this explanation by solving for the implied value of V in equation (2). If C_K is $60,000/MW-Year and H_s is 46 hours, then the implied value of V in equation (2) is about $1,300 per MWh. If C_K is $30,000/MW-Year, the implied value of V is about $650/MWh. If we focus instead on the Op-4 action 11 hours (thirty-two hours on average) then the implied values of V are $1,875/MWh and $937/MWh, respectively. While these implied values for V are below the limited number of estimates of the value of lost energy used in other countries (e.g., England and Wales during the 1990s, Australia today)[40] to set price caps, the numbers are not directly comparable. Recall that V in equation (2) is defined as the marginal consumer's opportunity cost of consuming more or less *averaged over all reserve deficiency hours* and not just during the tiny number of hours when load is actually curtailed. We would expect the implied value of V as defined here to be below the value consumers place on consuming more or less energy during the very small number of hours they are actually subject to significant curtailments. Accordingly, the implied values of V as defined here and the prevailing levels of reliability do not seem to be out of line with the limited evidence on consumer valuations.

The conclusion that I draw from this analysis is that the spot hourly energy and ancillary services markets in New England have not provided scarcity rents that are nearly sufficient to make it profitable for reserve "peaking" capacity to enter the market through new investment or to continue operating consistent with conventional levels of reliability. These results are consistent with those contained in related studies done for PJM and the New York ISO.[41] While there appears to be abundant generating capacity in most regions of the country at the present time, this is a potential problem that may undermine future investment and lead to premature retirement of some existing generating capacity.

Transmission Governance and Investment

I do not want to conclude without a brief discussion of transmission governance and investment issues. Transmission networks provide the essential supporting platform upon which competitive wholesale markets depend. Transmission congestion effectively reduces the geographic expanse of competition, increases the incidence of locational market power, and can limit entry of competing generators. A well-functioning transmission network is a critical component of a program to create robust competitive wholesale and retail markets for electricity. Yet the legacy transmission network that we inherit from the era of large numbers of vertically integrated regulated firms was not designed to promote competition among generators over large geographic areas, focused on interconnecting generators and loads within individual utility control areas, and did not take local market power and other market performance problems into account when investments were made. It should come as no surprise that the legacy network is not well suited for supporting competitive wholesale markets and that significant investments will be required to adapt the legacy network to its new role.

As I have already discussed, many countries that have implemented competitive electricity market programs have created independent regional or national transmission companies with responsibilities for system operations (broadly defined) and transmission investment. In the United States, we have taken a different approach. Most transmission assets are owned, operated, and maintained by vertically integrated utilities. There is very significant geographic balkanization of ownership and operation with many companies owning, operating, maintaining, and potentially responsible for investing in new transmission facilities at particular locations on the same AC network.

Rather than promoting vertical and horizontal restructuring of asset ownership and operation to deal with these independence and balkanization issues, the FERC has taken the existing ownership structure as a constraint and promoted the creation of new not-for-profit ISOs or Regional Transmission Operators (RTO) to deal with these issues. The RTOs are to be responsible for scheduling and dispatching generators on regional networks; implementing market-based mechanisms for allocating scarce transmission capacity; monitoring generator, marketer, and transmission owner behavior and market performance; coordinating maintenance performed by transmission owners; coordinating regional planning processes for new transmission facilities; and operating voluntary public spot markets (real time and day ahead) for energy and ancillary services. However, these independent entities own no transmission assets, have no linemen or helicopters to maintain transmission lines and respond to outages, and are not directly responsible for the costs of operating, investing in, or the ultimate performance of the transmission networks they "manage."

These organizational arrangements are further complicated by the distribution of regulatory authority and responsibilities between state and federal regulators. The states are responsible for reviewing applications for major new transmission facilities and granting any necessary permits. The FERC has been responsible for regulating the prices for unbundled (wholesale) transmission service, but has no authority over transmission planning or siting approvals, while the states are responsible for regulating charges for bundled transmission service charged by vertically integrated companies to their retail customers, though exactly the same facilities and people are involved in both. Until recently, the FERC's policies on transmission investment responsibilities and cost recovery rules have been confusing and, in my view, much too heavily focused on flawed models that rely primarily on merchant transmission investment (Joskow and Tirole 2003). Moreover, the FERC has not embraced any program to adopt performance-based regulatory mechanisms focused on improving transmission network performance and reducing costs. Very recently, the FERC has begun to use its rate-making authority to reward transmission owners that divest their transmission assets, that form independent transmission companies, that operate under the supervision of RTOs, and that improve network performance.[42] This is a step in the right direction. However, there is much work to be done.

Current institutional arrangements governing transmission operations and investment are simply not well matched to creating the transmission network platform necessary to support well-functioning competitive markets that can operate with a minimal amount of continuing regulatory "mitigation" measures to respond to market power and related market performance concerns. Stimulating transmission investment has been especially problematic. While generation investment in generating capacity grew enormously during the last five years, transmission investment has been declining for many years (U.S. Department of Energy 2002). Transmission congestion has

Figure 1.7. Transmission line relief loadings (TLR): Twelve-month average

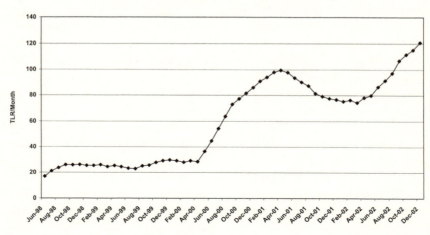

Source: North American Electric Reliability Council (NERC), ftp://www.nerc.com/pub/sys/all_updl/oc/scs/logs/trends.htm.

grown steadily over the last several years. Figure 1.7 displays the moving average of the number of monthly administrative transmission line relief actions (TLRs) ordered by regional security coordinators to respond to transmission constraints, primarily in the Midwest. Between June 1998 and December 2002, the number of monthly TLRs has increased by a factor of 6. In New England, new generating capacity that has been built in Maine and Rhode Island cannot be run to meet regional energy needs economically because there is inadequate transmission to get it out of these areas. At the same time, Southern Connecticut faces reliability problems because of transmission constraints that significantly limit imports into that part of New England. These trends in transmission congestion are not limited to areas that have not implemented LMP. Table 1.12 displays the number of hours of transmission congestion on the PJM system from 1998 to 2002, the first ISO to implement an LMP system.[43] Table 1.13 displays congestion charges in PJM between 1999 and 2002. By both measures congestion has continued to grow rapidly in PJM, the FERC's poster model for its SMD proposals.

It is often argued that the primary problem causing the decline in transmission investment is local "Nimby" opposition to new transmission lines. This is certainly a problem. However, many transmission investment opportunities do not involve opening up major new transmission corridors or significantly expanding the footprint of the transmission network. There are

Table 1.12 PJM congestion event hours

Year	Total	500KV	345KV	230KV
1998	1,244	203	71	588
1999	2,134	189	148	818
2000	6,941	562	14	869
2001	8,435	759	38	744
2002	11,657	1,926	1,107	2,056

Source: *PJM State of the Market Report 2002,* http://www.pjm.com/markets/market-monitor/reports.html.

Table 1.13 PJM congestion charges ($million)

Year	Charge
1999	53
2000	132
2001	271
2002	430

Source: *PJM State of the Market Report 2002,* http://www.pjm.com/markets/market-monitor/reports.html.

many potential opportunities to increase the capacity of transmission networks other than by building major new lines involving new rights of way and
expansion of the network's footprint. They vary from no- or low-cost upgrades of the reliability of breakers and other components on the network,
better monitoring, communication, and control capabilities, to more costly
investments in static var compensators, capacitors, substation enhancements,
and reconductoring of existing transmission lines. These types of investment
opportunities are typically intertwined with and inseparable from the incumbent transmission owners' (TOs) transmission networks from a physical,
maintenance, and operating perspective.

An ISO or RTO like PJM running a security-constrained dispatch, resulting in a set of ex post LMPs is not in a position to undertake this broader set of
transmission network management actions. It does not have the people, the
trucks, the materials, the money, or, at the present time, the financial incentives
to do it. Instead, what an ISO does on a day-to-day basis is to take into account
the transmission capacity that is available and, using the bids made by generators and demand response, then calculates the most efficient way to allocate the
transmission capacity that is available. The LMPs themselves do not "manage
congestion" in any meaningful way. The ISOs' security constrained dispatch
allocates scarce transmission capacity based on the bids submitted by competing users of the network, supply and demand conditions, and available trans-

mission capacity. The LMPs themselves merely provide ex post measures of congestion on the system given the transmission capacity available, the price and quantity bids made at different locations, and the security criteria specified by the independent transmission provider (ITP) and included in its central economic dispatch program. Few, if any, consumers actually see LMPs, so there is little if any response to them on the demand side either.

While an efficient security constrained dispatch that results in an efficient utilization of a given quantity of scarce transmission capacity is an important part of a comprehensive congestion management system, there are other important aspects of congestion management that need to be taken into account by policymakers. The experience in England and Wales over the last decade indicates that substantial transmission investment, operating performance improvements, reductions in congestion and ancillary services costs, and lower overall transmission costs can be achieved with the right organizational and regulatory incentive institutions in place. This is a goal that electricity policymakers in the United States need to place higher on the restructuring and regulatory reform agenda.

Conclusion

The development of well-functioning competitive wholesale and retail markets for electricity in the United States is a work in progress. It has encountered more problems and proceeded less quickly than some had anticipated when the first restructuring and competition programs were first being implemented in the late 1990s. The most visible success of these initiatives to date has been the substantial investment in new generating capacity completed by merchant generating companies in the last few years, and the shifting of the associated construction cost, operating performance, and market risks to suppliers rather than to consumers as under regulation. There has also been substantial growth in the fraction of electricity supplied through competitive wholesale-market transactions (physical and financial) as a result of restructuring of incumbent vertically integrated utilities, the entry of new generating capacity built by merchant generating companies, and the development of public and private wholesale power–trading institutions. Load-serving entities in all parts of the country rely more on competitive wholesale-market purchases to supplement or replace owned generation subject to cost-based regulation than they did in the mid-1990s. Despite their imperfections, Order 888 and the FERC initiatives that have built on it have substantially increased access to transmission networks and associated support services, facilitating these wholesale market developments. Reforms aimed at adopting best practices are being implemented in many regions of the country with strong support and encouragement by the FERC. Retail customers in a number of states have benefited from lower regulated retail prices negotiated as a component of state restructuring programs, though the direct benefits attributable to retail competition per se have been limited and have flowed primarily to the largest electricity customers.

The transition to competitive wholesale and retail electricity markets has also been plagued by problems and disappointments. The boom in merchant generating investment and the growth in wholesale power trade has now turned into a bust. Many merchant generating and trading companies are in serious financial trouble and cannot raise capital to build or acquire projects. Many generating projects under construction and development have been canceled. While a significant reduction in investment in new generating capacity should have been expected due to basic supply and demand fundamentals, the financial problems faced by this sector reflect a number of other market and regulatory phenomena. It is fairly clear that the next generation of merchant investment activity will take place in an environment where capital is much more costly than it was during the late 1990s bubble and where lenders will be looking for supporting portfolios of supply contracts of longer durations. Investors will also be looking for much more stability in wholesale-market rules, reforms in wholesale-market institutions to support investment or continued operation of peaking capacity, more efficient and transparent congestion management arrangements, and stable federal regulatory policies. Many wholesale trading companies have either completely or substantially withdrawn from trading activity beyond trading around their own generating assets and market liquidity has fallen dramatically, reducing the efficiency of short-term markets and making it very difficult for buyers' and sellers' risk preferences to be well matched in liquid markets for longer-term forward markets. Market power problems and other market imperfections have reduced the efficiency of wholesale power markets and increased costs to consumers.

In California, the combination of market design imperfections, market power problems, and poor federal and state policy responses has managed both to increase retail prices enormously (30 percent to 40 percent) and to leave the utility and merchant generating sectors littered with financially crippled and bankrupt suppliers. The performance of retail competition programs has been disappointing almost everywhere, especially for residential and small commercial customers. Imperfections in retail competition programs investments in new generating capacity undermine the performance of wholesale spot markets as well.

Investment in transmission capacity has stagnated while network congestion has increased. This in turn has increased local market power problems and complicated the smooth operation of wholesale power markets. System operators in many parts of the country continue to rely on inefficient non-price rationing mechanisms to manage congestion and property rights to scarce transmission capacity continue to be poorly defined. The transmission system remains fragmented with too many system operators relying on incompatible scheduling, transmission pricing, and emergency management mechanisms. The bulk of the transmission capacity is owned by companies that also own and operate generating facilities connected to these transmission facilities and trade power in the same regional markets, creating opportunities to increase rivals' costs and reduce competition. The FERC has responded to the failure to restructure the industry to match the needs of competitive electricity markets with new institutional arrangements (ISO, RTO) that may be well suited for operating public markets for energy and ancillary services and real-time physical system dispatch but whose long-run performance attributes from the broader perspective of transmission network operating costs, transmission line availability, and transmission investment are not particularly promising.

The positions that the various states have taken regarding electricity-sector reforms in general, and the FERC's SMD in particular, reflect their assessment of the costs and benefits of the electricity competition and restructuring initiatives to date. The states in the Northeast, Texas, and a few states in the Midwest that have gone the farthest down the restructuring path are committed to making these initiatives work better and to implement the wholesale- and retail-market reforms necessary to do so. They have gone too far to easily reverse course and return to the old system of regulated vertically integrated firms. Their strategies and the basic framework established in the FERC SMD seem to be reasonably well aligned. California remains in shock from the experiences of 2000 and 2001 and its long-run electricity strategy remains murky at best. The majority of the states, clustered in the Southeast, the South, and the West, have either taken a cautious wait and see attitude or have simply rejected restructuring and competition initiatives. These states tend to have relatively low regulated retail prices, do not face looming supply shortages or reliability problems, and face little consumer pressure for change. Why take the risk that a California-like crisis will come home to roost? Because restructuring to rely on wholesale and retail electricity markets involves turning much more of the electricity value chain over to federal from state jurisdiction, these states are also concerned that the FERC will not act promptly or responsibly to protect consumers in their states when problems arise.

(Texas is the only state that has been in a position to implement fundamental reforms while retaining state jurisdiction of the reform process.)

If the states that have not embraced competitive market reforms move forward voluntarily in the future it will be because the other states that have committed to restructuring, wholesale, and retail competition can demonstrate to them that it has in practice, rather than just in theory, brought long-term benefits to consumers. This will require solid *empirical* analysis of the performance of the electric power sectors in those states that have restructured and implemented comprehensive wholesale and retail competition programs.

***

REFERENCES

Borenstein, S., J. Bushnell, and F. Wolak. 2002. Measuring market inefficiencies in California's restructured wholesale electricity market. *American Economic Review* 92 (5): 1376–1405.

Department of Trade and Industry (DTI). 2000. *UK energy sector indicators.* London: HMSO.

———. 2003. Energy white paper: Our future—Creating a low carbon economy. London: HMSO, February.

Energy Argus, Inc. 2003. *New power plant spreadsheet.* Hoboken, NJ: Energy Argus, Inc.

Federal Energy Regulatory Commission (FERC). 2003a. *Proposed pricing policy for efficient operation and expansion of the transmission grid.* Docket no. PL-03-1-000. January 13. Washington, DC: FERC.

———. 2003b. *Notice of proposed rulemaking.* Docket no. RM01-12-000. July 31. Washington, DC: FERC.

Giulietti, M., C. Waddams Price, and M. Waterson. 2003. Consumer choice and industrial policy: A study of UK energy markets. University of Warwick. Mimeograph.

Green, R. 2000. Can competition replace regulation for small utility customers? Centre for Economic Policy Research Discussion Paper no. 2405. London: CEPR.

Hogan, W. 1992. Contract networks for electric power transmission. *Journal of Regulatory Economics* 4:211–42.

Hogan, W. 1993. Markets in real networks require reactive prices. *Energy Journal* 14 (3): 171–200.

Joskow, P. L. 1974. Inflation and environmental concern: Change in the process of public utility price regulation. *Journal of Law and Economics* 17 (2): 291–387.

———. 1987. Contract duration and relationship specific investment. *American Economic Review* 77 (1): 168–85.

———. 1989. Regulatory failure, regulatory reform and structural change in the electric power industry. *Brookings Papers on Economic Activity, Microeconomics:* 125–99.

———. 1996. Restructuring to promote competition in electricity: In general and regarding the POOLCO vs. bilateral contracts debate. Paper presented at the American Economic Association Annual Meeting. 8 January, San Francisco. Mimeograph.

———. 1997. Restructuring, competition and regulatory reform in the U.S. electricity sector. *Journal of Economic Perspectives* 11 (3): 119–38.

———. 2000a. Deregulation and regulatory reform in the U.S. electric power sector. In *De-*

regulation of network industries: The next steps, ed. S. Peltzman and Clifford Winston, 113–18. Washington, DC: Brookings Press.

———. 2000b. Why do we need electricity retailers? You can get it cheaper wholesale. http://econ-www.mit.edu/faculty/pjoskow/files/RETAILV2.pdf.

———. 2001. California's electricity crisis. *Oxford Review of Economic Policy* 17 (3): 365–88.

———. 2002. Electricity sector restructuring and competition: A transaction cost perspective. In *The economics of contracts: Theories and applications*, ed. Eric Brousseau and Jean-Michel Glachant, 1–35. New York: Cambridge University Press.

Joskow, P. L., and E. Kahn. 2002. A quantitative analysis of pricing behavior in California's wholesale electricity market during summer 2000. *The Energy Journal* 23 (4): 1–35.

Joskow, P. L., and R. Schmalensee. 1983. *Markets for power.* Cambridge, MA: MIT Press.

Joskow, P. L., and J. Tirole. 2000. Transmission rights and market power on electric power networks. *RAND Journal of Economics* 31 (3): 450–87.

———. 2003. Merchant transmission investment. MIT, Center for Energy and Environmental Policy Research. Working Paper.

Littlechild, S. C. 2003. Wholesale spot market passthrough. *Journal of Regulatory Economics* 23 (1): 61–91.

Office of Gas and Electricity Markets (OFGEM). 2001. *Review of domestic gas and electricity competition and supply regulation.* November. London: OFGEM.

Patton, D. S. 2002. *Summer 2002 review of New York electricity markets.* New York Independent System Operator. Unpublished Manuscript.

Public Utility Commission of Texas (PUCT). 2003. *February 2003 report card on competition.* Austin, TX: PUCT.

Stoft, S. 2002. *Power system economics.* Piscataway, NJ: Wiley Interscience.

Tirole, Jean. 1988. *The theory of industrial organization.* Cambridge, MA: MIT Press.

U.S. Department of Energy. 2002. *National transmission grid study.* Washington, DC: U.S. DOE.

U.S. Energy Information Administration. 1997. *Inventory of power plants: 1997.* Washington, DC: U.S. EIA.

———. 1998. *Inventory of power plants: 1998.* Washington, DC: U.S. EIA.

———. 1998–2003, various issues. *Electric Power Monthly.* Washington, DC: U.S. EIA.

———. 1999. *Electric power annual: 1999.* Washington, DC: U.S. EIA.

———. 2000. *Electric power annual: 2000.* Washington, DC: U.S. EIA.

———. 2002: *Annual review of energy: 2002:* Washington, DC: U.S. EIA.

———. 2003. *Monthly Energy Review,* March. Washington, DC: U.S. EIA.

White, M. 1996. Power struggles: Explaining deregulatory reforms in electric power markets. *Brookings Papers on Economic Activity, Microeconomics:* 201–50.

Wolfram, C. 1999. Measuring duopoly power in the British electricity spot market. *American Economic Review* 89 (4): 805–26.

Notes

Paul L. Joskow is Elizabeth and James Killian Professor of Economics and Management and director of the Center for Energy and Environmental Policy Research at the Massachusetts Institute of Technology.

Research support from the MIT Center for Energy and Environmental Policy Research (CEEPR) and the Cambridge-MIT Institute (CMI) is gratefully acknowledged.

1. My views on the causes of the California electricity crisis can be found in Joskow (2001) and my analysis of price formation and market power during the summer of 2000 in Joskow and Kahn (2002).

2. So, for example, hotel rooms are nonstorable. An empty room cannot be stored for another day. However, the demand for hotel rooms is likely to be quite elastic, "stockouts" fre-

quently occur when demand is high, average utilization factors are 80–90 percent, one hotel cannot affect the supply of rooms at another hotel in the city by closing down several rooms, and we do not expect hotels to rent all of their rooms at a uniform price equal to the hotel's short-run marginal cost.

3. Otherwise the magnitude and speed of stranded cost recovery was threatened.

4. A few utilities in these states chose voluntarily to divest their generating assets anyway.

5. They typically become electric wholesale generating (EWG) companies as provided for in the Energy Policy Act of 1992.

6. The United States has about 760,000 MW of generating capacity in 1995.

7. In 1990, virtually all of the nonutility generation was accounted for by cogenerators, industrial plants, and renewable energy facilities.

8. Unlike a first-class postage stamp that allows one to send a letter to anywhere in the United States for thirty-seven cents, "postage stamp" transmission tariffs only provide for transit to or through an individual utility's transmission network. The number of postage stamps required for transmission service depended upon how many utilities with transmission facilities happen to be on the contract path available between an injection point and a delivery point. This phenomenon is known as "pancaking."

9. The SMD NOPR is much less successful in dealing with transmission investment, organization, and incentive issues. See the comments that I submitted to the FERC on these issues at http://econwww.mit.edu/faculty/pjoskow/papers.htm

10. The ESP may, however, bundle the regulated delivery services and competitive services together, reimbursing the distribution company for P_R.

11. Some states (e.g., Massachusetts) define the default service price, "price to beat," or "price to compare" with reference to the competitive component P_C only as the P_R component is set by regulation and must be paid to the distribution company, regardless of which ESP supplies a customer with unbundled competitive services. Other states (e.g., Texas) define the "price to beat" with reference to the total of the regulated and competitive components $(P_R + P_C)$. In the latter case, ESPs quote customers a price for the combination of the regulated T&D charge and the competitive generation service charge they are offering. Arithmetically, the two approaches are the same, but they may have different implications from a marketing perspective.

12. Duquesne's stranded costs have now been recovered and the associated charges eliminated from the prices that it charges for distribution service.

13. The Pennsylvania Public Utilities Commission required PECO to auction off 64,000 commercial customers because too few customers had chosen voluntarily to be served by ESPs. The average discount offered by the winning bidders was 1.25 percent off the default service price. Customers can opt out of the "draft" if they fill out a postcard or call PECO. See Dow Jones Business Service, February 27, 2003 at http://biz.yahoo.com/djus/030227/1853001167_1.html

14. It is difficult to accept the view that it is appropriate to attribute fuel price reductions and the end-fuel surcharges as a benefit of restructuring. These costs were traditionally treated as pass throughs under regulation. Moreover, the relevant comparison is not with the 6 percent mandatory reduction from 1999 prices but what prices would have been if standard regulatory procedures had been followed.

15. See the Public Utility Commission of Texas, Retail Electric Service Rate Comparisons for May 2002 and February 2003 Report Card on Competition.

16. Many ESPs offer flat-rate annual rates while the incumbent supplier's price to beat may vary from month to month. Accordingly, annual comparisons provide a better picture than do monthly comparisons.

17. These price data come from the March issue of the EIA publication *Electric Power Monthly*. They are far from ideal as they include municipal and cooperative as well as investor-owned utility sales and revenues. The 2002 data are preliminary and the numbers for California look wrong to me. Further analysis as additional data become available would be desirable.

18. Retail competition states, Connecticut, Rhode Island, Michigan, Maryland, and Delaware, also had above-average retail prices in the mid-1990s. Texas and Michigan are the only states that have introduced retail competition (both in 2002) for residential customers that had regulated prices below the national average. Oregon, which has very low retail rates, technically introduced retail competition for large industrial customers only in 2002. However, no customers have chosen to be served by an ESP in Oregon because the rate options offered by the local utilities (including a floating market-based rate option) are cheaper.

19. This is not the case in Texas where customers that cease being served by an ESP are put on a POLR rate that is market based (through an auction) and reflects the attributes of customers who are likely to be dropped by their ESP. However, it also is not the case in Massachusetts and in New York City where default service customers are served on a separate market-based default service tariff.

20. See Littlechild (2003) for a different view.

21. This payment mechanism was dropped when the New Electricity Trading Arrangements (NETA) system was introduced in 2001.

22. See the Sithe Energy presentation, IAEE, Boston Chapter, February 19, 2003.

23. This will, of course, also be the value consumers place on this energy at the margin where supply and demand are equal.

24. This is to distinguish it from contrived scarcity resulting from suppliers withholding supplies from the market to drive up prices.

25. The FERC SMD NOPR proposes to require that under certain "non-competitive conditions" (e.g., local market power problems caused by congestion) generators be required to offer all available energy (must-offer requirement) to the system operator subject to a prespecified bid cap. See the FERC Docket No. RM01-12-000, Notice of Proposed Rulemaking, July 31, 2002, ¶ 409 (FERC 2003b). It also invites ITPs to propose additional mitigation measures that could apply under certain conditions where market power would be a significant problem, (¶ 415). Finally, the NOPR provides for a regional "safety-net bid cap" that would apply to the day-ahead and real-time markets under all conditions, (¶ 433).

26. This is obviously an oversimplification. P_s will vary during scarcity hours.

27. For simplicity, this presentation is a little different from the traditional presentation that focus only on the cost of lost energy when load is curtailed. In reality, measuring V is very difficult. It varies from consumer to consumer, with the severity of scarcity conditions, and with the methods used to ration demand when curtailments are required. See, generally, Stoft 2002, chapters 2–5.

28. There were five hours in May 2000 when spot energy prices exceeded the cap and the analysis reduces those prices to $1000/MWh. However, the conclusions that flow from the analysis would not be changed if the actual prices realized in these hours had been used instead.

29. This discussion assumes that market power mitigation mechanisms are successful, that prices for energy and operating reserves are competitive, and the market power does not lead to contrived scarcity. To the extent that scarcity conditions reflect the exercise of market power in New England during the period studied here, my estimates would *overestimate* the true competitive scarcity rents produced by the spot energy and operating reserve markets in New England under competitive conditions. The same is true for the data for PJM and NY described in the previous footnote.

30. There is no reason in principle why a system operator should not be able to respond to projected reserve deficiencies by making forward (e.g., two-day ahead) commitments if that is a lower cost option. If system operators had the right financial incentives it would make sense to expand their contracting options in this way.

31. See http://www.iso-ne.com/operating_procedures/Op4Fin.doc/.

32. Price formation in the real-time markets will work its way back into day-ahead and forward contract price formation through intertemporal arbitrage.

33. There are only five hours during this period (in May 2000) that are "trimmed" in this way, but the effect on scarcity rents associated with energy supplies (though strangely not operating reserves) is substantial. See the footnote to table 1.1.

34. The revenue effect is relatively small.

35. However, the relationship between energy prices and operating reserve prices on an hourly basis vary from theoretical predictions, especially in 1999 when the operating reserve prices are often very strange.

36. One must wonder if 1999 is just an unusual year, with the ISO and market participants learning how to operate within the new wholesale-market institutions in New England. There are many more Op-4 hours than in other years, but only one hour when the energy price exceeded $1000/MWh (and as I understand it no price caps were in effect). The scarcity rents are much higher than in other years.

37. A similar analysis has been done for the New York ISO and comes to similar conclusions. See Patton (2002, 25, 42–64). Patton's analysis of the New York ISO suggests that the reliance on out-of-market mechanisms and associated discretionary behavior by the New York ISO during reserve deficiency hours plays a much more important role than do the price caps.

38. These older plants also typically face costly environmental mitigation obligations if they continue to operate and these costs should be factored in as well.

39. See Stoft 2002, chapters 2–5.

40. Australia now uses a value of lost load of about $6,500/MWh ($AU 10,000/MWh).

41. Data available from the PJM Market Monitor's annual "State of the Market" report provides information that can help us to define an upper bound on the measure of scarcity rents that I have produced for New England. These PJM reports calculate the net revenues earned from spot energy sales for units with different marginal supply costs. The values calculated for units with marginal costs greater than $50 and $100 respectively are upper bounds for the values that would emerge by applying the same methods to PJM as I applied to New England. They are upper bounds, because they include all hours during each year and not just scarcity hours and reflect rents earned in other hours when there may be some market power. It is evident that the energy market rents for high heat-rate units appear to be much higher in PJM than in the New England-ISO. Nevertheless, even in this case, the average rents earned from the energy market are roughly 50 percent of the PJM target effective annualized capacity cost of about $63,000/MW-year. Of course, New England, New York, and PJM have had capacity obligations and owners of generating capacity can receive an additional stream of revenues from sales of capacity. And there is no shortage of generating capacity in New England, PJM, or New York (except in New York City where investment in new generating capacity faces additional challenges) and in most other regions of the country. In addition, as I have already discussed, the New England market frequently is cleared on the margin with generation from the large quantity of existing older oil/gas/coal fueled generating capacity with relatively high heat rates. The CCGT capacity coming into the market could earn net revenues to cover capital costs during many "nonscarcity" hours from the spark spread representing the difference between the heat rate of the old steam units that clear the market and define the competitive spot-market price and the lower heat rates of the CCGTs. Accordingly, CCGT capacity expands more quickly than demand grows, the older steam capacity will be pushed higher up in the merit order and can contribute to reliability as long as these units can earn enough in scarcity rents to cover their fixed-O&M costs and the costs of required environmental mitigation investments.

42. See Federal Energy Regulatory Commission Docket Number (FERC 2003a).

43. The 2002 data include the incorporation of PJM-West into PJM and are not directly comparable to the data for previous years.

2

Restructuring the Electricity Industry in England and Wales

Richard Green

Introduction

The British sometimes exaggerate their own importance. For example, we claim that the electricity market introduced in April 1990 was the first of its kind in the world, neglecting the Chilean reforms of 1978. Another boast is that Britain was the first country in the world to give all of its domestic electricity consumers a choice of where to buy their power, although all Norwegians had been able to switch retailer (for a fee) since 1995, and the switching fee was abolished in 1997. Although some of our claims for priority are exaggerated, there is no denying that the overall package of measures that was introduced in 1990 was substantial and did go beyond what many people thought would be possible. The existing generation and transmission board was broken up, generators were allowed free entry to the industry, and customers were promised a choice of retailer—if not immediately, then by 1998. Most of the industry was privatized. The aim was to create a competitive electricity industry with improved performance.

The restructuring has brought significant benefits, at least in terms of prices, which have fallen by around 30 percent in real terms. The price reductions have been driven by increases in efficiency, in the coal industry as well as the electricity companies, which have gradually been passed on to consumers. However, benefits to consumers were not guaranteed, and inadequate levels of competition in the early years allowed the generating companies (in particular) to retain most of the efficiency savings that they made. The level of performance experienced by customers comes from the interaction of market structure, market rules, and regulatory oversight. Proactive regulation may offset the impact of an uncompetitive market structure or poorly designed rules, but regulatory intervention is almost always a poor second best to a competitive market structure and well-designed rules. It took a decade of regulatory pressure to get an adequately competitive market structure in generation, while the governance of the wholesale market was so bad that the regulator and the government eventually decided to start again with a completely new set of rules.

Other features of the reform worked to consumers' advantage, however. Most wholesale trading took place through long- or medium-term contracts, giving stability to both generators and retailers while reducing the generators' incentive to raise prices in the spot market. Large customers quickly learned to shop around, and competition ensured that they were offered good deals. Small customers who were willing to shop around have also done quite well, but those who have stayed with their local incumbent (about three-fifths of the total) are typically paying 10 percent more than switchers. Competition was only possible, however, because the transmission and distribution networks were regulated in a way that required incumbents to allow other companies to use their networks. The United Kingdom's RPI – X incentive regulation has converged on rate-of-return regulation in terms of the calculations required to reset a control, but the regulators have continued to search for ways to give companies incentives to improve performance, and the companies seem to have responded well to these.

I will return to these themes at the end of this chapter, arguing that they represent "lessons learned" from the experience of the industry in England and Wales, while also pointing out some questions that remain open. The chapter itself, however, starts with a brief account of the process leading up to the restructuring, to put it in context, followed by a chronological tour of the main events after privatization. I then discuss a number of aspects of the restructuring in more detail.

Privatization

The electricity industry was the last of the four major utilities (the others being gas, telecoms, and water) to be privatized in the United Kingdom but the first to be restructured to introduce competition. The ideological beliefs underlying the restructuring were that private ownership and the profit motive gave far better incentives than the most benevolent kind of state control (let alone the state interference that seemed to be the best that British governments could achieve) and that competitive private industries gave better results than monopolies. This second belief was strengthened by the experience of privatizing British Telecommunications (BT) and British Gas as effective monopolies. By the time that Mrs. Thatcher asked Cecil Parkinson, the secretary of state for energy, to plan the privatization of the electricity industry, in June 1987, BT's quality of service was believed to have declined significantly since privatization ("believed," because the company had stopped publishing the information), and British Gas was on the brink of being referred to the Monopolies and Mergers Commission (MMC). Parkinson decided that he could do better than this and that when the electricity industry was privatized, it would be restructured to promote competition. Competition was thus a means of improving performance rather than an end in itself, although some of its proponents may take the latter view.

In February 1988, the government published a white paper (Department of Energy 1988) that announced this decision. The white paper had a vision of a competitive electricity industry, in which the transmission grid previously owned by the Central Electricity Generating Board (CEGB) would be owned by a new company (owned in turn by the distribution companies) and open to anybody who wished to generate electricity. The CEGB's power stations would be divided between two competing companies, and distributors would be able to buy electricity from them, from France and Scotland, and from new, independent stations. Some large customers would also be given access to the grid. The decision to create only two incumbent generators was driven by the desire to privatize the CEGB's nuclear power stations: a company with 30 gigawatts (GW) of conventional plant might be able to absorb the risks of 10 GW of nuclear plant.[1] The remaining 20 GW of conventional capacity were given to a second company in the hope that it would act as a counterbalance to "Big G." The government had considered a more competitive structure, with five conventional generators that would jointly own a nuclear company, but decided against this. One argument was that this complex structure could not be successfully marketed to investors: another is that it could not have been sustained, as a concentrated industry was needed if an inherited overhang of excess capacity was to be closed in an orderly manner.

The white paper did not contain much detail because most of the detail behind the vision had not been worked out. Its authors appear to have thought that competition in generation would be organized around bilateral physical contracts between generators and distributors. In the event, a "spot market," the Electricity Pool of England and Wales, became the formal centerpiece of competition, although financial contracts were used to hedge much of the trading in this market. The nuclear stations had to be withdrawn from the privatization when new estimates of their costs and risks proved too much for investors to accept without guarantees that the government was not willing to give. The plans for competition in retailing became more ambitious—every customer would be allowed to choose their retailer—but their full realization was postponed to April 1998, eight years after the reforms were due to commence. Vertical integration would be allowed—generators could sell directly to customers, and distributors could build power stations—but would be limited. Hundreds of special contracts were agreed, aiming to ensure that there would be no unpleasant financial surprises in the first few years of the new system. Everything was just about ready by March 31, 1990, the Vesting Day on which the new structure came into legal being. The twelve distribution boards, now known as Regional Electricity Companies (RECs), were privatized in December 1990, and the two major conventional generators, National Power and PowerGen, in March 1991. There have been other share sales since: the government kept 40 percent of the shares in the generators until March 1995, and the RECs divested the National Grid Company in December 1995. Finally, the more modern nuclear stations improved their performance to the point where their owner, British Energy, could be privatized in July 1996.

Events after Privatization — An Overview

Subsequent sections will discuss specific parts of the industry in greater detail, but it might be helpful to give a chronological overview. The new system came into being on schedule on Vesting Day, March 31, 1990, although temporary patches were being used while the permanent market software was being written. Three-year contracts between the generators and British Coal, and the generators and the RECs, required the generators to buy a fixed quantity of coal (more than they really needed) and the RECs' captive customers to pay for it. Large customers, however, were free to switch between retailers, started to do so, and most of them (switchers and nonswitchers) saw real price reductions of about 10 percent. This was because their prices were now based upon Pool prices expected to be set in relation to the (lower) cost of imported coal. A few very large industrial customers, who had had particularly good terms from the CEGB, would have faced price increases, but special contracts, backed by the state-owned Nuclear Electric, ensured that no one's bill rose in real terms that year.[2]

The following year, some of these customers' prices rose, and they started to complain, particularly as the rest of the economy was in a recession. Prices in the Pool, which had actually been lower than had been expected in 1990–1991, also rose significantly, and the regulator held an inquiry into Pool prices (Offer 1991). This criticized one particular tactic adopted by PowerGen but did not object to the price increase, as Pool prices had been less than the generators' avoidable costs—with most of their revenues determined by contracts for differences (CfDs), a low Pool price had been acceptable to them in the short term but was obviously not sustainable.

The RECs responded to the likelihood of future price increases, and the chance to acquire some unregulated profits, by building new power stations using combined-cycle gas turbines. These stations, and others built by National Power and PowerGen, meant that the demand for coal was going to fall significantly after the three-year coal contracts agreed upon in 1990 expired. Impending job losses in the coal industry caused a political crisis in October 1992, but the new stations' contracts had been signed, and there was no room in the market for any more coal—the Conservative government accepted that its energy policy would, in general, be to accept whatever the market decided. A new set of five-year contracts, beginning in April 1993, linked a reduced volume of coal purchases, at a lower price, with the RECs' needs for their franchise customers, less the power they were buying from their new stations.

In July 1993, the regulator announced that Pool prices had risen above avoidable costs, that there was insufficient competition in the wholesale market, and that he was starting a study into National Power and PowerGen's costs and margins to decide whether he should refer them to the MMC. In February 1994, the generators agreed an undertaking on prices (holding them below current levels for the next two years) and an undertaking to use all reasonable endeavors to sell or otherwise dispose of 6 GW of plant within two years, in return for which the regulator agreed not to refer them to the MMC during that period. Both companies leased their plant to Eastern, one of the RECs, which had its own generation limit relaxed in order to allow the acquisition.

The regulator announced an apparently generous set of price-control revisions for the RECs in the summer of 1994, and their shares, which had outperformed the stock market since privatization, continued to rise rapidly. In November of that year, Trafalgar House launched the first takeover bid for a REC, which lapsed when the regulator unexpectedly announced that he was revisiting the price controls. Several successful bids followed the regulator's announcement of revised controls in July 1995, however. British water companies, U.S. electric utilities, and Scottish Power were allowed to acquire RECs without any government intervention, but when National Power and

PowerGen each announced an agreed takeover of a REC in the early Autumn of 1995, the bids were referred to the MMC. The MMC found that the mergers would act against the public interest as formulated, but most members of the panel examining the mergers believed that they should be allowed, subject to conditions to reduce the damage to competition. One member, however, believed that competition in the industry was still at too delicate a stage for the mergers to be acceptable. Unusually, the report was leaked to the press, a consensus developed in favor of the minority report, and the minister responsible for the final decision blocked the merger in May 1996.

The RECs had floated the National Grid Company (NGC) in November 1995, selling the company's pumped storage stations to Edison Mission Energy in the process, and entry into generation continued, but prices stayed high. The impending end of the five-year coal contracts threatened more miners' jobs in the autumn of 1997, and the new Labour government, more interventionist than its predecessor, wanted to take action. A moratorium on new entry by gas-fired power plants was more symbolic than immediately effective, but the government also encouraged the regulator to carry out a review of electricity trading arrangements, which recommended the abolition of the Pool. This became government policy, and the New Electricity Trading Arrangements (NETA) went live on March 27, 2001.

The government also wanted more competition in generation, and Power-Gen and National Power were required to divest another 4 GW of plant apiece, in return for permission to acquire a REC and a REC's retail business, respectively. The licensing regime was changed, first to allow and then to require, retail businesses to be separately licensed from distribution, allowing for separate ownership. The limits on vertical integration had now effectively been abandoned, for British Energy, owner of the privatized nuclear stations floated in 1996, was allowed to buy a retail business (which it later sold), and Electricité de France acquired London Electricity. One justification for relaxing the limits on vertical integration was that all households became able to choose their retailer by May 1999, ending the RECs' legal franchise, and that competition in generation was increasing—National Power and Power-Gen both sold other power stations voluntarily. National Power then split itself into two, with its international stations (and one in the United Kingdom) becoming International Power, and the rest of the company becoming Innogy in October 2000.

Competition in retailing was arguably becoming more effective, as an increasing proportion of customers switched away from their local REC, and price controls on all final prices were lifted beginning in April 2002. At the same time, however, the industry was consolidating—Innogy, London Elec-

Table 2.1 The electricity supply industry in March 2003

Group	Centrica	Innogy	London Electricity	PowerGen	Scottish & Southern Energy	Scottish Power
Parent		RWE	EdF	E.On		
Customers	5.5 m	4.8 m	4.2 m	6.0 m	3.4 m	2.4 m
Generation	1.7 GW	8.2 GW	6.8 GW[a]	9.9 GW	4.5 GW[a]	6.9 GW[a]
Main businesses	British Gas	Midlands,[b] Northern,[b] Yorkshire[b]	London, Seeboard, SWEB[b]	East Midlands, Eastern,[b] Norweb[b]	Hydro-Electric, Southern, Swalec[b]	Scottish Power, Manweb

[a]London Electricity's generation includes the 2 GW capacity of the interconnector with France (although this may be accessed by other companies, the ultimate source of incremental flows is likely to be an EdF plant). The Scottish companies' generation includes plants throughout Great Britain, adjusted for the output-sharing contracts arranged at privatization.
[b]Supply (retail) business only—distribution has a different owner.

tricity, and TXU Europe (the renamed Eastern Electricity) all acquired other RECs or retail businesses. The last independent REC, Southern Electric, had merged with Hydro Electric of Scotland to form Scottish and Southern Energy in 1998. These mergers were at least partly driven by the belief that five million customers were required to achieve economies of scale in retailing to domestic customers, given the information technology (IT) systems needed—and there are about twenty-five million domestic customers in Great Britain.

Wholesale prices fell sharply before the introduction of NETA, to the point where a number of generators faced financial difficulties. Some independent power stations went into administration, and British Energy required a government-organized rescue that left both shareholders and bondholders facing heavy losses. TXU Europe, which was a net buyer in physical terms, had an unfavorable portfolio of contracts and sold most of its U.K. assets to PowerGen. PowerGen, by this time, had been acquired by E.On of Germany, while Innogy was owned by RWE, another German utility.

In early 2003, England and Wales thus has six major integrated energy companies, listed in table 2.1, together with a number of generation-only companies. Wholesale power prices are low, almost certainly below the level that can be sustained in the long term. Retail prices for large customers have followed wholesale prices downward, and all customers have gained from large reductions in transmission and distribution prices over the last ten years, but there are concerns that retail prices for small consumers are not passing on the recent reductions in wholesale prices. Prices for all customers, however, are 30 percent below those of 1990 in real terms. The rest of this chapter discusses the processes that have given us this structure in greater detail.

How Was It Meant to Work?

The Electricity Pool of England and Wales was often presented as the most important and the most radical part of the 1990 reforms. It also proved to be one of the most controversial features, perhaps the least popular with large customers, and the least enduring, for it was abolished in March 2001. The many criticisms of the way in which the Pool *has* worked make it hard to assess how it *should have* worked, but that assessment is a crucial part to understanding what the reforms were meant to achieve.

The Wholesale Market

The reformers wanted competition in generation, but they also wished to maintain the merit order system, under which the cheapest generators were dispatched first. The first attempt at market design, based on physical contracts that had to be continuously exchanged to ensure that the cheapest stations were running, collapsed under its own weight. The Pool was based on the CEGB's old dispatch software, run every day, twenty-four hours before operation, but used price bids instead of internal cost data. The bid of the most expensive station in normal operation set the System Marginal Price (SMP).

SMP was intended to reflect the short-run marginal cost of electricity, but the price of electricity has to rise above its short-run marginal cost from time to time, or peaking capacity would never cover its fixed costs. The CEGB had dealt with this by charging the Area Boards a fixed amount (about £16/kWh in 1988–1989) for each unit of electricity that they took in the three peak half hours of the year. Retailers might have been required to back all of their energy demand with "capacity tickets," but at the rare times when capacity grew short, this would have given generators more market power than the buyers were willing to countenance. In a very competitive market with no explicit payment for capacity, we might expect that prices would equal marginal cost as long as there is any spare capacity at all, but that they would rise almost without limit at the rare times when there is no spare capacity.[3]

In the end, the industry decided to smooth the cost of capacity, charging for it on the expected cost of power cuts rather than on the actual cost. A computer program calculated the loss of load probability (LOLP) and the government set the value of lost load (VOLL). The capacity payment was set equal to LOLP × (VOLL − SMP): the probability of a power cut multiplied by its expected cost.[4] Power stations which were available would receive a capacity payment,[5] whether or not they generated. If they generated, they would receive SMP as well.

The Pool was the centerpiece of the new market in that almost all generation had to be sold to the Pool at the Pool Purchase Price (PPP) of (1 − LOLP) × SMP + LOLP × VOLL. Various other costs were recovered in an Uplift charge, and this was added to PPP to give the Pool Selling Price, which had to be paid by almost all demand. This eliminated free riding, at the expense of some cost smearing. Because all parties had the option of trading at Pool prices, we would expect any other prices at which trading took place to converge to their level. In that sense, the Pool was the center of the wholesale market.

In practice, however, most participants want to trade at prices that are less volatile than the Pool's half-hourly prices. Contracts for differences (CfDs) allowed them to do this, and between 80 percent and 90 percent of electricity trades through the Pool were hedged with CfDs. With a two-way CfD, the parties agree a strike price for a fixed quantity of electricity, and whenever the Pool price was below the strike price, the buyer paid the seller the difference between the two. When the Pool price was higher, the seller refunded the difference. If a generator produced the amount of electricity covered by its CfD, then its revenues were fixed by the strike price. With this type of CfD, however, the Pool price still determined the generator's incentives at the margin. Bidding marginal cost would maximize a single station's profits while ensuring it only ran when it was efficient to do so.

The capacity payments mechanism could also be combined with appropriate CfDs to promote efficient decisions about plant closures. For at least twenty years, the level of capacity in England and Wales has been fine-tuned, not by new investment, but by bringing forward or delaying the closure of old stations. Annual CfDs that made payments with reference to the capacity payment alone had prices based on the expected value of capacity payments over the year. Because these were intended to reflect the expected value of the energy that would be lost through capacity shortages, a single station was worth keeping open if (and only if) it could cover its costs with the revenues from such a CfD. As with other revenue-hedging CfDs, the station's day-to-day incentives still depended on the expected Pool prices. The efficient course of action in both the short run and the long run should thus have been privately profitable, for the owner of a single station.

That caveat is critical. For most purposes, we can treat the owner of a single station as a price taker who should have responded in an efficient manner to the signals provided by the Pool. Most of the capacity in England and Wales, however, was owned by larger companies with many stations each. These companies were not price-takers, and if they withdrew some of their capacity from the market, the capacity payments received by the remainder would rise (Newbery 1995). The larger generators would maximize their profits by keeping the industry's capacity at less than the efficient level unless the smaller companies were able to provide enough capacity to offset any withdrawals. Similarly, the larger companies maximized their profits by bidding some of their stations above their marginal costs: the stations that raised their bids might be displaced in the merit order, sacrificing market share, but the inframarginal stations earned more from the higher level of SMP (Green and Newbery 1992).

There are two ways in which this market power could be restrained. One is through the contract market, for a generator that had covered most of its output with CfDs was practically indifferent to the Pool price in the short term (Green 1999). In the medium term, however, the generator was likely to be aware that contract prices depend on expected Pool prices and that raising Pool prices, even though it was not immediately profitable, would raise the company's future revenues. The second route was through entry. Unless there are barriers to entry, the incumbents must keep prices just below the level at which entry is profitable or lose market share to new stations. The industry rapidly developed a package of linked contracts—a CfD for electricity, a long-term gas purchase contract, and project finance for building the station—that allowed a power station to enter the market with little risk and made the market for very long-term contracts contestable.[6] At the time of the restructuring, when a large number of three-year contracts between the major generators and the RECs were signed, the government was relying on these two mechanisms to produce an acceptable outcome in the generation market (Hunt 1992). Wolak's chapter suggests that the lack of similar vesting contracts in California was a key contributor to the disaster in that market.

Competitive Retail and Regulated Distribution

Competition in electricity retailing (or supply, as the activity is known in the United Kingdom) was a new concept in 1990. Before then, the physical distribution of electricity was not distinguished from retailing it—the activity of dealing with the consumer and collecting payment. The regulatory licenses issued in 1990 separated the two businesses, however, and required the

RECs to keep separate accounts for each business. More importantly, each REC had to publish a tariff at which any licensed retailer could use its distribution system to sell to customers in its area and had to ensure that this tariff applied to its own retail business as well. The level of the tariff was regulated with the kind of RPI – X price cap that was fast becoming traditional in British utility privatizations. This "common carriage" provision made competition in electricity retailing a reality and contrasted with the initial situation in the gas industry, where British Gas was expected to use its control of the distribution system to block any attempts at retail competition.[7]

The prices that the RECs' retail businesses charged final customers in their own areas (so-called first-tier customers) were also regulated. The controls contained an RPI – X component for the retail business' own costs and profits and passed through the regulated costs of transmission and distribution. Generation costs were also subject to a pass-through, although a yardstick control, linking allowable costs to the average incurred by the industry, would have given the RECs more incentive to keep their costs down. Instead, there was an "economic purchasing condition," to be enforced by the regulator, requiring the RECs to buy electricity "at the best effective price reasonably obtainable having regard to the sources available" (Trade and Industry Committee 1993, 55).

The government realized that existing electricity companies moving into new activities might be the most important source of new competition but was worried about the potential for "sweetheart deals." Vertical integration was therefore allowed but limited. National Power and PowerGen's direct sales (so-called second-tier supply) were initially limited to a total of 15 percent of the demand in each REC's area. Each REC was given a limit (in MW) for its equity investment in generation capacity, again representing around 15 percent of the peak demand in its area.[8]

The final piece in the jigsaw was the Fossil Fuel Levy, which was intended to raise about £8.5 billion (in 1990 prices) toward the costs of decommissioning nuclear power stations and reprocessing their fuel. This was linked to the difference between the amount that the nuclear industry was expected to spend and the amount that it was expected to earn in the market. Preparations for the privatization had revealed that these costs were much higher than the CEGB had anticipated, and the Levy appeared (to the government) to be the best way of building up the necessary funds. The Levy was applied to all the electricity produced from fossil-fueled stations, or those which received payments from it, initially at a rate of 10.6 percent of the final price. A small part of the proceeds would be used to support renewable generation—wind power, waste burning, and the like—with developers bidding for contracts awarded by the government in biennial tender rounds. The Levy was originally intended to last only until 1998 but was then extended (at a much lower rate) to allow continued support for renewable generators until succeeded by the Renewables Obligation, a system of tradable certificates, in 2002.

To oversee all of this, a regulator was appointed. The first director-general of electricity supply was Professor Stephen Littlechild, appointed for a five-year term beginning in September 1989. This followed the model adopted for the earlier privatizations, in which a single person acted as regulator, hopefully insulated from political pressure by a fixed-term appointment and with a set of legal duties that centered on ensuring that all reasonable demands for electricity were met, that the companies involved could be financed, and, as a secondary duty, that consumers were protected. Professor Littlechild, who was to be reappointed for a second term, was supported by the staff of the Office of Electricity Regulation (Offer), but Offer documents from this period are clear that there was a single person responsible for all the major decisions. This model was criticized as time went on due to the risk that it could become overly personalized, while the gas and electricity industries became increasingly interrelated. When the government looked for a new gas regulator in 1998, they made it clear that the same person would become the next electricity regulator once that post became vacant, and Professor Littlechild stepped down a few months early, at the end of 1998, to allow Callum McCarthy to take over. Offer merged with the Office of Gas Supply to form Ofgem, the Office of Gas and Electricity Markets. The Utilities Act 2000 replaced the individual regulators with a Gas and Electricity Markets Authority, with five executive and six nonexecutive members, and Mr. McCarthy as its first chairman.

The industry is regulated through licenses, contracts that can only be amended by agreement, or after a reference to the Competition Commission (previously the MMC). This structure was adopted for the privatization of BT, when there was a real fear that a future Labour government would adopt confiscatory policies towards the company, and was designed to protect it against expropriation. Price controls will expire after a fixed time period unless the regulator explicitly changes the license, and this requires the company's agreement, or the Competition Commission's approval. Every company has to have a license, but most of the licenses for generation and supply contain few clauses intended to affect the companies' economic behavior. The regulator does have powers to refer companies to the Competition Commission under the United Kingdom's standard antimonopoly legislation, however, and is consulted by the competition authorities when mergers in the electricity sector are being reviewed.

Incentive Regulation

Large parts of the electricity industry are natural monopolies and will therefore need regulation for the foreseeable future. When BT was privatized in 1984, a new system of regulation was adopted in which prices were to be controlled, rather than the profits that were the subject of traditional methods. This was because price regulation was expected to be a temporary measure "to hold the fort" until competition could arrive, rather than a permanent feature of the industry (Littlechild 1983). A control on profits would reduce the company's incentive to keep its costs down or to act in an innovative manner, while a control on prices allowed the company to keep all of the savings from lower costs. In the medium term, of course, the level of the price control would become increasingly divorced from the level of the company's costs. This would not be a problem if competition had taken over as the main restraint on the firm, but if competition had not become effective, it would become necessary to reset the price control and to take the company's costs into account. This could reduce the company's incentives to reduce those costs in the run-up to the review of its prices.

Although this RPI – X system of price controls had originally been designed for an industry where competition was expected, it was soon adopted for the gas industry, where there were no plans to introduce competition for smaller customers. The scheme was adapted to allow the cost of buying gas from the North Sea to be passed through to consumers. The water industry was the next utility to be privatized, and a similar scheme was chosen, with two special features. First, the presence of ten regional water and sewerage companies and more than twenty local water-only companies allowed the regulator to base future revisions to the price controls on comparisons between the companies. This weakens the link between each company's own costs and its allowed prices and hence strengthens the incentive to keep its costs down (Shleifer 1985). Second, prices would be allowed to rise to finance much-needed investment, and so RPI – X was replaced by RPI + K when it was time to name the scheme.

British Telecommunications' price control expired during the run-up to the electricity privatization, and as competition was still limited, the telecommunications regulator reset the control, tightening it from RPI – 3 to RPI – 4.5 and increasing its coverage. The regulator later stated that the level of the control was chosen so that BT's predicted return on capital at the end of the review period would equal its cost of capital, but this information was not made public at the time. This reflected a fear of the regulators, that the companies might challenge their decisions through the route of judicial review of the process followed by the regulator. This could have overturned the regulator's decision on the basis that he had followed the incorrect procedures or taken a manifestly unreasonable decision.[9] Regulators believed that they could reduce the risk of a judicial review by minimizing the information they provided on the reasons behind their decisions, while plainly stating that they had followed their statutory duties.[10] The companies could still appeal to the MMC, the U.K. Competition Authority, over the level of the control, but it was possible that the MMC would substitute a tougher price control than the regulator had chosen. In fact, at least one regulator believed that his duty to protect consumers implied that he should set the toughest price control that the company would accept rather than going to the MMC. On this basis, resetting the price control was more a matter of negotiation than the judicial process common in the United States.

The Early Price Controls — Closed but Simple

Given the precedents and the apparently successful resetting of a price control, it was inevitable that RPI – X would be chosen for the price controls in electricity. There were three main controls—on transmission charges, on distribution charges, and on the retail element of most customers' bills. Transmission charges were held in real terms for three years beginning in 1990, while distribution charges were allowed to rise by up to 2.5 percent a year for five years. The exact amount varied by company and was arguably to finance future investment—the investment could of course have been financed by the companies' new owners, but that would have reduced the price the government received from selling them. Furthermore, if prices had been below long-run marginal costs, and the industry's return on capital during the 1980s was certainly very low, then an increase would be economically efficient. The retail element was held constant in real terms for four years.

This retail element was not the final bill seen by the customer but that part of it that would cover the costs of retailing—that is, of dealing with the customer. The largest customers' final bills were unregulated, while the maximum price that the companies could charge their other customers was the sum of the other regulated charges for transmission, distribution, and retailing; of the cost of buying electricity in the wholesale market; and of the Fossil Fuel Levy. Finally, a supplementary charge condition required the companies to keep price increases to customers with maximum demands of less than 1 MW below the rate of inflation until April 1993. The other controls covered customers with higher demand levels, who would be subject to competition, giving the RECs an incentive to rebalance their tariffs in favor of those customers. This condition would prevent any price increases due to rebalancing, at least until after the next general election, due in 1992 at the latest.[11]

British regulators always aimed to announce their proposed changes to price controls in good time so that the process of appeal to the MMC could be completed, if necessary, before the old control expired. It was thus in 1992 that the regulator announced his first price control, for NGC's transmission charges. He seems to have followed the principle of avoiding the risk of judicial review by giving very little information, for a five-page press release stated that he had taken his statutory duties into account, reiterated his belief in the principles behind $RPI - X$, and announced that the new value of X would be 3. The following year, the control on the retail element of final prices was also tightened, and the control on final prices was redefined to exclude customers who were in the competitive part of the market—those with maximum demands of over 1 MW at the time and those with maximum demands above 100 kW beginning in April 1994.

The 1994 Distribution Price-Control Review

Preparations for the price-control review of distribution charges also began in 1993, with the publication of a consultation paper on the issues involved, giving a little financial information on the companies. In May 1994, a leak from one of the companies suggested that their prices would be reduced by up to 25 percent. The companies had been making significant profits in the midst of a recession, and two Select Committee reports from Parliament had recommended that the regulator should bring forward the scheduled review of their price control in order to reduce these profits, widely seen as excessive. The regulator decided against bringing forward the review, arguing that the companies' long-term incentives for efficiency depended on the belief that they would be allowed to keep the benefits of any cost reductions until the next scheduled review. Bringing forward the review would produce short-term gains for consumers but long-term losses.

When the regulator's proposals for the distribution price control appeared in August 1994, most commentators were surprised that the initial cut in prices was to be not 25 percent but between 11 percent and 17 percent. To have any one-off reduction was in fact an innovation, as the regulators in other sectors had simply increased the X-factor when the company had been making too much money. This allowed the price control to converge on the regulator's desired level of prices by the end of the period, allowing the company to retain the benefits of unexpected efficiency gains for longer, and strengthening its incentives. In this case, however, the regulator argued that the companies had been making so much more than had been anticipated when the original price controls were set that their incentives for future cost reductions would not be unduly blunted if these exceptional profits were clawed back quickly. The companies' unexpected profitability had come from reductions in their operating costs and from the fact that investment had not risen after privatization to the extent previously predicted.[12]

While the regulator pointed out that the distribution price control review had "returned" more money to customers than any previous price review, the expectations created by the earlier leak meant that most commentators believed that the RECs had been let off lightly. Their share prices rose significantly after the announcement and continued to rise. In December 1994, Trafalgar House, a U.K.-based conglomerate, announced a bid for Northern Electric, one of the RECs. In its defense document, released in February 1995, Northern promised to give shareholders a special dividend and the company's shares in NGC (about to be floated by the RECs) in a package valued at over £5 a share and to continue to raise its regular dividends in the future. The company's shares had been privatized for £2.40 each just over four years previously.

The Northern defense document led to another round of criticism for the regulator, who had just announced a period of formal consultation over the legal draft of the license conditions required to implement the new controls. This should have been a formality, but on March 7, the regulator announced that he would be extending the consultation and seeking views on whether he should reopen the price control. The RECs' shares fell by 20 percent that day. Unfortunately for the regulator, the shares of National Power and Power-Gen also fell by 10 percent, although the impact of the announcement on their business should have been, at most, indirect.[13] Since the government had completed the sale of £4 billion of shares in the two companies just the day before, the timing was embarrassing.

At the end of the new consultation period, the regulator announced that he would implement the originally announced price controls for the year about to start but that he would reconsider the controls for the following four years. In July, he was able to justify a further one-off cut of between 10 percent and 13 percent and tightened the control for the following three years from RPI − 2 to RPI − 3. Most of the one-off cut came from reinterpreting the implicit contract between the regulator and investors in the companies. The cost of capital for the companies, as measured by their dividend yield, had fallen from 7.3 percent when they were floated to around 4.8 percent in 1994. If investors had bought a bond-like asset, with a given promised return in cash terms, then a reduction in other interest rates would lead to an increase in the capital value of the bond. In the first review, the regulator adopted a procedure that mimicked this feature of the bond market, uprating the regulatory asset base of the companies by 50 percent to offset the reduction in the cost of capital. By the summer of 1995, he had received a report from the MMC (Monopolies and Mergers Commission [MMC] 1995) on the price control for Hydro-Electric, one of the Scottish companies,[14] which had rejected its price control. The MMC report had rejected any adjustment in response to changes in the cost of capital, and the regulator reduced his uprating to 15 percent in his revised proposals for the RECs.

The MMC report on the Hydro-Electric price control included an explicit financial methodology for calculating the price control, given figures for predicted operating costs, investment, the regulatory asset base, and the cost of capital. An earlier report on a price control for British Gas (MMC 1993) had deliberately restricted itself to giving ranges for these figures and no explicit methodology. If a methodology became set in stone, then the companies would perhaps have a greater incentive to manipulate the figures that it relied upon than if the setting of a price control was known to be a matter of overall judgement. Following the Hydro-Electric report, however, and given the criticism of the regulator's botched reviews,[15] all the subsequent price-control reviews have been run on the basis of the MMC methodology and in a far more transparent manner. The regulator has typically published four or five consultation papers per review, starting with an initial review of the issues. This is followed with papers on the financial position of the companies and their predicted costs, then an indicative proposal, and eventually a final proposal, showing how this has been adjusted from the indicative proposal in the light of additional information.

The Later Price-Control Reviews — Open but Complex

The first company to be reviewed under the new, more transparent, methodology was NGC. The company had been making significant profits through the mid-1990s, and so the regulator was able to propose a one-off cut of 20 percent in 1997–1998, followed by three years of RPI – 4, which NGC accepted. This seems to have been set at an appropriate level in that there was no proposal for a one-off cut when the company's prices were next reviewed in 2000. The regulator proposed a control of RPI – 1.5 for the company's transmission asset owner function, and a new, separate control for its role as system operator.

This second control had evolved from an initiative taken in 1994 to control the costs of Uplift in the Pool. Uplift was the charge used to recover the cost of adjusting station outputs to deal with unplanned outages, forecast er-

rors, and transmission constraints and was at first simply passed through to retailers. During the first four years of the Pool's life, uplift rose significantly, in
part because of the amount of work required to connect new stations and cope
with the loss of older stations that had been providing support to particular
parts of the transmission system—while circuits were taken out of action to
perform this work, transmission constraints increased.

To give NGC an incentive to keep these costs down, by better forecasting,
contracting in advance with generators or customers, or by rescheduling
maintenance, the Uplift Management Incentive Scheme (UMIS) was adopted
in April 1994. NGC was given a cash target for the parts of Uplift that it could
influence, and exposed to a share of the gains or losses against that target. In
1994–1995, the company earned almost the maximum amount allowed under
the scheme (potential gains and losses were both capped), and repeating the
scheme the following year was an easy decision to take. The negotiating process was becoming increasingly complex, however, as NGC was reluctant to
give information on its predictions of Uplift costs to those retailers who were
also generators lest they infer something about NGC's plans for transmission
outages and try to exploit the information. Another difficulty concerned the
incentive for NGC to invest to reduce Uplift costs when the annual scheme
had a tendency to ratchet down the targets, taking each year's outturn as the
following year's starting point.

These problems have been reduced, but not completely eliminated, by
passing responsibility for the incentive schemes to the regulator. The schemes
gradually became more complicated, giving greater sharing factors for those
cost categories that NGC could influence more easily, until the company was
facing five separate incentive schemes in 2000–2001. This potentially gave
NGC the chance to arbitrage between schemes, incurring costs wherever it
was most advantageous for the company to do so. When the wholesale trading arrangements were reformed in March 2001, the regulator eliminated
these opportunities by combining the schemes into a single incentive for all
of NGC's system operator costs. The level of costs under the new arrangements was uncertain, and the regulator allowed NGC to choose between a
menu of contracts, trading off a lower target against a higher share of the gains
if NGC beat the target. In practice, NGC chose an intermediate target and
sharing factors.

In the following years, the regulator has continued to implement annual
incentive schemes, although there have been proposals for a longer-term
scheme, linked to other changes in NGC's charges that have not yet been
agreed. In particular, the regulator would like NGC to sell rights to use the
transmission system to generators and to have to buy them back if the system

becomes congested. A similar scheme has been introduced in the gas industry, but is being resisted by most electricity companies, believing that it would be far more complicated to implement in an electricity network. The regulator's view is that the scheme would ensure that NGC had an incentive to keep as much as possible of its system available to users. The issues are related to those in the debate over merchant transmission investment, discussed in the chapters by Hogan and Joskow.

The RECs are also facing direct incentives to provide a good level of service. In their most recent distribution price control, which started in April 2000, the regulator imposed another one-off cut of between 25 and 30 percent. Part of this cut (9 percent on average) was because some costs were transferred from the distribution businesses to retailing (which was allowed a higher margin in consequence), and so the RECs' customers saw no impact on their bills. The size of the remaining cut, however, does rather suggest that even the second attempt at cutting the RECs' charges in 1995 had not gone quite far enough. The package also included proposals for an "information and incentives" mechanism, which was eventually introduced in April 2002. If the number and duration of interruptions to supply rose above target, the companies could lose up to 1.75 percent of their revenues. A second measure would reward or penalize companies by up to 0.125 percent of revenue, depending on the quality of their telephone services, as measured by customer surveys. The hope is that companies regulated through such schemes will have a strong incentive to deliver a high level of quality—at least where it can be measured and incentivized!

Incentive regulation in the United Kingdom has thus come a long way from the early days in which it was seen as an alternative to the mechanistic process of rate-of-return regulation, as practiced in the United States. What was once almost a process of negotiation has now become much more a matter of finding the correct numbers to place inside a formula. However, Ofgem is attempting to ensure that the companies are still given incentives to improve their efficiency and their standards of service. The efficiency incentive comes from the built-in regulatory lag implicit in fixed intervals between price-control reviews, while standards of service are being more directly controlled.

Competition in Retailing

The best guarantee of a high standard of service is usually a competitive market in which informed customers will go elsewhere in response to poor service. Competition in retailing was an innovation when it was introduced in

1990, but it has turned out to be a successful one, at least as far as large customers are concerned.

Large Customers

In 1990, roughly 5,000 customers with a maximum demand of more than 1 MW, representing 30 percent of electricity consumption, were allowed to choose their retailer.[16] Those who did so had to pay charges for half-hourly metering and data processing, but these charges were small in proportion to their bills, or to the savings available from shopping around. Large customers had the incentive and the ability to seek out the best deals, and 27 percent chose to buy from a second-tier supplier in 1990–1991. There were two main complaints—the technical process of installing a meter and arranging data collection did not always go smoothly, and a regulatory restriction on National Power and PowerGen meant that some customers could not get the best deals available.

In an effort to limit the amount of vertical integration and ensure that other companies got a fair chance to enter the market, the major generators were (jointly) limited to 15 percent by volume of the sales in any one REC's area. The companies were generally offering lower prices than their rivals, however, and the limits meant that they were soon turning customers away. The regulator responded to the resulting complaints by raising the limits in the areas of four RECs with the greatest proportion of industrial customers. The following year, the limits were raised again and then abolished. Competition in retailing for these customers became firmly established, and 1993's abolition of price controls on the overall prices paid by all customers in the competitive market was uncontroversial.

In 1994, the competitive market was opened up to a further 45,000 customers with maximum demands of over 100 kW, representing a further 20 percent of electricity sales. These customers were also to prove adept at shopping around, but the market opening did not go smoothly. The industry had been left to design the processes for market opening, although the incumbent retailers had little incentive to give the task any urgency, and at a late stage, the regulator decided that customers would be responsible for choosing their own meter operator. This had been the task of the retailer, which had almost always appointed the local REC, but the regulator wanted to promote competition in metering. The relationship between retailer and customer was often a short-term one, giving neither time nor incentive for the retailer to avoid the incumbent meter operator. Unfortunately, many customers either did not learn of this decision, or did not act on it, until there was very little time to install the meters and communication links and then register them with the market operator. It soon became apparent that many customers would not be able to complete these formalities in time for the market's expansion in April 1994, but the regulator insisted that the market should open on time and that consumers should be allowed to join it without a registered meter.

The results should have been predictable. Many consumers received no bills for several months, while others received two sets of bills. Most of the bills were based on estimated levels of consumption, in any case, and proved to be wildly inaccurate. It took several months before the regulator and the industry could agree to stop the problems from getting worse by stopping new consumers joining the competitive market without a meter. Once this step had finally been taken, the industry could sort out the backlog. The whole episode was a public relations disaster, compounded by the fact that the following year, the charge for metering and settlement services was raised to recover the cost of sorting out the mess—from the customers!

Small Customers

The one good effect of the 100 kW fiasco (and I should add that these customers, too, quickly learned to shop around for good deals and were therefore adequately protected by competition) was that the industry, the regulator, and the government woke up to the importance of avoiding similar problems when the market for domestic customers was opened up. The key problem was the need to assign customers' consumption to their retailers within the time periods used in the wholesale market, which means every half hour. Large customers could afford half-hourly metering, and the decision was taken to require all over-100 kW customers to install half-hourly meters, whether or not they were currently taking a second-tier supply, to ensure the costs of serving them were measured accurately and to create a level playing field between incumbent and entrant retailers.

It would be inconceivably expensive to require all domestic consumers to install half-hourly meters, and so a system of profiling was developed. A customer's meter might only be read once a year, and the profile would be used to assign their consumption in the period since the last reading across each of the half hours since that time. The negotiations involved in designing this system were complex, as a fundamental principle of the wholesale market was that the sums paid in and paid out on any one day had to be equal, and as a number of the companies appeared to believe that any inaccuracy in the way in which a profile allocated costs to individual customers would create commercial risks for them.[17] In the end, the industry agreed that the wholesale market's settlement program would be run several times for each day, with the final run fourteen months after the day in question so that new data could be fed in to the results as it arrived.

Agreeing the rules was one thing; writing the software to implement them and for keeping track of every customer in the country was quite another. Learning from the problems with the 100 kW market, the regulator appointed a team of project management consultants to manage the task, and a strict regime of testing was imposed before any company could be declared ready for the competitive market. As the original date for market opening drew near, it became clear that the companies would not be ready in time, and the sensible decision to delay the start of domestic competition was taken. It is possible that some companies may have delayed spending money on the preparations for "1998," believing that the Labour government that everyone expected to be elected in 1997 might decide not to go ahead with the plans for full-scale competition. When the new government announced that it did in fact favor the project, the companies had to accelerate their preparations. This may have accounted for the high cost of opening the market, some £850 million (including Scotland).

In the event, the first companies started to open their markets in September 1998, and the last customers were allowed to choose their retailer beginning in May 1999. Each company opened its market in stages, using defined geographical areas, to ensure that its systems were not overloaded at the beginning. The process was a technological success although there were a number of human errors. Some customers managed to sign up with several retailers at once, but some sales agents transferred customers who had not known that they were signing a contract for electricity. The number of consumer complaints over erroneous transfers and other errors rose significantly, but most consumers have found the process of changing retailer an easy one.

Has the introduction of retail competition been worthwhile? To some, competition may be an end in itself, but a more pragmatic view would be that retail competition is a good policy if it makes price regulation unnecessary. In other words, are competitive pressures strong enough to protect consumers? We have already seen that larger customers quickly learned to shop around, and incumbents and entrants both generally offered competitive deals. When the domestic market opened, there was a steady stream of customers switching away from their local incumbent, implying that a similar process was taking place.

The discounts available, however, were much greater than those offered to larger customers. This was not because the new domestic retailers were selling at a loss but because the incumbents had been allowed to set prices well above the marginal cost of selling to a domestic customer. In the early 1990s, they had signed long-term contracts with independent power producers at prices that turned out to be well above the levels prevailing at the end of the decade. When the market was opened to competition, retaining a retail price control was an obvious precaution, and this was based on the level of each incumbent's average costs, including its past contracts. This allowed the entrants to undercut incumbents by up to 12 percent—even though many of the entrants were in fact RECs and hence incumbents in other areas.[18] There were three major entrants that were not, at the time, affiliated to RECs—National Power, PowerGen, and Centrica, which trades in the United Kingdom as British Gas. Centrica had been opening its own market in stages since 1996, and losing market share to RECs using their existing relationships with electricity customers. It was eager to start winning electricity customers. "Dual fuel" deals, in which the customer buys electricity and gas from the same company, were to become a prominent feature of domestic energy competition in Great Britain.

The price controls set in 1998 lasted two years as a transitional measure. When the time came to reset them, the great majority of consumers were still with their local incumbent, and competitive pressures were therefore limited. The regulator, now Callum McCarthy, therefore proposed to continue the controls for a further two years, but at a lower level, passing on some of the reductions in the RECs' costs to their consumers. His predecessor, however, argued that this would inappropriately stunt the development of competition (Littlechild 1999). If the incumbents' prices were driven down too quickly, entrants would find it difficult to win any more market share, and the competitive pressure on the incumbents would weaken. Littlechild argued that it was better to maintain the entrants' headroom and allow competition to develop to the point where it might become self-sustaining. Regulation could then be abolished. A similar logic appears to underlie the "price to beat" mechanism that puts a floor under incumbents' retail prices in Texas, as described by Baldick and Niu. The regulator did revise his proposed price controls, leaving more scope for entrants to undercut the incumbents, the number of customers switching continued to rise, and price controls for domestic electricity consumers were lifted in April 2002. This decision was justified on the basis of the number of consumers switching, and the fact that some companies were now pricing below the level of their price cap although the differences were generally very small (several had been allowed to raise nominal prices by 1 percent or so, had not done so, and were therefore below their price caps). However, in the period since then, the majority of incumbents have raised their prices slightly, even though wholesale prices and transmission and distribution charges have been falling. It is difficult to avoid the conclusion that they may prefer to increase the margins that they can obtain from their loyal customers than to compete actively to regain those that have left. If that is the case, retail competition has not been totally effective in protecting consumers.

Competition in Generation

At the time of privatization, the government had hoped that the generation market would be competitive, but one legacy of the failed attempt to privatize the nuclear stations was the duopoly of National Power and PowerGen. These companies started their lives with three-year contracts for coal and electricity arranged to meet a number of objectives. The coal contracts required the generators to buy almost all of their fuel requirements from British Coal and to pay much more than the world market price. The excess cost of this was passed on to the RECs' captive franchise customers in the electricity contracts. Customers in the competitive market could not be made to share in this cost, as they would have the option of buying electricity from a retailer paying Pool prices, and those were expected to reflect the world price of coal, not the British price. Pool prices were also expected to reflect the generators' inherited excess capacity, and the contracts included a capacity allowance to raise the generators' revenues until they had brought the market into equilibrium by closing plant (Henney 1994). The British government did not face the legal problems over the recovery of stranded costs that have been common in the United States, and are discussed in the chapter by Joskow, because it owned the industry. Nonetheless, it wanted to obtain a good price when it sold the generating companies, and there would have been political and economic disadvantages to letting prices fall for a short period only to rise once the market was in equilibrium.

In a competitive market with excess capacity, prices would be kept low and might only cover the industry's variable costs. If the industry has deep pockets, it can wait until demand rises, but otherwise it must either reduce the amount of capacity or collude to raise prices above short-run costs. Hunt (1992), who was an advisor during the privatization process, doubts that the industry would have been able to close plants in an orderly manner if it had been divided into a larger number of companies. In her view, the conventional duopoly was not just a side effect of the failed nuclear privatization but also the only way of dealing with the overhang of excess capacity. National Power and PowerGen had the ability to raise Pool prices, but their ability to raise contract prices was limited by the threat of entry, and most electricity was sold through contracts, not the Pool.

Entry

The problem is that the one-off overhang expected in 1990 turned into an almost continuous excess of capacity because of the amount of entry. The RECs had been given the opportunity to make some unregulated profits by investing in new power stations, and eleven of them took it. The contract structure developed for these stations, and the fact that their regulation allowed them to pass their purchase costs straight through to their captive customers meant that these investments appeared almost riskless. The regulator agreed that the stations met the RECs' economic purchasing condition, given the unattractive nature of the generators' initial offers for renewed contracts.[19] The RECs might have been less enthusiastic if yardstick regulation had been used for their purchase costs, rather than a pass-through, although the desire to reduce their dependence on the major generators was another justification for the new stations.

Following this first "dash for gas" in the early 1990s, a second wave of stations was built, with outside investors playing a larger role. The major generators also built gas-fired stations, in part to reduce their sulphur emissions by switching away from coal-fired generation. However, they also closed or mothballed 22.1 GW of capacity, almost matching the 25.9 GW that has been added (in total) since 1990. If the incumbents had not been willing to reduce their capacity in this way and to keep prices at about the level of entrants' costs, much of the new capacity would have been unprofitable. Figure 2.1 shows the way in which the entrants (and increased nuclear output) have displaced output from National Power and PowerGen.

Combined-cycle gas turbines are clearly the cheapest form of new generation, and building CCGTs will often be a cheaper way to reduce sulphur emissions than retro-fitting existing stations with flue gas desulphurisation equipment.[20] The problem in England and Wales was that the CCGTs were built while the industry had excess capacity and before sulphur emissions became a binding constraint. It is hard to avoid the conclusion that they raised the industry's costs.

The switch to gas-fired generation also had a large impact on the coal industry. The United Kingdom's coal output fell by one-third between 1982 and 1992, from 125 to 85 million tonnes, but British Coal's employment fell by nearly four-fifths as the corporation concentrated its output on its more productive mines. In 1982, British Coal employed around a quarter of a million workers, but this had fallen to roughly 50,000 by 1992. During that year, it became clear that the generators wanted to reduce their purchases from 70 million tonnes (in 1991–1992) to 30 million tonnes a year (from 1994 to 1995

Figure 2.1. Electricity generation in England and Wales

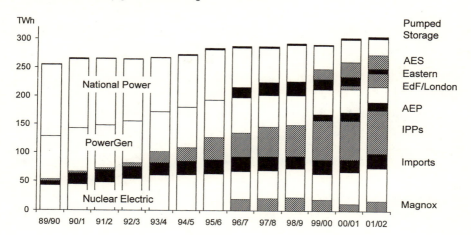

onward) and that this would result in the loss of another 30,000 jobs. This sparked a political crisis, resolved with promises of government assistance, but the stations that were crowding coal out of the industry's fuel mix already had contracts. The government was not willing to tear up these contracts and was unable to increase the amount of coal burned. It was able to persuade the electricity industry to agree to another set of linked coal and electricity contracts, passing on the excess cost of British coal to the RECs' franchise consumers. The coal price was falling, however, reducing the premium in the electricity contracts. These had to expire in 1998, when the franchise was due to end, in case competition made it impossible to pass on further premia.

In the autumn of 1997, it became clear that the generators' demand for coal would fall further. By that time, however, Britain had a Labour government, with historical ties to the miners and a more interventionist mindset than the Conservatives. Existing contracts remained sacrosanct, but the government announced a temporary moratorium on new power stations.[21] This would not affect the amount of coal burned in the next two years (as it only affected stations not yet under construction) but had symbolic importance as a statement of support for the coal industry.

Professor Littlechild, however, "was concerned about the consequences of the proposed policy of restricting new entry both for competition and for prices to customers." Allowing himself a degree of criticism unusual for a civil servant, he advised the government that "[t]he distortions in the market . . . would not seem to justify [the] policy," and that "it would be helpful if . . . an early opportunity could be taken to relax and then remove it" (Offer 1998a). His concerns stemmed from his belief that the generation market was still insufficiently competitive and that removing the threat of entry would allow the incumbents to raise prices.

Competition and Prices

The regulators issued a dozen reports on competition in generation between 1991 and 2000, and all of them have reflected concern over the state of competition in the Pool. At first, National Power and PowerGen were clearly dominant, but Pool prices were below the companies' avoidable costs (most of their sales were hedged by contracts at much higher prices) and the regulator did not object to increases. By 1993, however, he found that prices were higher than they would have been in a competitive market. Even so, Wolfram (1999b) found that the companies had only exploited part of their market power and could have maximized their short-term profitability by selling at a higher price. This may have been because their CfDs reduced the generators' short-term incentive to raise prices (Green 1999) or because the generators were trying not to provoke the regulator. In 1994, they agreed to sell 6 GW of their capacity (about 15 percent) and to restrain prices in the Pool and for new contracts, rather than face a reference to the MMC for investigation and possible action. Ironically, many of the duopolists' sales were already covered by their five-year coal-related contracts with the RECs, and the reduction in short-term prices probably had a bigger impact on Nuclear Electric than on the companies that agreed to the deal!

The undertaking on prices was promptly followed by a winter of record prices caused by plant failures that reduced the amount of spare capacity and raised capacity payments (figure 2.2). Capacity payments were formula-driven, based on a calculated LOLP multiplied by the VOLL, and intended to give the correct incentive to keep rarely used plant on the system when this was necessary for security of supply. The largest price component was SMP, based on the bid of the most expensive station in normal operation, while the costs of keeping the system stable (in electrical terms), mostly incurred by NGC, were recovered in a charge called Uplift (later split into Uplift and Transport Uplift). The high capacity payments of early 1995 were followed in turn by two months of very low prices, as the companies made sure that the annual averages were close to the levels in the undertaking. The regulator accepted that these plant failures were unusual and that the high prices did not breach the companies' undertakings but warned them to avoid a repetition. Capacity payments were even higher the following year, but the companies

Figure 2.2. Electricity spot prices in England and Wales (rebased to 1999–2000 prices)

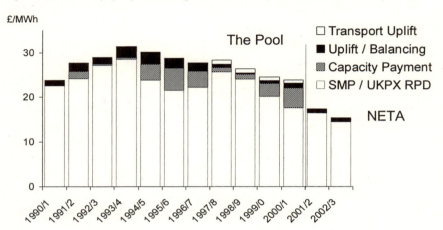

kept the annual average price down to the level they had agreed with the regulator. The regulator made no attempt to extend the restraint on prices, which was only ever intended as a temporary relief, and had significant effects on companies that were not parties to it. His long-term hopes for the deal agreed upon in 1994 depended on the generators selling part of their capacity to increase competition in the midmerit part of the market.

By the mid-1990s, a large number of CCGT stations were competing for continuous, baseload running alongside Nuclear Electric, imported electricity, and the duopolists. This part of the market was probably adequately competitive, but most Pool prices were set by midmerit stations that only generated for part of the time: by definition, SMP was a *marginal* price. Most of the time, this price was set by one of the stations owned by National Power or PowerGen, and they clearly had enough inframarginal capacity to benefit from price increases. Furthermore, the threat of baseload entry would not prevent them from changing the balance of peak and off-peak prices, deterring entry by keeping the time-weighted average low but raising their own revenues. Forcing the companies to sell some of their price-setting plants should reduce both their ability and their incentive to raise prices—a company that raised its bids would face a greater risk of losing market share to one of its larger number of rivals. Generating less, it would also gain less from the higher prices that resulted.

Eventually, both National Power and PowerGen leased some of their plant to Eastern, one of the RECs. The regulator relaxed the limit on the company's investment in generation to allow this. One feature of the deal was an "earn-out": Eastern paid the lessors £6 for each MWh it generated. This solved the difficulty of valuing the stations, for the generators did not want to agree on a sale price based on the earnings from midmerit running and find that Eastern was running them on base-load. It also raised Eastern's opportunity costs, however, and hence the level of its likely bids. In the event, Pool prices were slightly lower in real terms in the first year after the plant was transferred, but price increases during the winter of 1997–1998 prompted the regulator's tenth report on competition in generation. He found that the companies had reacted to lower capacity payments by raising SMP (a logical strategy if they were targeting the Pool Purchase Price that they receive) and called for further plant divestitures.

In due course, the government agreed that it would be desirable for the generators to sell more plant, and the generators' desire to merge with RECs provided a suitable opportunity. PowerGen sold 4 GW of capacity in return for permission to buy East Midlands Electricity, and National Power sold 4 GW in return for permission to buy Midlands Electricity's retail business. These sales took place in the first half of 1999, but over the next eighteen months, the generators voluntarily sold an additional 5 GW. The market should have been becoming more competitive, but the industry's new regulator was concerned that even relatively small companies might have the ability to manipulate the market.

Following another episode of high prices, in July 1999, Mr. McCarthy proposed a Market Abuse License Condition, which would prohibit the abuse of a position of substantial market power. This would give the regulator power to order companies not to repeat behavior that his investigations determined was abusive and to fine them if they ignored such an order. While Professor Littlechild had attempted to influence the generators' conduct, he had concentrated on making the structure of the market more competitive. This condition marked a shift toward conduct regulation, similar to the one that Bushnell describes the Federal Energy Regulatory Commission as making. The plan was to impose the condition on any generators with a market share of 8 percent or more, and six of the eight generators concerned accepted it. Two did not, however, and the matter was referred to the Competition Commission.

The Competition Commission (2000) decided that the condition was unnecessary—the contractual position of the two companies that had rejected it meant that they would have no incentive to manipulate the Pool in the last months before the start of NETA, while the Commission also doubted that the companies on their own could cause significant problems after the start of NETA. It is perhaps unfortunate that the Commission felt it was restricted to look only at these two companies, even though the regulator had said that a rejection of the condition would force him to withdraw it from the licenses of those companies that had accepted the condition. The Commission might have reached a different conclusion if it had looked at the eight largest generators together. There were problems with the way that the condition might be applied, however, and doubts whether it was even necessary, given the rest of U.K. competition law.[22] Furthermore, the regulator had planned to offer confidential guidance to the larger companies, telling them if a proposed strategy would be consistent with the condition, which could have created important asymmetries between larger and smaller generators. With hindsight, the industry was about to enter a period of very low wholesale prices, with no apparent need for regulatory constraints, and the debate over the Market Abuse License Condition has faded away.

The New Electricity Trading Arrangements

The reduction in electricity wholesale prices has been linked to the abolition of the Pool, which had acquired a lot of influential enemies. The coal industry had long believed that the Pool was biased against it because nuclear and CCGT stations could bid zero, guaranteeing that they would run but still receive the Pool Purchase Price or a contract price which might be even higher. It is certainly possible that some CCGTs had contracts that made it attractive for them to run, even when SMP was below the value of the gas they were burning.[23] This would have distorted the merit order, although it ought to have been possible to renegotiate the contracts, reaching a more efficient outcome and sharing the resulting benefits among the parties involved. Many large industrial customers seemed to believe that the single-price auction raised their prices and that they would pay less if each station received its own bid. This would certainly be the case if some stations had continued to bid zero, but that was not a likely outcome! Other customers may have believed that they would be able to negotiate discounts if the industry moved toward a system of bilateral contracting, as they did in the days of the CEGB. The regulator had become frustrated by the Pool's inability to change its rules—a governance system designed to protect minority interests against changes being imposed by the larger companies had allowed opponents of potentially beneficial reforms to drag out the change process for months or years.[24]

Although economists poured scorn on many of these arguments (Newbery 1998; Wolfram 1999a; Hogan 2000), enough of them were accepted by the regulator and the government to seal the Pool's fate. The Review of Electricity Trading Arrangements started in late 1997 and reported in July 1998 (Offer 1998b). Its conclusions were accepted by the government in October 1998 (Department of Trade and Industry [DTI] 1998). A series of bilateral markets were to replace the Pool in what became known as NETA. Most of these would be allowed to evolve, and over-the-counter markets for contracts have indeed developed as well as two organized markets for short-term trades.[25] The only centralized market is for the period immediately before real time. At Gate Closure, initially three and a half hours before real time but now only one hour in advance, all generators and retailers must inform NGC of their contracts and intended physical positions. NGC has to keep the system in electrical balance by trading electricity bilaterally with those generators and retailers (or large consumers) who bid into a balancing mechanism, paying for each accepted trade at its own bid price. NGC also uses longer-term contracts to give it access to a wider range of resources and is allowed to trade electricity in the run-up to Gate Closure. Typically NGC would need to buy power from some stations but would sell power back to others.

The average cost of most of NGC's purchases for each half hour, including an allocation of the costs of its longer-term arrangements, was defined as the system buy price (SBP), while the average cost of NGC's sales (and longer-term arrangements) was defined as the system sell price (SSP). The caveat "most of" was included because some trades were assumed to be required to deal with constraints on the transmission system, rather than to keep the system in (energy) balance, and their costs were to be removed from the calculation of (energy) imbalance prices. Because it is practically impossible to tell whether a given trade is for energy or system balancing, the mechanism for assigning costs between the two was inevitably arbitrary, and the calculation of the imbalance prices is less than transparent.

Companies that have a net short position (have generated less than they sold or taken more than they bought) have to pay the SBP for their imbalance. Companies with a net long position (generated more than they sold or took less than they bought) are paid the SSP. These imbalances are aggregated across power stations or distribution areas, but not between generation and consumption, so as not to advantage vertically integrated companies. The intention was to give all companies an incentive to predict their demand and generation accurately and to trade in advance to balance their position. In practice, companies have an incentive to enter the balancing mechanism expecting to be "long," because SBP has been far higher and much more volatile than SSP. A company that is long in the balancing mechanism will expect to sell some power at the relatively unattractive SSP (roughly £5/MWh less than the average level of prices in the short-term markets) but reduces the chance that it will have to buy at SBP, which has averaged nearly £15/MWh above short-term prices. Portfolio generators have also part-loaded many of their stations so that they can increase generation from other units if one suffers an unexpected failure.[26] This has given NGC access to lots of cheap spinning reserve but has reduced the thermal efficiency of the system.

Generators with unpredictable output levels have done relatively badly under NETA. This could be argued to be simply a reflection of the costs that unpredictability imposes on the system, but the unpredictable generators include combined heat and power schemes and wind generators, both politically favored. Many of these generators have struggled to find buyers for their output, except at low prices, as many retailers want to avoid the risk of exposure to the balancing mechanism inherent in buying from unpredictable sources. Ofgem has tried to promote "consolidation services" that would aggregate the output of a number of generators, reducing the variability of the portfolio's output, but these have not yet had much impact. The fact that consolidation services could reduce costs for participating generators highlights one of the flaws in NETA's logic—many individual imbalances in fact cancel out, and generators who are heavily penalized for being short may in fact be helping a system that is normally long overall, with a surplus of power. This point was finally accepted when the market rules were amended so that neutral imbalances, those in the opposite direction to the overall system imbalance, would be cashed out at a market price based on prices reported from the short-term markets rather than at SSP or SBP as previously calculated. This amendment took effect at the end of February 2003 and has greatly narrowed the spread between the imbalance prices.

This is only one of a large number of amendments to NETA's rules, the Balancing and Settlement Code. One of the genuine problems with the Pool was its governance and the way in which rule changes could be delayed by minority interests. Under NETA, there is a Balancing and Settlement Code Panel, made up of industry representatives, which is required to consider all proposed amendments to the code, and pass a recommendation to Ofgem. This recommendation should be based on whether the proposed amendment will further the defined objectives of the code. The final decision is made by the Gas and Electricity Markets Authority, Ofgem's governing board. A number of rule changes have been made quickly, but others have allegedly been held up inside Ofgem, and there have been occasions when the Authority has overruled the recommendation of the industry's experts. That is not necessarily a bad thing, but the lack of appeal may be a worry (although the Authority itself is of course acting as a review body, and too many appeals could create gridlock). At least one of Ofgem's favored policies, to create geographical transmission charges by auctioning entry rights to the grid, does seem likely to create far more costs than benefits. Unlike the rights discussed by Hogan, these would be physical rights to be used as the primary means of resolving congestion. This means that they will have to be fairly narrowly defined so that trading in any given right will be illiquid. Keeping track of generators' rights holdings and penalizing them when they do not have enough rights will require a large IT program. Ofgem claims that experience in the gas market, where entry rights to six terminals have been auctioned, shows that the same system should be applied to electricity (with half-hourly, rather than daily, trading and many more entry points), but the gas auctions have received mixed reviews.

The most important question about NETA is whether it has made any difference to prices. Bower (2002) uses a regression of monthly prices from April 1990 to March 2002 to claim that NETA has led to an increase in the energy-only price and a reduction in the overall price of electricity that was less than the level of capacity payments in the last year of the Pool. Because capacity payments might have been abolished by administrative fiat (given that an Act of Parliament was needed to introduce NETA, a different Act could have changed the Pool rules in this regard), he argues that NETA was in fact counterproductive.

Evans and Green (2003) use data for the shorter period from April 1996 to September 2002 and reproduce Bower's conclusion about the impact of NETA on prices, as long as the effect is expected to happen at the time that NETA was introduced. However, they also noticed a sharp drop in margins in October 2000, six months before NETA. Sweeting (2002) has found evidence of tacit collusion between the major generators during 1999, declining in the first half of 2000. Evans and Green suggest that if the generators had been colluding, the impending introduction of NETA could have caused this collusion to break down, reducing prices. Their results with a dummy variable from October 2000 onwards imply that almost all of the reduction in prices between 1998 and 2002 was due to this dummy rather than to the reductions in concentration over the period. However, it is also possible that plant disposals in October 2000 finally moved the market into a state where price reductions were inevitable, implying a threshold effect that regressions are badly placed to pick up.

The uncertainty over NETA's actual impact on prices makes it hard to produce an overall assessment of the changes. The Pool had certainly become discredited, so that there were public relations gains from the changes, but we have no firm evidence on whether imbalance pricing based on a single-price auction (as in many other electricity markets) or NETA's system of dual cash-out prices based on average costs gives superior results in practice. Nor have we any evidence of whether the lack of a capacity payment is affecting the long-run efficiency of the market, as no rational capacity payment mechanism would be having a significant impact on prices with the current overhang of spare capacity.

Whatever the cause, electricity prices have been extremely low in the period since NETA. The market has become fragmented, there is an overhang of excess capacity, and prices have fallen to short-run marginal cost. A number of independent power producers have been driven into administration, and British Energy needed a government-led rescue plan, with losses to shareholders, bondholders, and the (state-owned) reprocessing company. Prices are unlikely to rise above short-run marginal cost until the overhang of spare capacity is eliminated, either by plant closures or by the gradual increase in demand over time, or the industry returns to a more concentrated structure.

The Overall Record So Far

The preceding sections have discussed particular aspects of the reforms in England and Wales, but what of their overall impact? Figure 2.3 shows the prices paid by the three main customer classes, reflated to 1995 levels using the gross domestic product (GDP) deflator. The data cover the United Kingdom as a whole, but England and Wales account for nearly nine-tenths of the electricity consumed in the United Kingdom and will therefore dominate the figures. All three averages fell slightly in the run-up to privatization but then diverged. The average price for industrial customers fell in 1990, for many of them stopped contributing to the high cost of British coal. In the competitive part of the market, there was no mechanism for passing through the cost of the effective subsidy that the coal industry received, and industrial sales are dominated by large users who gained by no longer having to contribute to British Coal. The very largest users lost out from the introduction of competition, however, because they had effectively received a subsidy before the restructuring. Their representatives have been among the industry's fiercest critics ever since. Smaller customers' prices went up slightly at the time of privatization (which increased the value of the companies to be sold) but have since fallen. Many commercial customers saw significant reductions in 1994 when they in turn entered the competitive market and stopped contributing to the British coal subsidy (which has declined throughout the period). Domestic customers saw a similar reduction in 1998 at the end of the second set of above-market coal contracts. In the second half of the 1990s, lower prices

Figure 2.3. U.K. electricity prices

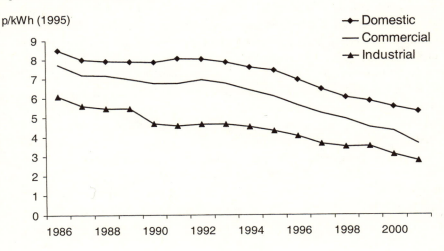

came from reductions in the regulated charges for distribution and transmission and in the Fossil Fuel Levy, which fell from 11 percent (in 1991–1992) to less than 1 percent. Retail competition offered lower prices to some domestic consumers after 1998, while falls in wholesale prices could have been passed on. Overall, most customers have seen reductions of more than 30 percent since 1989, after adjusting for inflation.[27]

Figure 2.4 breaks the average price into fuel costs, other costs, and the industry's operating profits. While not going into the same level of detail as the studies cited by Wolfram, this gives us a broad-brush account of the sources of price reductions. Most of the early price reductions were financed by lower fuel costs, rather than reductions in the electricity industry's value added. The top line shows the average price across all consumers, and the next line down deducts fuel costs. The line is based on the present cost of nuclear fuel, now that a deal for reprocessing services has been agreed; the dotted line just below it in the left-hand part of the graph includes the higher figures that had previously been included in the accounts of the nuclear companies. The industry's revenue net of fuel costs actually peaked in 1993 and then declined by about 30 percent by 2000. The reductions in fuel costs partly come from lower prices, particularly for coal, and partly from an increase in thermal efficiency, as older stations were closed and combined-cycle gas turbines replaced conventional thermal plant.

The bottom line shows the electricity industry's nonfuel operating costs.

Figure 2.4. Average electricity price and its components, United Kingdom 1986–2001

p/kWh (1995)

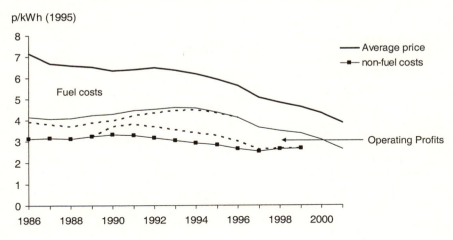

Some of the increase in the late 1980s may have been due to a better recognition of nuclear costs rather than a real increase in cost levels. From 1991 to 1997, however, the industry's costs were falling at around 4 percent a year. If we deduct uncontrollable costs, such as depreciation, the figure is over 5 percent: a significant fall, if not quite as dramatic as some of the headline cuts in employment.[28] The industry's profits are given by the gap between its revenues, net of fuel costs, and its other operating costs. (The area below the lower dotted line shows the portion of the industry's profits that was due to the Fossil Fuel Levy and a similar premium paid to Scottish Nuclear.) Profits were quite low (measured as a return on assets) in the 1980s, and some increase could be justified on grounds of allocative efficiency. In the event, current cost operating profits nearly doubled in the early 1990s. They stayed close to this level for much of the decade before finally falling at its end.[29] This increase had not been foreshadowed in the companies' sale prices, however, and shareholders made large gains. Some of those gains were extracted with the windfall tax levied in the Labour government's first budget of 1997, although where the company had already changed hands at a high price, the new owners paying the tax were not the people who made the earlier gains.

Overall, the data on prices and on costs imply that the industry has performed reasonably well in the period since restructuring, reducing costs and (eventually) passing most of the gains on to consumers. One key question, however, is whether consumers will gain from any future cost reductions, given the current trend towards vertical integration in the industry.

The Future: Vertical Integration?

Figure 2.5 shows the industry's structure at the time of privatization. Three large groups dominated generation, and while retailing appears to be fragmented, each of the twelve regional markets was in fact dominated by the local incumbent, particularly as 70 percent of the market was not even open to competition. Given the limited extent of competition, the government imposed a number of measures to limit vertical integration. The fear was that vertically integrated companies would have an advantage over others and would make entry by nonintegrated companies much harder.

As competition grew within retailing and within generation, the barriers to vertical integration were gradually lowered. Scottish Power was allowed to take over Manweb, and Eastern was allowed to lease the stations that National Power and PowerGen were required to divest in the mid-1990s. When those two generators attempted to merge with two Regional Electricity Companies in 1995, however, the mergers were blocked by the government, with the support of most independent commentators. By 1998, however, a new government was willing to allow a major generator to buy a REC, in return for further plant divestiture. Both generators took the opportunity to turn themselves into integrated groups and have now become net buyers in the wholesale market.

Figure 2.6 shows how radically the market appears to have changed. There are now ten large generators, plus a fringe of smaller companies, which looks like a competitive market structure, while the number of major retailers has fallen to six. All the major retailers also own generation, but almost all of them appear to be net buyers in the wholesale market, even Innogy (the former National Power) and PowerGen. The caveat about appearances is important, because some generators had tolling arrangements with retailers that effectively amounted to vertical integration by contract. In particular, TXU was badly exposed to low wholesale prices during 2002, which would imply that it had many of the characteristics of a net seller—its exposure was in fact so bad that it has disappeared from the industry!

The largest generator, British Energy, is the only net seller among the major integrated groups, and its recent financial troubles have been mentioned already. There are several other net generators in figure 2.6, and some of those have also reported financial problems. The combination of excess capacity, a fragmented generation sector, and the presence of a significant number of generators that would actually prefer low wholesale prices, given their overall position as net buyers, has pushed wholesale prices down to what must be unsustainable levels. At the same time, while final prices for large consumers

Figure 2.5. Supply and generation in England and Wales, 1990

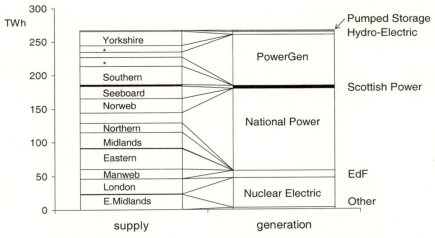

Notes: The RECs' supply figures are derived from turnover. Swalec is below Yorkshire; SWEB is above Southern.

Figure 2.6. Supply and generation in Great Britain, 2003

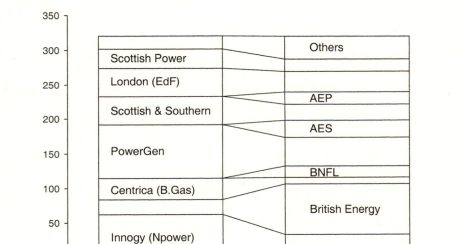

Note: Based on 2001–2002 estimates adjusted for the London/Seeboard, Innogy/Northern, and PowerGen/TXU mergers.

have followed wholesale prices down, prices to small customers have not, leaving large margins in the domestic market.

This would seem to imply that generation and retailing to large customers are currently competitive, but that competition is less effective in retailing to small customers. Should that worry us? The issue really hinges on how we expect to pay for the investment in generation that will eventually be needed, if only to cope with ever-tougher restrictions on coal-fired plants and their sulphur emissions. That investment will only happen if generators expect prices to be high enough to give them an adequate return.

If the industry remains unconcentrated, prices will be low whenever there is spare capacity (including off-peak times during periods of peak scarcity), but prices should rise once there is a shortage of capacity. With little or no spare capacity, the industry becomes a sellers' market and prices can rise above variable costs. However, the total costs of peaking capacity must be recovered over the periods in which capacity is scarce. This either requires very high prices for a few half hours or more moderate prices lasting for a longer period. These high prices could cause political problems for the industry—Ofgem's statements imply that it is aware that a competitive electricity market should produce such prices when capacity is scarce, but politicians may not be able to resist interfering if these prices actually occur. In an ideal world, generators would add or close capacity at the right rate to keep prices in line with costs from year to year. In reality, however, cycles of over- and underinvestment are a danger, as discussed by Joskow (chap. 1 in this volume). This could produce long periods of surplus capacity and low prices, greatly raising the level of costs that have to be recovered in the intervening periods of scarcity. Investment would only be attractive once prices were approaching levels that promised to cover these costs over a relatively short period. The resulting pattern of prices is unlikely to be attractive.

The mechanisms described relate to short-term prices, and so long-term contracts might allow companies to smooth out these fluctuations. One potential problem is that if retailing becomes too competitive, then companies will be unwilling to lock themselves into long-term contracts, as they face a risk of losing money on those contracts if short-term prices drop and competitors without long-term contracts can undercut them. Newbery (2002) describes this issue, and the problems that reliance on short-term markets caused in California, but Green (2004) uses a parameterized model to suggest that companies might in practice be willing to accept the risk of contracts.

In a best-case world, therefore, we might have a competitive generation market in which investment is financed with the help of long-term contracts and capacity rises smoothly in line with demand. The retail market would also be competitive, but retailers would be willing to sign the contracts necessary to support investment by generators. If we do not have a fully competitive retail market, this might even ease the problem of supporting investment in generation, as retailers would be more willing to contract in advance.

The dangers come from the combination of vertical integration and an imperfectly competitive retail market. Vertically integrated companies are unlikely to sign long-term contracts with new entrants to generation if this means that they will be supporting competitors. If entrants cannot obtain contracts, then entry into generation will be riskier, raising the limit price that the incumbents could charge without encouraging entry. The end result could be an unattractive combination of high wholesale prices and high retail margins for many customers, with only those prepared to shop around benefiting from retail competition.

If we have moved from having too few generators but a reasonable number of retailers to having enough generators in the short term but too few retailers, was there a point at which we could have stopped the clock and established a better industrial structure? At the end of the 1990s, generation was becoming competitive enough, and Pool prices were on the point of falling, even before NETA took effect. Looking forward to NETA, however, the major generators were determined to integrate vertically in order to protect themselves from the new wholesale market. They were allowed to do so, putting further downward pressure on wholesale prices but making unintegrated entry much harder. If the major generators had not been allowed to integrate, then future entry into generation would have been made easier. There are serious doubts about whether NETA was responsible for the (welcome) reductions in wholesale prices—if it was the catalyst for a move to a disadvantageous industry structure, then the change in trading arrangements will have been very unfortunate.

Lessons Learned

Because the British reforms were among the earliest in the world and received so much publicity, they have acted as a source of lessons learned for other countries. The first and most important lesson is that restructuring can bring significant benefits—prices to most consumers have fallen by around 30 percent in real terms since the restructuring, while the industry's overall profits have remained healthy. (In a competitive market, individual companies can face financial problems even in a market which is profitable overall, of course, and a number of generators, in particular, have recently done so.)

The second lesson is that these benefits are not guaranteed—a lesson that has become obvious since the California energy crisis but should have been clear from the early days of the British experience. The market structure, market rules, and regulatory oversight interact to produce the level of performance experienced by customers. If the structure is uncompetitive, prices are likely to be too high, while poorly designed market rules will also tend to raise prices and reduce efficiency. Proactive regulation can counteract these tendencies, but regulatory intervention is almost always a poor second best to a competitive market structure and well-designed rules.

In particular, wholesale electricity markets are very susceptible to the exercise of market power if even moderately concentrated. If it is possible to create an unconcentrated market structure as part of the original reform package, the opportunity should be taken. The government may still own the industry, while the reform process involves opportunities for "log-rolling" that may persuade private companies to make concessions. To impose a more competitive structure later will almost inevitably reduce the future profits of private shareholders. That cannot be done lightly in an economy subject to the rule of law (and the other sort rarely perform well). Increases in competition can only be brought about by the slow process of market entry (if conditions allow it), by government or regulatory action following due process (which also requires time for the evidence of unsatisfactory performance to build up), or by voluntary divestitures by the dominant companies. Such divestitures are likely to require a quid pro quo that may have subsequent disadvantages—the British increased competition in generation at the cost of allowing two of the largest generators to integrate with retail businesses, cementing the trend toward vertical integration.[30] The speed with which the British industry became vertically integrated also shows that while desirable changes to market structure can take a long time to achieve, undesirable trends can become established very quickly. A third lesson is thus that a good market structure is hard to create except at the start of a reform and, once achieved, is still fragile.

While structural changes are always likely to be hard to impose once the market has started up, the extent to which the market rules can be changed is an endogenous variable. Lesson four is that the governance of market institutions is very important and that it must be possible to deal with flaws in the market rules speedily and fairly. The Electricity Pool of England and Wales was set up as the central market place, and its governance was designed to make rule changes difficult to achieve in order to guard against coalitions forming to change the rules to the detriment of outsiders. In practice, this meant that desirable changes were equally difficult to achieve, and the Pool was abolished when further attempts at reform were perceived as unprofitable. Klevorik discusses the danger of gridlock in Independent Transmission Providers that are controlled by stakeholder boards.

Even if the market structure is competitive, it is desirable that most wholesale trading should take place through long- or medium-term contracts (lesson five). Contracts lasting a year or more give stability to both generators and retailers, while reducing the generators' incentive to raise prices should they have market power. Experience in the British market implies that these contracts could be either physical or financial, while still delivering the same benefits. The nature of the final spot market dictates the nature of the bilateral contracts that overlie it. For the first eleven years, the Pool was a "gross" pool so that practically all electricity was bought and sold through this centralized market, and the bilateral deals were financial contracts for differences. Beginning in March 2001, the central market was restricted to the net imbalances,[31] and bilateral deals changed to contracts for physical delivery.

A sixth lesson is that retail competition is clearly capable of protecting large customers, who are able and motivated to shop around for good deals. Retail competition has proved less effective in protecting small consumers, many of whom are unwilling to switch retailer for relatively small price savings. Some 40 percent of domestic customers have changed retailer, frequently buying gas and electricity from the same company, but this is in response to savings of up to a tenth. The regulators deliberately created headroom for entrants by setting relatively lenient price controls for the incumbents and then removed those controls on the basis of the high level of switching that had been observed. Few of the incumbents have responded to the loss of customers by reducing their prices, however. The level of switching that would cause the incumbents to reduce their prices, the price differential that would promote it, and the political acceptability of such a differential remain open questions.

A seventh lesson concerns the appropriate regulation for the remaining monopoly elements of the industry. A focus on these elements may seem inappropriate for a volume on restructured electricity markets, but they play a vital role in making competition possible. The U.K. system of incentive regulation based on $RPI - X$ price controls has worked well, but the original belief that price controls were a radical departure from rate-of-return regulation has not stood up to experience. Projected costs and revenues and the cost of capital have proved to be central elements in the setting of new price controls. At the same time, the regulator has been innovative in seeking ways to create additional incentives for good performance by the regulated companies. The split-savings regulation used to control the National Grid Company's costs of operating the transmission system has been particularly effective, but it has not been simple to implement.

A final lesson concerns the importance of the demand side of the market. The Pool set prices by combining generators' bids with a demand forecast that explicitly excluded any short-run price responsiveness on the part of customers. As Borenstein's chapter shows, demand responsiveness can be a vital curb on generators' market power. A somewhat unsatisfactory demand-side bidding scheme was added to the Pool, through which a few large customers offered demand reductions as a kind of negative generation, but the impact of this was limited. The replacement New Electricity Trading Arrangements were designed to give the demand side a potentially much greater role in price setting, although active demand-side participation in the short term remains limited.[32] Spurred on by its incentive schemes, however, NGC has been much more proactive in finding customers willing to provide short-notice reserve capacity by reducing load on demand, and this has resulted in a reduction in system operation costs.

Open Questions

Despite the passage of time, some important questions are still open. I have already referred to the effectiveness of retail competition in protecting small consumers. A second open question concerns the need for a separate payment for capacity, as opposed to energy. Theoretically optimal prices for electricity include a payment for capacity, over and above the marginal cost of producing energy, which is proportional to the risk of losing load. The Pool included such a payment, which proved extremely volatile (as designed and expected and mostly hedged via contracts) but was set by a computer program that appeared to lose touch with reality as time went on. NETA does not contain a capacity payment, in part because the demand side is intended to play a more active role in price setting. (The theoretically optimal price referred to previously is based on consumers' willingness to pay to avoid having to reduce load, which an active demand side should discover directly.) In theory, such an active demand side should be able to avoid the need for a separate capacity payment, while still giving incentives for generators to keep the right amount of capacity on the system. Since NETA was implemented at a time of substantial excess capacity, we have not yet experienced any conditions where the lack of a capacity payment might have affected market outcomes.

A third open question concerns the optimal mechanism for wholesale price setting. The Pool used a uniform pricing rule in which the bid of the marginal unit set the SMP for all generators. While most generators' actual revenues were modified by the impact of CfDs, the Pool's critics argued that the uniform pricing rule made the market particularly vulnerable to the abuse of market power. The New Electricity Trading Arrangements were therefore designed to have no "focal" central price. There were two prices for settling imbalances between traders' physical positions and their contractual obligations, based on the average of a large number of bilateral transactions made by NGC and the companies that helped it to balance the system. The mean spread between these prices was originally more than the lower of the two prices, but a number of subsequent rule changes have brought them much closer together at most times. This dual-price cash-out, and its impact, are still controversial features of NETA.

A final open question concerns the impact of vertical integration. Retailing to small consumers is now dominated by six vertically integrated groups, and large-scale entry seems unlikely. If the retail market is insufficiently competitive, this integration could have knock-on effects in the generation sector, and its long-term consequences are not yet clear.

These doubts for the future are not to deny the impressive achievements of the industry since 1990. Prices have fallen by more than 30 percent in real terms, costs are down, and quality remains generally high. Consumers have gained enormously from the restructuring of the electricity industry in England and Wales. The challenge is to ensure that they continue to do so.

***

REFERENCES

Bower, J. 2002. Why did electricity prices fall in England & Wales: Market mechanism or market structure? Oxford Institute for Energy Studies, Working Paper no. EL02.

Competition Commission. 2000. AES and British Energy: A report on references made under section 12 of the Electricity Act 1989. Competition Commission Report no. 453. London: HMSO.

Department of Energy. 1988. *Privatising electricity.* Cm 322. London: HMSO.

Department of Trade and Industry. 1998. *Conclusions of the review of energy sources for power generation and government response to fourth and fifth reports of Trade and Industry Committee.* London: HMSO.

Evans, J. E., and R. J. Green. 2003. Why did British electricity prices fall after 1998? University of Cambridge, CMI Electricity Project Working Paper no. EP26.

Green, R. J. 1999. The electricity contract market in England and Wales. *Journal of Industrial Economics* 47 (1): 107–24.

———. 2004. Retail competition and electricity contracts. University of Cambridge, CMI Electricity Project Working Paper no. EP33.

Green, R. J., and D. M. Newbery. 1992. Competition in the British electricity spot market. *Journal of Political Economy* 100 (5): 929–53.

Henney, A. 1994. *A study of the privatisation of the electricity industry in England and Wales.* London: Energy Economic Engineering Limited.

Hogan, W. W. 2000. Making markets in power. Cantor Lecture to the Royal Society for the Encouragement of Arts, Manufactures and Commerce. 21 February, London.

Hunt, S. 1992. *The first year: How is the England and Wales privatisation working?* NERA Topics 6. London: National Economic Research Associates.

Littlechild, S. C. 1983. *Regulation of British telecommunications profitability:* London: HMSO.

———. 1999. Promoting competition in electricity supply. *Power UK* (68): 12–19.

Monopolies and Mergers Commission (MMC). 1993. *British Gas plc: Volume 1 of reports under the Gas Act 1986 on the conveyance and storage of gas and the fixing of tariffs for the supply of gas by British Gas plc.* Cm 2315. London: HMSO.

———. 1995. *Hydro-electric plc: A report on a reference under section 12 of the Electricity Act 1989.* London: HMSO.

Newbery, D. M. 1995. Power markets and market power. *The Energy Journal* 16 (3): 41–66.

———. 1998. The regulator's review of the English electricity pool. *Utilities Policy* 7 (3): 129–42.

———. 2002. Problems of liberalising the electricity industry. *European Economic Review* 46:919–27.

Office of Electricity Regulation (Offer). 1991. *Pool price enquiry.* Birmingham, England: Office of Electricity Regulation.

———. 1998a. Offer response to the government's consultation on the review of energy sources for power stations. Press Release no. R57/98. Birmingham, England: Office of Electricity Regulation.

———. 1998b. *Review of electricity trading arrangements: Proposals.* Birmingham, England: Office of Electricity Regulation.

Office of Electricity Regulation (Offer) and Office of Gas Supply (Ofgas). 1999. *A review of competition in the designated electricity market, June 1999.* London: Office of Electricity Regulation and Office of Gas Supply.

Shleifer, A. 1985. A theory of yardstick competition. *RAND Journal of Economics* 16:319–27.

Sweeting, A. T. 2002. Market outcomes and generator behaviour in the England and Wales wholesale electricity market. MIT, Department of Economics. Mimeograph.

Trade and Industry Committee. 1993. *British energy policy and the market for coal: First report of session 1992–1993.* HC 237. London: HMSO.

Wolfram, C. D. 1999a. Electricity markets: Should the rest of the world adopt the United Kingdom's reforms? *Regulation* 22 (4): 48–53.

———. 1999b. Measuring duopoly power in the British electricity spot market. *American Economic Review* 89 (4): 805–26.

NOTES

Richard Green is professor of economics at the University of Hull Business School.

I would like to thank Jim Griffin and Steve Puller for helpful comments. The views expressed are mine alone. This chapter was written during 2003.

1. Nuclear Electric's capacity in March 1990 was only 8 GW, but some of the company's stations were later uprated, and the total rose to 10 GW by 1995 when the pressurized water reactor (PWR) at Sizewell B was commissioned.

2. These contracts were actually customer specific, and there were arrangements to transfer the contract to the customer's new retailer if it switched away from its local REC.

3. If enough customers can react to prices in real time, then they could reduce their demand as prices start to rise, and the equilibrium price would be just sufficient to keep demand down to the level of capacity. If customers cannot react in this way and random power cuts are needed, then there is no limit to the price that the generators could set, if they were allowed to do so after the shortage has appeared. In Australia, a (very high) administered price is used in these circumstances.

4. The expected cost is the economic value of the load that cannot be met (deemed to be VOLL), less the short-run marginal cost of meeting it, believed to equal SMP.

5. For a station that was not operating, the formula used a price based on the station's own bid in place of SMP—because this bid would be above SMP (as the station was out of merit), the payment it received would be slightly lower than the regular capacity payment.

6. Generation itself is not a contestable activity, for a station remains a sunk investment. The contract market is contestable, however, for it costs relatively little to arrange the package of contracts, and once they are signed, the new entrant is protected from most price risks.

7. I have not heard that British Gas actually did block any such attempts: the obstacles to potential retailers appeared so overwhelming that none of them bothered to try.

8. The average demand is about two-thirds of the peak demand, and only half of this is taken by customers with demands below 100 kW, who would remain in the RECs' legal franchise until 1998. A REC that used all of its allowable investment could have met half of these customers' demand, and more if it had equity partners that did not take any electricity.

9. The test of reasonableness is a weak one in English law—it does not require the court to test whether the decision was the correct one but merely whether it was one that a reasonable person might have made.

10. This account draws on a meeting between one of the regulators from this period and researchers on the Economic and Social Research Council (ESRC) project R0001811, "Privatisation and Re-regulation of Network Utilities."

11. British prime ministers can choose the timing of the General Election, with a maximum interval of five years. While Mrs. Thatcher had always gone to the country at four-year intervals, she was replaced as Prime Minister in November 1990, and her successor did indeed wait until 1992 before calling an election, which he won unexpectedly.

12. The regulator's statistics on standards of performance, such as the number and duration of power cuts, imply that the unexpectedly low investment was not associated with a reduction in the quality of supply.

13. A reduction in distribution prices might, if anything, have increased the demand for electricity and hence the generators' profits, but investors took fright at the news that the sector's regulator was less predictable, and perhaps tougher, than they had previously assumed.

14. The price controls for the Scottish companies were announced in September 1994 and were widely acknowledged to be tougher than the RECs' controls.

15. The regulator had given the revised price controls to the RECs, in confidence, twenty-four hours before he planned to announce them to the stock market, but numbers, correct or incorrect, started circulating almost immediately, and the regulator convened a hurried press conference to announce the actual controls that afternoon, ensuring a further round of bad publicity. The cuts were, yet again, less than many commentators had expected.

16. The exact definition of a 1 MW site did cause some problems—for example, what if a road cut an industrial site in two, or a hospital included some shops in its reception areas?—but these were determined on appeal by the regulator.

17. This is unlikely to have been the case in practice, as in the absence of half-hourly metering, no one would ever know which consumers were being given an inaccurate cost allocation, and so there was no commercial opportunity to exploit.

18. See table 21 in Offer and Ofgas (1999).

19. It is possible that the generators planned to make better offers at a later stage in the contract negotiations, but the RECs built their own stations instead.

20. The comparison depends on fuel prices and on the remaining life of the coal station, over which the investment has to be amortized.

21. Section 36 of the Electricity Act 1989 requires new stations to obtain a consent from the government, but this had not previously been a significant barrier.

22. U.K. and European Competition Law prohibits the abuse of a dominant position, and

the issue was whether a company too small to count as dominant could still cause significant problems in the context of an electricity market.

23. This is partly because their gas is on "take or pay" contracts that ban its resale and partly because some electricity sales contracts only pay the station if it operates, unlike the CfDs discussed earlier.

24. One example of this concerns geographical charging for transmission losses, which had been considered in 1990 but rejected as too complicated to implement in the time available before privatization. Instead, the Pooling and Settlement Agreement required the industry to consider its implementation by 1994. When this consideration led to a proposal to introduce differentiated charges (although somewhat muted compared to the marginal cost of losses), the decision was appealed to the regulator, who supported geographical charging. The Pool then had to approve the work program to implement this, and this decision was also appealed to the regulator. When he supported geographical charging for the second time (and implied that he really did not want to have to hear a third appeal on the issue), the dissenting companies launched a judicial review through the legal system, which held things up until the approach of NETA made the case irrelevant.

25. The liquidity in each of these markets is quite low, and it is arguable that if a single short-term market had been organized by Offer and the Department of Trade and Industry, as some had suggested, it would helpfully have concentrated liquidity.

26. In theory, they should not change the output of these other units after they have submitted their final physical notifications to NGC, but NGC has few powers to stop such practices.

27. This ignores the imposition of VAT in the mid-1990s.

28. Some companies have halved employment over this period, with the generators (including the then publicly owned Nuclear Electric) leading the (privately owned) RECs.

29. Changes to the industry's structure mean that a few of the final years' profit figures have had to be estimated.

30. I am conscious of the tension between encouraging "log-rolling" at the start of the reform process and being wary of giving firms a *quid pro quo* at a later stage, but would argue that the authorities have more degrees of freedom in the earlier stages.

31. Given the history of the word in the United Kingdom, the designers of NETA would probably be insulted if I was to use the common term in the industry, a "net" pool, for their market design.

32. There is a difference between retailers arbitraging between markets in order to meet a fixed demand at the lowest price (which certainly happens under NETA) and customers actually reducing the amount they wish to buy because the price is too high—only the latter will genuinely curb market power.

3

Lessons from the California Electricity Crisis

Frank A. Wolak

Introduction

This paper provides a diagnosis of the causes of the California electricity crisis. It assesses the impact of actions taken by state and federal regulators in response to the crisis and determines those actions that ultimately ended the crisis. The main point of this paper is that the California electricity crisis was fundamentally a regulatory crisis rather than an economic crisis. It is also important to emphasize that a number of conditions in California electricity supply industry discussed in the following contributed to the events that occurred during the summer 2000. However, it is difficult to see how the market meltdown that occurred in late 2000 and during the first six months 2001 could have occurred without a significant lapse in wholesale-market regulatory oversight and several ill-conceived responses to events in California during the period June 2000 to June 2001 by the Federal Energy Regulatory Commission (FERC).

The most important lesson from the California crisis relates to how the FERC carries out its statutory mandate under the Federal Power Act of 1935 to set just and reasonable wholesale prices in a market regime. There are a number of important lessons for governments and public utilities commissions (PUCs) in states that have already formed wholesale electricity markets and those that are currently considering forming these markets. Because the FERC has recently issued a Notice of Proposed Rulemaking (NOPR) outlining a standard market design (SMD) that it would like the entire United States to adopt, it is essential that the FERC and the state PUCs learn the correct lessons from this regulatory failure. Otherwise, it is very likely that these standard market rules combined with the retail-market rules implemented by state PUCs will increase the likelihood of future regulatory failures like the California electricity crisis.

A correct diagnosis of the California crisis requires a clear understanding of the federal and state regulatory infrastructure that governs the U.S. electricity supply industry. Many observers fail to recognize that wholesale electricity prices are subject to a much tighter performance standard than are the prices for virtually all other products. Consequently, they miss this key explanatory factor in the California electricity crisis. The retail-market policy of the California PUC (CPUC) is the second key explanatory factor. I will describe the important inconsistencies between California's retail-market policies and the FERC's wholesale-market policies that enabled the California crisis to occur.

I will then discuss the conditions in the western U.S. electricity supply industry that enabled the California crisis to occur. Another important factor that is often unexplained by observers who blame the crisis on California's "flawed market design" is that a strong case could be made that, according to a number of standard metrics, the California market outperformed all of the wholesale markets in the United States during the period April 1998 to April 2000. This paper will provide an explanation for these first two years of market outcomes and discuss the conditions that enabled the events of the summer of 2000 to occur.

I will then describe and analyze several regulatory decisions by the FERC that allowed a manageable problem to develop into an economic disaster during the latter part of 2000. As part of this discussion of the FERC's response to the events of the summer of 2000, I will provide evidence to dispel a number of the misconceptions that circulated beginning in the late summer of 2000 about the causes and consequences of the California electricity crisis. It is important to clarify the factors that led to the summer of 2000 because a number of apparent misconceptions about conditions in California were used to justify the FERC's inactivity during the late summer and autumn of 2000 as well as the ill-conceived remedies it implemented in December of 2000. A number of factors suggest that these remedies directly led to the economic disaster of early 2001, when all three investor-owned utilities in California threatened bankruptcy, with one eventually declaring bankruptcy, and whole-sale electricity prices and natural gas prices rose to unprecedented levels.

I will then discuss the actions taken at the state and federal level that ulti-mately stabilized the California electricity market. This is followed by a dis-cussion of what I believe are the major lessons for electricity market design that should be learned from the California crisis. The paper concludes with recommendations for how the FERC should change the way it carries out its statutory mandate to set just and reasonable wholesale prices and how state PUCs should revise their retail-market policies to prevent a future California crisis. In this discussion, I describe a worst-case scenario for how another Cal-ifornia electricity crisis could occur if these recommendations are not fol-lowed. Unfortunately, only a few states appear to be moving forward with plans to make their retail-market policies consistent with a workably compet-itive wholesale market.

Diagnosing the California Electricity Crisis

For the most part, market participants in California behaved exactly as one would predict, given the federal and state regulatory processes and wholesale-market incentives they faced. The unilateral actions of privately owned suppliers to maximize the profits they earn from selling wholesale power, government-owned entities to minimize the costs of supplying their captive customers, and privately owned retailers to maximize the profits they earn from selling electricity to final consumers in this regulatory environment can explain the market outcomes observed in 1998, 1999, and 2000. In order to understand the complete set of incentives faced by these market participants it is necessary to understand the essential features of the federal and state reg-ulatory processes governing the California electricity market.

Federal Regulatory Oversight of Wholesale Electricity Markets

In 1935, Congress passed the Federal Power Act, which imposed a statu-tory mandate on the Federal Power Commission, the predecessor to the FERC, to set "just and reasonable" wholesale electricity prices. An accepted standard for just and reasonable prices are those that recover production costs, including a "fair" rate of return on the capital invested by the firm. Moreover, if the FERC finds that wholesale electricity prices are unjust and unreason-able, the Federal Power Act gives it the authority to take actions that result in just and reasonable prices.[1] Finally, the Federal Power Act requires that the

FERC order refunds for any payments by consumers for prices in excess of just and reasonable levels.

Without a legal mandate from Congress, approximately ten years ago the FERC embarked on a policy to promote wholesale electricity markets throughout the United States. Under this policy, the price a generation-unit owner receives from selling into a wholesale electricity market is determined by the willingness of all generation-unit owners to supply electricity, rather than by an administrative process that uses the firm's production costs and a rate of return on capital invested.

The just and reasonable price standard for wholesale electricity prices required by the Federal Power Act presented a significant legal and regulatory challenge for the FERC because markets can set prices substantially in excess of the production costs for sustained periods of time. This occurs because one or more firms operating in the market have market power—the ability to raise market prices through their unilateral action and profit from this price increase.

Rationale for Federal Power Act Protection

Spot wholesale electricity markets are particularly susceptible to the exercise of market power because of how electricity is produced, delivered, and sold to final customers. The production of electricity is characterized by binding capacity constraints because a generation unit with a nameplate capacity of 500 megawatts (MW) can produce only slightly more than 500 megawatt-hours (MWh) of energy in a single hour. These capacity constraints limit the magnitude of the short-run supply response of each firm to the attempts of its competitors to raise market prices.

Electricity must be delivered to all customers over a common transmission grid that is often subject to congestion (a form of capacity constraints), particularly along transmission paths to major metropolitan areas and isolated geographic locations. Transmission congestion limits the number of generators able to sell power into the congested region. This reduces the potential supply response to the attempts of firms selling into this smaller market (caused by congestion into the region) to raise local prices through the unilateral exercise of market power.

Finally, the retail-market policies that currently exist in most states, including California, make the hourly demand for electricity virtually insensitive to the value of the hourly wholesale price, particularly in the real-time energy market. Generators collectively recognize that bidding higher prices will not significantly reduce the risk that less electricity will be consumed during that hour. Consequently, the only factor disciplining the bidding behavior of electricity suppliers is the aggressiveness of bids submitted by their competitors, rather than the expectation of any tangible reduction total demand in response to higher prices, as is the case most other markets.

When the demand for electricity is high, the probability of transmission congestion is usually very high. During these system conditions, generation-unit owners can be confident that at least some of their capacity will be needed to serve the price-insensitive aggregate wholesale demand. These firms also recognize that any reduction in the quantity of electricity sold because of high bid prices will be more than compensated for by the significantly higher market prices they will receive for all sales they do make. For this reason, the unilateral exercise of market power by these firms through their bidding behavior leads to higher profits than they could achieve if they did not bid to influence market prices.

The time lag necessary to site and construct new generation capacity can result in substantial periods of significant market power in an electricity market. This feature of the electricity industry makes the potential economic damage associated with the exercise of market power extremely large. In California, even under the most optimistic scenarios, the time from choosing a site for a sizable new generating facility (greater than or equal to 50 MW in capacity) to producing electricity from this facility can range from eighteen to twenty-four months.[2] This estimate does not include the time necessary to obtain the permits needed to site the new facility, which can sometimes double the time necessary to bring the new plant on line. In California, there are several examples of significant permit approval delays for power plants sited close to large population centers, with the Calpine Metcalf facility south of San Jose being perhaps the most well known. Because of this time lag between conception of the new facility and production of energy from that facility, once market conditions arise that allow existing generating facilities to exercise substantial amounts of unilateral market power, as was the case in California during the summer of 2000, these conditions are likely to persist for a long enough period of time to impose substantial economic hardship on consumers. At a minimum, this interval of significant economic hardship is the shortest time period necessary to site, obtain permits for, and construct enough new generation capacity to create the competitive conditions necessary to reduce the ability of existing firms to exercise their unilateral market power.

Federal Power Act Requirements Applied in Wholesale Market Environment

Because of the very large potential harm from the exercise of unilateral market power by firms in a wholesale electricity market, the FERC determined that its statutory mandate under the Federal Power Act implies that unless a firm could prove that it did not possess market power, it was not eligible to receive market-based prices. The supplier could, however, receive prices for any electricity produced that are set through a cost-of-service regulatory process administered by the FERC. The FERC's logic for granting market-based price authority is that if all firms participating in a market possess no market power, the price set by the market will satisfy the just and reasonable standard of the Federal Power Act. This logic is consistent with a standard result from economic theory that states if all firms are unable to exercise any market power, the market price will equal to the marginal cost of the highest-cost unit produced. As noted earlier, the conditions necessary for all firms to possess no market power are unlikely to hold in a wholesale electricity market.

Because the FERC allows any market participant to receive a market price rather than a preexisting cost-based price set through a regulatory process, the FERC requires that each participant demonstrate that it does not have market power or has adequately mitigated any market power it might possess. In other words, each market participant must submit sworn testimony to the FERC demonstrating it does not have the ability to raise market prices and profit from this behavior. Those generators unable to demonstrate that they do not have market power or have not adequately mitigated that market power are not eligible to receive market-based rates but do have the option to sell at cost-of-service prices set by the FERC.

Each of the new generation-unit owners and power marketers made these market-based rate filings before they began selling into the California market and, in many cases, before the California market began operation in April 1998. Each firm had its authority to receive market prices approved by the FERC for a three-year period. Because of the timing of the transfer of assets from the California investor-owned utilities—Pacific Gas and Electric, Southern California Edison, and San Diego Gas and Electric—to the new owners—Duke, Dynegy, Reliant, AES/Williams, and Mirant—some of these entities did not begin selling into California at market-based rates until a later date.

Flaws in the FERC Market-Based Price Regulatory Review

A major source of potential error in determining whether a market participant is eligible to receive market-based prices is the fact that it is extremely difficult to determine on a prospective basis if a firm possesses market power. This is particularly likely to be the case for wholesale electricity for the reasons discussed in the section on the rationale for Federal Power Act protection. A second source of potential errors is that the methodology used by the FERC to make this determination uses analytical techniques for market power assessment based in supplier concentration indices. Market structure indices have long been acknowledged by the economics profession as inadequate for measuring firm-level market power in other product markets. The characteristics of the electricity supply industry makes these indices even less useful for quantifying the extent of market power possessed by an electricity supplier.

The FERC market power analysis was based on concentration indices applied to geographic markets that do not account for the fact that electricity must be delivered to final customers over the existing transmission grid. The analysis does not recognize the crucial role that demand and other system conditions, such as transmission capacity availability, play in determining the amount of unilateral market power that a firm can exercise.[3] Most important, it does not acknowledge the crucial role played by bidding, scheduling, and operating protocols in determining the extent of market power that can be exercised by a firm in a wholesale electricity market. Finally, an important lesson from recent research on wholesale electricity markets is that very small changes in market rules can exert an enormous impact on the ability of a firm to exercise market power, and this methodology does not account for differences in market rules in assessing the amount of market power a supplier possesses. Bushnell (2003) reviews the FERC market power assessment methodology and suggests and implements an alternate approach that addresses many of these shortcomings.

Besides the extreme difficulty in accurately determining on an ex ante basis whether a market participant possesses substantial market power, the FERC's methodology for protecting consumers against the exercise of unilateral market power has an even more troubling property. Once a supplier has received market-based price authority it is free to maximize profits, which is equivalent to exercising all available unilateral market power, because the FERC's market-based price process has determined that the firm has no ability to exercise unilateral market power. This creates the following logical inconsistency for the FERC that it has still not dealt with: it is not illegal for a firm with market-based rate authority to exercise all available unilateral market power, but it is illegal for consumers to pay prices that reflect the exercise of significant unilateral market power because these prices are unjust and unreasonable. Prices that reflect the exercise of significant market power are unjust and unreasonable because they are not cost reflective.

Stated differently, according to the FERC's market-based price policy it is not illegal for a firm to receive a market price that reflects the exercise of significant market power, but it is illegal for a consumer to pay this unjust and unreasonable price. This logical impossibility is the result of an assumption

implicit in the FERC's methodology that market power is a binary variable—
a firm either does or does not have the ability to exercise market power. Unfortunately, as the events in California and all other bid-based electricity markets operating around the world have demonstrated, depending on the system
conditions, almost any size firm can possess substantial unilateral market
power. The issue is not whether a firm possesses substantial unilateral market
power, but under what conditions the firm possesses substantial unilateral
market power and whether these system conditions occur with sufficiently
high probability that the firm will bid and schedule its units to take advantage
of these system conditions to raise market prices and cause substantial harm
to consumers.

As I discuss in the section on lessons learned from the California electricity crisis, protecting consumers from prices that expose them to significant
harm is a more logically consistent strategy for the FERC to pursue in fulfilling its statutory mandate to set just and reasonable prices in a wholesale market regime. This strategy involves first determining what pattern of prices and
for what duration of time causes significant consumer harm and, second, specifying what actions the FERC will take in response to these harmful prices.

Enabling Retail-Market Policies in California

There are two features of the California market that enhanced the ability
of suppliers to exercise unilateral market power. The first is that the CPUC
shielded all final consumers from wholesale price volatility by offering them
the option to purchase all of their demand at a frozen retail price equal to 90
percent of the regulated retail price during 1996. This price reduction was financed by California issuing rate-freeze bonds that would be repaid over the
first few years of the wholesale-market regime. At the start of the California
market, all consumers could shop around for lower prices from competing retailers, but at any time in the future they could switch back to their default
provider and purchase at this frozen retail rate.

The second enabling feature of the California retail market was the requirement that the three large load-serving entities (LSEs), Pacific Gas and
Electric (PG&E), Southern California Edison (SCE), and San Diego Gas and
Electric (SDG&E), purchase all of their wholesale electricity needs from the
California Power Exchange (PX) day-ahead market and the California Independent System (ISO) hour-ahead and real-time markets. This purchasing
requirement was imposed primarily to administer a transparent mechanism
implemented by the CPUC to recover the stranded assets of the three LSEs.

Under the CPUC's stranded asset recovery mechanism, the following equation held on a monthly basis for each investor-owned utility (IOU):

(1)   CTC = P(retail) – P(wholesale) – P(T&D) – Bond Payments,

where P(retail) is the frozen retail rate set by the CPUC, P(T&D) is the regulated price of transmission and distribution services, Bond Payments is the administratively determined amount of bond payments used to fund the reduced fixed retail rate, and P(wholesale) is the average wholesale energy and ancillary services price. CTC is amount of the competitive transition charge, or stranded asset recovery paid to each IOU—PG&E, SCE, and SDG&E— for each MWh of energy consumed in their former service territory, whether or not they sold that electricity to the final consumer.

To implement equation (1) as a stranded asset recovery mechanism, the CPUC needed a transparent wholesale price of electricity to use for P(wholesale). If it used the average wholesale price that each of the three IOUs paid for their power through bilateral transactions, these firms would have an incentive to negotiate deals with their unregulated affiliates to reduce P(wholesale) as a way to increase the amount of CTC recovery they earned, because on a dollar-for-dollar basis, a $1/MWh lower price for P(wholesale) means a $1/MWh higher value for CTC for that month. The CPUC recognized this problem and therefore decided to use the California PX price as its primary reference price for P(wholesale). To insure that it was a deep spot market, the CPUC required all purchases by the LSEs of three IOUs to be through this market.[4]

In spite of this requirement to purchase their entire load through this spot market and the ISO's real-time market, the CPUC *did not* prohibit the three IOUs from entering into forward contracts to hedge this spot price risk. The CPUC just did not guarantee full cost recovery of these forward contract purchases. I also want to emphasize that the CPUC could not prohibit these three firms from hedging this spot price risk in other ways. For example, all of these firms own unregulated affiliates that are not subject to CPUC regulation. These unregulated affiliates could have purchased the necessary forward contracts to hedge the spot risk borne by the regulated affiliate subject to CPUC oversight.

For example, had PG&E Corporation wished to hedge the spot price risk faced by its CPUC-regulated affiliate, it could have used any of its unregulated affiliates to purchase forward financial contracts from suppliers serving the California market. The regulated affiliate could have continued to make purchases from the PX and ISO markets, but difference payments between the sellers of the forward contracts to the PG&E affiliate not subject to CPUC regulation would have hedged PG&E against this spot price risk. For example, assuming PG&E's load is 10,000 MWh, the unregulated affiliate could have purchased forward financial contracts for 10,000 MWh at a fixed price from a number of suppliers. The difference payments associated with this contract would exactly offset any spot price and CTC payment risk the CPUC-regulated affiliate might face because of the requirement to purchase all of its energy from the PX and ISO markets.

It is unclear why the three IOUs did not hedge their spot price risk in this manner or even make full use of the authority given to them by the CPUC to hedge spot price risk though the PX block forwards market. One explanation is that they did not believe that wholesale prices would reach the level for a sustained period of time so that equation (1) produced negative values for CTC on a monthly basis, as it did throughout the summer and fall of 2000. It seems very plausible that the three IOUs believed that if wholesale prices reached this level, the FERC would intervene and declare that wholesale electricity prices were unjust and unreasonable. Evidence for this view is that the average value of the difference between P(retail) and P(T&D) and Bond Payments was roughly between $65/MWh and $70/MWh, depending on the IOU. However, during the first two years of the market, the average value of P(wholesale) in equation (1) was slightly less than $35/MWh, which meant that CTC averaged between $30/MWh to $35/MWh, depending on the IOU.[5]

Average wholesale prices on the order of $70/MWh were difficult to fathom unless one was willing to assume substantial unilateral market power was being exercised, which would cause the FERC to intervene, or extremely high natural gas prices, which did not occur in California until very late 2000. Consequently, as of the start of the market, and even as late as April 2000, it is difficult see how the IOUs could have forecasted average wholesale prices above $70/MWh for an entire month, which could explain their lack of interest in hedging this spot price risk.

Events Leading Up to the California Electricity Crisis

In July of 1998, California's energy and ancillary services markets experienced the first episode of the exercise of significant market power. Perhaps the most dramatic illustration of this activity took place in the ISO's replacement-reserve market. A generator providing replacement reserve is paid a $/MW capacity payment to provide standby generation capacity available with sixty minutes notice. A generation-unit owner providing this service also submits a bid curve to supply energy in the ISO's real-time energy market if the unit's capacity bid wins in the replacement-reserve market. Because a generation-unit owner providing this service has the right to receive the ISO's real-time price for any energy it provides from this reserve capacity, the market price for this product averaged less than $10/MW during the first three months of the California market.

On July 9, 1998, because capacity was withheld from the ancillary services markets—some suppliers did not make capacity available at any price and others bid extremely high prices—the price of replacement reserve hit $2,500/MW. In the subsequent days, the ISO cut its replacement reserve demand in half, but these attempts were largely unsuccessful in limiting the amount of market power exercised in this market. On July 13, 1998 the price of replacement reserve hit $9999.99/MW. A rumor circulating at the time claimed that the only reason the market participant had not bid higher than $9999.99/MW was because of a belief that the ISO's bid software could not handle bids above this magnitude. During this same time period, prices in the California PX day-ahead energy market and ISO real-time energy market reached record-high levels.

As a result of these market outcomes, the ISO management made an emergency filing with the FERC for permission to impose hard price caps on the ISO's energy and ancillary services markets at $250/MW in the ancillary services markets and $250/MWh in the real-time energy market, which the FERC quickly granted. The FERC also directed the Market Surveillance Committee (MSC) of the California ISO to prepare a report on the performance of the ISO's energy and ancillary services markets. The August 19, 1998 (MSC) report (Wolak, Nordhaus, and Shapiro 1998) noted that the ISO's energy and ancillary services markets were not workably competitive. This report identified a number of market design flaws that enhanced the ability of generators to exercise their unilateral market power in the California electricity market. The report contained a number of recommendations for correcting these market design flaws.

In response to the August 1998 MSC report, the FERC issued an order implementing various market rule changes and asked the MSC to prepare a report analyzing the impact these market rule changes had on the performance of the ISO's energy and ancillary services markets. The March 25, 1999 MSC report (Wolak, Nordhaus, and Shapiro 1999) provided an analysis of the market power impacts of the redesign of the ISO's ancillary services markets and its reliability must-run contracts. The major focus of this report was whether the FERC should continue to grant the ISO the authority to impose "damage control" price caps on the ISO's energy and ancillary services markets. The MSC concluded that the California market was still not yet workably competitive and was susceptible to the exercise of unilateral market power because of an overreliance on day-ahead and shorter time-horizon markets for the procurement of energy and ancillary services and the lack of price responsiveness in the hourly wholesale electricity demand. As noted earlier, all customers had the option to purchase at their IOU's frozen retail rate. For these reasons, the MSC strongly advocated that the FERC extend the ISO's authority to impose price caps on the real-time energy and ancillary services markets, which the FERC subsequently did.

On October 18, 1999, the MSC filed a report (Wolak 1999) with the FERC reviewing the performance of the market since the March 25, 1999 report. The focus of this report was a comparison of the performance of the California electricity market during the summer of 1999 versus the summer of 1998. The measure of market performance used in this report was based on a preliminary version of the methodology for measuring market power in wholesale electricity markets described in the study by Borenstein, Bushnell, and Wolak (2002), hereafter BBW.

This measure of performance compares average actual market prices to the average prices that would exist in a market where no generators are able to exercise market power. This analysis controls for the changing costs of production for generation owners due to input fuel price changes, forced outages, and import availability. This standard of a market where no supplier possesses market power was selected because it is consistent with the perfectly competitive market benchmark and the standard the FERC uses to determine whether a market yields just and reasonable prices.

Based on this measure of market performance, as well as other factors, the October 1999 MSC report concluded that the potential to exercise significant market power still existed in California's wholesale energy market, despite the fact that the performance of the California electricity market significantly improved during the summer of 1999 relative to the summer of 1998. The October 1999 MSC report emphasized that a major reason for the superior performance of the market during the summer of 1999 versus the summer 1998 was the much milder weather conditions and corresponding lower peak-load conditions during the summer of 1999 and the greater availability of imports from the Pacific Northwest in 1999 relative to 1998.

This report also noted that the two major retail market design flaws allowing generation-unit owners to exercise market power in the California energy and ancillary services markets—the lack of forward financial contracting by the load-serving entities and the lack of price-responsive wholesale demand—remained unaddressed. The October 1999 MSC report provided several recommendations for redesigning California's retail market policies in order to address these market design problems. This report also noted that if these retail market issues were not addressed as soon as possible, generators would have significant opportunities to exercise market power in the California electricity market during the summer of 2000.

In March of 2000, the MSC was asked by the board of governors of the ISO to provide an assessment of whether the California energy and ancillary services markets were workably competitive and offer an opinion on the appropriate level of the price cap on the ISO's energy and ancillary services markets for the summer of 2000. In its March 9, 2000 opinion, the MSC concluded that these markets were not likely to be workably competitive for the summer of 2000 for the same reasons that it concluded in previous MSC reports that these markets were not workably competitive during the summers of 1998 and 1999 (Wolak, Nordhaus, and Shapiro 2000). This opinion also summarized an update of the market power measures of BBW (2002) through the summer and autumn of 2000.

This opinion also provided a prospective assessment of the impact on average wholesale electricity prices of the exercise of market power for various levels of the price cap on the ISO's real-time energy market during the summer of 2000. Because of a divergence of viewpoints among the members of the MSC about the increased opportunities to exercise market power at a higher price cap during the summer of 2000, the MSC did not offer an opinion on the level of the price cap but instead explained to the ISO board the tradeoffs it should take into account in setting the level of the price cap for the summer of 2000.

In spite of the problems that occurred during the summer of 1998, average market performance over the first two years of the market, April 1998 to April 2000, was close to the average competitive benchmark price. The average difference between the actual electricity prices and those that emerged from the BBW (2002) competitive benchmark pricing algorithm over this two-year period differed by less than $2/MWh. The average electricity price over this two-year period was approximately $33/MWh.

It is also important to emphasize that other wholesale electricity markets operating over this time period also experienced the exercise of significant unilateral market power. Bushnell, Mansur, and Saravia (2002) compare the extent of unilateral market power exercised in the California market to that in the Pennsylvania, New Jersey, and Maryland (PJM) and ISO-New England wholesale markets. The major conclusion from this three-market comparison is that unilateral market power is common to all of these wholesale markets, particularly when the demand for electricity is sufficiently high that a large fraction of the within-control-area generating capacity is needed to meet this demand. Over their sample period, Bushnell, Mansur, and Saravia (2002) find that the amount of market power exercised in California to be quantitatively similar to the amount exercised in the other two ISOs. In fact, over their sample period of the summer of 1999, they found that PJM experienced the greatest amount of unilateral market power.

Although the performance of the California market during its first two years of operation compared favorably to that in eastern ISOs, there were two danger signals not present to as great of an extent in the eastern ISOs as they were in California. The first, and by far most important, was the lack of hedging of spot price risk by California's LSEs. The eastern ISOs had virtually their entire final load covered by forward contracts either because of explicit forward contract purchases or because very little divestiture of vertically integrated firms was ordered as part of forming the eastern ISOs. In contrast, California LSEs purchased all of their supplies through day-ahead or shorter-horizon markets. While it is true that the three IOUs retained ownership of enough generation capacity to serve between 1/3 to 1/2 of the hourly load obligations of their LSEs, this left a substantial amount of their daily energy needs for the short-term markets.

Another important factor is California's significantly greater import dependence than the eastern ISOs. California historically relies on imports to meet between 20 percent and 25 percent of its electricity needs. Moreover, these imports are primarily from hydroelectricity from the Pacific Northwest, and water availability does not respond to electricity prices. A fossil-fuel-based system can usually supply more electricity in response to higher prices because more input fuel sources become economic. In case of hydroelectricity, a supplier can only sell as much energy as there is water behind the turbine, regardless of how high the electricity price gets. This implies that LSEs in California should have hedged an even greater fraction of their expected wholesale energy needs than the eastern ISOs because they were much more dependent on hydroelectric energy.

The California Electricity Crisis

Low hydro conditions during the summer of 2000 throughout the Pacific Northwest and high-demand conditions in the Desert Southwest left significantly less energy available from these regions to import into California. Borenstein, Bushnell, and Wolak (2002) show that the average hourly quantity of imports during the late summer of 1998 was 5,000 MWh; 6,800 MWh in 1999; and 3,600 MWh in 2000. This substantial drop in imports in 2000, relative to 1999, implied that generators located in California faced a significantly smaller import supply response when they attempted to raise prices through the unilateral exercise of market power. Borenstein, Bushnell, and Wolak found that suppliers to California were able to exercise market power at unprecedented levels during the summer of 2000. Using a similar methodology to that employed by BBW and public data sources on generation-unit-level hourly output, Joskow and Kahn (2002) quantified the enormous amount of market power exercised during the summer of 2000. Moreover, they provided firm-level evidence of supply withholding to exercise market power during many hours of the summer of 2000.

Wolak (2003b) provides evidence that the substantially higher prices during the summer of 2000 were the result of the unilateral profit-maximizing actions of suppliers to the California electricity market. Building on the model of expected profit-maximizing bidding behavior in a wholesale market given in Wolak (2000), this paper shows that a firm with the marginal cost curve given in figure 3.1 would formulate its expected profit-maximizing bid curve, $S(p)$, as follows, given that it faces two possible residual-demand realizations—$DR_1(p)$ and $DR_2(p)$. It would compute the profit-maximizing price and quantity pair associated with each realization of the residual-demand curve. If residual-demand realization $DR_1(p)$ occurs, the firm would like to produce at the output level q_1, where the marginal revenue curve associated with $DR_1(p)$ crosses $MC(q)$, the firm A's marginal cost curve. The market price at this level of output by firm A is equal to p_1. The profit-maximizing price and quantity pair associated with residual-demand realization $DR_2(p)$ is equal to (p_2, q_2). If the supplier faced these two possible residual-demand realizations, its expected profit-maximizing bidding strategy would be any function passing through the two profit-maximizing price and quantity pairs (p_1, q_1) and (p_2, q_2). The curve drawn in figure 3.1 is one possible expected profit-maximizing bidding strategy. Extending this procedure to the case of more than two possible states of the world (or residual-demand realizations) is straightforward so long as distribution of the residual-demand curves satisfies the regularity conditions given in Wolak (2000). In this case, the firm's expected profit-maximizing bid curve, $S(p)$, is the function passing through all of the ex post profit-maximizing price and quantity pairs associated with all of the possible residual-demand curve realizations.

This logic has the following implication. Regardless of the residual-demand realization, the following equation holds each hour of the day, h, and for each supplier, j:

Figure 3.1. Derivation of expected profit-maximizing supply curve, $S(p)$, for two residual demand realizations.

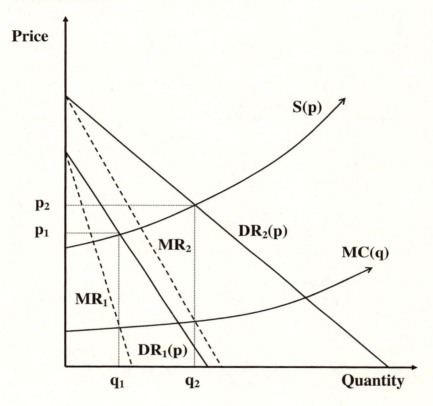

$$(2) \qquad \frac{(P_b - MC_{jb})}{P_b} = -\frac{1}{\varepsilon_{bj}},$$

where P_b is the market price in hour b, MC_{jb} is the marginal cost of the highest cost MWh produced by firm j in hour b, and ε_{bj} is elasticity of the residual demand curve facing firm j during hour b evaluated at P_b. Mathematically, ε_{bj} = $DR_{jb}'(P_b) (P_b)/DR_{jb}[P_b])$. Define $L_{bj} = -1/\varepsilon_{bj}$ as the Lerner index for firm j in hour b derived from this hourly residual demand elasticity. By the logic of figure 3.1, it is expected profit-maximizing for supplier j to submit a bid curve in hour b, $S_{jb}(p)$, such that all points of intersection between it and any possible residual-demand curve firm j might face in that hour occur at prices where the equation (2) holds for that residual-demand curve realization and resulting market-clearing price, P_b. If supplier j is able to find such a bid curve, then it cannot increase its expected profits by changing $S_{jh}(p)$, given the bids submitted by all of its competitors and all possible market-demand realizations Q_b^d during hour h.

By this logic, the value of $L_{hj} = -1/\varepsilon_{hj}$ is a measure of the unilateral market power that firm j possesses in hour h. Using bids submitted by all participants in the California ISO's real-time market, it is possible to compute L_{hj} for each supplier j and for all hours. The calculation differs from the usual approach to computing the Lerner index for a supplier that uses an estimate of the marginal cost of the highest-cost unit operating during the hour for supplier j and the market-clearing price for that hour. Using bids into the ISO's real-time market, I only require the assumption of expected profit-maximizing bidding behavior to recover a supplier's Lerner index from the bids submitted by all other suppliers besides supplier j and the market price. The average hourly value of L_{hj} for each supplier for the period June 1 to September 30 is a measure of the amount of unilateral market power possessed by that firm.

Although the conditions required for equation (2) to hold exactly for all possible residual-demand realizations are not strictly valid for California Independent System Operator (CAISO) real-time market, deviations from equation (2) are unlikely to be economically significant. As discussed in Wolak (2000), the market rules may prohibit the firm from submitting a bid curve that is sufficiently flexible to intersect all possible residual-demand curve realizations at their ex post profit-maximizing price and quantity pairs. Figure 4.1 of Wolak (2003a) gives an example of how market rules might constrain the bid curves a supplier is able to submit for the case of the Australian electricity market. In this market, suppliers are able to submit up to ten quantity bid increments per generating unit each half hour of the day, subject to the constraints that all quantity increments are positive and they sum to less than or equal to the capacity of the generating unit. Associated with each of these quantity increments are prices that must be set once per day. In the ISO's real-time energy market, suppliers are able to submit ten price-quantity pairs each hour for each generation unit, which affords them considerably more flexibility in satisfying equation (2) each hour than suppliers in the Australian market.

Using bid data from the California ISO's real-time electricity market, Wolak (2003b) computes ε_{jh}, the elasticity of the hourly residual-demand curve for hour h facing supplier j evaluated at the hourly market-clearing price for each of the five large in-state suppliers to the California electricity market—AES/Williams, Duke, Dynegy, Mirant, and Reliant—for the period June 1 to September 30 for 1998, 1999, and 2000. Consistent with the market-wide estimates of the extent of unilateral market power exercised presented in BBW (2002), Wolak (2003b) demonstrates that for all of these suppliers the average hourly value of $1/\varepsilon_{jb}$ was substantially higher in 2000 relative to 1998 and 1999. This result implies that the ability of each of these five suppliers to raise market prices by bidding to maximize their profits from selling electricity in the California ISO's real-time market was much greater in 2000 than in the previous two years. The average hourly value of $1/\varepsilon_{jb}$ in 1998 was somewhat higher than the same value in 1999, indicating that the unilateral profit-maximizing actions of these suppliers in 1999 were less able to raise market prices than in 1998. This result is also consistent with the market-wide estimates of the extent of unilateral market power computed in BBW for 1998 versus 1999.

The FERC's Response to the Summer and Autumn of 2000

On November 1, 2000, the FERC issued an order that concluded wholesale electricity prices during the summer and autumn of 2000 were unjust and unreasonable and reflected the exercise of significant market power. This order also proposed remedies for these unjust and unreasonable prices in the California wholesale electricity market. It proposed replacing the $250/MW($h$) hard cap on the ISO's real-time energy and ancillary services market with a soft cap of $150/MW($h$).[6] This soft price cap required all generators to cost-justify bids in excess of $150/MWh. If this quantity of energy or ancillary services was needed by the ISO, then the firm would be paid as bid for its sales. This order also proposed to eliminate the requirement that all California investor-owned utilities buy and sell all of their day-ahead energy requirements through the California PX. In addition to several other market rule changes, this preliminary order required that the ISO implement a penalty on all loads of $100/MWh for any energy in excess of 5 percent of their total consumption that is purchased in the ISO's real-time energy market. The FERC also invited comment on these proposed remedies.

On December 1, 2000, the MSC filed comments on these proposed remedies (Wolak, Nordhaus, and Shapiro 2000). The MSC concluded that "the Proposed Order's remedies are likely to be ineffective to constrain market power and, in fact, could exacerbate California's supply shortfalls and, thereby, increase wholesale energy prices" (Wolak, Nordhaus, and Shapiro 2000, p. 2). The MSC concluded that the proposed remedies would be likely to cause the California PX to declare bankruptcy with little impact on wholesale electricity prices. The MSC and the PX's Market Monitoring Committee, as well as a number of other commenters, observed that the FERC's soft cap would function very much like no price cap because market participants could use affiliate transactions or other means to make the cost (paid by the affiliate that owns the generation unit) of providing energy or ancillary services to California consumers extremely high. The MSC also argued that the order's penalty on load for purchasing excessive amounts of energy in the real-time market would do little to solve the significant reliability problems that the California ISO was facing as a result of the enormous amounts of generation and load that appeared in the ISO's real-time energy market, given the profitability to suppliers of withholding power from the California market until the real-time market under the FERC's proposed remedies.

On December 8, 2000, the ISO management and board unilaterally implemented the FERC soft cap at a $250/MWh level. This meant that from this date going forward, any generator that could cost-justify its bid above $250/MWh would be paid as bid for the electricity they supplied in the ISO's real-time market. In its final order directing remedies for the California electricity market on December 15, 2000, the FERC reiterated its statement that wholesale electricity prices in California were unjust and unreasonable and reflected the exercise of market power. This order adopted its November 1, 2000 proposed remedies with only minor modifications. Effective January 1, 2001, when all of the remedies ordered by the FERC were implemented, the ISO's soft cap was reset at $150/MWh.

On February 6, 2001, the MSC filed with the FERC a further elaboration and clarification of its proposed market power mitigation plan outlined in the December 1, 2000 MSC report (Wolak 2001). This report noted that many of the warnings about the likely impact of the remedies in the FERC's December 15, 2000 order given in the December 1, 2000 MSC report had been borne out by the events of January 2001. The February 6, 2001 MSC report noted that the average real-time wholesale energy price (the quantity weighted-average price of real-time energy purchases) during January 2001 was approximately $290/MWh, despite the existence of a $150/MWh soft cap on the ISO real-time energy market. Moreover, California experienced, for the first time, two days with rolling blackouts due to insufficient generation capacity available to serve the California market.

It is important to emphasize that these rolling blackouts occurred during a month when the daily demand for electricity is near its lowest annual level. For example, the peak demand in January 2001 was approximately 30,000 MW. The peak demand during the summer of 2000 was slightly less than 44,000 MW. This occurred during August of 2000 when the average price of wholesale electricity was slightly less than $180/MWh. Consequently, despite a significantly lower peak demand and significantly less energy consumed daily, real-time prices in January of 2001 (when the FERC's remedies were in place) were more than \$100/MWh more than prices during August of 2000, the month with the highest average price during the summer of 2000. Moreover, the California ISO experienced no stage 3 emergencies and no rolling blackouts during August of 2000, whereas it experienced almost daily stage 3 emergencies and two days with rolling blackouts during January of 2001.

The February 6, 2001 report also described the perverse incentives the FERC soft cap created for generators with natural gas affiliates selling into California. This report outlines logic that illustrates how these firms can use affiliate transactions to raise the announced spot price of natural gas in California and thereby cost-justify higher electricity bids under the FERC soft cap. It also presented evidence that the persistent divergence in natural gas prices in California relative to the rest of the western United States could be attributed to this activity. Finally, this report described a fundamental difference in the incentives faced by a generation-unit owner in wholesale electricity markets versus the former vertically integrated monopoly regime: the enormous potential profit increase to generators selling into an electricity market from declaring forced outages at their facilities. By declaring a forced outage, a generation-unit owner is able to create an artificial scarcity of generation capacity and therefore precommit itself not to provide an aggressive supply response (because some of its capacity is declared out of service) to the attempts of its competitors to raise market prices through their bidding behavior. Under the former vertically integrated monopoly regime, the generation owner has little incentive to declare forced outages because it still retains the obligation to serve final retail demand. A forced outage requires this firm to operate more expensive units or purchase power from other firms to meet its demand obligations.

This report also noted the practical impossibility of verifying whether a declared forced outage truly means that the plant is unable to operate. An analogy is drawn to the labor market, where an employee might call his boss to claim a sick day. It is virtually impossible for the employee's boss to determine whether that employee can in fact work despite his request for a sick day. Similar logic applies to the attempts of the ISO, the FERC, or any other independent entity to verify if a declared forced outage in fact means that the plant is truly unable to operate. By this logic, planned or unplanned outages can be very powerful tools that owners of multiple generation units can use to exercise their unilateral market power.

In assessing the plausibility of "sick days" as a mechanism for creating an artificial scarcity of available generation capacity, it is important to bear in mind the following facts. The California ISO control area has slightly over 44,000 MW of installed capacity. Consequently, for a capacity shortfall sufficient to cause rolling blackouts to occur when peak demand is 30,000 MW, over 14,000 MW of capacity must be either forced or planned out. For stage 3 emergencies to occur, only slightly less capacity must be forced or planned out. All of these calculations assume that no imports are available to sell into the California market. With some imports, these numbers must be even larger. California has over 12,000 MW of available transmission capacity to deliver energy into the California market, with a historical peak transfer of energy into California of more than 10,000 MWh in early 1999, so that unless the amount of energy available to import in California is limited, this use of generation outages to exercise market power is likely to be unprofitable. However, these calculations provide strong evidence for the view that the unprecedented magnitude of forced outages during the late autumn of 2000 and winter of 2001 was due in part to the increased ability of suppliers to exercise unilateral market power in response to less import availability. This ability to exercise market power was enhanced by the remedies implemented by the FERC in its December 15, 2000 order that increased the potential profitability of withholding power until the ISO's real-time market.

The FERC's Response to Further Evidence of Substantial Market Power

Despite the growing volume of evidence from a number of independent sources on the extent of market power exercised in the California electricity market following the imposition of the December 15, 2000 remedies, the FERC took no further action to fulfill its statutory mandate to set just and reasonable prices for wholesale electricity in California for almost four months. The average real-time price over this period was more than $300/MWh, even though these months are typically the lowest demand months of the year.

On April 26, 2001 the FERC issued an order establishing a prospective mitigation and monitoring plan for the California wholesale electricity market that was implemented by the California ISO on May 29, 2001. This plan provided price mitigation only under stage 1, 2, and 3 system emergencies but placed no requirements on the bid prices of generators during other system conditions.[7] Because of the requirement in the FERC order to limit bid prices during periods of system emergencies, the incentives for generators to supply as much capacity as possible were significantly dulled precisely at the time when the capacity was needed most. For many of the same reasons that the soft cap and other market rule changes implemented under the December 15, 2000 FERC order were ineffective at mitigating the significant market power exercised in the California electricity market from January 1, 2001 to June 2001, these market rules did not significantly improve market performance.

In response to increasing pressure from other states in the west as well as California, the FERC imposed a west-wide mitigation plan on June 19, 2001. This plan set a west-wide price cap subject to cost justification, similar to the previous soft cap, which applied to all western U.S. generation units. Moreover, power marketers and importers were required to bid as price takers, which meant they could not set the market-clearing price with their bid and would be paid the market-clearing price for any energy they sold. This west-wide mitigation measure applied to all hours, rather than just system emergency hours. However, the mitigation mechanism only applied to the ISO's real-time market, which by that time was serving less than 5 percent of California's load. In mid-January of 2001, the State of California Department of Water Resources had begun purchasing the net short of the three LSEs, the difference between their total demand for energy and the amount they could supply from their own generation units, through bilateral transactions.

In spite of its laudable goals, the mitigation measure was, for the most part, too late because as I discuss in the section on the regulatory dispute that led to the California crisis, the state of California had already essentially solved the California crisis, albeit at a significant cost to California consumers, by substantial purchases of forward contracts during the winter of 2001 that began to make deliveries in June of 2001.

Fundamental Enabler of Supplier Market Power in California

I will now describe the primary factor that allowed suppliers serving the California market to raise prices vastly in excess of competitive levels during the period May 2000 to June 2001. When California sold off approximately 17,000 MW of fossil-fuel generation capacity owned by PG&E, SCE, and SDG&E to Duke, Dynegy, Reliant, AES, and Mirant, the five new entrants to the California market, it was done without an accompanying provision that the new owners agree to sell back to these three firms a large fraction of the expected annual output from these units at a fixed price in a long-term contract with a duration of at least five years. These mandatory buy-back forward contracts sold along with the generation units are typically called "vesting contracts." A vesting contract on a 500 MW unit might require the new owner to sell an average of 400 MWh each hour back to the load-serving entity that sold the generation asset at a price set by the regulator (before the asset is sold) for a period of at least five years. There are a number of modifications to this basic vesting contract structure, but the crucial feature of these forward contracts is that they obligate the new owner to sell a fixed quantity of energy each year at a fixed price to the LSE affiliate of the former owner.

Vesting contracts have been a standard part of the restructuring process in virtually all countries around the world and in a number of U.S. markets. Green (1999) discusses the role of vesting contracts in the England and Wales electricity market. Wolak (2000) discusses the Australian electricity market's experience with vesting contracts. In the New England market, a number of investor-owned utilities (IOUs) had energy buy-back arrangements with the purchasers of the divested units that resembled vesting contracts. Although vesting contracts are not essential to the success of a restructured electricity market, an active forward market where the vast majority of energy is bought and sold substantially limits the incentive suppliers have to exercise market power in the spot market. In restructured markets where active forward markets did not previously exist, such as in countries where the process started with a state-owned monopoly, vesting contracts are a transition period to an active forward market. In markets where an active forward energy market already exists, there is less need for vesting contracts to stimulate the level of forward market participation necessary for a workably competitive spot market.[8]

Forward contracts set up an extremely powerful incentive for the seller to produce at least the contract quantity from its generation units each hour of the day. The new owner must purchase any energy necessary to meet its forward contract obligations that it does not supply from its own units at the spot market price and sell it at the previously agreed upon contract price. Consequently, the supplier only has an incentive to bid to raise the market price if it is assured that it will produce at least its forward contract obligations from its own units. However, this supplier cannot be assured of producing its forward contract obligation unless its bids for this quantity of energy are low enough to be accepted by the ISO. If each supplier knows that other suppliers have forward contracts and are eager to supply at least their forward contract obligations from their own units, then all suppliers will have strong incentives to bid very close to their marginal cost of production for their forward contract obligation. This aggressive bidding brought about by the desire of suppliers to cover their forward contract positions will set market prices very close to competitive levels in all but the highest-demand periods, when at least one supplier is confident that it will be needed by the ISO to produce more energy than its forward contract quantity, regardless of how high it bids.

In contrast, if suppliers have little or no forward contract obligations, their incentive to bid substantially in excess of the marginal cost of supplying electricity from their units can be much greater. That is because they will earn the market-clearing price on all electricity they produce. Because these suppliers have no forward contract obligations to meet, they are net suppliers of electricity with the first MWh of electricity they produce. To understand this dramatic change in the incentive to raise prices caused by having no forward contract obligations, consider the 500 MW unit described earlier. Suppose this supplier actually produces 450 MWh of energy. In a world with 400 MWh committed in a forward contract, if the supplier manages to raise market prices by $1/MWh, this will increase its revenues by the difference of 450 MWh (the amount of energy it actually produces) and 400 MWh (the amount of its forward contract obligation) times $1/MWh, or $50. In contrast, in a world with no forward contract obligation, if this firm manages to increase the market price by $1/MWh, it earns an additional $450 in revenues because it receives this price for all of its sales. In this simple example, the lack of any forward contract obligation for the supplier resulted in a nine times greater incentive to raise market prices by $1/MWh than would be the case if the firm had a forward contract obligation to supply 400 MWh. Extending this example to the case of a supplier that owns a portfolio of generation units, one can immediately see the tremendous increase in the incentive to bid in excess of marginal cost during certain system conditions caused by the lack of sufficient forward contract commitments. The five new entrants to the California market had very limited forward contract commitments to the three large load-serving entities in California. Besides limited sales in the PX block forwards market to the three LSEs, virtually all of the energy the five merchant generation companies sold to the three LSEs was purchased in the day-ahead PX and real-time ISO markets. Consequently, any increase in these short-term market prices could be earned on virtually all of the energy produced by these suppliers.

This same incentive for suppliers to raise spot prices in the eastern ISO is limited to extreme demand conditions because all of the large load-serving entities in these markets either own sufficient generation capacity to meet most all of their final demand obligations or have forward contracts with other suppliers for a substantial fraction of the expected output from their units. Consequently, the exercise of significant market power only occurs during very high demand conditions in which one or more suppliers is net long relative to their forward contract position. This is consistent with the evidence presented in Bushnell, Mansur, and Saravia (2002) for PJM and New England, two ISOs with substantial forward contract coverage of final demand. Although it is difficult to get precise estimates of the extent that final demand is covered by forward contracts, estimates for the PJM, New York, and New England markets suggest that between 85 and 90 percent of annual demand is covered by forward financial obligations either in the form of generation ownership or forward financial contracts. In California during the period May 2000 to June 2001, this figure was close to 40 percent, which is the approximate average percentage of the total demand of the three large investor-owned utilities that could be met from their own generation units.

The very limited forward contract obligations to the three LSEs by the five new fossil-fuel capacity entrants combined with low import availability during the second half of 2000 created an environment where, as shown in Wolak (2003b), the unilateral profit-maximizing bidding behavior of these suppliers resulted in prices vastly in excess of competitive levels. If California had forward contract coverage for final demand at the same levels relative to annual demand as the eastern ISOs, it is difficult to understand how California suppliers would have found it unilaterally profit maximizing to withhold capacity to create the artificial scarcity that allowed them to raise market prices dramatically starting in the summer of 2000. In addition, even if the five suppliers had been able to raise market prices, California consumers would have only had to pay these extremely high prices for approximately 10 percent of their consumption rather than for close to 60 percent of their consumption.

The lack of forward contract obligations to final load in California created a much faster rate of harm to consumers in California than in other states in the west. These states only used the spot market for approximately 5 percent of their annual electricity needs. The substantially larger spot market share in California meant that the same $/MWh electricity price increase resulted in wholesale energy payments increases in California that were more than ten to twelve times higher than the wholesale energy payments increases in the rest of the western United States.

Regulatory Dispute that Led to California Crisis

The discussion in the sections on the FERC's response to the summer and autumn of 2000 and the FERC's response to further evidence of substantial market power are consistent with the view that the California electricity crisis that occurred in the latter part of 2000 and the first six months of 2001 was primarily the result of the conflict between the FERC and the state of California over the appropriate regulatory response to the extremely high wholesale electricity prices in California during the summer and autumn of 2000. The state of California argued that wholesale electricity prices during the summer and autumn of 2000 were unjust and unreasonable, and it was therefore illegal under the Federal Power Act of 1935 for California consumers to pay these wholesale prices. However, not until it issued a preliminary order on November 1, 2000 did the FERC first formally state that wholesale prices in California were unjust and unreasonable and reflected the exercise of significant market power by suppliers to the California market. Although the FERC reached this conclusion almost four months after California, the ultimate conflict between the FERC and the state of California does not appear to be over whether wholesale prices in California during the summer and autumn of 2000 were illegal under the Federal Power Act. Instead, the ultimate regulatory conflict that led to the California crisis appears to be over the appropriate remedy for these unjust and unreasonable prices.

As should be clear from the events in California from June 2000 to June 2001, the process the FERC uses to determine whether a firm is eligible to receive market-based prices does not guarantee market prices that satisfy the FERC's statutory mandate under the Federal Power Act. First, the dichotomy implicit in the FERC process that a firm either possesses market power or does not possess market power does not reflect the realities of wholesale market operation. Depending on conditions in the transmission network and the operating decisions of all market participants, almost any firm can possess substantial market power in the sense of being able to impact significantly the market price through its unilateral actions. Second, it is extremely difficult, if not impossible, to determine on a prospective basis the frequency that a firm possesses substantial market power given the tremendous uncertainty about system conditions and the incentives they create for the behavior of other firms in the market.

Because the FERC granted market-based price authority to all sellers in the California market using an inadequate methodology without any accompanying regulatory safeguards, given the discussion in the previous section, it is not surprising that a sustained period of the exercise of significant market power and unjust and unreasonable wholesale prices occurred because of the substantially lower import availability in 2000 and the overdependence of California's three large LSEs on the spot market. The FERC's remedies implemented in its December 15, 2000 order are more difficult to understand. Despite filings by a large number of parties arguing that these remedies (also proposed in the November 15, 2000 preliminary order) would be ineffective at best and most likely harmful to the market, the FERC still implemented them without significant modification. As I noted earlier, in its December 1, 2000 comments, the MSC concluded that the proposed order's remedies would most likely be ineffective at constraining the exercise of market power and, in fact, could exacerbate California's supply shortfalls and thereby increase wholesale energy prices. Unfortunately, this is precisely what happened following the implementation of these remedies in January of 2001. The California PX went bankrupt, PG&E declared bankruptcy, SCE came close to declaring bankruptcy, and rolling blackouts of firm load occurred in January, March, and May of 2001.

As noted in the December 1, 2000 MSC report, the FERC's soft price cap policy contained in its December 15, 2000 final order amounted to no price cap on wholesale electricity prices because all suppliers had to do was cost-justify their bids in excess of the $150/MWh soft price cap, something they found increasingly easy to do over time because at the time the FERC only did a very limited review of the prudency of these cost justifications. Rather than remedying the unjust and unreasonable prices of the summer and autumn of 2000 noted earlier, the December 15, 2000 remedies appear to have produced real-time wholesale prices from December 2000 to the end of May 2001 that were substantially higher than average wholesale prices during any preceding or following six-month period, along with the rolling blackouts and bankruptcies and near bankruptcies described previously.

Solution to the California Electricity Crisis

I now address the question of the solution to the California electricity crisis. As described in the preceding, the lack of forward contracts between California suppliers and the three large LSEs created strong incentives for suppliers to withhold energy from the market in order to increase spot prices. By this logic, if enough California suppliers had a substantial amount of their capacity committed in long-term contracts to California LSEs, the incentive California suppliers had to withhold capacity from the market would be substantially reduced and the accompanying very high average spot prices created by this artificial scarcity would be largely eliminated. For this reason, the December 1, 2000 report of the MSC proposed a joint/federal state regulatory mechanism to implement what amounted to ex post vesting contracts between California's LSEs and suppliers to the California market at fixed prices set by the FERC. This regulated forward contract remedy was not adopted by the FERC in its December 15, 2000 final order. Consequently, if the state of California wished to purchase the quantity and mix of forward contracts necessary to commit suppliers to the California market during the summer 2001 and the following two years, it would have to pay prices that reflected the market power that suppliers expected to exist in the spot market in California over the coming two years. Profit-maximizing suppliers would not sell their output in forward contracts that covered this time period at a fixed price that is below the average price that they expected to receive from selling this energy in the spot market over the duration of the contract.

Thus, the only way for California to lower the price it had to pay for a forward contract was to increase the duration of the contract or the fraction of energy purchased in the later years of the contract. By committing to purchase more power from existing suppliers at prices above the level of spot prices likely to exist in California more than two years into the future, California could obtain a lower overall forward contract price. However, this was simply a case of paying for the market power that was likely to exist in the California spot market during the period June 2001 to May 2003 on the installment plan rather than only during this two-year time period.

A simple numerical example illustrates this point. Suppose a supplier expects that it will be able to sell electricity in the spot market at prices that average $300/MWh for the period June 2001 through May 2002, $150/MWh for the period June 2002 through May 2003, and $45/MWh for all years following May 2003. Consider a forward contract that offers 1/20 of its energy in the first year, 1/10 in the second year, and 17/20 in years three to ten. Only if California officials were willing to pay at least $68.25/MWh (= $[0.05 \times 300]$ + $[0.1 \times 150]$ + $[0.85 \times 45]$) for this forward contract would a profit-maximizing generator be willing to offer it.

This example shows that the forward contracts California signed during the winter and spring of 2001 did not allow it to avoid paying for the considerable market power that market participants expected to exist over the coming two years when the contracts were signed during the winter of 2001. One might ask why the forward prices for deliveries in 2003 and beyond during the winter of 2001 were significantly lower than prices for deliveries in the two intervening years. This occurred because suppliers recognized that new generation units could be sited and put into service before the start of the summer of 2003, so the market for electricity deliveries made after that date is very competitive. Even during the winter of 2001, existing firms faced significant competition to supply electricity at time horizons beyond the start of the summer of 2003 from many potential entrants using combined-cycle gas turbine technologies that are almost twice as efficient at converting natural gas into electricity than most existing gas-fired facilities in California.[9]

During the late winter and early spring of 2001, the state of California signed approximately $45 billion in forward contracts with durations averaging approximately ten years. These forward contracts committed a significant amount of electricity to the California market during the summer of 2001 and even more in the summer of 2002 and beyond. While a few of the forward contracts signed during the winter of 2001 began making deliveries in late

March and the beginning of April and May of 2001, a substantial fraction of these contracts began delivering power to California on June 1, 2001. The vast majority of the remaining contracts delivering power during summer of 2001 began July 1, 2001 and August 1, 2001.

The FERC price mitigation plan described in its June 19, 2001 order was implemented June 20, 2001. This plan established a west-wide price cap and required power marketers to bid as price takers in the California market. However, all sellers other than power marketers were still allowed the opportunity to cost-justify and to be paid as bid for their electricity at prices above this west-wide price cap.

To assess the relative impact on spot market outcomes of this price mitigation plan relative to the forward contracts purchased by the state of California, it is important to bear in mind the following facts. First, the FERC price mitigation plan only applied to sales in the California ISO real-time market. During this time period, less than 5 percent of the energy consumed in California was paid the ISO real-time price. The vast majority of sales during the summer of 2001 were made through the long-term forward contracts signed during the winter of 2001 and medium-term commitments to supply power negotiated by the California Department of Water Resources. Second, according to the California ISO's Department of Market Analysis, average prices for incremental energy were slightly below $70/MWh during July of 2001 and less than $50/MWh for the remaining months of 2001. Throughout this entire time period the west-wide price cap was slightly above $91/MWh. Third, according to the July 25, 2001 market analysis report of the ISO's Department of Market Analysis, the extent to which real-time prices exceeded the competitive benchmark price during the period June 1, 2001 to June 19, 2001 was substantially smaller than it was in any previous month during 2001 (Sheffrin 2001). The result is consistent with the logic that the forward contracts beginning delivery on June 1, 2001 provided incentives for more aggressive spot market behavior. Finally, it is important to note that demand during each month of 2001 was approximately 5 percent less than demand during the same month of 2000 in part because of significant conservation efforts by California consumers. All of these facts suggest that the June 19, 2001 price-mitigation plan was not a binding constraint on real-time prices during the vast majority of hours of the second half of 2001.

Monthly average real-time incremental energy prices from January 1, 2002 to September 30, 2002, the end of the price-mitigation period, averaged between $50/MWh and $60/MWh, which provides evidence that this price-mitigation plan was not the binding constraint on prices for the vast majority of hours of the first nine months of 2002 as well. Average prices for near-term (forward market horizons longer than day-ahead) energy during the period July 1, 2001 to September 30, 2002 were significantly lower than average incremental real-time energy prices over this same time period. This result provides evidence that the long-term contracts signed during the winter of 2001 caused suppliers to exhibit more competitive behavior in the near-term energy market during this time period. More recent analyses of market outcomes by the Department of Analysis of the California ISO, which accounts for the impact of the forward contract obligations of the large suppliers, finds additional evidence consistent with the view that these forward contract obligations increased the competitiveness of the near-term and real-time electricity markets during the period July 2001 to September 2002.

Although the preceding evidence suggests that the FERC June 19, 2001 price-mitigation order at most had a very limited impact on the competitiveness of the medium-term and real-time spot markets for electricity in California relative to the impact of forward contracts signed by the state of California during the winter of 2001, it did have substantial impact on the behavior of market participants. Following this imposition of the June 19, 2001 order, the FERC clearly demonstrated a greater willingness to support the actions of the California ISO operators and Department of Market Analysis in their attempts to restore order to the California market. Following the implementation of the June 19, 2001 order, the FERC was much more willing to take tangible actions in support of the ISO's efforts to make suppliers comply with the FERC's must-offer requirement as well as a number of other provisions of the ISO tariff. These actions demonstrated to California market participants that the FERC was now taking a far more active role in regulating the California market. This more active presence by the FERC in California appears to have subsequently benefited system reliability and market performance.

Lessons Learned from the California Electricity Crisis

Several lessons from the California electricity crisis follow directly from the diagnosis of the causes and solution to the California electricity crisis given in the previous sections of this paper. The most important lesson is that any restructuring process should begin with a large fraction of final demand covered by long-term forward contracts. Only a very small fraction of total demand should be purchased from the medium-term and real-time markets, particularly given the way that retail electricity is priced to final consumers throughout the United States. To the extent that the wholesale market in a geographic region is highly dependent on imports and highly dependent on hydroelectric power, the fraction of total demand that should be left to the medium-term and real-time market is even smaller. For this reason, the forward contract coverage of final load at the start of the market in California should have been even greater than what exists in any of the markets in the eastern United States because none of them are as dependent on imports and hydroelectric energy as California.

The second lesson is that state and federal regulators must coordinate their regulatory efforts to protect consumers. Because the FERC appears to have disregarded much of the input from California regulators and policy-makers and other independent monitoring entities intimately acquainted with the performance of the California market during autumn of 2000 in for-mulating its December 15, 2000 order implementing remedies for the Cali-fornia market, this order had many unintended consequences that only made matters worse rather than remedying the extreme market power exercised in the spot electricity market in California. This outcome underscores an im-portant component of this lesson that is particularly relevant for states that have not yet restructured. State regulators cannot protect consumers from market power in the wholesale market without the cooperation of the FERC because it is the only regulatory body charged with setting just and reasonable wholesale electricity prices. To provide the necessary assurance to states that another regulatory crisis between the FERC and state regulators will not oc-cur at some future date, I believe it is necessary for the FERC to implement a formal mechanism that guarantees it will fulfill its statutory mandate to set just and reasonable wholesale prices in the most timely manner possible should market outcomes that reflect significant market power arise in any wholesale electricity market that it regulates. I am extremely skeptical that the national political process will allow further restructuring of the electricity supply industry unless the FERC is able to provide a greater degree of assur-ance to state regulators that it will provide the same or a superior level of pro-tection to consumers relative to what they received in the former vertically in-tegrated utility regime. The tremendous resistance to the FERC's standard market design NOPR expressed by politicians and policymakers in the ma-jority of U.S. states appears to be due in part to the perception that the FERC cannot or will not provide this level of protection to electricity consumers.

An important corollary to the necessity of coordinating federal and state regulatory policies is that a successful wholesale-market design must take into account the existing retail-market design. Federal wholesale-market policies must be coordinated with state-level retail-market policies. The details of state-level retail-market policies can have potentially enormous unintended consequences for wholesale-market performance. For example, designing a wholesale market assuming the existence of active participation by final consumers when virtually all U.S. retail markets do not support such participation will not create a workably competitive wholesale market. Consequently, a national policy for a standard wholesale-market design should at least recognize that certain conditions in the retail market are necessary to support a workably competitive wholesale market. For example, one retail-market precondition for FERC approval of a wholesale-market design would be that all customers above some peak-demand level, say 200 KW, have hourly meters at their facility and face a default wholesale price equal to the hourly spot price of electricity at their location. The FERC may also wish to consider preconditions on the retail infrastructure to support participation by small business and residential customers in the wholesale market, but some preconditions on the retail infrastructure for large, sophisticated electricity customers is essential.

A third lesson from the California crisis is that the FERC cannot set ex ante criteria for a supplier to meet in order for it to be allowed to receive market-based prices without an ex post criteria for assessing whether the subsequent market prices are just and reasonable. As discussed previously, it is impossible to determine with certainty on an ex ante basis whether a supplier owning a portfolio of generation units has the ability to exercise significant market power. Consequently, I see no way for the FERC to avoid devising a transparent methodology for determining what constitutes a just and reasonable price in a wholesale-market regime. Despite over six-years experience with wholesale markets in the United States, the FERC is still unwilling to define what constitutes unjust and unreasonable prices. This FERC policy creates unnecessary regulatory uncertainty and increases the likelihood of another California electricity crisis, where there is a disagreement between the FERC and state regulators over the extent to which wholesale prices are unjust and unreasonable and the appropriate regulatory remedies for these prices. This policy does not serve the interests of electricity suppliers either. A major complaint of electricity suppliers at the present time is that they want to be assured that any price they are paid will not be subject to an ex post refund obligation. Setting an ex post standard for what constitutes a just and reasonable market price along the lines of the twelve-month competitiveness index that is part of the California ISO's Market Design 2002 proposed market power mitigation measures satisfies this goal.[10]

If one is willing to acknowledge that suppliers attempt to exploit all of the unilateral market power that they possess and that conditions in the transmission network and the production and consumption decisions of other market participants determine whether a firm possesses substantial market power, then it follows that a supplier cannot be immunized against the ability to exercise market power on an ex ante basis. By this logic, the issue is no longer whether any supplier possesses market power but whether the unilateral actions of all market participants exercising all available market power results in prices that impose significant harm to consumers. In other words, do wholesale prices reflect the exercise of a substantial amount of market power for a sustained enough period of time to impose sufficient harm to consumers to justify regulatory intervention? This is the fundamental question that the FERC must answer in order to provide a transparent definition of what constitutes unjust and unreasonable prices in a wholesale-market regime. Specifically, the FERC should be required to define the extent of market power exercised, the geographic market over which it is exercised, and the time interval over which it is exercised that results in unjust and unreasonable wholesale prices worthy of regulatory intervention. A transparent definition of unjust and unreasonable prices in a wholesale-market regime that can be applied to any wholesale market considerably simplifies the process of regulating wholesale markets. If this transparent standard (that can be computed by all market participants) for prices is exceeded, then regulatory intervention should automatically occur.

This perspective on just and reasonable wholesale market prices suggests a logical inconsistency in the FERC's current approach to enforcing the just and reasonable price provision of the Federal Power Act. Specifically, in a number of public statements and orders, the FERC has stated that it is important to find the bad actors and punish them for causing unjust and unreasonable prices. While it is important to find market participants that have violated market rules and take back their ill-gotten gains as well as penalize them for any market rule violations or illegal behavior, these statements by the FERC seem to suggest that bad behavior on the part of a market participant is necessary for unjust and unreasonable prices worthy of refunds to occur. However, as emphasized in the preceding discussion, the unilateral actions of all privately owned market participants to serve their fiduciary responsibility to their shareholders and the unilateral actions of all publicly owned market participants to serve the interests of their captive customers can result in market outcomes that reflect the exercise of enormous market power. In short, there is no need for any malicious behavior by any market participant for a wholesale electricity market to produce unjust and unreasonable prices. Moreover, the Federal Power Act does not specify that prices must be the result of malicious behavior by a market participant in order for them to be deemed unjust and unreasonable. The Federal Power Act only requires that if the FERC determines that prices are unjust and unreasonable, regardless of the cause, then it must take actions to set just and reasonable prices, and it must order refunds for any payments in excess of just and reasonable levels.

The Federal Power Act does not say that these refunds must be paid only by firms that violated market rules or engaged in illegal behavior. This is the fundamental logical inconsistency that the FERC faces in attempting to introduce wholesale markets without an explicit statutory mandate to do so. Firms can be required to refund wholesale-market revenues despite the fact that no market participant engaged in any illegal behavior or violated any market rule because their unilateral profit-maximizing actions jointly resulted in unjust and unreasonable market prices. This means that the legal actions of market participants in compliance with the market rules can result in market prices that are illegal and worthy of refunds. I believe the best way for the FERC to deal with this problem is once again to set a transparent standard for what constitutes unjust and unreasonable prices in a wholesale-market regime and set a prespecified regulatory intervention that will occur if this standard is violated along the lines of the California ISO's proposed twelve-month competitiveness index for market power mitigation. This will minimize the potential for future FERC versus state regulatory conflicts that can create another California electricity crisis.

Recommended Changes in the FERC's Regulatory Oversight of Wholesale Market

A final lesson from California crisis is that the FERC must regulate, rather than simply monitor, wholesale electricity markets. As should be clear from the previous sections and the description of the earning warning signs of the exercise of market power in the California market discussed previously, there was no shortage of effective market monitoring in California from the start of the market on April 1, 1998 to the present time. The Department of Market Analysis of the California ISO, the Market Monitoring Committee of the California Power Exchange, the Market Surveillance Committee of the California ISO, as well as a number of state agencies all documented the exercise of market power in California. However, none of these entities had the authority to implement any market rule changes or penalty mechanisms to limit the incentives firms had to exercise market power or violate California ISO market rules. Only the FERC has the authority to implement market rule changes and make regulatory interventions to improve market performance. Rather than focusing its attention on monitoring market performance, the FERC should instead concentrate on designing proactive protocols for rapid regulatory intervention to correct market design flaws as quickly as possible and order refunds as soon as unjust and unreasonable prices are found. What allowed the California crisis to exist was not a shortage of observers with radar guns recording the speed of cars on the highway; it was the lack of traffic cops writing tickets and imposing fines on cars that exceeded the posted speed limit.

On the topic of the necessity of the FERC regulating rather than simply monitoring the wholesale market, I would like to use the FERC's soft price cap policy during the period January 2001 through June 2001 to illustrate this point. As discussed previously, the soft cap policy stated that if a generator could cost-justify a bid in excess of the $150/MWh soft price cap, then it could be paid as bid for its energy if it was needed to meet demand. However, regulation that simply says a firm must justify its costs in order to be reimbursed can yield the same outcome as no regulation at all. The recent revelations that energy traders in California misreported natural gas transactions prices during the crisis period suggests that it would be easy for an electricity supplier to obtain an invoice for its natural gas input fuel purchase at prices in excess of the actual cost to its energy trading affiliate. Consequently, without a rigorous prudency review of how input costs are actually incurred and disallowances for imprudently incurred costs, there is little limit on the prices that firms might be able to cost-justify. In fact, during the period January 1, 2001 to June 30, 2001, electricity suppliers often cost-justified and were paid as-bid prices substantially in excess of $300/MWh under the FERC soft cap policy. For this reason, anytime the FERC caps the bids that a firm might submit based on its costs of production, it must perform a prudency review of these costs and be prepared to disallow any cost that cannot be adequately justified.

A final point related to the importance of the FERC regulating rather than simply monitoring is the necessity of very accurate data on the physical characteristics of plants, input fuel prices, other input prices, and many other aspects of the operation of the wholesale market to carry out this task. For example, in order to perform a satisfactory review of the prudency of costs a firm would like to recover, the FERC must have the best available data on these variables. Moreover, in order to compute the best possible estimate of what constitutes a just and reasonable wholesale market price, the FERC will need, at a minimum, the best available information on the operating characteristics of generation units, input fuel prices, and the physical state of the transmission network. Finally, in order to provide tangible evidence on how well it is doing in delivering economic benefits (in the form of lower prices) to consumers that they would not have received in the former vertically integrated utility regime, the FERC will need to be able to determine what prices would have been under the former vertically integrated utility regime. This will require the same information. Consequently, particularly during the initial transition to a wholesale-market regime, the FERC should substantially increase, and certainly not reduce, the amount of data that it collects from market participants if it would like to be an effective and credible regulator.

***

REFERENCES

Borenstein, Severin, James Bushnell, and Frank A. Wolak. 2002. Measuring market inefficiencies in California's restructured wholesale electricity market. *American Economic Review* 92 (5): 1376–1405.

Bushnell, James. 2003. Looking for trouble: Competition policy in the U.S. electricity industry. Center for the Study of Energy Markets (CSEM) Working Paper no. 109. http://www.ucei.berkeley.edu/PDF/csemwp109.pdf.

Bushnell, James, Erin Mansur, and Celeste Saravia. 2002. An empirical assessment of the competitiveness of the New England electricity market. University of California Center for the Study of Energy Markets (CSEM) Working Paper, May.

Green, Richard. 1999. The electricity contract market in England and Wales. *The Journal of Industrial Economics* 47 (1): 107–24.

Joskow, Paul, and Ed Kahn. 2002. A quantitative analysis of pricing behavior in California's wholesale electricity market during summer 2000: The final word. *The Energy Journal* 28 (4): 1–35.

Schmalensee, Richard, and Benett Golub. 1994. Estimating effective concentration in deregulated wholesale electricity markets. *RAND Journal of Economics* 15 (1): 12–26.

Sheffrin, Anjali. 2001. Market analysis report. http://www.caiso.com/docs/2001/07/26/200107260820387855.pdf.

Wolak, Frank A. 1999. Report on the redesign of the California real-time energy and ancillary services markets. http://www.stanford.edu/~wolak.

———. 2000. An empirical analysis of the impact of hedge contracts on bidding behavior in a competitive electricity market. *International Economic Journal* 14 (2): 1–40.

———. 2001. Proposed market monitoring and mitigation plan for California electricity market. http://www.stanford.edu/~wolak.

———. 2003a. Identification and estimation of cost functions using observed bid data: An application to electricity markets. In *Advances in economics and econometrics: Theory and applications*, Vol. II, ed. M. Dewatripont, L. P. Hansen, and S. J. Turnovsky, 133–69. New York: Cambridge University Press.

———. 2003b. Measuring unilateral market power in wholesale electricity markets: The California market 1998 to 2000. *American Economic Review* 93 (2): 425–30.

Wolak, Frank A., Robert Nordhaus, and Carl Shapiro. 1998. Preliminary report on the operation of the ancillary services markets of the California Independent System Operator (ISO). http://www.stanford.edu/~wolak.

———. 1999. Report on the redesign of the markets for ancillary services and real-time energy. http://www.stanford.edu/~wolak.

———. 2000. Analysis of order proposing remedies for California wholesale electric markets (issued November 1, 2000). Market Surveillance Committee of the California Independent System Operator. http://www.caiso.com/docs/2000/12/01/2000120116120227219.pdf.

Wolak, Frank A., Brad Barber, James Bushnell, and Benjamin F. Hobbs. 2002. Comments of the Market Surveillance Committee of the California ISO on the proposed October 1, 2002 market power mitigation measures. http://www.caiso.com/msc.

NOTES

Frank A. Wolak is a professor at Stanford University in the Department of Economics and chairman of the Market Surveillance Committee of the California Independent System Operator.

I would like to thank Paul Joskow and Al Klevorick for helpful comments on a previous draft.

1. To illustrate the wide-ranging authority the Federal Power Act gives to the FERC to set just and reasonable prices, I quote the following text from section 206(a) of the Federal Power Act:

> Whenever the Commission, after a hearing had up its own motion or upon complaint, shall find that any rate, charge, or classification, demand, observed, charged or collected by any public utility for transmission or sale subject to the jurisdiction of the Commission, or that any rule, regulation, practice, or contract affected such rate, charge, or classification is unjust, unreasonable, unduly discriminatory or preferential, the Commission shall determine the just and reasonable rate, charge, classification rule, rule, regulation, practice or contract to be thereafter observed and in force, and shall fix the same by order.

2. The California Energy Commission processes all applications for licensing of thermal power plants that are 50 MW or larger. Plants smaller than 50 MW are licensed by city and county agencies and, as a result, may face a shorter time from conception to operation.

3. Schmalensee and Golub (1994) first noted the crucial role played by transmission constraints in market power assessment in wholesale electricity markets.

4. Wolak (1999) discusses the stranded asset recovery mechanism in detail and its impact on retail competition in the California market.

5. Another explanation is that the three IOUs felt that if wholesale prices rose above $65/MWh to $70/MWh, the CPUC would be forced to raise retail rates above this level under the "filed rate doctrine," which roughly states that any wholesale price that has been filed with and approved by the FERC must be passed through in retail electricity prices.

6. Specifically, the soft price cap for energy was $150/MWh, and the soft price cap for each ancillary service was $150/MW.

7. Stages 1, 2, and 3 are various levels of system-reserve deficiencies, with a stage 3 emergency being when the ISO forecasts less than 1.5 percent available reserves on the system or less than the largest contingency within the service area.

8. In this regard, the difference between the origins of California ISO and the Eastern ISOs is informative. The Eastern ISOs were formed from tight power pools where presumably active forward markets had ample time to develop during the power pool regime. In contrast, the California ISO was formed by combining the control areas of three vertically integrated IOUs that primarily used their own units to serve load.

9. Subsequent events in the California market bear out this logic. More than 3,000 MW of incremental capacity (net of unit retirements) has been put into service in the California ISO control area between the winter of 2001 and the summer of 2003.

10. In the April 19, 2002 MSC comments on the ISO's proposed market power mitigation measures, Wolak, Barber, Bushnell, and Hobbs (2002) discuss this twelve-month competitiveness index and how it should be used as a mechanism for determining consumer harm worthy of regulatory intervention.

4

Lessons Learned: The Texas Experience

Ross Baldick and Hui Niu

Introduction

Electricity market reform has taken place over the last fifteen years in various countries. There are more than a dozen existing restructured electricity markets in the United States and around the world.[1] The markets vary in terms of the market organization, system operation, transmission charges, congestion management, and investment incentives. These differences are often related to the history of the particular system, asset ownership, operational practices, and philosophical perspectives. Some markets have a day-ahead market for spot trading while some others have just a day-ahead scheduling process together with a short-term market to facilitate real-time operations.

Because of various difficulties and problems experienced, each market has changed in some aspects. Some markets have undertaken big changes, such as in the California market and the England and Wales market. The California market ended its zonal Power Exchange and is implementing "MD02," which is similar to the Federal Energy Regulatory Commission's (FERC) standard market design (SMD). The England and Wales market changed from a centrally dispatched bid-based power pool to the New Electricity Trading Arrangements (NETA) based on bilateral trading in a forward market and a balancing market. Other markets, including that of the Electric Reliability Council of Texas (ERCOT), have changed more incrementally.

This paper presents a review of the electricity market in the ERCOT system and draws lessons from the experiences. The main focus is on the ERCOT market design and its development after July 31, 2001 until approximately April 2003. The conclusions should be tempered with the understanding that the restructured ERCOT market has been in place for only about two years, so some conclusions can only be tentative at best.

This paper is based on a variety of reports, filed comments of stakeholders, and the records of workshops related to wholesale market design at the Public Utility Commission of Texas (PUCT) from 2001 to 2003. The information resources are the commission's *Reports on the Scope of Competition in Electric Markets* to the 77th Legislature (PUCT 2001a) and to the 78th Legislature (PUCT 2003b), the white paper (PUCT 2002h), the report (PUCT 2003d), and the presentations in workshops of the ERCOT wholesale market design project (PUCT 2002k), the ERCOT protocols (PUCT 2000), the comments of stakeholders in response to the commission's questions about day-ahead markets (PUCT 2002c), congestion management issues (PUCT 2003a), and lessons learned (PUCT 2002g).

The organization of the paper is as follows. The second section is an overview of ERCOT, beginning with a brief history of legislation, market milestones, and statistics and then continuing with an overview of the market design. The third section describes and assesses in detail the components and characteristics of the ERCOT market. Comparisons to other markets are made and the changes to the market structure will be discussed. Where appropriate, lessons will be drawn from the Texas experience. The fourth section summarizes the lessons and concludes. An appendix lists the acronyms introduced in the paper.

The Electric Reliability Council of Texas

The Electric Reliability Council of Texas (ERCOT) is the corporation that administers the part of Texas's power grid that is not "synchronous" (Bergen and Vittal 2000) with the Eastern or the Western Interconnection. Although some Texas statewide statistics will be presented in some of the figures and tables, the parts of Texas that are served by the Eastern Interconnection will not be discussed in detail. That is, this paper will mainly discuss the ERCOT system, which covers approximately 200,000 square miles and has its peak demand in summer, driven by air-conditioning loads.

In the section on history and statistics, we briefly review the history and development of ERCOT and the ERCOT electricity market, presenting various statistics, and then in the next section, we describe the principal characteristics of ERCOT market design.

History and Statistics

Officially founded in 1970, ERCOT is one of ten regional reliability councils in North America operating under the reliability and safety standards set by the North American Electric Reliability Council (NERC). Figure 4.1 shows the regions of the ten reliability councils of NERC and shows that the ERCOT system covers most of the geographical area of Texas. As a NERC member, ERCOT's primary responsibility is to facilitate reliable power grid operations in the ERCOT system by working with the region's electric utility industry organizations. An independent board of directors comprised of electric utility market participants governs ERCOT.

Because ERCOT is entirely within the state boundaries of Texas, the production and sale of electricity in ERCOT is not subject to regulation by the FERC but instead falls exclusively under the jurisdiction of PUCT, with laws established by the Texas legislature. The jurisdictional arrangement for ERCOT is unlike the case in the other lower forty-seven states where jurisdiction is split between the FERC and state public utility commissions. As discussed by Wolak (chap. 3 in this volume) the jurisdictional split between the FERC and the California Public Utility Commission appears to have contributed to the electricity crisis in California. The presence of a single regulatory authority over ERCOT avoids such regulatory disputes in the ERCOT system.

In 1995, the Texas legislature amended the Public Utility Regulatory Act (PURA) to restructure the wholesale generation market. In 1996, ERCOT was authorized by the PUCT to operate as a not-for-profit independent system operator (ISO) to facilitate the efficient use of the electric transmission system by all market participants. In its initial operation, the ERCOT ISO did not fulfill all the functions specified in FERC Order 888 (FERC 1996). In particular, the ERCOT ISO was not the "control area operator" for ERCOT.

On May 21, 1999, the Texas legislature passed Senate Bill 7 (SB7; PUCT 1999). Under SB7, the ERCOT ISO was given the responsibility to develop the market structure, infrastructure, and business processes to facilitate retail competition in Texas. During 1999 and 2000, the ERCOT ISO and market participants developed "protocols," which are rules and standards that the

Figure 4.1. Regional reliability councils of NERC

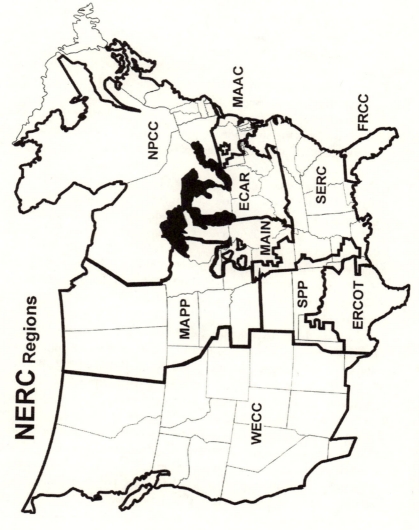

NERC Regions

NPCC
MAAC
FRCC
ECAR
SERC
MAIN
MAPP
SPP
ERCOT
WECC

Source: NERC (www.nerc.com).

ERCOT ISO uses to implement its market functions. The PUCT approved the market rules of the Texas wholesale electricity market (ERCOT protocols) on June 4, 2001, and the ERCOT market began to operate as a single "control area" under the ERCOT ISO on July 31, 2001.

The PUCT began implementing SB7 shortly after former Governor Bush signed the bill into law. Several rulemaking projects were opened by the PUCT to define the retail market in Texas, including rules relating to the code of conduct, electric reliability standards, a renewable energy credit-trading program, and wholesale market rules. As of December 2002, forty-one rulemaking projects related to SB7 have been completed to implement the act, and twelve more were opened in 2003.

The ERCOT ISO serves approximately 85 percent of the state's electric load and oversees the operation of approximately 77,000 megawatts of generation and over 37,000 miles of transmission lines. During the eight years between the introduction of wholesale competition to ERCOT in 1995 and early 2003, generation capacity in ERCOT has increased by 30 percent, while the peak demand increased about 20 percent. That is, there is currently a large amount of generation capacity relative to demand in ERCOT. About 18,000 MW of mostly independent generation capacity was added in ERCOT over this period, increasing the installed capacity from 59,000 MW to 77,000 MW, while peak demand increased from 46,668 MW to 55,703 MW. (The highest ERCOT peak demand was recorded at 57,600 MW in August 2000.) Much of the resource growth has occurred in the last couple of years and was built primarily by nonutilities.

Based on the NERC report "Summer Assessment of Reliability of Bulk Electricity Supply in North America" (NERC 2003), the summer available resources, projected peak demand, and actual peak demands (ERCOT 2002b) in ERCOT from 1996 to 2002 are summarized in figure 4.2. *Available resources* in figure 4.2 are defined to be the existing generation capacity plus new units scheduled for service by the given summer peak month and year, plus the difference between firm capacity purchases and sales, less existing capacity that is unavailable due to planned outages. Projected peak demand is the projected peak-hour demand for the given summer peak month and given year, including standby demand, less the sum of direct control load management (monthly coincident) and interruptible demands.

During the same period, transmission facilities were actively planned and built in the ERCOT region to ensure that the transmission grid could transfer the increased power supply. Over 900 miles of transmission facilities of various voltages were built between 1996 and 2003, an increase of approxi-

Figure 4.2. Available resources and peak demand of ERCOT (1996–2002)

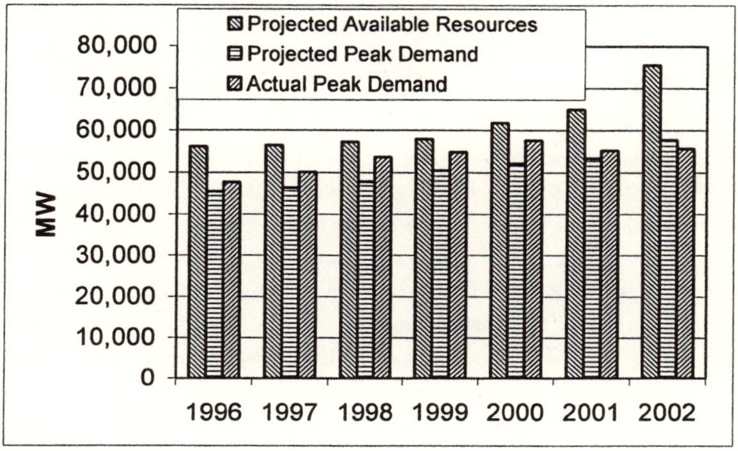

Source: NERC (2003).

mately 2.5 percent. While this lags the rate of generation and demand growth in ERCOT, in many other regions of North America transmission growth has been smaller still.

Nevertheless, even with the large increases in generation capacity and some increase in transmission capacity, ERCOT stakeholders have been facing various problems and addressing market design issues on an ad hoc basis since the ERCOT protocols were implemented on July 31, 2001. This has led stakeholders to think about systematic approaches to fix problems and about the future direction for the wholesale market design. Whether ERCOT should move toward the FERC's SMD is becoming a key policy issue. In the next section, we present an overview of the ERCOT market design.

Overview of ERCOT Market Design

Four years elapsed from the opening of the wholesale market in ERCOT to competition until Senate Bill 7 (SB7) was enacted in 1999. SB7 changed the wholesale market and introduced competition to the retail sale of electricity in Texas. Each investor-owned electric utility (IOU) was required to be unbundled into three distinct kinds of companies: a power generation company (PGC), a transmission and distribution service provider (TDSP), and a retail electric provider (REP). These entities could remain affiliated.[2] The PGCs operate as wholesale providers of generation services. The REPs operate as retail providers of electricity and services and as contacts with the retail customers in the new market. We will first describe PGCs and REPs and then return to TDSPs. Then we will discuss retail customers, municipal utilities and Co-Ops, and then discuss how these entities interact in the market.

In ERCOT, PGCs could and have remained affiliated with REPs, which has produced implicit vesting contracts between generators and retailers. Vesting contracts or other long-term contracts have been put in place in most restructured markets. In contrast, there were no such contracts between generators and retailers in California, as explained in Wolak (chap. 3 in this volume). The generation in California was divested to unaffiliated companies (Bushnell, tables 6.1 and 6.2, this volume) and there were only limited long-term contractual links between generators and retailers. As discussed in Wolak (chap. 3 in this volume), the lack of long-term contracts or other vesting arrangements created incentives for generator owners in California to profit from withholding from the market to increase wholesale prices. This differs from the incentives faced by PGCs in ERCOT that have affiliated REPs and is a key difference between ERCOT and the California market.

The TDSPs remain regulated by the PUCT, and are required to provide nondiscriminatory access to the transmission and distribution grid. The PUCT sets the rates for transmission and distribution service. Although transmission and distribution facilities remain regulated by the PUCT, the prices for the production, transmission congestion, and sale of electricity to both wholesale and retail customers are predominantly dictated by the market, except that customers with a peak demand of one megawatt (MW) or less can continue to purchase at the regulated "price-to-beat" rate until 2007, to be discussed in detail in the section on retail competition.

Customers have various options in the market after the introduction of retail electric competition in ERCOT. Prior to it, all retail customers were served by IOUs, electric cooperatives (Co-Ops), or municipally owned utilities (MOUs). Very few customers had a choice of companies to supply their power. Senate Bill 7 established a framework to allow retail electric customers of IOUs to select their provider of electricity beginning January 1, 2002.

Municipally owned utilities and co-ops were granted the authority to decide whether and when to open their service areas to retail competition under the so-called opt-in or non-opt-in provision. They are allowed to continue bundled operations regardless of their choice to open their service areas to retail competition. Evidently, the Texas legislature did not believe that it could or should impose the same requirements on MOUs and Co-Ops as it did on IOUs. As in most other state jurisdictions, restructuring in ERCOT left various entities grandfathered to operate under preexisting arrangements.

ERCOT uses the term *resources* to describe the entities able to meet system demand. A resource can be a PGC, a qualifying facility (QF), a MOU or a Co-Op, or a load-serving entity (LSE) representing a load acting as a resource. A PGC is the entity registered by the PUCT that generates electricity to sell at wholesale. A PGC does not own transmission or distribution facilities and does not have a PUCT-certified service area. Qualifying facilities (QFs) are a category of cogeneration or small power-generating facility that meets ownership, operating, and efficiency criteria established by the FERC. An independent power producer (IPP) is a nonutility power generator that is not a regulated utility, government agency, or QF.

Load-serving entities (LSEs) is the term used in ERCOT for entities that provide electric service to customers. They include REPs, competitive retailers (CRs), and non-opt-in Entities (NOIEs). A CR could be a REP, a MOU, or a Co-Op that offers customer choice in the restructured competitive electric power market. The LSEs forecast their customer load and negotiate privately with other market participants, such as resources or power marketers, to buy energy to provide for their customer load.

The plethora of categories of generation resources and of LSEs reflects the coexistence of grandfathered entities with restructured IOUs and with new entities such as CRs. We will refer to generation resources and LSEs generically, omitting some of the detailed differences between types of generation resources and types of LSEs.

The matching of generation from a generation resource to load for an LSE constitutes a "schedule." Market participants are required to submit their schedules of energy to the ERCOT ISO through qualified-scheduling entities (QSEs), which are qualified by the ERCOT ISO in accordance with the protocol to submit balanced schedules and ancillary services (AS) bids and settle payments with the ERCOT ISO for the entities in their portfolio.

For every fifteen-minute interval, the ERCOT ISO compares the sum of the schedules submitted by QSEs to its own load forecasts and determines balancing energy and AS requirements. If the submitted schedules result in congestion of the transmission system, then the ERCOT ISO will redispatch system resources to resolve the congestion. As will be discussed in the section on congestion management, the method of allocating costs of redispatching to the market participants has been changed since February 2002.

In contrast to ISOs in other restructured markets in the United States, the

Figure 4.3. Overview of ERCOT market participants

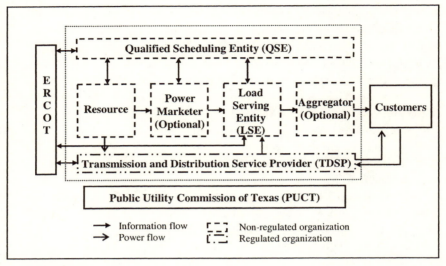

Source: ERCOT (2001).

ERCOT ISO also serves as the registration agent for all retail transactions, including switching requests, move-in and move-out requests, and monthly electricity usage data. The TDSPs are responsible for load and resource meter installation as well as submitting meter data for all loads and resource meters that are not directly polled by ERCOT.

Figure 4.3 shows the relationship between major market participants in the ERCOT market. In addition to the entities already described, figure 4.3 also shows "power marketers" and "aggregators." A power marketer is an entity that becomes an owner or controller of electric energy for the purpose of buying and selling electric energy at wholesale. A power marketer does not own generation, transmission, or distribution facilities in Texas and does not have a certified service area but has been granted the authority by the FERC to sell electric energy at market-based rates or has registered with the PUCT as a power marketer. Aggregators join two or more customers into a single purchasing unit to negotiate the purchase of electricity from retail electric providers. As of early 2003, there are 46 QSEs, 52 CRs, 153 aggregators, 16 REPs, 17 power marketers, 37 Co-Ops, 16 MOUs, 8 IOUs, and 5 IPPs (PUCT 2003e; ERCOT 2003c). In the next section we will describe the interaction between these entities in more detail.

Market Components and Characteristics

In the following sections, we describe the components and characteristics of the ERCOT market design from the following perspectives: bilateral energy market, balancing energy market, congestion management, AS market, operational issues, capacity adequacy, generator interconnection policy, transmission planning, market power mitigation, retail competition, and load response. We will then summarize the revisions to the ERCOT market and compare it to other markets.

Bilateral Energy Market

In this section, we first introduce and describe the bilateral energy market then describe a change to the market and the implications for price discovery and liquidity.

Introduction

One fundamental issue of electricity market design is whether the market incorporates a central bid-based pool where resources are dispatched by the ISO based on bid prices and quantities. Electricity markets that have a day-ahead centrally dispatched energy market include the (now defunct) California Power Exchange (PX), the California MD02, the England and Wales market prior to March 2001, and the markets in the northeastern United States. In these markets, bilateral transactions between generation and demand are essentially "financial" in nature in that the actual dispatch is decided by the pool rather than specified by the bilateral contracts. The role of bilateral contracts in these markets is to financially hedge against pool price variation.

Unlike the pool markets, the ERCOT wholesale market only has a day-ahead portfolio energy schedule process. The ERCOT portfolio schedule process is broadly similar to the California market absent the PX and to the England and Wales NETA that has been in place since March 2001. Under the ERCOT scheduling process, each QSE submits schedules for their bilateral transactions with total generation and demand, specified at zonal level, and bid curves for zonal balancing up and balancing down energy. The schedules for generation and demand are required to be "balanced" in that supply equals demand for each QSE individually. The balancing energy market, which compensates for deviations between scheduled and actual generation and between scheduled and actual demand, will be discussed in the section titled "Balancing Energy Market," which is followed by the section on congestion management.

Bilateral transactions represent the bulk of delivered energy in the ERCOT system, and much of the bilateral transactions are between affiliates. These schedules account for about 95 percent to 97 percent of the end-user electric energy requirements in ERCOT, which is close to 300 million MWh on an annual basis. In contrast to the financial bilateral transactions in pool markets, the bilateral transactions in ERCOT have a "physical" flavor in that, in principle, a bilateral transaction that is scheduled by a QSE is expected to occur.

An important philosophical question in the design of electricity markets is whether day-ahead central dispatch is necessary. The ERCOT market shows that a centrally dispatched day-ahead market may not be necessary, at least given the circumstances in ERCOT where there is a large amount of generation capacity (see the section on operational issues) and where most of the bilateral transactions are between affiliates. Scheduling by affiliated PGCs and REPs can be interpreted as implicit vesting contracts, which act to decrease the effect of significant market concentration in ERCOT. These circumstances contrast with the initial California market, for example, where there was central day-ahead dispatch by the PX for most generation. But, for reasons set out in Wolak (chap. 3 in this volume), there were few long-term contracts in California and, moreover, affiliations between generation and distribution companies had been removed.

Relaxed Balanced Scheduling

The stakeholders included the balanced schedule requirement in the original protocols to be consistent with a "min-ISO" philosophy as a way of minimizing balancing energy volumes. It creates less credit and financial risk for the ERCOT ISO. However, some market participants have been concerned that the requirement for balanced schedules makes market participants unable to buy and sell energy actively. Industrial loads may want the ability to go short by contracting for less power than they need and then purchase the remainder from a spot market or curtail their demand.

In November 2002, the ERCOT ISO implemented "relaxed balanced scheduling" on a trial basis. Until that revision, the protocol required that each QSE submit a balanced day-ahead energy schedule based on the QSE's load forecast for the following day. Under the relaxed balanced schedule, QSEs can schedule any amount of their demand and are not expected to schedule demand equal to their forecast. The expectation is that a larger fraction of energy would be transacted in the balancing market, increasing the liquidity in this market.

After several bankruptcies due to exposure to high balancing market prices, relaxed balanced scheduling was modified in April 2003 to limit the allowable deviation between the schedules and forecast.

Price Discovery and Liquidity

Two main concerns about the ERCOT bilateral market are price discovery and liquidity. As buyers and sellers generally negotiate in private and do not have to disclose the price and terms of contracts to others, it may be difficult for buyers and sellers to know the prevailing market price. The lack of price transparency makes it difficult to value the offers for services appropriately.

Liquidity is related to the volume of trades in a market. Lack of liquidity makes it difficult for a party to sell the excess or buy the deficiency in the market. The volume of wholesale trading between nonaffiliates has been a small fraction of the total energy in the ERCOT market, and some stakeholders have expressed concerns about the lack of liquidity (PUCT 2002e). A day-ahead energy market with a third-party intermediary is supported by some market participants in part to improve liquidity (PUCT 2002b). According to the 2003 reports to legislature by the PUCT, several parties have expressed concerns that REPs and their affiliated PGCs in ERCOT have largely contracted with each other in bilateral contracts, thereby limiting the ability of new generation plants to compete to serve retail customers. This problem should decrease over time as customers switch to alternate suppliers, placing increased pressures on the affiliated REPs to procure the least expensive power available. (See the section on retail competition.) On the other hand, a weakened connection between PGCs and REPs will increase incentives for PGCs to withhold to increase wholesale prices. (See the section on market power.)

The PUCT is currently exploring these issues in several pending rule-making proceedings and projects (PUCT 2002f,i,j). The elements of the FERC's SMD, which could add transparency and liquidity to the ERCOT markets, are also under consideration. Some stakeholders believe that the ultimate solution to the problem is to implement a spot market similar to SMD.

Balancing Energy Market

The ERCOT market design reflects the philosophy of minimizing the involvement of the ISO (min-ISO) in the electricity market, where the ISO just operates a residual market or a "net pool" (Hogan 1995). The ERCOT ISO is only involved in the transaction of the imbalances of the bilateral generation and load schedules and in clearing congestion and other actions to keep system reliability. About 2 percent to 5 percent of the total energy is transacted through the balancing energy market operated by the ERCOT ISO.

According to the ERCOT market guide (ERCOT 2001), the market operations process contains three major periods: day-ahead AS market, adjustment period, and operating period. The day-ahead AS market occurs from 6:00 a.m. to 6:00 p.m. on the day prior to the operating day. The QSEs submit portfolio schedules and AS bids. As will be discussed in the section on the AS market, the ERCOT ISO assesses the needs for and procures AS for the following operation day.

The adjustment period happens between the close of the day-ahead AS market and one hour prior to the operating hour (the current clock hour). The QSEs may adjust their energy and AS schedules and update their resource plans during this period. The QSEs may also submit, remove, or adjust their balancing energy and replacement reserve bids during the adjustment period. Based on the analysis of schedule changes, resource plans, load forecasts, and other system conditions, the ERCOT ISO may procure additional AS during the adjustment period by announcing the need to procure additional services and opening subsequent markets. By the end of the adjustment period, ERCOT ISO receives final bids for balancing up and down energy services.

The operating period includes the operating hour and the hour prior to the operating hour. Based on the submitted portfolio schedules, forecasted load, and bid prices, the ERCOT ISO clears the balancing market to keep system balance and so that flows on the interzonal commercially significant constraints (CSCs) are within their transmission capacities. The ERCOT ISO also conducts the security-constrained reliability analysis by distributing the generation portfolio dispatch and forecasting demand at the nodal level. If necessary, the ERCOT ISO requests unit-specific energy bids, as well as out-of-merit energy, reliability-must-run units, or nonspinning reserve energy. Ten minutes prior to the settlement interval (which is itself of duration fifteen minutes), the ERCOT ISO clears the balancing energy market, and instructs those QSEs whose bids were selected to provide balancing energy for the settlement interval.

Settlements of the balancing energy are based on the zonal aggregate load imbalance and resource imbalance for each QSE. The load imbalance is the difference between the scheduled load and actual load from each QSE, while the resource imbalance is the difference between the scheduled generation and actual generation for each QSE. The actual load and generation amounts are derived from the load and resource meter readings.

Congestion Management

In this section, we introduce the process of transmission congestion management in ERCOT. The general process of redispatch to relieve transmission congestion is discussed in the following section. The ERCOT ISO uses a flow-based zonal congestion management scheme. The ERCOT transmission grid, including generation resources and loads, is divided into several congestion zones that are determined on an annual basis. Each congestion zone is defined such that every generation resource or load within the congestion zone boundaries has a similar effect (characterized by its shift factor) on the transmission facilities that limit transfer between congestion zones. These transmission facilities are called CSCs. The CSCs will be discussed in a later section.

The ERCOT ISO categorizes congestion management as either zonal congestion or local congestion. The former encompasses managing congestion on CSCs or predefined closely related elements (CRE). The QSEs specify portfolio bid prices for zonal balancing energy to the ERCOT ISO, and these bids are used to relieve zonal congestion. Generators are exposed to locational prices that reflect the average effect of location in zones on CSCs.

In addition to congestion on CSCs and CREs, congestion can occur on transmission paths within a zone, which is called "local congestion" and will be discussed in the section on the difficulties in adequately hedging congestion rent. Local congestion management relies on a more detailed operational model to determine how each particular resource or load influences the transmission system. The cost of the redispatch used to solve local congestion is uplifted to each QSE based on its load ratio share (LRS). The same method of uplift was used for zonal congestion before February 15, 2002. After this date, direct assignment of zonal congestion rent was implemented, which will be discussed in a later section.

Redispatch to Relieve Congestion

The ERCOT ISO analyzes schedules submitted by the QSEs to determine whether the resulting flows are within the system transmission capability. When the power scheduled to be transferred on a transmission facility element or set of elements would exceed the transfer capability of the elements, the ISO has to redispatch generators to ensure the reliability of the system. We will illustrate this redispatch process with a simple two-zone system and clarify some definitions related to congestion before discussing congestion management in ERCOT.

Figure 4.4. A two-zone system

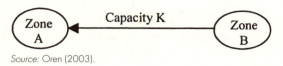

Figure 4.4 shows a two-zone system with zones A and B. The generation resources in zone A are more expensive than in zone B. Zone A is a net-load zone, while zone B is a net-generation zone. The marginal cost of net supply at A and the marginal avoided cost at B are shown in figure 4.5. If there were no transmission capacity limit, then QSEs can schedule the cheap resources at zone B to supply the demand at zone A. As shown in figure 4.5, neglecting distortions due to market power, the market price at node A and node B would both be P_C, and the import to zone A and the export from zone B would both equal $K1$.

However, suppose that the transmission capacity between zone A and zone B were limited to K, as shown in figure 4.5. If K is less than $K1$, then the ISO has to redispatch the system. The generation output at B is decreased by $(K1 - K)$, and the output of generators in zone A is increased by $(K1 - K)$ to meet the demand in zone A. In the absence of market power, the market clearing prices at A and B are P_A and P_B, respectively. The difference between these prices is the "shadow price" of the transmission capacity between node A and node B. The redispatch cost (Stoft 2002; Oren 2003a,b) under a marginal clearing mechanism (the rectangular area *DIEF*) is $(P_A - P_B) \times (K1 - K)$, which is the net payment by the ISO to increase the output of expensive generators in A and decrease the output of cheap generators in B. The rectangular area *DIGH* and the triangular area *DIC* in figure 4.5 are called congestion rent and congestion cost, respectively (Oren 2002a, 2003a,b; Joskow, chap. 1 in this volume). The congestion cost is the loss of social welfare due to the constraint.

In ERCOT, the term *congestion cost* is (confusingly) used to refer to either the congestion redispatch cost or the congestion rent, depending on the context. We will avoid this usage and instead use terms as defined in the previous paragraph.

Commercially Significant Constraints

The effect of a generator or load on a transmission facility is characterized by its shift factor. In ERCOT, busses with similar shift factors are combined into a zone. Zonal generation-weighted average shift factors, determined by

Figure 4.5. Congestion costs and rents

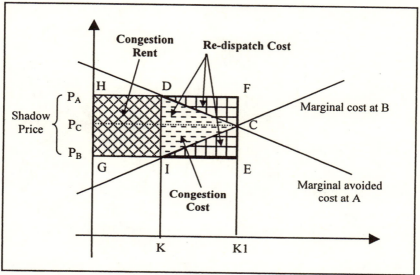

Source: Oren (2003).

the ERCOT ISO, are used as an approximation to the actual shift factors to manage congestion on CSCs.

Assuming a single shift factor for all resources and load in each zone allows the resources and load in a zone to be considered without regard to their specific location. This enables resource scheduling and bidding as a portfolio rather than as specific units. The portfolio energy schedules submitted by each QSE specify its total generation and demand in each zone. Any imbalance between loads and generation resources in a congestion zone is assumed to have the same impact on a given CSC.

ERCOT reassesses CSCs annually, based on the changes of the system topology. New congestion zones may be identified based on the reassessed CSCs. In 2001, there were three congestion zones in ERCOT: North Zone; South Zone; and West Zone; and two CSCs: transmission from Graham to Parker and from Limestone to Watermill. There have been four congestion zones for 2002 and 2003: North Zone, South Zone, West Zone, and Houston Zone. The transmission from Sandow to Temple, Graham to Parker, South Texas Project (STP) to Dow Chemical Company (DOW), and Parker to Graham were the CSCs for 2002. There are only three CSCs in 2003, involving transmission from STP to DOW (South to Houston), from Graham to Parker

Figure 4.6. CSCs and congestion zones of ERCOT in 2003

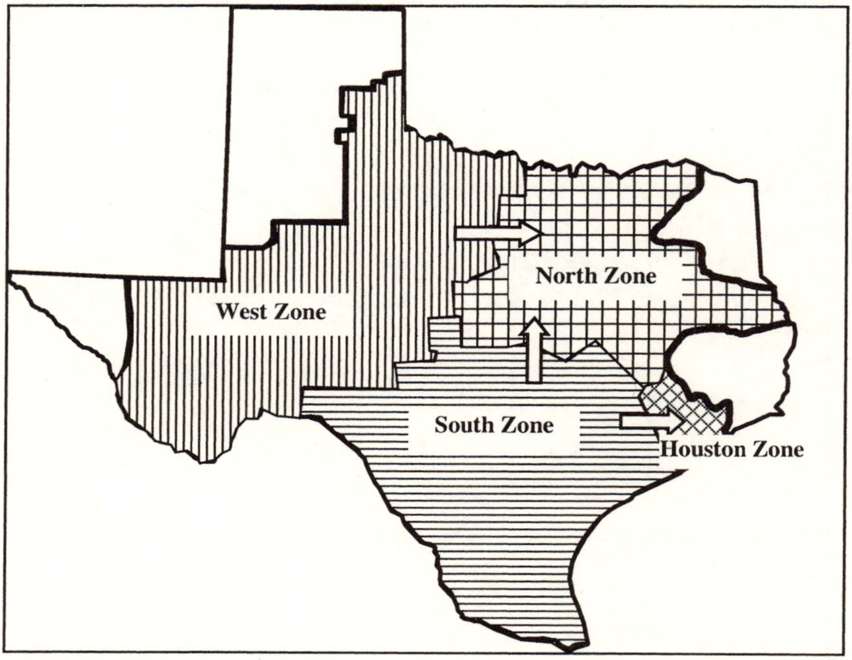

Source: ERCOT (2002b).

(West to North) and from Sandow to Temple (South to North). The CSCs and congestion zones of ERCOT in 2003 are shown in figure 4.6.

The zonal model feature of ERCOT is related to the geographical arrangements of each utility's generation and load before ERCOT began to operate as a single area. There were ten control areas within ERCOT prior to July 2001. The companies scheduled and operated their generation and load within each area as an entity. Under portfolio scheduling and zonal congestion management, market participants can maintain their preexisting portfolio management approaches, including self-commitment of generation resources.

When only transmission congestion on CSCs needs to be managed within the ERCOT region, only portfolio-balancing instructions are issued on a zonal basis. QSEs only need to meet their portfolio obligations zone by zone and no unit-specific deployment instructions are issued. The market clearing price of energy (MCPE) is determined for each zone based on the zonal portfolio offer curves for the balancing energy, forecasted load, and interzonal transmission constraints. If there is intrazonal congestion, however, ERCOT uses unit-specific bids to relieve local constraints and to issue unit-specific instructions to clear local congestion. This will be discussed in the section on local congestion.

The zonal aggregation and use of a single weighted-average shift factor means that the economic signals for congestion are approximate. Empirical data shows that the assumptions underlying the use of the zonal average shift factors to approximate the actual shift factors are violated in ERCOT. The implication is that, under some circumstances, the average shift factors provide incentives that deviate significantly from the efficient level (Baldick 2003). Moreover, interaction between the zonal and local congestion management process (to be discussed in the section on local congestion) poses operational difficulties for the ERCOT ISO.

The portfolio market structure and zonal congestion management model have provided operational flexibility to the ERCOT market participants but also brought difficulties to the operation of ERCOT ISO. If the ERCOT transmission system were less robust or the supply more limited, then the inefficiencies due to zonal aggregation would be more problematic.

Direct Assignment of Zonal Congestion Rent

When ERCOT began operation as a single control area on July 31, 2001, interzonal congestion redispatch costs were uplifted among market participants on a load-ratio-share basis. This presented an opportunity for profiting by overscheduling and then being paid to relieve congestion. This is similar to the "Inc and Dec" game in the California market. Serious overscheduling was observed in August 2001. The redispatch costs and the costs related to load imbalance, resource imbalance, and uninstructed deviation are aggregated as balancing energy neutrality adjustment (BENA) charges. The BENA charges for August 2001 alone were approximately $75.9 million. Six QSEs received more than $2 million each in load imbalance revenues for that month. A settlement was reached with them agreeing to refunds of gains from the ERCOT market.

The potential for this problem was anticipated (Oren 2001) and the PUCT required ERCOT to switch to a "direct assignment" methodology (that is, charging zonal congestion rents) by January 1, 2003 or six months after interzonal redispatch costs rose above $20 million on a rolling twelve-month period, whichever came first. It also required ERCOT to implement a system of transmission congestion rights (TCRs), which would allow market participants to hedge their interzonal congestion charges.

The $20 million threshold for interzonal redispatch costs was reached on August 15, 2001, just fifteen days after the beginning of the operation as a single control area. Direct assignment and the TCR system were implemented on February 15, 2002. Under it, the charge or payment to a QSE is based on the product of its scheduled flow and shadow prices on the congested CSCs. That is, a QSE is exposed to the variation of the shadow price for the CSC.

Transmission congestion rights and preassigned congestion rights (PCRs) were implemented as financial hedges against the zonal congestion rent. The TCR and PCR holder receives an amount equal to the congestion rent for an equivalent quantity of scheduled flow. The TCRs are awarded in yearly and monthly simultaneous combinatorial auctions based on the auction clearing prices. As discussed in the following, PCRs are allocated to MOUs and Co-Ops rather than awarded by the TCR auction process and are priced differently to TCRs. For all other purposes, PCRs are functionally and financially equivalent to TCRs.

The MOUs and Co-Ops that made a long-term (greater than five years) contractual commitment for annual capacity or energy from a specific remote-generation resource prior to September 1, 1999 are eligible for PCRs between the zone of their resource and the zone of their demand. The PCRs are available on an annual basis until the date upon which an MOU or Co-Op implements retail customer choice or, alternatively, until such other date as may be specified by order of the PUCT. The cost of PCRs equals 15 percent of the applicable annual TCR auction clearing price for each CSC for which a PCR is allocated. The PCRs may be traded in the secondary market. Holders of PCRs are not precluded from participating in the market to purchase additional TCRs.

The ERCOT ISO initially conducted a simple single-round TCR auction for each CSC. The auction awarded the TCRs from the highest prices to the lowest prices until 100 percent of the TCR capability is awarded. The lowest awarded price becomes the market clearing price for the TCRs for the CSC. However, a transaction from one zone to another requires capacity on several CSCs simultaneously. Consequently, the value of a TCR on one CSC depends on the amount of TCR awarded on other CSCs (Oren 2001). That is, TCRs for the various CSCs are closely interrelated products. Having separate markets for them poses difficulties for achieving efficiency.

To respond to this issue, the Congestion Management Working Group of the Wholesale Market Subcommittee drafted the Protocol Revision Request (PRR) 329 in May 2002 to implement the PUCT order to convert the simple auction to a combinatorial auction of TCRs. This PRR was approved on May 9, 2002, and it became effective on January 1, 2003. By this revision, the ERCOT ISO conduct a single-round, simultaneous combinatorial auction for selling the TCRs available for each annual or monthly auction for all

Figure 4.7. Zonal redispatch cost (August 1, 2001–February 14, 2002) and congestion rent (February 15, 2002–December 30, 2002)

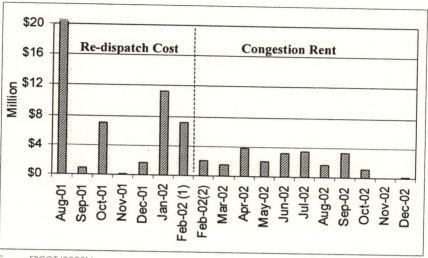

Source: ERCOT (2003b).

CSCs. In this auction, bidders can reflect their needs for TCRs on multiple CSCs simultaneously. The clearing price for each TCR equals to the corresponding shadow price of the marginal TCR awarded on that CSC.

Under some circumstances, PCRs and TCRs have the potential to enhance electricity seller or buyer market power (Oren 1997; Joskow and Tirole 2000). As an ad hoc approach to mitigating market power, no entity combined with its affiliates may, directly or indirectly, own, control, or receive the revenue from more than 25 percent of the total available TCRs at a CSC interface for any single direction and a given hour. Market power will be discussed in a later section.

Figure 4.7 shows the monthly zonal redispatch costs (until February 14, 2002) and congestion rent (after February 15, 2002) in ERCOT. Until February 14, 2002, zonal redispatch cost was uplifted to all QSEs in the system based on their load-ratio share. From February 15, 2002, direct assignment of zonal congestion rent was implemented in ERCOT, under which the congestion charge or payment for each QSE is based on the shadow prices and power flow it scheduled on the congested CSCs. Zonal congestion rent after February 15, 2002 was significantly less than the redispatch cost prior to February 15, 2002. This strongly suggests that significant overscheduling was taking place prior to

February 15, 2002. Overscheduling across the CSCs has stopped and should not reoccur because the change to direct assignment of zonal congestion rent removed the incentives for QSEs to overschedule load across the CSCs. The same problem still remains for local congestion, as will be discussed in a later section.

Difficulties in Adequately Hedging Congestion Rent

One of the goals of a zonal congestion model is to simplify the commercial model to facilitate trading. However, the need to change the model on an annual basis has a deleterious effect on long-term commercial activities. The annual revision of congestion zones creates uncertainty and results in a lack of liquidity in the forward market for zonal products. Because the boundary shifts are difficult to predict, trading of long-term zonal products is risky for a power generation company if it has assets near the zone boundaries or if zones are subdivided.

A similar problem is the inability to make long-term purchases of TCRs. It is difficult for REPs and QSEs to hedge congestion rent adequately in the long term. Ownership limitations on TCRs (opt-ins limited to 25 percent of total available TCRs per CSC, non-opt-in limited to same 25 percent of TCRs, plus their PCRs) has also been cited by market participants as an obstacle to fully hedging risk, although the limit on TCR ownership is aimed at mitigating exercise of generation market power.

To address this problem, the creation of trading hubs has been proposed as a solution to provide certainty regarding delivery expectations. The ERCOT managed hubs are expected to enhance the market stability by allowing participants to arrange transactions, despite annual rezoning. Long-term hedging of congestion is a problem in other markets as well as in ERCOT; however, the annual rezoning in ERCOT exacerbates the problem.

Local Congestion

A similar situation continues to exist for local congestion as existed for zonal congestion prior to February 15, 2002. However, ERCOT relies on a more-detailed operational model to determine how each particular resource or load affects the transmission system, and this model does not use portfolio bids. Each resource is required to submit resource-specific premiums (positive or negative) and the resource-specific dispatch ranges. The resource-specific premiums and unit-specific shift factor are used to relieve local congestion through a set of balanced adjustments to local resources in each zone. Resources in other zones may be chosen when there is no solution within local resources.

The ERCOT protocols define a "market solution" for local congestion as when at least three unaffiliated resources, with capacity available, submit bids to the ERCOT ISO that can solve the local congestion and no one bidder is essential to solving the congestion. If there is no market solution, then bid prices are mitigated based on verifiable operating costs.

There has been no market solution for local congestion in ERCOT in most cases. That is, local market power (to be discussed in a later section) is deemed to exist most of the time when local transmission constraints are binding. Instead of relying on a market process to determine prices, ERCOT obtains commitments to provide capacity and energy at a prespecified cost level. These are called out-of-merit-order energy (OOME) and out-of-merit-order capacity (OOMC). The OOME services are provided by resources selected by ERCOT ISO outside the bidding process in order to resolve local congestion when no market solution exists. Out-of-merit-order capacity provides generation capacity needed such that balancing energy is available to solve local congestion or other reliability needs when a market solution does not exist. Out-of-merit-order capacity can be provided from any resource or load acting as a resource that is listed as available in the resource plan.

Sometimes a reliability must run (RMR) unit may be needed to provide generation capacity or energy resources when there is no market solution. A RMR unit is a generation resource unit operated under the terms of an annual agreement with ERCOT that would not otherwise be operated except that they are necessary to provide voltage support, stability, or management of localized transmission constraints under first contingency criteria where market solutions do not exist.

The local congestion cost is uplifted to each QSE based on the load-ratio share of the QSE. Figure 4.8 shows the local redispatch costs in ERCOT from August 2001 to December 2002.

In docket 23220 of 2001, the PUCT ordered the ERCOT ISO to implement direct assignment of local congestion costs if the redispatch costs for resolving local congestion rose above $20 million in a rolling twelve-month period. The direct assignment of local congestion cost tries to eliminate opportunities for market participants to profit from scheduling that result in congestion on local transmission lines and to send appropriate signals to locate new generation facilities in places that have sufficient transmission capacity to deliver the power to electric consumers. The $20 million threshold for local redispatch costs was met on March 5, 2002, after seven months of operation as a single control area.

Several proposals have been suggested for solving the local congestion

Figure 4.8. Local redispatch cost of ERCOT

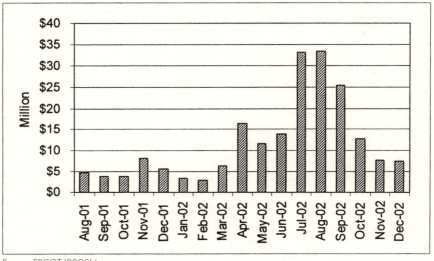

Source: ERCOT (2003b).

problem, including implementing nodal locational marginal pricing (LMP). Currently ERCOT is implementing a Texas nodal market design process.

Summary

The clear lesson from both California and ERCOT is that uplifting redispatch cost is a serious flaw in market design. The problems with uplifting redispatch cost were recognized at the time the ERCOT Protocols were approved, and the triggers to implement the change were set to deal with this issue (Oren 2001). In the case of zonal redispatch costs, the change from uplifting to charging congestion rent was relatively straightforward and has been implemented. In the case of local redispatch, however, the issue cannot be resolved without finer-scale disaggregation of the system including unit-specific scheduling and bidding, which will render the zonal portfolio scheduling process untenable.

The TCRs for the three CSCs are closely interrelated products. Auctioning them separately, as in the original implementation, leads to inefficiencies. Such closely interrelated products should be auctioned simultaneously.

The approach to defining "market solutions" accepts the transmission and generation system as given and then mitigates market power by regulating the prices. This approach provides no long-term solution to the problem because it does not encourage new entry to contest the local market power. Moreover, the lack of transparency due to the uplifting of congestion costs tends to entrench local monopoly power.

Ancillary Services Market

Ancillary services (AS) are the services necessary to maintain electric system reliability and security. In ERCOT, each market participant is assigned an obligation to provide AS based on its historical load. Market participants may provide the AS themselves or rely on ERCOT to acquire the AS through a centralized auction. From August 2001 to December 2002, market participants self-procured between 80 percent and 90 percent of their AS obligations.

ERCOT operates a day-ahead AS market for regulation down services (RgDn), regulation up services (RgUp), responsive reserves services (RRS), non–spinning reserve services (NSRS), and replacement reserve services (RPRS) as needed. These AS are procured day-ahead for each hour of the following day.

One concern about AS markets is price reversal (Oren 2000), where the market clearing prices of capacity (MCPC) for the higher-quality AS are lower than the prices for the lower-quality AS. This occurs because, in the initial ERCOT implementation, the markets for regulation services RRS and NSRS are cleared in sequence. Sometimes lower-quality AS were offered from generating units that are capable of producing higher-quality AS when lower-quality services were anticipated to receive higher prices. This may result in a shortage of higher-quality services such as RgUp and RgDn. From August 2001 to September 2002, the monthly average percentage of price-reversal hours in ERCOT was about 35 percent.

Because AS are interrelated products and because generators can provide several types of AS, having separate markets for AS poses difficulties for achieving efficiency. This is analogous to the case for auctions of TCRs for CSCs. In order to procure AS efficiently and prevent price reversal, PRR 342 for simultaneous selection of AS services was submitted in May 2002. It was approved by the ERCOT Board on January 22, 2003 and will be in place after the ERCOT systems are changed accordingly.

Operational Issues

Market participants and the ERCOT ISO are currently discussing how to improve the operational efficiency and the system reliability. The QSEs that represent resources are required to submit to the ERCOT ISO a resource plan about the availability of their resources and the planned operating level of each resource for each hour of a day. The capacity indicated in the resource plan must be sufficient to support the portfolio schedules that the QSE has submitted.

In some instances, the ERCOT ISO has encountered problems with inaccurate resource plans, which have the potential to cause problems in maintaining system reliability. Schedule control error (SCE; the difference between the QSE's actual resource output and its base power schedule plus instructed AS) resulting from inaccurate resource plans may lead the ERCOT ISO to acquire additional ancillary services. In addition, as resource plans are used by the ERCOT ISO to identify available units that can solve a congestion problem, an inaccurate plan may make it difficult for ERCOT to manage transmission congestion.

A special team of stakeholders has been formed to develop recommendations for the resolution of this issue to improve the accuracy of resource plans. In June 2002, PRR 287 imposed stricter requirements for generators to adhere to their production schedules in order to improve reliability.

Although portfolio scheduling and the adjustment period bring flexibility to market participants, they cause other problems for system operation. For example, in order to issue a portfolio instruction, shift factors of each bus within a zone on CSCs are assumed to be the same and effects on local congestion in other zones are ignored. As discussed previously, this is in conflict with the physical laws of electricity (Baldick 2003) and means that incentives are distorted compared to efficient signals. It also potentially causes some QSEs to commit inefficient generation on line because there is no central unit commitment and dispatch in the ERCOT market. Several market participants have expressed concerns that older and inefficient generation appears to be running at times when newer, more efficient generation is idle, raising a concern about the efficiency of the current market design.

Moreover, as the ERCOT ISO does not issue a unit commitment and does not dispatch all resources of the commercial model, it has to make assumptions based on limited information available ahead of real time to procure balancing energy services and manage congestion. These assumptions may not be consistent with real-time operations because ERCOT lacks details about the QSEs' internal dispatch rationales. Accurate nodal information is necessary to efficiently operate the electric system and maintain system reliability.

It is hard to evaluate the trade-off between the market participant flexibility and the technical inefficiency that the portfolio structure brings to the market. Moreover, the deviation of the ERCOT market process from other market structures, such as SMD, means that analysis of and solutions to operational inefficiency problems cannot easily benefit from experience in other North American markets.

Capacity Adequacy

In order to meet reliability criteria, there must be adequate installed capacity. The reserve margin is used to characterize capacity adequacy and is defined as the difference between total electricity generation capacity and peak demand, divided by the peak demand.

The ERCOT ISO periodically determines the minimum reserve margin required to ensure the adequacy of installed generation capability. The ERCOT utilities have traditionally been required to maintain a reserve margin of 15 percent. In mid-2002, the ERCOT ISO Board approved a 12.5 percent reserve-margin requirement; however, there is no formal mechanism currently in place to enforce the reserve margin. The PUCT is in the process of developing a reserve-margin mechanism.

The strong gas delivery infrastructure and the regulatory environment, including the introduction of wholesale competition in Texas and the generation interconnection policy (see the next section) have attracted the investment of new, efficient generation facilities. A significant amount of new generating capacity has been added in Texas since wholesale competition was introduced in 1995. About 22,000 MW of new capacity has been added between 1995 and early 2003, with another 7,500 MW under construction. Of this amount, more than 12,500 MW was added in 2001 and the first three quarters of 2002. As of early 2003, ERCOT generation capacity is approximately 77,000 MW. Another 7,000 MW is expected to be added by the end of 2003.

According to PURA's Goal for Natural Gas, at least 50 percent of new generating capacity (in MWs) installed in Texas, excluding renewables, should use natural gas as its primary fuel. Since January 1, 2000, 100 percent of the new nonrenewable generating capacity added in Texas has been gas-fired. The total gas-fired capacity added in Texas since January 1, 2000 has been 16,800 MW. Figure 4.9 shows the installed generation mix in Texas in 2002.

Because of the nationwide economic turndown and a mild summer, the actual peak for ERCOT in summer 2002 was below the projection. (See figure 4.2.) Consequently, the effective reserve margin (based on actual generation capacity minus peak load, divided by peak load) of approximately 34 percent was higher than predicted. ERCOT predicts a 21.0 percent reserve margin in 2003, 21.6 percent in 2004, 18.3 percent in 2005, and 16.1 percent in 2006, and 13.6 percent in 2007. Figure 4.10 shows the projected available resources and peak demands from 2003 to 2007.

Figure 4.9. Generation mix in Texas

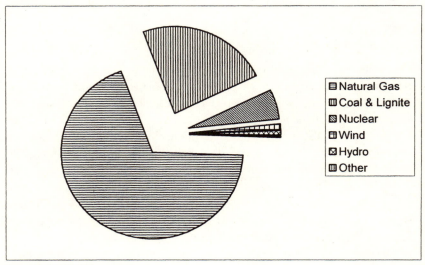

Source: PUCT (2003b).

Several issues have enabled new generation construction in ERCOT (and the "dash for gas" in England and Wales), including the availability of natural gas, the electric transmission interconnection policy (to be discussed in the next section), and the environmental permitting process. The large amount of new generation has put pressure on older plants to be retired or mothballed. The nationwide economic slowdown and the potential availability of mothballed units and imports suggest that the preceding estimated margins for the coming years may be conservative. That is, the actual margins, including use of all mothballed units and imports, could be higher by several thousand MW.

As a countervailing effect, the pace of development and construction of new generation has reduced in response to slower demand growth and the nationwide economic downturn. More than 9,700 MW of announced new generation capacity planned for Texas has been delayed and more than 4,400 MW has been cancelled. Additionally, American Electric Power (AEP) and CenterPoint Energy announced in fall 2002 that they plan to mothball, collectively, a further 7,000 MW of older, less efficient generating capacity, which may reduce the projected ERCOT reserve margins. That is, the actual margin may be lower by many thousands of MW if mothballing and cancellation occurs. Consequently, there is considerable uncertainty in the future reserve margins.

Figure 4.10. Summer peak demand, capacity and resource

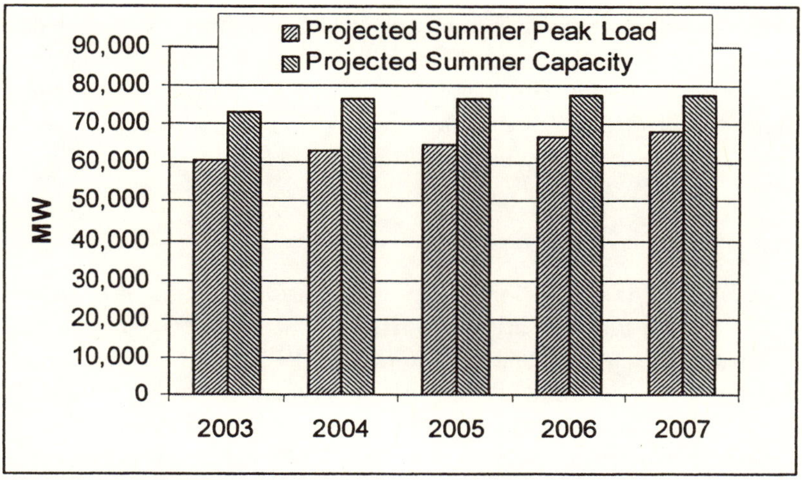

Source: ERCOT (2002k).

In ERCOT, the absence of an installed capacity market (ICAP) market or other mechanism to ensure adequacy implies that the large reserve margins reflect expectations by investors in new generators that their capacity would be profitable based on energy and AS prices alone. However, the extremely high reserve margins mean that considerable capacity is not being used and that, in the absence of transmission constraints, competitive pressures will presumably drive down wholesale energy prices in ERCOT (Cunningham, Baldick, and Baughman 2003). While this will yield low prices in the short term, the large expenditure on capital beyond the needed reserve margins represents a significant cost to society. This may be indicative of a boom and bust cycle in generation expansion.

Generator Interconnection Policy

ERCOT has been proactive in encouraging new generation through its interconnection policy. In some other jurisdictions, developers of new generation projects pay upfront for upgrades to the transmission network necessary to deliver their energy to demand. New generation facilities in ERCOT pay upfront only for the "shallow" costs of interconnecting with the transmission network and not for "deep" interconnection costs of upgrading the network to accommodate moving power from the resource to demand centers.

The choice between charging shallow versus deep interconnection costs has important implications for efficient growth of generation. In the England and Wales market, a similar choice of shallow interconnection costs led to considerable gas-fired generation being built near the North Sea but far from demand centers, posing considerable problems for transmission network planning. Analogous issues are arising in ERCOT. The following section discusses the transmission planning process in ERCOT.

Transmission Planning

The ERCOT ISO is responsible for transmission planning on a regional basis in ERCOT. Planning criteria for ERCOT were set by combining the NERC planning standards and the criteria that the ERCOT market participants proposed. The ERCOT Planning Assessment and Review Working Group (PARWG) review the planning criteria every three years to ensure that they meet the requirements outlined in the NERC planning standards. The ERCOT PARWG also periodically reviews the planning criteria, procedures, and practices of individual TDSPs to ensure the consistency with NERC and the ERCOT criteria.

Section 39.155 of the PURA, as amended by SB7 in 1999, requires the ERCOT ISO to submit an annual report to identify existing and potential transmission constraints and recommend actions for meeting system needs. The ERCOT ISO currently leads three regional planning groups (North, South, and West) to determine if additional actions are needed to resolve transmission constraints.

New transmission lines are constructed by the TDSPs. A utility is required to obtain a certificate of convenience and necessity (CCN) from the PUCT before constructing transmission facilities in Texas. In order to encourage the construction of new transmission facilities, transmission access rules were revised in 2001 (PUCT 2001b). The transmission cost recovery factor (TCRF) was established to permit a utility to receive expedited cost recovery of additional transmission investments. The TCRF only recovers the capital costs associated with new investments in transmission facilities and reflects the costs in the nonbypassable rates charged to REPs. All REPs must pay TDSPs for delivering electricity to the REPs' customers. The charges are called nonbypassable fees because every customer pays these charges, regardless of which REP the customer chooses.

Transmission facilities have been actively planned and built in the ERCOT region. Between 1996, when ERCOT ISO began conducting regional transmission planning, and early 2003, over 900 miles of transmission facilities of various voltages in ERCOT (including over 400 miles of 345 kV transmission facilities) have been built. Major finished transmission projects include the Limestone–Watermill project, which was intended to increase transmission capacity from South Texas to North Texas, and numerous projects in the Houston and Corpus Christi areas, which were also intended to reduce the likelihood of voltage collapse and provide dynamic voltage control (Bergen and Vittal 2002).

Although a relatively large amount of new transmission facilities has been installed in ERCOT, transmission constraints in ERCOT limit the deliverability of some generation resources, especially wind power from the Mc-Camey area in west Texas, where there is now considerably more generation capacity than there is transmission capability to export the power. The proactive interconnection policy has encouraged new generation, but this has put strong pressure on the transmission system.

An important issue in most restructured electricity markets is the disconnection between generation construction and transmission planning. Although ERCOT has been active in building and upgrading transmission, ERCOT is not immune from this problem, which has been exacerbated by the generation interconnection policy and lack of local congestion price signals.

For example, as mentioned in the preceding, in the McCamey area of west Texas, transmission resources are inadequate to transmit the wind energy generated there to load centers. New wind-power capacity of 758 MW has been installed in the area as of the end of 2002 and another 300 MW is expected to be in service by the end of 2003. However, the local transmission network currently can only export 400 MW and, under the ERCOT interconnection policy, the wind turbines were permitted to interconnect with ERCOT despite the lack of transmission capability. This has resulted in routine wind-power curtailments, higher local redispatch costs, and damages to transmission equipment due to overloading. The transmission utilities serving the Mc-Camey area are seeking approval for upgrades that would increase export capacity to 2,000 MW, but these improvements would not be finished until 2007.

The uncertainty regarding the expiration of the federal production tax credit (PTC) for renewable energy caused the rush to install wind capacity despite the lack of transmission capacity. The PTC, currently $18 per MWh, will expire at the end of 2003 unless it is extended by Congress and the president. Section 39.904 of the PURA, *Goal for Renewable Energy*, required that 400 MW of new renewable capacity be installed in Texas by 2003. As of October 1, 2002, approximately 1,000 MW of new renewable capacity had been installed and the majority of installed renewable capacity is wind generation.

Retail-market participants have an incentive to contract for more wind power to gain more PTC and share of the limited transport capacity. However, entities throughout ERCOT are paying for excessive amounts of OOME due to the concentration of wind power in areas where there is not adequate transmission available. Similar problems could arise elsewhere, depending on where the future generation is sited.

In order to find ways to address this problem, project 25819, *PUC Proceeding to Address Transmission Constraints Affecting West Texas Wind Power Generators,* has been opened. The methods for allocating transmission access and PTC in the highly constrained area would be examined.

The lack of nodal wholesale price signals has contributed to the generation siting problem. If there were proper locational signals, new generators would have had an incentive to avoid the McCamey area and locate in places where transmission was sufficient. Locational pricing issues are addressed in project 26376, *Rulemaking Proceeding on Wholesale Market Design Issues in the Electric Reliability Council of Texas.*

The ERCOT interconnection policy has enabled IPPs to interconnect in advance of adequate transmission capability. When coupled with tax credits and the state legislative requirement for installation of renewables, the result has been generation development outpacing transmission construction. The lack of coordination between generation siting decisions and transmission analysis and planning poses serious problems for ERCOT. Transmission planning remains an extremely difficult issue in restructured electricity markets, including ERCOT.

Market Power

Market power is the ability of a firm to set price profitably above competitive levels reflecting marginal costs. Market power becomes problematic when a firm has the ability to significantly influence market prices and cause them to vary from competitive levels for an extended time. Participants may have market power through controlling a large share of the market, by being pivotal or through exercising control under certain market conditions. A bid cap is a common approach in almost all markets to mitigate market power. The PUCT has established bid caps of \$1000/MWh for energy and \$1000/MW per hour for capacity.

The notion of a "market solution," as defined previously, is used as an indicator of when local market power may be exercised. If there is no market solution, then market power is deemed to exist and prices are mitigated.

The PUCT's Market Oversight Division (MOD) has developed another market power mitigation approach called the competitive solution method (CSM) (Oren 2002b; PUCT 2002a). The implementation of CSM for the balancing energy service market depends upon the congestion management method adopted by the commission in project 26376 (PUCT 2003c).

In PUCT project 26736, other market power mitigation methods have also been discussed, such as automatic mitigation procedure (AMP) and zonal-ERCOT-nodal (ZEN) (Siddiqi 2003). An AMP is an automated ex ante measure based on behavioral mitigation. Its ex ante nature implies that market participants avoid the regulatory risk and disruptions to settlements and financial accounting caused by refunds. It was first implemented by the New York ISO (NYISO). The ZEN approach tries to distinguish between changes in bidding pattern due to true scarcity in the market as opposed to locational market power. This approach is aimed at providing price signals to the market that reflect scarcity when it occurs.

Even absent local congestion, the ERCOT market is concentrated in the sense that there are a small number of IOUs owning the bulk of generation. If this market power were not mitigated, then wholesale prices could be expected to be well above competitive levels (Cunningham, Baldick, and Baughman 2003). However, the retail load obligations of the IOUs are implicit vesting contracts that considerably blunt the incentives for exercising market power. As explained in Wolak (chap. 3 in this volume), this contrasts with the absence of any vesting arrangements or long-term contracts in the ostensibly less-concentrated California market. As will be discussed in the following section, the extent of these retail load obligations will change as the market share of competitive retailers changes.

When there is local congestion, local market power is mitigated in ERCOT by ad hoc procedures that are aimed at keeping prices relatively low while maintaining transmission flows within limits. As described in Joskow (chap. 1 in this volume), however, the prices may be too low when there is local scarcity. In particular, the prices may not be high enough to attract efficient new entry to provide long-term solutions to the local market power problems. It is difficult for new entrants to contest such local markets so that the local monopoly positions are essentially entrenched.

Retail Competition

Senate Bill 7 required the creation of competitive retail electricity market that gave customers the ability to choose their retail electric providers starting on January 1, 2002. On June 1, 2001, a Texas Electric Choice Pilot Project (or pilot project) was started in advance of full retail competition in order to inform customers how to participate in the new competitive electric market and to make the system ready for the full implementation of retail competition. In the pilot project, 5 percent of electric load within each investor-owned electric utility's service was permitted to buy power from competitive retail electric providers. At the end of the pilot project, over 115,000 customers had enrolled in the pilot project. Approximately 90 percent of these customers were residential, 9 percent were small nonresidential (peak demand less than one megawatt), and 1 percent were large nonresidential (peak demand over one megawatt).

In contrast to fixed-price regimes established in electricity retail markets as in, for example, the initial California market (Wolak, chap. 3 in this volume), the PUCT adopted the "price to beat" (PUCT 2001c) to encourage competitive retail market for residential and small customers. The rule requires a 6 percent reduction from the rates in effect on January 1, 1999 for residential and small commercial customers (peak demand of 1 MW or less) who choose to take service from the affiliated retail electric provider. However, in contrast to the initial California retail market, the price to beat allowed for adjustments based on fuel costs, and affiliated REPs could charge above the price to beat. These issues will be discussed in the next paragraphs.

The price to beat can be adjusted by a "fuel factor" for the integrated utility as of December 31, 2001. The fuel factors are adjusted to reflect changes in the prices of fuel to approximately track average wholesale prices and to prevent the price to beat from falling below the wholesale prices. This avoids a problem that arose in California's retail competition, where the incumbent utilities were required to provide service to retail customers at rates that were below their actual costs to serve customers. On the other hand, the adjustment of rates through a fuel factor means that there are not strong incentives for the affiliated retail electric provider to seek contracts with the most efficient generation plant.

Affiliated REPs are required to sell electricity at or above the price to beat to residential and small commercial customers (1 MW of peak demand or less) until January 1, 2007. They can offer rates lower than the price to beat beginning January 1, 2007 or earlier if at least 40 percent of their customers (1 MW of peak demand or less) move to competitors. Customers who did not choose a new REP were transferred automatically to their utility's affiliated retail electric provider in January 2002.

The objective of the price to beat is to encourage entry of new retail providers for residential and small commercial customers. The price to beat freezes the incumbent retailers' rates at a level that was chosen so that the new competitors should be able to undercut it. The intent was that it would be easy for new competitors to enter the market by providing a large amount of head-room: that is, the difference between the price to beat and the competitive market price. In contrast, if the rate charged by the affiliated REPs were be-low the competitive price, then other REPs would be unable to compete for customers and make a profit.

Interestingly, this suggests that, although the rates in ERCOT were low by national standards, the rates were nevertheless well above competitive prices for energy in ERCOT. This simultaneously allows retail price reduc-tions and significant headroom. The situation is evidently similar to the En-gland and Wales experience (Green, chap. 2 in this volume). However, it con-trasts with the experience in California where retail rate reductions were financed by bonds and did not, apparently, represent a sustainable reduction in prices (Wolak, chap. 3 in this volume).

Based on the publicly available information from the REPs, the approved price-to-beat rates, and representative usage levels (calculated using a histor-ical load profile for each service area), the PUCT has estimated that residen-tial customers have saved approximately $900 million on electric bills in 2002 as compared to 2001. Competing REPs were estimated by the PUCT to be offering up to 14 percent in additional savings off the price to beat to residen-tial customers (PUCT 2003f). However, it is difficult to assess the veracity of the PUCT assessment and whether this is a sustainable reduction. For ex-ample, as indicated by Joskow (chap. 1 in this volume), some of the savings are due to issues that would have occurred in the absence of restructuring and, moreover, the large reserve margins in ERCOT now suggest overbuilding of generation and, consequently, relatively low wholesale prices if the market were functioning efficiently. Retirements of generation may increase whole-sale prices and retail prices in the medium term.

Whatever the long-term prognosis for the market, customers have taken advantage of the opportunities to switch providers. As of February 2003, about 467,029 retail customers were taking service from nonaffiliated REP. Over 7 percent of residential customers were served by a nonaffiliated REP. About 11 percent of small nonresidential and 50 percent of large nonresiden-tial customers (peak demand larger than 1 MW) received service from a non-affiliated REP (ERCOT 2003a).

The price to beat has enabled retail competition in ERCOT by setting prices for formerly regulated entities that allow competitive retailers to un-dercut them. It is a transition measure to foster competition in the retail mar-ket. As discussed in the context of England and Wales by Green (chap. 2 in this volume), the incentives for retail customers to switch have come from a regulatory decision to set the headroom to be large. While this has certainly enabled CRs to enter the market, the long-term prognosis is unclear. ERCOT retail prices prior to restructuring were simultaneously relatively low compared to other regions in North America and (given the implication of large headroom) nevertheless well above competitive levels. This combination is potentially unique to ERCOT.

Load Response

The QSEs can, in principle, bid their load resources into AS and other markets as loads acting as resources (LaaR). Many traditional demand-side resources, however, have found it difficult to meet all of the performance criteria set out in the protocols all of the time. Consequently, the number of LaaRs that can compete in the provisioning of the services has been low, resulting in a less-competitive market than would otherwise be the case. Larger QSEs have an advantage over smaller QSEs due to their superior ability to use load diversity to smooth out performance and have more chance to bid in their LaaRs.

Some market participants think this situation can be ameliorated by defining a reasonable performance criterion to recognize the unique operating characteristics of fluctuating loads. Others think a better mechanism is needed so that retail customers can access and respond to real-time prices by either increasing or decreasing their usage as prices increase or decrease.

The importance of incorporating demand response into electricity markets has been observed (Borenstein 2001). However, implementing demand responsiveness poses challenges because of the difference between generation resources and load, particularly regarding dispatchability.

Revisions to ERCOT Market

In the process of the ERCOT protocols review, Dr. Oren, senior consultant of the PUCT, made recommendations in his report to the PUCT regarding market power mitigation, congestion management, simultaneous auction of TCRs, relaxed balanced scheduling, and simultaneous auctions for the AS (Oren 2000, 2001). All the recommendations have been adopted by the commission as part of the final approval of the protocols with the exception that the congestion management recommendation (for assignment of interzonal and local congestion) was predicated on a $20 million trigger in redispatch cost over twelve months. When the PUCT approved the ERCOT protocols in June 2001, it was decided to phase in all the recommended changes gradually.

Subsequent to the approval of the ERCOT protocols, the protocols have undergone significant changes to improve the wholesale market, including

Figure 4.11. Milestones and revisions of the ERCOT wholesale market

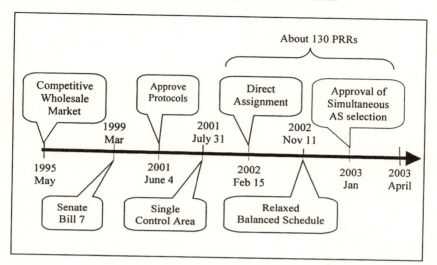

the changes that were anticipated in the June 2001 protocols. Between 2001 and 2003, there were about 130 PRRs approved by the ERCOT board. Among these, the PRRs of direct assignment of zonal congestion rent, relaxed balanced schedules, and simultaneous selection of AS are three of the major revisions to the ERCOT market. Figure 4.11 shows the milestones and principal revisions to the ERCOT market. In the future, ERCOT will change from a zonal to a nodal market.

The large number of rule changes and amendments in ERCOT are potential barriers to entry into the ERCOT wholesale market. Only large companies were able to track, discuss, and implement rapid changes in a timely fashion. The level of changes has potentially discouraged some new entry. Although it was important to correct the deficiencies in the market, it may have ultimately been better to spend more time developing the market in advance of implementation to minimize the necessity for changes. In some cases, such as the problems with uplift charges, experiences from other markets such as California were not heeded in the initial implementation although they were anticipated to be problematic.

Comparison to Other Markets

In table 4.1, we summarize the current ERCOT market design versus other U.S. electricity markets in relation to day-ahead, hour-ahead, and real-

Table 4.1. Summary of major U.S. electricity market design

Market	Day-ahead market	Hour-ahead market	Real-time market	Congestion management	ICAP market	Price/ bid cap	AMP
ERCOT	Schedule		√	Zonal/flowgate		√	
California							
MD02	√	√	√	Nodal	√	√	√
ISO-NE	√		√	Nodal	√	√	
MISO	√		√	Nodal/flowgate	√	√	√
NYISO	√	Schedule	√	Nodal	√	√	√
PJM	√		√	Nodal	√	√	
SMD	√		√	Nodal	√	√	√

Source: PUCT, 2003d.

time energy markets, congestion management, and other attributes. The markets listed in the table are ERCOT, those of the California Independent System Operator (CAISO) MD02, NYISO, ISO New England (ISO-NE), the Midwest Independent System Operator (MISO), Pennsylvania-New Jersey-Maryland (PJM), and the FERC SMD.

Table 4.1 shows that there are various differences in detail between all markets such as, for example, the presence of an hour-ahead market and the market mitigation procedure. However, a striking aspect of table 4.1 is that the markets besides ERCOT are similar in a number of aspects, while the ERCOT market is different to them all. The ERCOT market demonstrates, for example, that an electricity market can be run without central day-ahead dispatch, albeit with implications such as limited price discovery and potential operational inefficiencies. It also demonstrates that a market can function with a zonal rather than a nodal congestion management system; however, again there are implications for operational efficiency.

Summary of Lessons Learned and Conclusion

This chapter presented a review of the electricity market development in ERCOT and the lessons learned from the market experience. In this section, we conclude by summarizing in point form the lessons discussed in the third section.

- The successful operation of the ERCOT market shows that an electricity market can be run without a centrally dispatched day-ahead market, at least given the current availability of generation and the affiliation between generators and retail providers in ERCOT. This observation should be tempered with the understanding that the market has been operating for only about two years. For example, if supply were to become tighter and transmission congestion more binding then the bilateral scheduling process might be much more problematic. An important aspect of mitigating the effects of market concentration in ERCOT is the implicit vesting contracts due to the affiliation between resources and LSEs. As more customers move to other CRs in the coming years, the potential for exercise of market power in the wholesale market may increase.

- Portfolio scheduling has provided considerable flexibility to market participants but has several negative implications, including reduced market efficiency, lack of price discovery, limited liquidity, and operational problems. The update of zones on a yearly basis and the lack of long-term financial transmission rights mean that there are transmission congestion risks that are difficult to hedge over long periods.

- The redispatch costs experienced in the zonal congestion process and, more recently, in the local congestion process show that uplifting redispatch costs provides poor incentives to market participants.

- For both the TCR and the AS markets, having separate markets for closely interrelated products reduced efficiency.

- ERCOT has attracted considerable independent generation development. Several aspects of the ERCOT market contribute to this, including the availability of natural gas infrastructure, the regulatory environment, having a standard interconnection agreement, and charging only shallow interconnection costs. The last aspect has negative implications in terms of poor incentives for siting generation and has enabled IPPs to interconnect in advance of adequate transmission capability being built.

- Market power mitigation that aims only at keeping prices low has the side effect of not encouraging long-term solutions to local market power problems. ERCOT has attracted considerable new independent generation but, for the most part, the generation has not located to help with local market power problems.

- The combination of regulated prices being high enough to enable significant headroom and yet low compared to the U.S. average is potentially unique to ERCOT. The price to beat has enabled retail competition in ERCOT by setting prices for formerly regulated entities that allow competitive retailers to undercut them. It is a transition measure to foster competition in the retail market.

- Implementing demand responsiveness poses challenges because of the difference between generation resources and load, particularly regarding dispatchability.

- There have been many changes to the ERCOT protocols, potentially posing a barrier to entry.

The ERCOT market continues to evolve. Similarly, the lessons learned from the restructured ERCOT market should be viewed as a work in progress with only two years or so of accumulated experience.

Appendix

AEP—American Electric Power
AMP—Automatic Mitigation Procedure
AS—Ancillary services
BENA—Balancing Energy Neutrality Adjustment
CAISO—California ISO
CCN—Certificate of Convenience and Necessity
Co-Op—Electric Cooperatives
CPL—Central Power and Light Company
CR—Competitive Retailer
CRE—Closely Related Elements
CSC—Commercially Significant Constraint
CSM—Competitive Solution Method
Entergy—Entergy Gulf States, Inc.
EIA—Energy Information Administration
ERCOT—Electric Reliability Council of Texas
FERC—Federal Energy Regulatory Commission
ICAP—Installed Capacity Market
IMO—Independent Electricity Market Operator of Ontario
IOU—Investor-Owned Electric Utility
IPP—Independent Power Provider
ISO-NE—ISO New England
ISO—Independent System Operator
LaaR—Loads Acting as Resources
LMP—Locational Marginal Pricing
LRS—Load-Ratio Share
LSE—Load-Serving Entity
MCPC—Market Clearing Prices of Capacity
MCPE—Market Clearing Price of Energy
MD02—California Market Design 2002
MISO—Mid-West Independent System Operator

MOD—Market Oversight Division
MOU—Municipally Owned Utilities
NEM—National Electricity Market of Australia
NERC—North American Electric Reliability Council
NOIE—Non-Opt-In Entity
NETA—New Energy Trading Arrangement of England and Wales
Nord Pool—Nordic Power Exchange
NSRS—Non–Spinning Reserves Service
NYISO—New York ISO
NZEM—New Zealand Electricity Market
OOMC—Out-of-Merit-Order Capacity
OOME—Out-of-Merit-Order Energy
PARWG—Planning Assessment and Review Working Group
PCR—Preassigned Congestion Rights
PDS—Parallel Decoupled Solution
PGC—Power Generation Company
PJM—Pennsylvania-New Jersey-Maryland Interconnection
PRR—Protocol Revision Request
PTC—Production Tax Credit
PUCT—Public Utility Commission of Texas
PURA—Public Utility Regulatory Act
QF—Qualifying Facility
QSE—Qualified Scheduling Entity
REP—Retail Electric Provider
RgDn—Regulation Down Service
RgUp—Regulation Up Service
RMR—Reliability Must Run
RPRS—Replacement Reserve Service
RRS—Responsive Reserve Service
SB7—Senate Bill 7
SCE—Schedule Control Error
SGIA—Standard Generation Interconnection Agreement
SMC—Simultaneous Real-Time Market Clearing
SMD—Standard Market Design
SWEPCO—Southwestern Electric Power Company
TCR—Transmission Congestion Right
TCRF—Transmission Cost Recovery Factor
TDSP—Transmission and/or Distribution Service Provider
TNMP—Texas-New Mexico Power Company
TXU—TXU Electric Company

WTU—West Texas Utilities Company

ZEN—Zonal-ERCOT-Nodal

***

REFERENCES

Baldick, R. 2003. Shift factors in ERCOT congestion pricing. Paper presented at PUCT workshop. 14 January, Austin, Texas. http://www.puc.state.tx.us/rules/rulemake/26376/26376.cfm.

Bergen, A. R., and V. Vittal. 2000. *Power systems analysis.* 2nd ed. Upper Saddle River, NJ: Prentice Hall.

Borenstein, S. 2001. The trouble with electricity markets (and some solutions). University of California Energy Institute POWER Paper no. PWP-081. http://www.ucei.berkeley.edu/ucei/PDF/pwp081.pdf.

Cunningham, L., R. Baldick, and M. L. Baughman. 2003. An oligopoly simulation of a restructured ERCOT: Will future prices be competitive? *The Electricity Journal* 16 (3): 59–71.

The Electric Reliability Council of Texas (ERCOT). 2001. The market guide: A guide to how the Electric Reliability Council of Texas (ERCOT) facilitates the competitive power market. http://www.ercot.com/Participants/marketoverviewinfo.htm.

———. 2002a. The ERCOT Capacity-Demand-Reserve (CDR) Report. http://www.ercot.com/tmaps/Login.cfm.

———. 2002b. Report on existing and potential electric system constraints and needs within the ERCOT region. http://www.ercot.com/tmaps/Login.cfm.

———. 2003a. ERCOT's Retail Transaction Report. http://www.ercot.com/Participants/PublicMarketInfo/RetailTransaction_reports.

———. 2003b. Market Information. http://www.ercot.com/Participants/PublicMarketInfo/PublicMarketInfo.htm.

———. 2003c. Market Participants; Members and Stakeholders. http://www.ercot.com/participants/mparticipants/mparticipants.htm; http://www.ercot.com/AboutERCOT/Members.htm.

The Federal Energy Regulatory Commission (FERC). 1996. Order number 888 final rule. Docket nos. RM95-8-000 and RM94-7-001. Washington, DC: FERC.

Hogan, W. W. 1995. To pool or not to pool: A distracting debate. *Public Utilities Fortnightly* 133 (1): 24–26.

Joskow, P. L., and J. Tirole. 2000. Transmission rights and market power on electric power networks. *RAND Journal of Economics* 31 (3): 450–87.

The North American Electric Reliability Council (NERC). 2003. Summer assessment of reliability of bulk electricity supply in North America. http://www.nerc.com/~filez/rasreports.html.

Oren, S. S. 1997. Economic inefficiency and passive transmission rights in congested electric systems with competitive generation. *Energy Journal* 18 (1): 63–83.

———. 2000. Review of the ERCOT ISO draft protocols for the ancillary services ancillary services markets. July 2000.

———. 2001. Report to the Public Utility Commission of Texas on the ERCOT proposals. February 2001.

———. 2002a. Congestion pricing and transmission rights. Paper presented at PUCT Work-shop, Elements on Market Design. 1 November, Austin, Texas.

———. 2002b. Market failure mitigation for ancillary services. Paper presented at PUCT Technical Conference. 19 July, Austin, Texas.

———. 2003a. Market-based congestion management. Paper presented at PUCT Workshop. 13 January, Austin, Texas.

———. 2003b. MOD's proposal for direct assignment of local congestion rents. Paper presented at PUCT Workshop. 14 January, Austin, Texas.

The Public Utility Commission of Texas (PUCT). 1999. Electric industry restructuring: SB7 implementation. http://www.puc.state.tx.us/electric/projects/20970/20970.cfm#general.

———. 2000. Petition of the Electric Reliability Council of Texas for approval of the ERCOT protocols, project no. 23220. http://interchange.puc.state.tx.us/WebApp/Interchange/application/dbapps/login/pgLogin.asp.

———. 2001a. The commission's 2001 report on the scope of competition in electric markets to the 77th Legislature. http://www.puc.state.tx.us/electric/reports/scope/archive.cfm.

———. 2001b. Rulemaking proceeding to revise PUC transmission rules consistent with the new ERCOT market design, project no. 23157. http://www.puc.state.tx.us/rules/rulemake/23157/23157.cfm.

———. 2001c. Rulemaking relating to price to beat, project no. 21409, order adopting new § 25.41. http://www.puc.state.tx.us/rules/rulemake/21409/21409.cfm.

———. 2002a. Application of competitive solution method to data from ERCOT ancillary capacity services. Market Oversight Division Staff Report. October 2002. http://www.puc.state.tx.us/WebApp/Interchange/Documents/24770_155_369127.pdf.

———. 2002b. Comments to commission's questions about a day-ahead market for ERCOT, project no. 26330, item no. 41. http://interchange.puc.state.tx.us/WebApp/Interchange/application/dbapps/login/pgLogin.asp.

———. 2002c. Comments to commission's questions about a day-ahead market for ERCOT, project no. 26376, item no. 39-45. http://interchange.puc.state.tx.us/WebApp/Interchange/application/dbapps/login/pgLogin.asp.

———. 2002d. Comments to workshop "Lessons Learned: Evaluation of the Performance of the ERCOT Wholesale Market." Project no. 26330. Item no. 7-25. http://interchange.puc.state.tx.us/WebApp/Interchange/application/dbapps/login/pgLogin.asp.

———. 2002e. Comments to workshop "Lessons Learned: Evaluation of the Performance of the ERCOT Wholesale Market." Project no. 26330. Item no. 19. http://interchange.puc.state.tx.us/WebApp/Interchange/application/dbapps/login/pgLogin.asp.

———. 2002f. Disclosure of information related to electricity transactions originating or terminating in Texas, project no. 26188. http://www.puc.state.tx.us/rules/rulemake/26188/26188.cfm.

———. 2002g. Lessons learned: Evaluation of the performance of the ERCOT wholesale market, project no. 26330. http://interchange.puc.state.tx.us/WebApp/Interchange/application/dbapps/filings/pgSearch.asp.

———. 2002h. A primer on wholesale market design issues. Market Oversight Division White Paper. http://interchange.puc.state.tx.us/WebApp/Interchange/Documents/26376_32_370797.PDF.

———. 2002i. PUC rulemaking on oversight of independent organizations in the competitive electric market, project no. 25959. http://www.puc.state.tx.us/rules/rulemake/25959/25959.cfm.

———. 2002j. PUC rulemaking proceeding on code of conduct for wholesale market participants, project no. 26201. http://www.puc.state.tx.us/rules/rulemake/26201/26201.cfm.

———. 2002k. Rulemaking proceeding on wholesale market design issues in the Electric Relia-

bility Council of Texas, project no. 26376. http://www.puc.state.tx.us/rules/rulemake/
26376/26376.cfm.

———. 2003a. Comments to Commission's questions about congestion management issues,
project no. 26376, item no. 79-103.

———. 2003b. The Commission's 2003 report on the scope of competition in electric markets
to the 77th Legislature. http://www.puc.state.tx.us/electric/reports/scope/index.cfm.

———. 2003c. Commission staff's response to Order 18, project no. 24770. item no. 205.
http://interchange.puc.state.tx.us/WebApp/Interchange/application/dbapps/login/
pgLogin.asp.

———. 2003d. Comparison of market design. http://www.puc.state.tx.us/rules/rulemake/
26376/010703rept.pdf.

———. 2003e. Electric business opportunities: Information for business that intend to participate in the Texas competitive retail energy market. http://www.puc.state.tx.us/electric/
business.

———. 2003f. Monthly retail electric service bill comparison for residential electric service.
http://www.puc.state.tx.us/electric/rates/RESbill.cfm.

Siddiqi, S. 2003. Superior LMP implementation with minimal changes to ERCOT market.
Paper presented at PUCT Workshop. 13–14 January, Austin, Texas. http://www.puc.state
.tx.us/rules/rulemake/26376/26376.cfm.

Stoft, S. 2002. *Power system economics.* Piscataway, NJ: IEEE Press.

Notes

Ross Baldick is professor at the University of Texas, Austin in the Department of Electrical and Computer Engineering. Hui Niu is a graduate student at the University of Texas, Austin in the Department of Electrical and Computer Engineering.

1. Restructured U.S. electricity markets identified by their independent system operators (ISOs) include the following: California ISO (CAISO); Pennsylvania-New Jersey-Maryland Interconnection (PJM); New York ISO (NYISO); ISO-New England (ISO-NE); and the Electric Reliability Council of Texas (ERCOT). The U.S. electricity markets undergoing development or changes include the following: California Market Design 2002 (MD02) and Mid-West ISO (MISO). Examples of international electricity markets are Independent Electricity Market Operator (IMO) of Ontario; Power Pool of Alberta; New Energy Trading Arrangement (NETA) of England and Wales; Nordic Power Exchange (Nord Pool); National Electricity Market (NEM) of Australia; and New Zealand Electricity Market (NZEM).

2. Affiliate means an entity who directly or indirectly owns or holds at least 5 percent of the voting securities of another entity; or an entity in a chain of successive ownership of at least 5 percent of the voting securities of another entity; or an entity that has at least 5 percent of its voting securities owned or controlled, directly or indirectly, by another entity; or an entity that has at least 5 percent of its voting securities owned or controlled, directly or indirectly, by an entity who directly or indirectly owns or controls at least 5 percent of the voting securities of another entity; or an entity in a chain of successive ownership of at least 5 percent of the voting securities of another entity; or a person who is an officer or director of another entity or of a corporation in a chain of successive ownership of at least 5 percent of the voting securities of an entity; or an entity that actually exercises substantial influence or control over the policies and actions of another entity; or any other entity determined by the PUCT to be an affiliate.

PART TWO

Policies for Successful Market Design

5

The Efficiency of Electricity Generation in the United States after Restructuring

Catherine Wolfram

Over the past eleven years, U.S. electric utilities have faced significant changes to their competitive and regulatory environments. The Energy Policy Act of 1992 opened access to transmission for nonutility generating plants. Then, beginning with California in 1996, nearly half the states passed and a smaller number enacted restructuring legislation that involved complete retail access. The industry restructuring is designed to enhance economic efficiency at all levels of operation, including distribution, transmission, generation, and retail services. The gains are likely to be largest in electric generation because generation costs are the largest component of end-use costs and restructuring has a larger impact on generation than on other segments of the electricity industry, such as transmission and distribution, which are likely to remain more heavily regulated.

The transition to new competitive and regulatory environments involves many market design challenges and potential pitfalls that other papers in this volume discuss. If restructuring does not promote economic efficiency, however, discussions about the appropriate design of restructured markets should be tabled. At the same time, any discussion about market design must also consider the likely effects on the participants' incentives to promote efficiency.

This chapter will evaluate changes in the efficiency of electric

227

generation from restructuring. It both summarizes the current state of knowledge on the topic and serves as a roadmap for future work. In the next section, I outline many of the changes brought about by restructuring, focusing on why they might affect generation efficiency. Section 2 discusses the aspects of production that could possibly be affected. Section 3 outlines some possible approaches for measuring the effects, and Section 4 discusses the existing empirical evidence. Section 5 concludes.

Why Might Restructuring Affect Generation Efficiency?

In this section, I outline several possible effects restructuring could have on generation efficiency. I begin by describing the effect of new incentives on existing plant owners. I then consider how changes in plant ownership could affect efficiency and conclude by describing how restructuring is changing which firms are building plants.

Existing Plant Owners Face New Incentives

Many investor-owned utilities (IOUs) began to see competition for their business before the Energy Policy Act of 1992. The Public Utility Regulatory Policy Act of 1978 (or PURPA) created a market for nonutility generators, specifically cogeneration facilities or plants using renewable resources. Also, initiatives to increase demand-side management led to competitive procurement processes in several states. The Energy Policy Act gave open access to transmission lines for any nonutility generator that built a new power plant in any state. In order to remain competitive and maintain market share in the face of increasing numbers of nonutility generators, the utilities may have taken steps to reduce their operating costs and improve their operating performance. For example, in Boston Edison Company's 1993 10-K, the company discusses its responses to increased competition: "The Company is responding to the current and anticipated competitive pressures with a commitment to cost control and increased operating efficiencies without sacrificing quality of service or profitability" (Boston Edison Company 1993, 6).

After 1992, the most dramatic changes to the regulatory structure came through state restructuring programs, and as the 1990s progressed, more and more companies saw restructuring legislation discussed and eventually passed in their states. The middle column of table 5.1 indicates whether a state had passed restructuring legislation as of April 2001. By way of comparison, column (1) summarizes the fraction of generating capacity in each state owned

Table 5.1. Changes to investor-owned utilities regulatory and competitive environment by state

State	Fraction of generating capacity owned by nonutility generators as of 1995	Restructuring legislation passed as of April 2001?	Number of plants divested as of December 2001
Alabama	4.6	No	0
Alaska	13.8	No	1
Arizona	1.0	Yes	0
Arkansas	4.5	Yes	0
California	20.3	Yes	29
Colorado	9.7	No	0
Connecticut	9.3	Yes	14
Delaware	7.5	Yes	7
District of Columbia	0.3	Yes	2
Florida	9.7	No	1
Georgia	5.8	No	0
Hawaii	33.5	No	0
Idaho	15.6	No	0
Illinois	2.1	Yes	37
Indiana	3.5	No	2
Iowa	3.8	No	0
Kansas	0.5	No	0
Kentucky	0.0	No	5
Louisiana	14.5	No	2
Maine	36.7	Yes	4
Maryland	3.2	Yes	19
Massachusetts	16.7	Yes	31
Michigan	12.2	Yes	0
Minnesota	6.7	No	0
Mississippi	5.1	No	0
Missouri	0.7	No	0
Montana	2.5	Yes	14
Nebraska	0.2	No	0
Nevada	12.7	Yes	0
New Hampshire	9.0	Yes	4
New Jersey	19.1	Yes	27
New Mexico	3.4	Yes	0
New York	15.7	Yes	33
North Carolina	8.2	No	0
North Dakota	0.8	No	0
Ohio	1.2	Yes	2
Oklahoma	5.8	Yes	0
Oregon	3.9	Yes	0

continued

Table 5.1. *continued*

State	Fraction of generating capacity owned by nonutility generators as of 1995	Restructuring legislation passed as of April 2001?	Number of plants divested as of December 2001
Pennsylvania	**7.3**	Yes	60
Rhode Island	**54.8**	Yes	1
South Carolina	2.3	No	0
South Dakota	0.0	No	0
Tennessee	3.5	No	0
Texas	**12.2**	Yes	0
Utah	2.7	No	0
Vermont	**6.2**	No	4
Virginia	**19.5**	Yes	3
Washington	4.4	No	2
West Virginia	3.8	No	1
Wisconsin	5.0	No	0
Wyoming	1.6	No	0

Sources: Column (1): The numerator is taken from *Electric Power Annual*, Vol. 2, table 55, U.S. Energy Information Administration (1995). The denominator is the numerator plus utility capacity from *Inventory of Power Plants: 1996*, table 17, U.S. Energy Information Administration, (1996). Column (2): Various Energy Information Administration and National Association of Regulatory Utility Commissioners publications and state public utility commission websites. See Markiewicz, Rose, and Wolfram (2004) for more details. Column (3): *Electric Power Monthly*, March (various years), "Electric Utility Plants That Have Been Sold and Reclassified as Nonutility Plants," U.S. Energy Information Administration.
Note: Bold type indicates that state has greater than median (5.1) nonutility generator capacity.

by nonutility generators as of 1995. Numbers in bold indicate that nonutility generators in that state had built more than the median share (5.1 percent) of total capacity. States with high penetration by nonutility generators, like California, Rhode Island, and Massachusetts, were also on the forefront of restructuring movements.

Restructuring has differed across states, and no one necessarily knew where it was going when it started, but I discuss several general features of restructuring programs that may change companies' incentives to operate their existing plants. Without knowing exactly what restructuring will look like, plant owners generally know that it means the end of cost-plus regulation—this is what restructuring is trying to replace. Details about what wholesale and retail markets will look like, how they will interact, and how they will contribute to IOUs' bottom lines have been the meat of the debates about restructuring.

Competitive wholesale electricity markets are the starting point for restructuring programs, formalizing and broadening the competition IOUs face for the right to sell electricity. In a typical competitive spot market, plant owners submit daily or hourly bids to supply power. An auctioneer (e.g., an independent system operator [ISO]) combines the bids into an aggregate supply schedule and intersects this schedule with a (usually vertical) demand curve to determine which units will be used to supply power. Nearly all the markets are run as uniform price auctions so that the bid of the marginal generating unit sets the price paid to all generators who have submitted winning bids. The fraction of total transactions made through the spot markets has varied across states. California reluctantly allowed companies to sign bilateral forward contracts while in other states long-term contracts are a more important component of trading. Even with extensive contracting, contract prices and dispatch decisions should be based on expected spot-market prices.[1]

The existing competitive wholesale markets are regional. Of the markets now in operation, the New England ISO is the smallest, with 2001 peak demand of 24,967 megawatts (MW), followed by the New York ISO, with 2001 peak demand of 30,982 MW, the California ISO, with 2001 peak demand of 41,155 MW, Pennsylvania, New Jersey, and Maryland (PJM), with 2001 peak demand of 54,030 MW and Texas, with 2001 peak demand of 55,201 MW. By comparison, the sum of peak demands in the United States is nearly 700,000 MW.[2]

In order to maximize the profits they earn through the wholesale market, companies want to ensure that they are operating their plants at low cost. If a plant is bid into the spot market at its marginal costs, lower costs will increase the chance that the bid will be lower than a competitor's bid, and the plant will increase its chances of being included in the dispatch schedule. Competing bids come from other IOUs in the region, government authorities like the Tennessee Valley Authority (TVA), merchant firms operating old plants and newly constructed plants, and imports from other regions. Even if it is not bidding its marginal cost (but is exercising market power), low costs yield higher profits at the market-clearing price. Similarly, companies can maximize their profits from long-term contracts by minimizing their operating costs.

In order to assess how the new competitive wholesale markets are changing generators' incentives to minimize costs, we need to think about how the dispatch was determined before restructuring. Suppliers organized themselves into regional power pools. Some of these power pools essentially worked like competitive wholesale markets and aggregated supplies to find the cost-minimizing mix of plants to meet demand. (These pools, such as the prerestructuring New England and PJM pools, are sometimes referred to as "tight.") Where power pools weren't as organized, bilateral short-term power purchase and sales agreements helped utilities minimize their production costs. If power pooling arrangements were able to mimic a wholesale market in finding the least-expensive mix of plants to meet demand, competition to sell into deregulated wholesale markets may not have much effect on the dispatch order.

What restructuring changes without question is the compensation firms receive for participating in the dispatch schedule. Under cost-plus regulation, utilities are guaranteed a service territory and regulators use reported costs to set the prices paid by the customers within the service territories. Consider an IOU that owned a cycling plant in Massachusetts and was part of the tight New England power pool. Prior to restructuring, its rates were set based on its reported costs to the regulator. Allowed fuel costs were adjusted quarterly to reflect changes in fuel procurement costs while rates were adjusted to reflect changes in operations and maintenance and capital costs during rate hearings. Given this, the company had little incentive to minimize its costs.[3] So while the power pool may have found the right mix of plants conditional on their costs, new links between costs and revenue could change firms' incentives to keep fuel, operation and maintenance, and capital costs down.

Restructuring programs have changed the way retail rates are determined and the way in which retail customers are allocated. Different states have used different approaches to linking retail rates under restructuring to the wholesale prices. Most states have implemented short-term rate freezes. These decouple the link between a utility's costs and its revenue so that now it can keep the difference between its rates and any savings it can squeeze out of its fuel costs, for instance. Some states, such as Pennsylvania, are aggressively trying to encourage entry by competitive energy suppliers to whom utilities are at risk of losing their retail customers. A utility's net position in the spot market can affect how aggressively it bids into the market, although it still maximizes profits by minimizing the cost of the energy it does sell there.

Finally, as cost-plus regulation is replaced by less-regulated wholesale markets, the political constraints faced by the plant owners change. For instance, all of the existing wholesale markets fall under the jurisdiction of the Federal Energy Regulatory Commission (FERC), so plant owners are much more beholden to federal regulators than to the local state utility commission. The FERC commissioners have different constituencies and different political agendas than state commissioners.

Existing Plants Owned and Operated by New Companies

As part of their restructuring programs, a number of states have encouraged the vertically integrated utilities to sell some or all of their generating plants. Divestitures fulfill several objectives. First, by separating the ownership of generating plants from the ownership and operation of transmission assets, divestitures alleviate fears that vertically integrated companies will operate transmission in a way that biases against competing generation owners. Also, there have been concerns that restructuring might lead to stranded costs, that is, that a plant's market value, based on prices in a restructured wholesale market, will be lower than its book value. Divestitures have been used as a means of determining the market value of assets and hence stranded costs.

Divestitures have led to a considerable turnover in plant ownership.[4] By the end of 2001, 305 plants accounting for over 156,000 MW, or nearly 20 percent of U.S. generating capacity had been transferred from utilities to merchant generators. The last column of table 5.1 lists the number of plants divested in each state. Divestitures have taken place in twenty-four states, although most of them have been in a handful of states, including Pennsylvania, New York, Massachusetts, Illinois, and California. Nearly three-quarters of the capacity has been sold to merchant generators that were unregulated subsidiaries of IOUs (Ishii 2003). For instance, while Pacific Gas & Electric Company divested most of their plants in California, their merchant subsidiary, National Energy Group, purchased plants in New England.

New merchant owners can differ from IOUs on several dimensions. First, the new owners are not vertically integrated into transmission and distribution (at least in the geographic market in which they purchase capacity), so the discussion in the previous subsection about how wholesale costs are reflected in retail rates is moot. Merchant owners earn revenue by selling into the wholesale markets and earning wholesale prices. As a result, they face clear incentives to minimize costs. On the other hand, they may also face incentives to exercise market power and raise wholesale prices. As discussed in several of the chapters in this volume, market power discussions have been central to the early experiences with restructuring.

On the cost side, the capacity reshuffling may allow owners to specialize in running a particular type of plant. Vertically integrated utilities traditionally have owned enough capacity to satisfy retail demand in their service territory. Occasionally, a given utility will be short for a while and rely on purchases from other utilities. Nonetheless, nearly all utilities hold portfolios of baseload, cycling, and peaking plants using different technologies (steam turbines, combustion turbines, combined cycle) and fuels (nuclear, coal, oil, and gas). Merchant generators are no longer constrained to meet demand in a particular geographic area and can specialize in operating particular types of plants. For example, Calpine specializes in operating natural gas-fired plants, primarily baseload combined-cycle plants. In their 2001 10-K, the company claims that they can "achieve significant operating synergies and efficiencies in fuel procurement, power marketing, and operations and maintenance" (Calpine Corporation 2001, 4).

New Electricity Generating Plants

More important over the long run than the changes at existing plants, restructuring will change how new capacity is added to the system. By making it easier for merchant power companies to sell the power from their plants, one of the primary goals of restructuring is to take the decisions about plant investments out of the hands of rate-of-return regulated companies. Some speculate that this is the source of the major benefits that will come out of restructuring. For example, Joskow (1997) states, "my sense is that the opportunities for cost savings in the United States in the medium run are significant, but not enormous. The most important opportunities for cost savings are associated with long-run investments in generating capacity" (125).

What Might Change?

Generators combine fuel, labor, materials, and capital to make electricity.[5] A single plant's cost of producing electricity is a function of the prices and amounts of each input. For instance, from a simple cost accounting perspective, a plant's costs of producing a given number of MWh over a year can be represented by the following equation:

$$C = P_F \cdot F + P_L \cdot L + P_M \cdot M + P_K \cdot K,$$

where F, L, M and K represent fuel, labor, material and capital, respectively and P_i is the price of input $i \in \{F, L, M, K\}$ measured in dollars per whatever unit is used to enumerate the respective input. For instance, if labor inputs were measured in person-hours per year, P_L would be the average hourly wage rate. C is measured in total dollars per year. Using this equation as a starting point, this section begins by considering how restructuring might affect the amount of each input used and the prices paid for each input. The end of the section goes beyond this equation to address how restructuring might change other dimensions of production, including plant-level reliability and the mix of plants used.

Inputs

A production function is a mathematical representation of the relationship between inputs and outputs. It can be used to define a production frontier, which defines the maximum possible output for any given combination of inputs. If a firm is fully using its inputs, it is on the technology or production frontier. An electric utility would *not* be on the technology frontier if, for instance, it were buying too many spare parts, and they were lying around and not contributing to the production of electricity.

Production functions describe the technological process of transforming inputs to outputs and ignore the costs of the inputs. Cost minimization assumes that, given the input costs, firms choose the mix of inputs that minimizes the costs of producing a given level of output. A firm could be on the production frontier, but not minimizing its costs if, for instance, labor were cheap relative to materials, yet a firm were using a lot of materials. Given the number of workers it was hiring and the amount of materials it was buying, it could have been producing the most possible output, but it may have been able to produce the same level of output less expensively by substituting labor for materials.

This framework helps us think about how new incentives might change the way companies produce electricity. In the face of new incentives, there are several general areas where new owners or old owners with new incentives might change their practices. Firms facing more competition might move closer to the technological frontier by figuring out how to generate the same amount of electricity with fewer inputs.[6] For example, impending restructuring may give utility management a bargaining chip they can use with unions to consolidate jobs at plants. For plants that are divested, the sales may be a way to break or weaken the union and eliminate jobs. Also, under cost-plus regulation, fuel adjustment clauses allow utilities to pass through to ratepayers all of their fuel costs, so they have little incentive to minimize the amount of fuel they burn to generate a given amount of electricity.[7]

On the other hand, new owners could at least temporarily require more inputs per MWh if intangible knowledge about running the plants cannot be transferred with the transfer of ownership. To the extent plant-specific knowledge is held by plant-level workers, the new owners may be able to avoid some of these losses by rehiring employees who have worked at the plant for some time. Similarly, restructuring may inhibit plant owners from sharing information with one another about best practices so that the diffusion of knowledge about how to operate plants optimally may be slowed.

To minimize the cost of producing a given level of output, a firm must also find the right mix of inputs given their relative costs. The ability of a firm to change the mix of inputs in response to factor prices is a function of how substitutable inputs are. For instance, if labor prices go down, a profit-maximizing plant owner may be able to hire more workers who can do maintenance to achieve lower heat rates at his plant (hence burning less fuel), but beyond a certain point, labor can no longer substitute for fuel.[8]

One noteworthy example of how restructuring might change the mix of inputs is suggested by the Averch-Johnson effect, which describes how rate-of-return regulation can bias companies in favor of capital-intensive projects (Averch and Johnson 1962). For one, regulated companies may be overusing capital at specific plants. It is also possible that rate-of-return regulation has distorted traditional IOUs' incentives to invest in the proper mix of generating plant technologies. Investments in nuclear power projects during the 1970s and 1980s, which frequently far exceeded their initial capital budgets, exemplify this notion.

Price of Inputs

Restructuring may permit utilities to lower the costs at which they procure some inputs. For labor costs, there is evidence from other formerly regulated industries that union wages fall after deregulation (Rose 1987). Older work specific to the electricity industry, however, finds that average wage levels for electricity workers are lower than wages for comparable workers in unregulated industries (Hendricks 1975, 1977).

For fuel costs, fuel adjustment clauses leave utilities little incentive to minimize the prices they pay for their fuel. As a result, utilities may overpay for flexible delivery schedules, and they may not take advantage of financial instruments to help them minimize their costs. Also, sometimes environmental compliance costs (e.g., permits) are included with fuel costs, so utilities may not take every possible step to minimize these costs. Hence, after restructuring utilities may pay lower fuel and environmental prices.

As more nonutility generators build and operate plants, the prices at which plant owners acquire capital may also change. Also, restructuring may change the rates at which utilities themselves can acquire capital. Because rate-of-return regulation all but guarantees that utilities cover their costs, they have traditionally been able to borrow money at low rates. Because nonutility generators' revenues are more at risk, investors demand higher returns. This affect is mitigated to the extent that nonutility generators can sign long-term contracts to insulate their revenue streams from adverse shocks.

To the extent that the relative levels of prices change (e.g., capital costs increase while labor costs fall), profit-maximizing plant owners will adjust the level of inputs they use, providing another reason why the level of inputs, discussed in the previous subsection, may change with restructuring.

Timing of Production — Preventative Maintenance and Forced Outages

Relaxing the assumptions embedded in the preceding framework highlights other possible changes to electricity production. For instance, the preceding discussion assumes that utilities are producing one output—MWhs. Because electricity is nonstorable, however, it makes more sense to think of electricity produced at 5 p.m. in July as a separate output from electricity produced at 5 a.m. in March. For a given plant, therefore, we care not only about how much electricity it produces but also when it produces it. Firms must decide how to balance the costs associated with taking their plant down to do maintenance against the probability that a poorly maintained plant will fail during peak-demand hours. It is likely that changes in incentives associated with restructuring change firms' assessments of the proper tradeoff although there are explanations that suggest plant owners would do more or less preventative maintenance after restructuring.

For instance, under cost-plus regulation, utilities may face strong political incentives to avoid blackouts or brownouts. They may do this both by overbuilding to maintain high reserve margins and by investing heavily in maintaining the reliability of their plants for times of peak demand. Unlike firms in restructured markets, regulated firms can pass on their maintenance costs to ratepayers. On the other hand, firms producing in restructured wholesale markets may face even stronger incentives to be available when demand peaks because this is when prices are highest. (If a firm has market power, however, it may not be optimal to have all of its capacity available even when demand levels are highest.) In order to determine the optimal balance between scheduled outages for preventative maintenance and the probability that a plant fails down the road, a firm would need to form expectations about the costs of a scheduled outage, primarily forgone wholesale-market profits in a restructured market.

Market Power

The above discussion has focused on changes in production processes at a given plant. Several of the changes associated with restructuring may change interplant or even interfirm efficiency. First, the restructured wholesale electricity markets have typically been dominated by a handful of large "strategic" sellers who face incentives to withhold capacity in order to boost the market price. Other sellers have less of an incentive to withhold capacity either because they are too small or because they are government-owned firms (e.g., Bonneville Power Administration) that do not have a clear profit-maximizing incentive. These so-called "fringe" firms are thought to sell power as long as the market price exceeds their cost. When the large, strategic firms withhold capacity and drive up the price, less efficient fringe plants find it profitable to produce. If the fringe firms' plants are less efficient than the strategic firms' plants that are withheld, the overall cost of electricity production can go up (see Borenstein, Bushnell, and Wolak 2002; Mansur 2001). Because of transmission congestion, firms may also exercise market power by withholding capacity from plants in specific locations (Borenstein, Bushnell, and Stoft 2000; Joskow and Tirole 2000).

System-Wide Investments

The Averch-Johnson effect, described previously, provides one explanation for why the overall mix of plants on the system may change with restructuring. If the Averch-Johnson effect causes utilities to overinvest in capital-intensive technologies at the plant level, the mix of plants brought online may change with restructuring. Also, if wholesale prices are high because firms are exercising market power, there may be too much new capacity built. This is because firms are building new plants to supply power that could have been supplied by existing plants in the market had firms not withheld the capacity to exercise market power. Also, Borenstein and Holland (2002) explore the relationship between the structure of retail prices and capacity investment. They start with the observation that in all restructured markets almost all customers still pay a flat per kWh rate that does not reflect real-time changes in the wholesale price. They point out that there will always be overinvestment in capacity relative to the first-best outcome with all customers on real-time prices. This occurs because customers who pay a flat rate, representing a weighted average of the time-varying (e.g., hourly) wholesale prices, are paying too little and overconsuming during peak periods when there is little excess capacity. They also show that competitive markets do not even achieve the second-best optimum that could be achieved through a specific form of cost-of-service regulation.

Increased Coordination across Plants

One of the main motivations for electricity industry restructuring is the observation that current generating plant technologies take advantage of economies of scale and have for some years (Joskow and Schmalensee 1983). As discussed previously, the fact that merchant firms buying divested plants seem to be specializing by plant type suggests that there may be further economies of scale at the firm level. In addition, the FERC appears to believe that regional coordination across firms has been incomplete and that significant gains are possible through improvements in pricing, congestion management, estimates of available transmission capability, and planning. For instance, a cheap plant in Montana may have excess generation capacity while a more expensive plant in California runs because there is incomplete coordination between the owners in Montana and California. The FERC's approach so far has been to improve market institutions through regional transmission organizations rather than to encourage geographic consolidation within firms. For instance, the Notice of Proposed Rulemaking on standard market design, the FERC's roadmap to competitive markets, states:

> The fundamental goal of the Standard Market Design requirements, in conjunction with the standardized transmission service, is to create "seamless" wholesale power markets that allow sellers to transact easily across transmission grid boundaries and that allow customers to receive the benefits of lower-cost and more reliable electric supply. For example, currently a supplier that seeks to serve load in a distant state may need to cross several utility systems or independent system operator systems (ISOs), all of which have different rules for such things as reserving and scheduling transmission and scheduling generation. This can either result in an efficient transaction not occurring at all or it can add significant time and costs to the transaction. Standard Market Design seeks to eliminate such impediments. (FERC 2002, 6–7, § 11)

How Should We Measure These Effects?

The previous section delineates several possible ways in which electricity generation efficiency could change with restructuring. On some of these issues, we already have some evidence, which I will discuss in the following section. The researchers who set out to obtain convincing empirical evidence on each of these issues face their own unique issues, although there are some common challenges that I lay out in this section.

Empirical Strategies

To determine empirically how restructuring has changed electricity generation, we need to come up with a counterfactual description of generation efficiency in the absence of restructuring. For the sake of exposition, assume we are trying to assess how restructuring has changed staffing at plants that are still owned by IOUs (i.e., at nondivested plants).[9] To answer this question, we need an estimate of staffing levels in the absence of restructuring. One obvious estimate is staffing levels prior to restructuring. We could evaluate whether staffing levels have fallen since 1992 and whether, perhaps, the rate of decline picks up as states construct and adopt their individual restructuring programs. Since, however, many other things change over time (such as information technology that makes staff obsolete or the power of unions to keep jobs), we would be confounding improvements over time that are independent of restructuring with the effects of restructuring.

Ideally, one would like to find a control group of plants with similar characteristics (fuel type, capacity, etc.) that experience exactly the same changes in unionization, technology exposure, and so on as plants in the United States faced with restructuring but are not themselves exposed to restructuring initiatives. Then, one could compare changes in staffing before 1992 at the control plants to changes at the plants facing restructuring. The difference in these two changes most likely reflects the effects of restructuring. (This approach is often referred to as difference-in-differences.) There are several possibilities for control groups, although each has its own sets of problems. For instance, if data were available, one could use plants in countries that are not currently restructuring as a control group. If, however, changes in unionization are driving changes over time in the United States but not abroad, this could be confounded with restructuring. Plants owned and operated by municipalities provide another potential control group to the extent that restructuring initiatives leave their incentives to minimize plant costs unchanged.

Another possible approach is to compare plants in states where restructuring is progressing quickly to states where it is moving more slowly with the hypothesis that utilities that do not see restructuring on their near-term horizon will be less likely to enact changes to their existing practices. Plants in the states where restructuring is moving slowly serve as the control group to pick up the effects of other changes in the United States over time. As mentioned previously, as of April 2001, twenty-three states and the District of Columbia had passed restructuring legislation. This approach is likely to underestimate the effects of restructuring as any changes due to restructuring in the slow states will be unmeasured. There are several reasons to expect employee reductions to begin as soon as managers see restructuring on the horizon (e.g., as soon as the state legislature passes a restructuring bill). First, there are a number of changes that take time to enact, so even if utilities had no immediate incentive to reduce their costs, they may have taken steps to do so immediately. For instance, if employment reductions are to be done through attrition rather than layoffs, this will take time. Second, if they anticipate that they will be selling plants, they may improve efficiency to make the plant look more attractive to potential buyers. Third, even before full retail access, utilities in some states were facing significant competition from nonutility generators (see the first column of table 5.1).

Also, for specific questions, it is possible to take advantage of other cross-sectional differences. For example, to evaluate whether changes in staffing levels depended on the political constraints faced by IOUs under regulation, one could assess whether changes in staffing varied across states where the public utility commission was more or less sympathetic to investor interests.[10]

Rather than using data from a control group to model the counterfactual outcome, one could also develop a model of the industry prerestructuring, simulate its progression through the 1990s and early 2000, and then compare actual developments to what actually happened. This is the approach taken by Newbery and Pollitt (1997) to assess the impacts of electricity industry restructuring and privatization in the United Kingdom. Also, Ishii and Yan (2002) take this approach to study investment decisions by independent power producers. The advantage of this approach is that it does not rely on constructing a control group. The disadvantage is that it relies on having a good model of the industry that captures the important forces.

The difficulties associated with describing a counterfactual are compounded for long-run investment decisions. First, we have to wait several years since the investment life cycle of plants is so long. Even after we have had several years to put merchant investors' power plant investment decisions to market tests, however, it will be difficult to assess whether they have made "better" decisions than utilities would have. This requires constructing a counterfactual description of what utilities would have built facing the same set of fuel price projections, environmental regulations, and so on.

Available Data

There are broadly four categories of data available to answer the types of questions raised in this chapter: (1) data collected under cost-plus regulation,

(2) data available from the existing competitive wholesale electricity markets, (3) data collected by environmental regulators, and (4) data from other sources.

One nice aspect of cost-plus regulation is that regulators collect detailed data on costs, including output and inputs. For instance, the FERC requires every utility to file annual operating and financial information in their FERC Form 1. The data include operating statistics such as fuel usage, number of employees, nonfuel operating expenses, total capacity factor, and many other firm- and plant-level statistics. The FERC has very clear and explicit reporting standards for this form, so subjective reporting differences between companies and across time should be minimized. Also, the FERC (formerly the Federal Power Commission) has collected data since it was created in 1935, so some trends can be tracked over a number of years. In addition to the FERC, several regulatory agencies collect data including the state public utility commissions (some of the information collected at the state level is aggregated by the National Association of Regulatory Utility Commissioners—NARUC), the Energy Information Agency (part of the Department of Energy), and the Nuclear Regulatory Commission for nuclear electric plants.

All of the existing competitive wholesale electricity markets have released publicly information on prices and total quantities transacted. Information on individual bidder's participation in the markets (e.g., their bids or their scheduled output) has generally been protected. Some markets have decided to release plant- or firm-specific bid curves that mask the identities of plants and bidders, although researchers have used other data to back out the firms' identities (Barmack 2003).

Because electricity producers are significant polluters, environmental compliance costs can comprise a significant component of their input costs. Unfortunately, environmental regulation is fragmented, so getting a handle on the costs for a given plant can involve collecting data from several regulatory bodies. For instance, plants in PJM are subject to the Environmental Protection Agency for SO_2 regulations and the Ozone Transport Commission for NO_x regulations. Fortunately, in the process of collecting information for environmental compliance, the Environmental Protection Agency collects hourly data on the fuel consumption and output of most fossil fuel–burning generating units in the country through their Continuous Emissions Monitoring System (CEMS) database. Information on inputs and outputs allows one to construct a generating unit's heat rate, one measure of short-run operating efficiency. This provides a rare level of detail on the production process.

In addition, as with any other firm or industry, data are available from Securities and Exchange Commission filings, stock market prices, and debt rating agencies.

What Do We Know Already?

This section discusses several pieces of evidence that speak to the size and importance of the various effects discussed so far. Using the framework developed above, I first consider changes to variable costs (prices for and amounts of fuel, labor, and materials) and capital costs (interest rates and capital expenditures).[11] For variable costs, I first discuss the effects of the new incentives faced by the utilities, then the effects of new ownership. The subsection on capital costs discusses these two effects but focuses on the effects of having new firms building new plants.

Variable Costs

Changes at Existing Plants by IOUs

A series of papers have used data on electric generating plants to estimate cost frontiers (see, for example, Christensen and Greene 1976; Greene 1990; Kleit and Terrell 2001). These give us some clues about how technical efficiency varies across plants and thus some indication of possible improvements. One view is that restructuring will push most plants to the frontier. Because the frontier is defined by observations on plants under cost-plus regulation, it is also possible that even the most efficient plants have room for improvement and that efficiency will improve by more than the measured inefficiency. The results suggest that under cost-plus regulation, the average plant could reduce costs by 10–15 percent by producing efficiently. Similarly, Joskow and Schmalensee (1987) find that some firms appear to be better than others at operating coal-burning power plants.

Newbery and Pollitt (1997) study the effects of the privatization and restructuring of the electricity sector in the United Kingdom. Among other things, they document significant labor force reductions although it is impossible to disentangle the extent to which this was a result of privatization as opposed to restructuring.

On the price side, electricity is the latest of a series of formerly regulated industries to go through a radical restructuring, including airlines, trucking, and telecommunications. In all of these industries, restructuring has led to wage reductions for at least some categories of worker (see Fortin and Lemieux 1997; Joskow and Rose 1987). In some industries, the wage reductions accompanying deregulation have been substantial. Rose (1987) finds that the union wage premia declined from 50 percent over nonunion wages to 30 percent over nonunion wages following deregulation of the trucking industry in the late

1970s. Early work by Hendricks (1975, 1977), however, suggested that electric utility workers earned less than their counterparts with similar job descriptions in other unregulated industries. It should be noted that while wage reductions may eventually lead to a better allocation of skilled workers across industries, the immediate effect of wage reductions is not an efficiency enhancement but rather a rent transfer from workers back to customers. No work, of which I am aware, has considered the effects of deregulation on a factor price other than labor.

In ongoing work with several coauthors, I am directly measuring whether existing plant owners have changed the amounts and prices of some inputs in response to restructuring discussions in their state (Markiewicz, Rose, and Wolfram 2004). As noted previously, restructuring initiatives have progressed at different paces in different states. We take advantage of this variation to compare how owners faced by more imminent restructuring have changed their operating practices compared to owners of plants in states where restructuring has seemed less likely. We separate states into two groups, *restructuring states* and *nonrestructuring states*, based on whether they passed restructuring legislation as of April 2001. We compare operating statistics across these groups using plant-level data from the FERC Form 1s from 1981 to 1999.[12]

Figures 5.1 to 5.3 compare employees per MW, nonfuel expenses per MW and fuel (coal) expenses per MWh at plants in restructuring states to plants in nonrestructuring states.[13] The pattern in figures 5.1 and 5.2 is most stark. Beginning in the early 1990s, plants in the restructuring states reduced their employment levels and nonfuel operating expenses relative to plants in nonrestructuring states. While average employment levels have been falling nearly every year since 1981, they began to fall faster at plants in restructuring states beginning in 1993. Average nonfuel operating expenses have risen nearly consistently in nonrestructuring states, while in restructuring states they began to fall in 1992. Notably, the first state-level initiatives to introduce restructuring occurred in late 1993 and 1994, when public utility commissions in California, Connecticut, Massachusetts, and Rhode Island began formal debates about restructuring initiatives. The results in figure 5.3 are less striking, though in our regression analysis, we analyze fuel inputs and fuel prices separately and find that there is a slightly larger reduction in coal prices at plants in restructuring states.

In Markiewicz, Rose, and Wolfram (2004) we find that the patterns depicted in figures 5.1 to 5.2—greater reductions in employment and nonfuel operating expenses at plants in restructuring states—persist when we use regression analysis to control for both time invariant plant characteristics using plant fixed effects and for time-varying plant characteristics (including

Figure 5.1. Average employees per MW in restructuring and nonrestructuring states

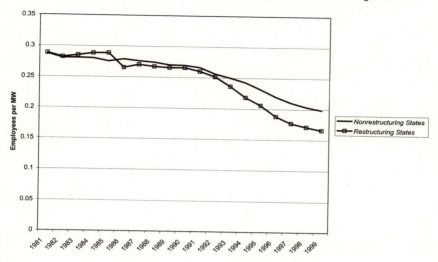

Figure 5.2. Average nonfuel expenses per MW in restructuring and nonrestructuring states

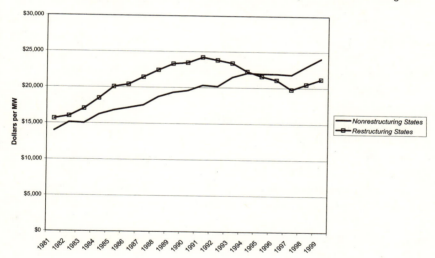

changes in nameplate capacity and the presence of environmental control technology). In addition, the regression analysis allows us to differentiate across restructuring states based on the year in which restructuring initiatives began. Generally, our results suggest that employees per MW fell by approximately 8 percent, and nonfuel operating expenses per MW fell by approxi-

Figure 5.3. Coal expenses per MWh in restructuring and nonrestructuring states

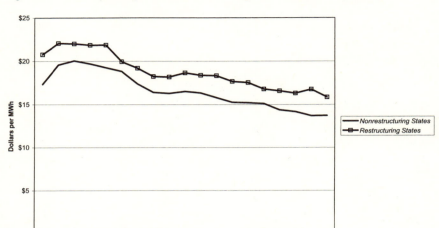

mately 14 percent following the initiation of restructuring discussions. These input reductions appear to have coincided with reductions in the plants' output, although we continue to investigate by how much.

To translate these percentage reductions into changes in costs, we need to make several assumptions. First, at the average plant in our database (750 MW), a 14 percent reduction translates into nonfuel expense savings of $2.3 million per year and an 8 percent workforce reduction amounts to fifteen employees. If total costs per employee (wages plus benefits) are $60,000, this translates into nearly $1 million. To scale this up to the industry level, note that there are nearly 800,000 MW of capacity in the United States. If every plant in the United States could achieve these savings eventually, annual industry costs would fall by $3–$4 billion.[14]

Several caveats are necessary. These are short-run effects, and it is possible that the efficiency gains could be reversed over the long run if there are reductions in knowledge sharing that affect productivity gradually over time. It is also possible, however, that longer-run effects will be more striking as firms with new incentives make investments in both human and physical capital that pay off over time. Also, as mentioned previously the price reductions are most likely simply transfers, not changes in efficiency.

One significant problem with the data set used to create figures 5.1 to 5.3 is the lack of data on plants purchased by merchant generators because they are not required to file the FERC Form 1. Merchant generators purchase existing generating capacity, often the plants that incumbents were required to divest during restructuring, and build new capacity. A potential selection problem would be of concern if the plants being purchased were either less or more efficient than other plants. One might expect that plants utilities knew they would divest were run differently before the divestiture. All regressions were also run excluding plants that did not have data through 1999 and results were consistent with those depicted in the figures.

Changes at Existing Plants by New Owners

In Bushnell and Wolfram (2004), we investigate whether plants divested to merchant generators perform differently after the divestiture. We use information from the CEMS database collected by the Environmental Protection Agency. The CEMS data are collected for all fossil-fueled power plant units that operate more than a certain number of hours a year. The data set contains hourly reports on heat input, electricity output, and pollutant output. The data provide a much finer picture of plant operations than the annual FERC Form 1 data, although they lack the comprehensive information on nonfuel inputs and fuel expenditures, and they are only available beginning in the last quarter of 1997. We analyze the data through December 2001.

We matched the CEMS data to information on divestitures taken from the "Electric Utility Plants That have Been Sold and Reclassified as Nonutility Plants" table in the Energy Information Administration (EIA), *Electric Power Monthly*, (EIA 2000, 2001, 2002). As of December 2001, divestitures have taken place in twenty-four states (see the last column of table 5.1).

We used the CEMS data to construct hourly heat rates, a measure of the heat input (measured in British Thermal Units [Btu]) used to generate a MWh of electricity. Table 5.2 reports changes in the average heat rates at plants that were divested before and after the divestiture (columns [1] and [4]) and before and after the divestiture compared to plants in the same states that weren't divested (columns [2] and [5]).[15] We report the results separately for plants divested in *market states*, which we define as states that had developed restructured wholesale markets by December 2001, and plants divested in *nonmarket states*. We do this because we believe that plants may be operated differently in states with markets, for example, because of the incentives to exercise market power. We also report results at five different points on the unit's heat-rate curve to assess whether the impact of divestitures is different at different operating levels.

The results suggest that plant heat rates improve (come down) after divestitures, and the results are particularly robust for divestitures in the market states. They suggest that when plants are operating at 40–100 percent of their capacity, plant heat rates come down by 2–2.5 percent following the divestiture.

Table 5.2. Average change in plant heat rates at divested fossil-fuel power plants

% of capacity at which plant operating	Market states			Nonmarket states		
	Change after divestiture (%)	Change after divestiture compared to nondivested plants (%)	Share of total output (%)	Change after divestiture (%)	Change after divestiture compared to nondivested plants (%)	Share of total output (%)
	(1)	(2)	(3)	(4)	(5)	(6)
0 >-20	2.6*	1.1	1.7	-13.7*	-9.5	0.2
20 >-40	0.1	-0.7	5.3	-2.7	<0.1	2.8
40 >-60	-2.0**	-2.3**	11.0	-3.3**	1.2	10.8
60 >-80	-1.9**	-2.1**	20.6	-1.4	2.7	22.4
80 >-100	-2.6**	-2.0*	61.3	-1.2	-0.2	63.4
0						

Source: Bushnell and Wolfram (2004).

Notes: Market states are those states where divestitures have taken place that also had restructured wholesale markets as of December 2001: California, Connecticut, DC, Delaware, Massachusetts, Maryland, Maine, New Hampshire, New Jersey, New York, Pennsylvania, Rhode Island, Vermont, and West Virginia. Nonmarket states are those where divestitures have taken place where no restructured wholesale market had been set up as of December 2001: Illinois, Indiana, Kentucky, Montana, Ohio, Virginia, and Washington. Share of total output is by quintile for all plants (divested and nondivested).

**Difference is statistically significant at the 1 percent level based on a test that accounts for serial correlation within a plant quintile.

*Difference is statistically significant at the 5 percent level based on a test that accounts for serial correlation within a plant quintile.

To put a dollar figure on this reduction, consider that for a plant with a heat rate of 10,000 Btu/kWh buying fuel for $4 per one million British thermal units (mmBtu; current natural gas price forecasts estimate $3–$4 per mmBtu), this implies a reduction of $1 per MWh. Columns (3) and (6) of table 5.2 demonstrate that over 90 percent of the energy is generated when plants are operating above 40 percent of their capacity. Given that total generation in the United States was 3.7 billion MWh in 2002, if every plant in the United States could achieve similar heat rate improvements, this would amount to savings of about $3.5 billion annually. This calculation assumes that divested plants were selected randomly from the population of U.S. plants and were not, for instance, particularly ripe for improvements. Also, because of data limitations, our study does not look at whether reductions in fuel use were achieved by increasing other inputs. At least anecdotally, however, there is evidence that the divested firms reduced labor inputs.

Capital Costs

Results in several papers suggest that rate-of-return regulation led to inefficient investment. For instance, a number of papers have found empirical support for the Averch-Johnson effect, including Courville (1974) and Spann (1974), although the regulatory climate considered by these papers (specifically the allowed rates of return and the willingness of commissions to disallow assets) was quite different from the one over the past twenty years.

Another way to quantify the potential reductions in capital-investment levels with restructuring is by looking at investments that were disallowed by state commissions. These were investments that the utilities expected to be able to pass on to ratepayers but which state commissions judged were not "prudently incurred" or were not "used and useful." If merchant power companies will avoid such "mistakes" (as defined ex post by state commissions), the disallowances provide a measure of the potential savings in capital-investment levels. Between 1980 and 1991, commissions disallowed $18.3 billion in nuclear plant costs and $782 million for coal and other plants (Lyons and Mayo 2000). Notably, over $4 billion of the $18 billion in nuclear disallowances were attributable to two plants, the Diablo Canyon plant in California and the Nine Mile Point 2 unit in New York (see Lyons and Mayo 2000). Nineteen billion dollars over twelve years amounts to roughly $1.6 billion per year, or 5–10 percent of annual investment in generation. If investments in nuclear power represented idiosyncratic mistakes made once by utilities during the 1980s and unlikely to be made now that most new plants use combined-cycle gas turbines, this measure overstates the likely savings going forward.

It is also instructive to think about the extent to which restructuring could affect the price of capital to firms building new plants and making capital improvements to existing plants. As table 4 in Joskow (chap. 1 in this volume) points out, most merchant generating firms currently have below investment-grade credit ratings. This is not true for most utilities. There is currently a 6 percentage point spread in yields on ten-year utility bonds with a mid-level investment-grade rating (A) compared to bonds with a rating just below investment grade (BB+).[16] This may overstate the difference in the overall weighted average cost of capital between utilities and merchant firms as utilities have less debt and more equity.

To assign a dollar value to the higher borrowing rates, we need to make an assumption about the level of investment. Over the past six years, there were on average 25,000 MW added in the United States per year (see table 2 of Joskow, chap. 1 in this volume). Assuming an approximate cost of $.5 million per MW, this represents $12.5 billion in investments per year. If the cost of capital for this $12.5 billion is 6 percentage points higher, capital costs will be higher by nearly $1 billion per year. Because the assets are long lived, however, this number escalates as merchant firms build more each year. In the long run, however, once the regulatory uncertainty gets resolved and the recent trading scandals have blown over, it is hard to see how merchant firms would continue to be rated so low. In fact, as recently as 2001, more than half the firms had investment-grade ratings. Similar to the case with the wage reductions, however, most of the increased capital costs reflect a transfer from creditors to customers rather than inefficiency. Rate-of-return regulation requires utility customers to pay for assets even if, for instance, demand is lower than expected and the asset is not used. With deregulated wholesale markets, however, creditors must bear the costs of an unused asset in the event of a default.

Dispatch Efficiency

Two papers have used data on existing wholesale markets to measure the production inefficiencies that arise when some suppliers withhold capacity to exercise market power. Production inefficiencies arise because more expensive fringe plants run to replace the withheld power. Borenstein, Bushnell, and Wolak (2002) consider the California market from June 1998 to October 2000. They estimate efficiency losses of $44 million in 1998, representing 2.6 percent of the total payments for wholesale electricity or a 3.4 percent increase over what total payments would have been had the market been perfectly competitive. For 1999 and 2000, the figures grow to $65 million and $347 million, respectively, representing 3.2 percent and 3.9 percent of the total payments or 3.8 percent or 7.1 percent increases over total payments estimated from a stylized competitive dispatch.

Using a slightly different approach, Mansur (2001) estimates higher production inefficiencies in PJM. His calculations suggest that production inefficiencies amounted to $160 million in the summer of 1999, or approximately 7.6 percent of total payments for electricity.

The FERC and other organizations have commissioned a handful of studies to measure the potential benefits of some aspect of restructuring (see, for example, Department of Energy 2003; ICF Consulting 2002). While the studies typically discuss several potential benefits of restructuring, the main analytical work in them is to simulate the benefits of improved coordination through regional transmission organizations by measuring trades that could have been made but were not under the current system. For instance, in a report prepared for the FERC, ICF Consulting used information on every generating unit connected to the transmission grid to simulate cost savings from increased interregional trading.[17] Their results suggest that savings could amount to $1–10 billion per year. The simulations do not account for some important aspects of wholesale-market operations such as the potential for plant owners to exercise market power.[18]

Conclusions

The California electricity crisis of 2000–2001 has slowed down restructuring initiatives in the United States. Also, it has focused attention on fixing market design and market structure issues believed to be at the root of the crisis. As we step back to assess the path restructuring is taking, it is useful to remind ourselves of some of the potential economic efficiency gains from restructuring. This paper lays out a framework for considering the potential changes to electricity generation efficiency. While some of the problems with competitive wholesale electricity generation markets highlighted by the California electricity crisis, such as market power, also have negative impacts on generation efficiency, this paper has outlined a number of possible avenues through which we could see gains in efficiency.

This paper focuses on changes to generation. Although transmission and distribution costs will continue to be subject to more heavy-handed regulation than generation, moves to introduce incentive-based regulation could also yield efficiency gains.

It would be convenient to have a single number to point to as the likely change in generation costs from restructuring. Unfortunately, the body of empirical evidence is still too sparse to even be able to speculate about the bottom line. In addition, the path of restructuring is still being laid. The studies I outlined in the fourth section suggest that IOUs have reduced their generating plant staff, operations and maintenance budgets, and fuel expenditures and that plants divested to merchant generators experience small improvements in their heat rates. This chapter intends to serve as a roadmap for policymakers and future researchers so that the remaining gaps in the empirical literature can be filled.

***

References

Averch, Harvey, and Leland L. Johnson. 1962. Behavior of the firm under regulatory constraint. *American Economic Review* 52 (5): 1052–69.

Barmack, Matthew. 2003. What do the ISO's public bid data reveal about the California market? *Electricity Journal* 16 (1): 63–73.

Baron, David P., and Raymond R. De Bondt. 1979. Fuel adjustment mechanisms and economic efficiency. *Journal of Industrial Economics* 27 (3): 243–61.

Borenstein, Severin, James B. Bushnell, and Steven Stoft. 2000. The competitive effects of transmission capacity in a deregulated electricity industry. *RAND Journal of Economics* 31 (2): 294–325.

Borenstein, Severin, James B. Bushnell, and Frank A. Wolak. 2002. Measuring market inefficiencies in California's restructured wholesale electricity market. *American Economic Review* 92 (5): 1376–1405.

Borenstein, Severin, and Stephen Holland. 2002. Investment efficiency in competitive electricity markets with and without time-varying retail prices. University of California Energy Institute, Center for the Study of Energy Markets. Working Paper no. 106.

Boston Edison Company. 1993. *Form 10-K.* Submitted to the Securities and Exchange Commission, March 31, 1994. http://sec.gov/edgar/searchedgar/webusers.htm.

Bushnell, James, and Catherine Wolfram. 2004. The impact of electricity generating plant divestitures on operating performance. University of California, Berkeley, Haas School of Business. Mimeograph.

Calpine Corporation. 2001. *Form 10-K.* Submitted to the Securities and Exchange Commission, March 29, 2001. http://www.sec.gov/edgar/searchedgar/webusers.htm.

Christensen, Laurits R., and William H. Greene. 1976. Economies of scale in U.S. electric power generation. *Journal of Political Economy* 84 (4): 655–76.

Courville, Leon. 1974. Regulation and efficiency in the electric utility industry. *Bell Journal of Economics and Management Science* 5:53–74.

Department of Energy. 2003. *Report to Congress: Impacts of the Federal Energy Regulatory Commission's proposal for standard market design.* April 30. Washington, DC: DOE.

Federal Energy Regulatory Commission. 2002. *Remedying undue discrimination through open access tariff and standard electricity market design: Notice of proposed rulemaking.* FERC Docket no. RM01-12-000. Washington, DC: FERC.

Fortin, Nicole M., and Thomas Lemieux. 1997. Institutional changes and rising wage inequality: Is there a linkage? *Journal of Economic Perspectives* 11 (2): 75–96.

Gollop, Frank M., and Stephen H. Karlson. 1978. The impact of the fuel adjustment mechanism on economic efficiency. *Review of Economics and Statistics* 60 (4): 574–84.

Greene, William H. 1990. A gamma-distributed stochastic frontier model. *Journal of Econometrics* 46 (1–2): 141–63.

Hendricks, Wallace. 1975. The effect of regulation on collective bargaining in electric utilities. *Bell Journal of Economics* 6 (2): 451–65.

———. 1977. Regulation and labor earnings. *Bell Journal of Economics* 8 (2): 483–96.

ICF Consulting. 2002. Economic assessment of RTO policy. Paper prepared for the Federal Energy Regulatory Commission. Washington, DC: ICF Consulting.

Ishii, Jun. 2003. From investor-owned utility to independent power producer. University of California Energy Institute, Center for the Study of Energy Markets. Working Paper no. 108.

Ishii, Jun, and Jingming Yan. 2002. The "Make or Buy" Decision in US Electricity Generation Investments. University of California Energy Institute, Center for the Study of Energy Markets, Working Paper no. 106.

Joskow, Paul L. 1997. Restructuring, competition and regulatory reform in the U.S. electricity sector. *Journal of Economic Perspectives* 11 (3): 119–38.

Joskow, Paul L., and Nancy L. Rose. 1987. The effects of economic regulation. In *Handbook of industrial organization*, Vol. 2, ed. R. Schmalensee and R. Willig, 1449–1506. New York: North Holland.

Joskow, Paul L., Nancy L. Rose, and Catherine Wolfram. 1996. Political constraints on executive compensation: Evidence for the electric utility industry. *RAND Journal of Economics* 27 (1): 165–82.

Joskow, Paul L., and Richard Schmalensee. 1983. *Markets for power.* Cambridge, MA: MIT Press.

———. 1987. The Performance of Coal-Burning Electric Generating Units in the United States: 1960–1980. *Journal of Applied Economics* 2 (2): 85–109.

Joskow, Paul L., and Jean Tirole. 2000. Transmission rights and market power on electric power networks. *RAND Journal of Economics* 31 (3): 450–87.

Kleit, Andrew N., and Dek Terrell. 2001. Measuring potential efficiency gains from deregulation of electricity generation: A Bayesian approach. *Review of Economics and Statistics* 83 (3): 523–30.

Lyons, Thomas P., and John W. Mayo. 2000. Regulatory opportunism and investment behavior: Evidence from the U.S. electric utility industry. Indiana University, Kelley School of Business and Georgetown University, McDonough School of Business. Mimeograph.

Mansur, Erin. 2001. Environmental regulation in oligopoly markets: A study of electricity markets. University of California Energy Institute. Power Working Paper no. 88.

Markiewicz, Kira, Nancy L. Rose, and Catherine Wolfram. 2004. Has restructuring improved operating efficiency at US electricity generating plants? University of California Energy Institute, Center for the Study of Energy Markets, Working Paper no. 135.

Newbery, David M., and Michael G. Pollitt. 1997. The restructuring and privatization of Britain's CEGB—Was it worth it? *Journal of Industrial Economics* 45 (3): 269–303.

Rose, Nancy L. 1987. Labor rent sharing and regulation: Evidence from the trucking industry. *Journal of Political Economy* 95 (6): 1146–78.

Spann, Robert M. 1974. Rate of return regulation and efficiency in production: An empirical test of the Averch-Johnson thesis. *Bell Journal of Economics and Management Science* 5:38–52.

U.S. Energy Information Administration. 1995. *Electric power annual: 1995.* Vol. 2. Washington, DC: U.S. EIA.

———. 1996. *Inventory of power plants: 1996.* Washington, DC: U.S. EIA.

———. 2000. *Electric Power Monthly*, March. Washington, DC: U.S. EIA.
———. 2001. *Electric Power Monthly*, March. Washington, DC: U.S. EIA.
———. 2002. *Electric Power Monthly*, March. Washington, DC: U.S. EIA.

NOTES

Catherine Wolfram is assistant professor of economics at the Haas School of Business, University of California, Berkeley, a faculty research fellow at the National Bureau of Economic Research, and a research associate at the University of California Energy Institute.

I am grateful to Jim Bushnell, Jim Griffin, Jenny Kaiser, Kira Markiewicz, Hethie Parmesano, Steve Puller, Nancy Rose, and Mike Rothkopf for valuable comments and discussions.

1. Contract prices will not equal expected spot prices if either buyers or sellers are risk averse.

2. The figures reported in this paragraph are from several sources, including websites listed on the UC Energy Institute web page (http://www.ucei.berkeley.edu/datamine/LINKS.html) and the North American Electric Reliability Council website (http://www.nerc.com/~esd/hcapdem.xls).

3. IOUs are not guaranteed recovery of every penny they spend for several reasons, including regulatory lag, reflecting the fact that firms' rates are fixed until the next rate hearing; selective performance programs, which tie companies' rates (often through the allowed cost of capital) to plant performance; and the threat that a regulator will disallow certain costs.

4. Outside the United States, electricity restructuring has accompanied privatization. Private companies face different incentives from government operators on a number of dimensions, but because privatizations don't factor into the U.S. experience, I do not discuss them here.

5. This is of course a simplification, and one could imagine other ways to categorize the inputs to electricity generation (distinguishing environmental inputs, for instance).

6. I am assuming that restructuring did not change the production function.

7. See Baron and De Bondt (1979) for a theoretical treatment of the efficiency characteristics of fuel adjustment clauses and Gollóp and Karlson (1978) for an empirical analysis.

8. Several papers report estimates of cross-price elasticities (e.g., by how much demand for labor increases when the price of fuel increases), and while the estimates vary considerably, they all suggest that fuel, labor, and materials are substitutes to some degree (see Christensen and Greene 1976; Kleit and Terrell 2001).

9. Markiewicz, Rose, and Wolfram (2004), which I discuss in the fourth section, examines this question.

10. In Joskow, Rose, and Wolfram (1996), we use measures of state commissions' attitudes toward investors to assess political constraints on executive compensation at IOUs.

11. Note that fuel, labor, materials, and capital account for roughly 55 percent, 8 percent, 22 percent, and 15 percent of generating costs, where capital here is defined as included in the rate base.

12. Plants are associated with the state in which they are regulated. A company may own a plant located in one state yet have its exclusive service territory in a different state, and that second state is the state by which we measure the restructuring policy. Some plants are owned by a company with service territories in more than one state, and some plants are owned by several companies that are regulated by different states. This creates a potential problem for allocating the plants to a particular state's deregulation policy. In separate analyses, we treat these two groups of plants independently. Our results from those analyses suggest that these issues are not affecting the differences between restructuring states and nonrestructuring states depicted in the figures.

13. This analysis assumes that firms have rational expectations regarding whether restruc-

turing legislation will be passed. Plants regulated by states that did initiate formal proceedings at some point in time but did not (as of April 2001) pass legislation are assumed to experience no influence from restructuring. Because states that have not yet passed the law are unlikely to do so for several years due to the problems experienced in California, this assumption is fair. Some states that did pass a restructuring law are in fact reconsidering the policy in light of the recent difficulties.

14. This calculation assumes nuclear plants could achieve the same reductions, although as our data set does not include nuclear plants, we have not analyzed them.

15. The reported results are based on regression specifications with unit-quintile fixed effects. For the results in columns (1) and (4) the specification only included plants that were divested at some point over the time period we analyze, and the reported changes are based on the coefficients on dummy variables equal to one after the divestiture (as our dependent variable is the log of the heat rate, we report the exponent of the coefficients minus one). The results in columns (2) and (5) include both divested and nondivested plants as well as month-year-state fixed effects.

16. See http://www.bondsonline.com/asp/corp/spreadbank.html.

17. The report is available at http://www.ferc.fed.us/Electric/RTO/mrkt-strct-comments/rtostudy_final_0226.pdf.

18. These studies take a different approach to quantifying the effects of restructuring than I have described in this chapter. Essentially, they take a "top-down" approach by plugging a number of assumptions into a big model. What I have described is more of a "bottom-up" approach that involves a number of analyses of detailed questions. The approaches are not mutually exclusive, and, ideally, the results from studies like I have described could be used to enhance the assumptions used in the simulations.

6

Looking for Trouble:
Competition Policy in the U.S. Electricity Industry

James Bushnell

Introduction

As the U.S. electricity industry has been transformed over the last twenty-five years, many of the laws and regulations that had formed the foundation of the industry's organization have become increasingly ill suited to the task of achieving the policy goals for which they were designed. The sets of laws and regulations that form competition policy in the electricity industry epitomize this trend. Competition policies have been stretched to accommodate the wide variety of market and regulatory contexts in which they have been applied. This is particularly true for market power screens, which are used to test whether a market has a sufficiently competitive structure. Procedures that had been developed primarily to review mergers and wholesale transactions between regulated, vertically integrated utilities have been applied with little change to the context of largely deregulated markets dominated by non–utility generation companies. The spectacular failure of the California market has drawn attention to the risks of this approach.

In the aftermath of the California crisis of 2000 and 2001, there has been a quiet revolution in the thinking of electricity regulators toward competition policy. In some contexts, the structural market power screens over which there had been much debate in the late 1990s are being set aside altogether in favor of more active pricing regulations to be applied by regional independent system operators (ISOs) under the rubric of market power mitigation. These policies constitute a shift in focus away from fostering a competitive structure and market *process* toward the application of regulations to specific market *outcomes*. Such a focus stands in marked contrast to the general principles governing competition policies in other industries.

This policy shift can be attributed in part to the fact that the traditional structural screens so clearly failed to achieve their purpose in California. The physical attributes of electric energy make it inherently vulnerable to the exercise of market power. If setting up a reliably competitive market structure is impossible, all that is left is to regulate prices. Yet such a reaction begs the question of whether the failure should be attributed to the professed goal of establishing a competitive structure that would require little subsequent regulation or to the specific tools that were applied to implement that concept. While California demonstrated the obsolescence of the traditional standards for a competitive market structure that were holdovers from the era of vertically integrated utilities, there were plenty of other warning signs of trouble. These warnings were largely ignored until the market was deep into crisis.

In this chapter, I describe the methods that have traditionally been applied as screens for competitiveness problems in the electricity industry, as well as some of the alternatives that appear to be much better suited to restructured electricity markets. One such alternative is the simulation of explicit market operations under various assumptions of oligopolistic competition. While there is extensive academic experience with the application of such models to electricity markets, they have had almost no impact on policymaking. Until recently, there also had been few attempts to test the veracity of such models. Evidence from Bushnell (2004) indicates that such models can provide relevant insights into the performance of electricity markets.

The richness of detail that is available from oligopoly models allows for the examination of counterfactual experiments about the impact of market structure. To demonstrate this potential, I utilize the model of Bushnell (2004) to explore the market impact of a more competitive industry structure on the California market during the summer of 2000. Such richness of detail also creates problems for policymakers. The models are much more complicated than the standardized approaches that have been applied to date. The increased sophistication of analysis creates the risk of bogging the process down in the examination of countless possible scenarios and outcomes. Increased complexity also makes it more difficult to interpret the impact of various assumptions on model results. One of the great challenges of adapting such models for policy analysis would be striking the proper balance between these considerations.

The results described here demonstrate that it is premature for policymakers to throw up their hands and abandon attempts at structural solutions to electricity-market competition. This is not to say that structural solutions are a panacea, only that their potential benefits are real enough to warrant a serious discussion about the methods that might be used to achieve more competitive market structures, the potential costs of such methods, and the potential costs of the alternative forms of regulation that are evolving as substitutes for competitive market structures.

Competition Policy in the U.S. Electricity Industry

For most industries, competition policy in the United States is generally concentrated within state and federal antitrust laws. The underlying philosophy of these laws is outlined in the Federal Sherman Act of 1890 and the Clayton Act of 1914. The focus of these acts is not on the pricing or production policies of dominant firms per se but rather on actions taken to achieve or maintain dominant status. The simple unilateral exercise of market power by a single firm is generally not subject to antitrust actions. Thus the spirit of U.S. competition policy is to *prevent* situations in which firms can exercise substantial market power, but not to regulate the behavior of firms that find themselves in dominant positions anyway.

Given this philosophy, U.S. antitrust policy has largely focused on preventing the formation of uncompetitive market structures, primarily through reviews of mergers, alliances, and joint ventures, as well as prosecuting attempts at explicit collusion between firms. Periodically there have been attempts to implement structural remedies in markets that are already dominated by a single firm, but with the exception of the AT&T case, these efforts have not met with much success.

Under the Federal Power Act (FPA) of 1935, the Federal Energy Regulatory Commission (FERC) has jurisdiction over wholesale electricity transactions and their supporting transmission arrangements and has a statutory mandate to ensure that rates meet a "just and reasonable" standard.[1] In defining its regulatory obligations in terms of pricing outcomes, rather than competitive process, the FPA gives the FERC a mandate that goes well beyond those of the antitrust authorities that oversee competition policies in other industries.[2] The FERC has wide discretion in determining a just and reasonable rate, however, and has at times chosen to define such rates in terms of the market environment from which they arose rather than in terms of pricing levels or cost-based measures.[3]

Until the late 1990s the vast majority of wholesale electricity trades were between utilities whose retail rates were regulated at the state level. Electricity policy at the FERC therefore naturally focused on the vertical relationship between generation and transmission facilities. In order to foster the development of "independent" nonutility generation, the FERC has attempted to implement a series of rulings intended to grant independent generators access to utility-owned transmission facilities. Horizontal market power concerns were much less prominent. The two areas in which horizontal market power issues were periodically addressed were in the review of mergers and the granting of "market-based" rate authority for wholesale transactions. Both of these processes involved a review of the market structure in which the subject producer would be operating. Although there was certainly large disagreement over the development and application of those structural screens, they were at their core attempts to ex ante promote a more competitive market structure. I explore the evolution of those screens in more detail in the following sections.

It is important to recognize that, until 1996, the analysis of both mergers and applications for market-based rates involved evaluating relatively incremental changes to the underlying markets. Most firms were still vertically integrated and regulated at the state level. Even the merger of large utilities produced a relatively modest impact on the wholesale markets because those markets accounted only for residual transactions, and the bulk of electricity was still produced internally by local utilities. The shortcomings of the FERC's standard analytic approaches were largely concealed by the incremental nature of these changes. The restructuring of regional markets, starting with California in 1996, changed all that. Instead of evaluating the incremental impact of market-based rate authority granted to a single utility, the FERC was now tasked with determining whether market-based rates applied to an entire regional market would produce just and reasonable outcomes. The problems with the FERC's traditional market-power screens were exposed to a dramatic extent by ensuing events in California.

Merger Review Policies at the FERC

Section 203 of the FPA provides that the FERC review all utility mergers or sales of facilities under its jurisdiction with a value in excess of $50,000. The act dictates that the FERC must determine that the proposed merger or transaction is "consistent with the public interest" before approving it.[4] In 1996, the FERC issued a policy statement intended to clarify its interpretation of the public interest standard and lay out a standardized framework for analyzing merger proposals.[5] The procedure drew heavily from the merger guidelines of the Federal Trade Commission (FTC) and Department of Justice (DOJ). In the policy statement, the FERC adopted a process for screening proposed mergers for the likelihood of anticompetitive effects.[6]

Appendix A of the policy statement outlines the procedure to be used as a horizontal market power screen. This has served as the blueprint for merger reviews in the industry since its adoption in 1996. The process involves first identifying the relevant products, then determining the geographic scope of the market for those products, and finally estimating the price impact of the proposed merger by measuring its impact on the concentration of suppliers in that geographic market. The FERC usually considered the relevant products to be nonfirm energy, short-term capacity (firm energy), and long-term capacity. These are the products most frequently traded between vertically integrated utilities in markets that have not been restructured around a market for "spot" energy, such as those in California and the northeast.

Defining Geographic Markets

The task of defining the scope of the relevant market has tended to be the most important, and therefore most contested, aspect of merger cases. The 1996 FERC policy statement describes the process of identifying a "destination" market of relevant consumers and applies a "delivered price" test to determine potential suppliers. The delivered price test includes as potential suppliers all generation units from which energy could be generated and transmitted to the destination market at a cost no more than 5 percent greater than the price in the destination market that would result if there were no merger. The delivered price test therefore boils down to an examination of whether a specific firm could profitably raise prices by 5 percent in the one target market, taking into consideration potential competition from neighboring suppliers.

The delivered price test has been criticized for its implicit assumption that firms can raise prices in the destination market without affecting prices in neighboring markets. In the absence of transmission constraints, such pricing separation is usually not the case in electricity markets (see Frankena 2001). Another problem with the delivered price test as described in the 1996 merger policy statement is that it does not give any guidance about how to deal with the potential for transmission congestion. Unlike most other markets of interest to antitrust authorities, geographic markets in electricity are determined not only by the *costs* to potential competitors of transporting their product but by their physical ability to ship it at *any* cost. In terms of potential impact on market prices, such transmission capacity constraints present a problem very different from that usually encountered in merger analysis in other industries.

In many other, durable goods, industries the type of "competitive harm" that is of concern is the ability of merging firms to sustain a modest but still significant (i.e., 5 percent) price increase. Large price increases would likely draw imports but still result in higher prices due to the higher transportation costs of those imports. In electricity, limits on transmission capacity, combined with the lack of economic storage, create circumstances in which there may be no additional competitive supply in the short term *at any price*. Such circumstances, in which a single supplier is *pivotal* (i.e., monopolizes a portion of the market demand), result in periodic extreme price increases rather than smaller increases sustained continuously over longer periods of time. Ironically, the focus on the ability to sustain small increases sometimes overlooks the more serious problem. In some cases an electricity supplier may not find it profitable to raise prices by 5 percent, but would find it profitable to raise prices by 500 percent.

The physical properties of electricity transmission carry implications both for the evaluation of firm incentives, which is discussed presently, and for the definition of a geographic market. Clearly, if transmission capacity limits power flow into a region, those limits also define the scope of the market. However, capacity limits bind only some of the time, and it is difficult to predict just how often they will be relevant. The physical properties of electricity transmission greatly complicate this task. Power is injected and withdrawn from an integrated network, rather than being "shipped" from one point to another, as in a railroad network. The actual path taken by power flows is determined by the physical characteristics of the network rather than by commercial transportation arrangements (see Schweppe, Caramanis, Tabors, and Bohn 1988).

Recognition of this problem, among others, within the FERC led to the convening of a technical conference in 1998 on the use of computer models in merger analysis (FERC 1998b). The FERC solicited comments on its proposals to utilize industry computer models to predict the impact of mergers on transmission congestion and prices. Specifically, a staff white paper outlined a proposal to utilize industry models, know as production cost models and power flow models, that optimize both the supply of power and the transportation of it, respectively. These models would help provide a more sophisticated picture of the cost of delivering power to the target market and, according to the proposal, allow for a more accurate application of the delivered price test.

While it is difficult to argue with the notion of using a computer to aid in merger analysis, the specific FERC proposals drew considerable skepticism. Many parties objected to the continued application of the delivered price test to a single "destination" market.[7] As described earlier, this amounts to an implicit assumption about the ability of the merging firms to price discriminate between submarkets. A firm that can price discriminate would potentially have more incentive to raise prices in a destination market and therefore raise more of a concern over a potential merger than if it could not price discriminate. Yet the adoption of models that simulate a market equilibrium over a much larger region implicitly assumes the opposite, that differential prices could not be sustained absent physical transmission limitations. It was argued that the delivered price test should be discarded in favor of a more global evaluation of regional price impacts.

Another set of comments was concerned with the proposal's potential to understate market power because it did not explicitly model the incentives of firms to create congestion, thereby creating smaller geographic markets (see, e.g., Borenstein, Bushnell, and Knittel 1998a). The models proposed by the FERC utilized an objective function of minimizing costs. Operating under such an objective function, the model would ascertain the least-cost set of generation available to satisfy demand and model the resulting power flows and transmission congestion accordingly. Thus the models would produce a prediction of the level of transmission congestion that would result from a perfectly competitive market, and then apply market power screens to the geographic markets produced by such models. However, to the extent that firms explicitly recognize that they can profit from creating additional congestion, such models will understate the level of congestion and produce unrealistically large geographic markets.[8]

The key problem with the 1998 proposals was that they tried to apply improved tools to a flawed process. The delivered price test has never reflected the reality of wholesale electricity markets. The focus on incremental price impacts sometimes missed the potential for far more significant, if less persistent, price impacts. The adoption of models utilizing an objective of least-cost production could understate the amount of congestion that could realistically be experienced when suppliers acted strategically. Finally, and most seriously, the proposals did not address a key shortcoming of the appendix A process, its reliance on a measure of supplier concentration, the Herfindahl-Hirschman Index (HHI) for the assessment of potential price impacts. This problem is discussed in more detail in the following section.

The Evaluation of Price Impacts

As described, the three steps to a merger analysis under the FERC's merger policy statement are the definition of the relevant products, the determination of the geographic scope of the market, and the measurement of potential price impacts on those markets. Although the greatest concern about mergers is their impacts on prices, in practice the potential market impacts are screened through the application of concentration measures. In particular, appendix A of the merger policy statement lays out explicit guidelines for the use of the HHI.[9] Unfortunately, concentration measures are very imperfect measures of potential market power, and the physical characteristics of electricity markets greatly magnify their shortcomings. The extent to which the FERC based important policy decisions upon concentration measures was one of the greatest problems with U.S. electricity competition policy in the 1990s.

The reliance upon HHIs as a screen for potential horizontal market power problems is derived from the FERC's interpretation of the FTC/DOJ merger guidelines, which also describe the application of concentration measures. Even so, the shortcomings of concentration measures are widely recognized at the FTC and DOJ, and most serious reviews of mergers go well beyond them. The FERC's merger policy, and its decisions on market-based rate authority for individual firms, by contrast, place much more importance on the HHI than do the agencies from which it was adopted.

The FERC's appendix A describes several thresholds that indicate a potential cause for concern and would trigger a call for more detailed analysis. A market with a postmerger HHI below 1,000 is considered unconcentrated, and a merger is considered unlikely to cause competitive harm regardless of the increase in HHI. A market with a postmerger HHI between 1,000 and 1,800 is considered to be moderately concentrated, and a merger that causes the HHI to increase by more than 100 would raise potential concern. A market with a postmerger HHI over 1,800 is considered to be highly concentrated, and an increase of more than 50 would potentially raise significant concerns.

Various measures of firm "size" are proposed. The two most commonly applied measures are that of *economic generating capacity*, which measures the amount of generation capacity a firm could supply to the destination market at a cost no greater than 105 percent of the estimated premerger price in that market, and *available economic generation capacity*, which subtracts a firm's internal demand obligations from its available economic capacity. This latter measure is appropriate for vertically integrated utilities that are obligated to serve their native demand at some cost-based rate. For example, a large firm with 10,000 MW of generation capacity that also has an obligation to supply power to 9,000 MW of demand is really only free to pursue wholesale sales on its "spare" 1,000 MW of generation capacity.

The application of appendix A, and related analyses are characterized as "screens" for potential competitive harm. If the screening thresholds are exceeded, then further analysis is called for. Such a practice assumes that the screen is a conservative measure that is likely to overstate the potential for market power. Thus, closer examination is warranted when the screen is triggered to reduce the likelihood of a false positive determination of competitive harm. However, these guidelines are far more likely to *understate*, rather than overstate, the potential severity of market power, at least in their application to restructured electricity markets.

Problems with Concentration Measures

The logic behind the application of concentration measures is derived from the obvious relationship between a firm's size and its ability to influence market prices. The essential question that a competition analysis is trying to answer is, what would happen to market prices if the subject firm attempted to raise offer prices or withhold its output? For a firm that is large relative to the market, any reduction in output would likely not be completely replaced by other firms. By contrast, the reduction in output by a small firm should have little impact on prices since the production could more easily be replaced by other firms. Such logic is much more persuasive in a circumstance where a product is inexpensive to store, production can be expanded relatively easily, and customers are responsive to changes in market prices.

Unfortunately, such conditions do not exist in electricity markets. Electricity, with the exception of some hydro facilities, cannot be economically stored. The lack of storage means that short-term limits on both generation and transmission capacity can create very "tight" markets, with little extra unused production capacity. Finally, while wholesale spot prices for electricity can vary significantly from hour to hour, the rates of the vast majority of end-use customers are at best adjusted annually. Thus, even if end-users were inclined to reduce their consumption in response to a price increase, they have no incentive to do so. The price increase is unlikely to show up on their bill for several months.

The problems with concentration measures under such conditions are best illustrated with an example of a tight electricity market. Consider a market with ten equal-sized producers, each with generation capacity of 1,000 MW. This would yield an unconcentrated HHI level of 1,000. If demand in this market were 5,000 MW, then any production withdrawn by a single producer would likely be nearly completely replaced from the large amount of remaining idled production. However, if demand on a hot summer day rose above 9,000 MW, then at least some production is required from *every* supplier. In other words, each supplier would be able to monopolize at least a portion of the market demand. As demand rises, each firm faces less risk that a reduction in output would be replaced by one of the other firms. In the absence of price-responsive demand, there is no market mechanism that can restrain the ability of firms to raise prices.

Importantly, appendix A declares that its guidelines are truly simply guidelines and not strict rules that would be rigidly applied. In practice, the FERC has indeed shown some flexibility in its application of its guidelines in merger proceedings. However, as will be described, similar criteria have also been applied to the granting of market-based rate authority and its application there has been more problematic. Because of the large number of requests the FERC receives for market-based rate authority, it has applied these guidelines much more literally as a screen of potential problems.

Unfortunately, while mergers have usually received more advanced scrutiny than applications for market-based rates, certain market-based rate proceedings have carried much greater risk of a false negative finding of a low potential for market power. This is because we have yet to see a merger that has significant impact on the market structure of a restructured U.S. market. Even if the FERC's merger policies bias against the finding of market power—and as a whole it is not obvious that they do, given the context in which they have been applied—the consequences of such a bias have been minimized by the fact that the merger parties have for the most part continued to be regulated by state or other authorities. As described presently, this is not the case with applications for market-based rates.

Market-Based Rate Authority

Unlike merger proceedings, proceedings over market-based rate authority have produced some of the key regulatory decisions that paved the way for the opening of restructured markets in California and the northeastern states. Many of the suppliers in these markets had no state-regulated retail load obligations. The granting of market-based rates therefore constituted the removal of the last significant regulatory constraint on the pricing practices of many of the firms in these markets. The potential consequences of a false-negative finding of low potential market power were therefore enormous. The FERC is aware of the problems with its market power screens, and has been trying to develop alternatives over the last several years. Interestingly, it appears that one of the leading alternatives is to abandon structural screens altogether in restructured markets in favor of a regime of more direct price regulation.

The FERC allows sales at market-based rates if "the seller and its affiliates do not have, or have adequately mitigated, market power in generation and transmission and cannot erect other barriers to entry."[10] For the bulk of its history, the FERC relied upon a market power screen known as the "hub-and-spoke" test for determining whether a firm was eligible to sell a given product at market-based rates. Although based upon the same principles as the appendix A merger analysis, the hub-and-spoke test applied standards that were much more favorable to the applicant.

The destination market, or hub, is defined as the applicant's home service territory, and the geographic market is defined to include all adjacent connected utilities that have filed open-access transmission tariffs with the FERC. The test then measures the ratio of the applicant's installed generation capacity divided by the capacity of all installed generation in the geographic market. It also measures the ratio of "uncommitted" capacity, where the load obligations of both the applicant and other firms are subtracted from installed capacity. If neither of these ratios exceeded 20 percent (i.e., if the applicant had less than a 20 percent share of both measures), the applicant was considered to have no market power in generation.

As described in an FERC staff white paper on the subject (see FERC 2001a), the hub-and-spoke test was developed during a period "when trading was predominantly between vertically integrated IOUs and market-based rates functioned as an incentive for vertically integrated utilities to file open access transmission tariffs into what were then largely closed and concentrated markets" (p. 1). When it was developed, the test reflected the FERC's focus on vertical concerns over horizontal ones. The horizontal screens were intentionally generous in order to provide incentives for firms to provide transmission access to outside generation sources. As observed in the white paper, "hub and spoke worked reasonably well for almost a decade when the markets were essentially vertical monopolies trading on the margin and retail loads were only partially exposed to the market" (p. 1).

By the second half of the 1990s, however, almost all utilities had filed open-access transmission tariffs with the FERC. The relevant geographic market for most applicants therefore encompassed the applicant's own control area and all adjacent ones, regardless of the transmission capacities connecting those regions. The result was a screen that almost no firms failed to pass. In markets dominated by vertically integrated, state-regulated utilities, this had little impact.

The restructured markets, however, were a different story. Because of the shortcomings of concentration measures described earlier, the test determined that firms had no market power in contexts, such as California, in which they clearly did. In the words of FERC Commissioner Massey, "the hub and spoke is much too primitive for these times. Clearly, the Commission must develop a more sophisticated approach to market analysis, and I would recommend that we proceed generically to do so" (see Massey 2000).

Beyond the Hub and Spoke

After declaring in December 2000 that the California market was "seriously flawed," producing the "potential for unjust and unreasonable rates" (see FERC 2000) despite the fact that the suppliers in the market had easily passed the hub-and-spoke screen, the commission began a search for alternative approaches to deal with market-based rate authority. In November 2001, it first applied a new screen based not on the concentration of supply but on the relationship of capacity ownership to overall demand in a market (see FERC 2001b). The new measure, called the supply margin assessment (SMA), aims to determine if a seller is a pivotal supplier of a given product in a given market. The screen is applied to the applicant's home control area. An applicant passes the screen if it controls an amount of generation that is less than the supply margin (generation in excess of load) in that control area. The measured amount of generation available to supply load in a control area includes the amount of generation available to be imported into that control area, limited by the total transfer capability (TTC) of the transmission system (i.e., the lesser of uncommitted capacity or TTC; see FERC 2001b).

Contrasted with the hub-and-spoke approach, the logic behind the SMA comes much closer to capturing the dynamics of supply competition in electricity markets. It takes explicit account of transmission capacity limits. It also considers the relationship of system capacity to peak demand, which is critical given the lack of economic storage and price-responsive demand. Despite its relative merits, however, the FERC's application of the SMA has been widely criticized (see, e.g., Morris 2002 and Hieronymus 2001).

The SMA as proposed has only been applied to markets that have not been restructured (i.e., markets without FERC-approved independent system operators, or ISOs). A firm operating in an ISO market is presumed to have its market power mitigated by its respective ISO's market power mitigation rules. Other regions tend to be dominated by large vertically integrated utilities, which are exactly the kind of firms most likely to fail the SMA test. Since such firms are still regulated at the state level, however, it is not clear what incentive such firms have to take advantage of their pivotal position. A large supplier with a concurrently large load obligation clearly has less interest in raising prices than one with no demand-side commitments. That said, firms that are allowed to "keep" some of their trading proceeds for their shareholders do have an incentive to sell their excess capacity at high prices.

For firms operating in restructured markets, the incentive question is still somewhat murky. State-regulated, vertically integrated utilities are major participants in many of these markets. Many other participants are pure generation companies or are selling power through generation affiliates that are unregulated at the state level. For these latter firms, the incentive to raise prices when the opportunity presents itself is more clear-cut. It has been argued that the application of the SMA screen is exactly backwards (see Morris 2002). Since firms in restructured markets are much more likely to behave as traditional profit-maximizing sellers, the SMA screen is much more appropriate for those markets, while it is largely irrelevant for markets dominated by players regulated at the state level.

An underlying motivation of this policy, however, is to further encourage the entry of firms into ISO-supervised markets. Just as the FERC once used market-based rate authority to encourage firms to file open-access tariffs, it can now use the same carrot to encourage firms to join ISOs or similar organizations. In those markets, the November order proposed to abandon structural screens altogether. Instead, it proposed to rely upon ISO market power mitigation rules to regulate the pricing behavior of firms and produce just and reasonable prices. This aspect of the order marked the culmination of a significant and underappreciated shift at the FERC away from policies more consistent with antitrust principles and toward a more activist regulation of market outcomes.

From Regulating Structure to Regulating Behavior

Until the height of the California crisis in November 2000, explicit competition policies at the FERC had focused on creating a competitive environment in which market mechanisms could be relied upon to produce just and reasonable prices. Under this doctrine, once a competitive environment had been created, the regulation of specific prices would no longer be necessary or desirable. This focus on the process used to create prices, rather than the specific market outcomes, was broadly similar to the philosophies applied by the federal antitrust authorities.

With the creation of the eastern ISOs, the FERC also approved the implementation of market power mitigation protocols that endowed the ISOs with limited powers to regulate the offer prices of firms. By focusing on the bidding behavior of specific firms and the impact of that behavior on prices, these measures constituted a departure from regulation based on structure.

Such measures were interpreted as limited, perhaps temporary tools, meant to deal with specific, infrequent conditions in which some part of the market would not be sufficiently competitive.[11] The forces of competition were expected to constrain prices in the vast majority of hours, and these regulations were intended as backup measures. Importantly, the California ISO did not possess a similar scope of regulatory powers. The only significant constraint on offer prices in the California market was a marketwide price cap.

In December 2000, the FERC had to address the California situation in the face of calls from many parties to revoke the market-based rate authority of sellers in that market.[12] The December 15th order from the FERC on the California market declared that the market was "dysfunctional" and as a consequence was producing rates that were not just and reasonable (see FERC 2000). The order did not identify specific parties as being at fault and did not move to revoke the market-based rate authority of any specific seller. The order did modify the price cap in the market, however, and in doing so introduced elements of cost-based regulation. The "soft cap" introduced in that order was set at $150/MWh starting in January 2001. Under the order, supply offers could be made at levels above $150 but would potentially have to be cost-justified to the FERC. By instituting a potential review of individual bids, the order signaled that the FERC was considering an approach in California that would involve at least partial regulation of specific offer prices. As it turned out, however, the scrutiny of offers made above the $150 took the form of a more flexible (and higher) marketwide price cap.[13]

Another order on April 26, 2001 (see FERC 2001c), expanded the scope of regulation of pricing behavior by firms in the western United States and also explicitly linked those regulations to conditions on market-based rate authority. In this order, the FERC identified certain anticompetitive bidding practices. The order stated that "the Commission is conditioning public utilities sellers' market-based rates to ensure that they do not engage in certain anticompetitive bidding behavior. Suppliers violating these conditions would have their rates subject to refund as well as the imposition of other conditions on their market-based rate authority." The anticompetitive bidding practices described in the order included "bids that vary with unit output in a way that is unrelated to the known performance characteristics of the unit," an example of which is "the so-called 'hockey-stick' bid where the last megawatts from a unit are bid at an excessively high price." The order also prohibited bids "that vary over time in a manner that appears unrelated to change in the unit's performance or to changes in the supply environment." Despite the apparently increased regulatory scrutiny, no firms to date have had their market-based rate authority revoked on these grounds.

The connection between market-based rate authority and specific pricing practices was further strengthened in November 2001. In a companion order to the order first applying the SMA screen to market-based rate applicants (see FERC 2001b), the FERC proposed altering *all* market-based rate tariffs to include the following provision: "As a condition of obtaining and retaining market-based rate authority, the seller is prohibited from engaging in anti-competitive behavior or the exercise of market power. The seller's market-based rate authority is subject to refunds or other remedies as may be appropriate to address any anti-competitive behavior or exercise of market power." In the order, the FERC defined anticompetitive behavior to include *physical withholding*, described as a failure "to offer output to the market during periods when the market price exceeds the supplier's full incremental costs," and *economic withholding*, described as a supply offer "at a price that is above both its full incremental costs and the market price."

Reactions to this proposal were strong and, to some extent, predictable. Sellers loudly protested the ambiguity of the behavioral standard and expressed dismay over the prospect of a potentially open-ended exposure to potential refunds (see, e.g., Williams Energy Marketing and Trading Co. 2002). Many public authorities countered that the proposed language was sufficiently specific and that limitations on the time frame for refunds would place undue pressure on the FERC and other potential investigators of market abuse (see, e.g., SMUD et al. 2002). Within the comments, however, were many signs that the FERC had overreached. The Federal Trade Commission (FTC; 2002) urged the FERC to revive its focus on structural conditions over behavioral remedies. It also cautioned that the ambiguous standards described in the order could prove unworkable to enforce. Alfred Kahn (2002) described the commission's proposal as a "substantial increase in regulation" of a "thoroughly novel kind, far more pervasive and intrusive than the institution we purport to be disassembling." He warned that the rules could "invite continuous scrutiny and second-guessing of what must inevitably be day-by-day, routine management decisions" (p. 8).

Despite the concerns raised in various comments, in November 2003 the FERC approved the incorporation of behavior rules into market-based rate tariffs and authorizations (FERC 2003). The final behavioral rules concerning market power took a much less specific form than those originally proposed. Market Behavior Rule 2 prohibits "transactions that are without a legitimate business purpose and that are intended to or foreseeably could manipulate market prices, market conditions or market rules for electric energy or electricity products." The phrase "legitimate business purposes" caused some consternation among parties to the proceeding because of its ambiguity. It is still unclear whether selling power at prices well above competitive levels is a legitimate business purpose in the eyes of the FERC. In the same order the commission states that "transactions with economic substance, in which a seller offers or provides service to a willing buyer and where value is exchanged for value, are not prohibited." This implies that transactions at high prices are not viewed as manipulation. However, the order also states that "an action or transaction which is anticompetitive (even though it may be undertaken to maximize a seller's profits), could not have a legitimate business purpose attributed to it under our rule."

While it is still not clear what kinds of actions the FERC may consider to be manipulative, this order, combined with parallel initiatives, does clearly signal that the FERC will rely upon the regulation of pricing practices and other behavior as its primary tool in implementing competition policy. Importantly, while firms participating in organized markets that are overseen by the FERC will apparently be exempted from horizontal structural screens for purposes of gaining market-based rate authority, they will not be exempted from the behavioral rules described above. To the extent that the markets that evolve from this point lack a competitive market structure, the behavioral rules contained in tariff authorization as well as the pricing regulations overseen by ISOs will be the major determinants of wholesale market prices going forward.

Standard Market Design

Most recently, policy efforts at the FERC have been directed at the implementation of a standard market design (SMD) for wholesale electricity markets (see FERC 2002). It is implied that sellers participating in markets conforming to the SMD will be granted market-based rate authority with no additional structural screens (see Breathitt 2002). The commission recognizes structural impediments to competition, in particular the "lack of price-responsive demand and generation concentration in transmission constrained" regions, but does not propose making corrections to these problems a condition for market-based rate authority. Instead, under SMD the commission would rely upon market power mitigation measures that would limit the market power of sellers by restraining their behavior.

The first element of the mitigation measures would be a "safety net" marketwide price cap that would be set at relatively high levels, such as $1,000/MWh. Another element would apply unit-specific regulation to generation deemed to possess local monopoly power due to transmission constraints. A third element would encourage, or perhaps require, long-term contracting by imposing a requirement that load-serving retail entities acquire some level of reliable generation supply commitments. A fourth element that is not de-scribed in the SMD Notice of Proposed Rule Making (NOPR) as mandatory but is strongly encouraged would be the application of some form of auto-mated mitigation procedures (AMPs). These measures apply continual screens of individual offer prices and alter the bids if an offer price exceeds some bound around a reference price level. Reference prices are usually set as some rolling average of accepted offer prices from previous hours.

The shift in policy focus from regulating structure to regulating behavior is unquestionably a significant event in the history of the industry. The rela-tive merits of this transformation will depend upon the ultimate impacts of the newly proposed regulations, both in terms of their ability to restrict the mar-ket power of suppliers and in terms of their indirect impacts on firms' behav-ior and investment choices. This topic is not the focus of this paper, but I pro-vide a brief discussion of the issues presently. A second aspect to an evaluation of these new policies is a consideration of how effective structural measures could be if they were applied with increased vigor. This is a topic explored in the following section.

Although the FERC implies that these measures may obviate the need both for structural review of firms and for imposing refund liability on sup-pliers, it is not at all certain that these measures would prove an adequate bul-wark against market power in a market with an uncompetitive structure. The aggregate impact of these mitigation measures, and particularly of AMP mea-sures, is not well understood at this time. The risks are twofold. First, they may prove to be too lax to significantly hamper market power. Both the con-tracting obligations and AMP are likely to lead to less volatile prices, but they may not lead to lower *average* prices.

Second, by adding a layer of regulation that monitors the daily transac-tions of firms, these measures could significantly distort the incentives of gen-eration and distribution firms and thereby lead to inefficient investment, op-erations, and transaction decisions. For example, a firm that expects the offer prices from one of its units to be restricted within some plausible range of the marginal operating costs of that unit may avoid efficiency-improving invest-ments in that unit. If some of that firm's units have higher marginal costs, it allows for that firm to set higher market prices while not running afoul of the mitigation measures. Although the mitigation measures contained in the SMD proposal are not the broadly phrased restrictions on the exercise of mar-ket power that had been earlier proposed for addition to market-based tariffs, they still constitute a potentially more intrusive form of regulation than tra-ditional cost-of-service regulation.

Market Structure and Competition

The previous sections have outlined a gradual but significant shift in FERC competition policy away from a focus on market structure and toward a focus on the regulation of pricing behavior. The Commission's traditional structural screen for market-based rates was widely viewed to be inadequate in the context of restructured electricity markets, and it contributed to the crisis conditions of 2000 in California. However, its attempts to refine its structural screens have not been well received either, and the commission's response has been to distance itself from the application of *any* structural screens in restructured (i.e., ISO-supervised or SMD-conforming) markets.

Given this trend, it is worthwhile to consider the alternative, a renewed and more aggressive focus on market structure in which firms in restructured markets would receive particular scrutiny, rather than blanket exemptions, when they apply for market-based rate authority. In assessing such an alternative path, one needs to confront two important questions: What kinds of structural screens should be applied, and how much of a difference could structural changes make? Models of oligopolistic competition have great potential to contribute to the analysis of the impacts of market structure on pricing outcomes in electricity markets. In this section I provide a brief overview of their application to electricity markets and utilize a specific implementation of the modeling concept to address the question of the impact of market structure on the California market during the summer of 2000.

Oligopoly Models of Electricity Markets

One of the first instances of the usage of a market simulation model in an electricity merger proceeding was the 1995 proposed merger of Wisconsin Electric Power and Northern States Power (to be called Primergy; FERC Docket no. EC95-16-000). The applicants in that case introduced a production cost model that represented the generation units in the region and modified it to examine the impact of energy price increases by the merged firm on various potential destination markets.[14] The Primergy model was an analysis of the potential profitability of incremental unilateral price increases by a single firm in a specific destination market. This was not necessarily inappropriate for the regulatory context in which the proposed merger was taking place. Such a model, however, is not capable of assessing the overall outlook for market power in a regional market featuring several unregulated producers. A model of *oligopoly* competition is required in order to provide this broader view. A few oligopoly models have appeared in regulatory proceedings. The Supply Function Equilibrium model developed by Rudkevich, Duckworth, and Rosen (1998) has been used in studies of the Wisconsin market, as well as the Western Resources Inc. and Kansas City Power & Light merger proceeding (see Rosen 1999). The Cournot model of Borenstein and Bushnell has been used to study the impact of restructuring in California and New Jersey, as well as a restructuring proposal in Wisconsin (see Borenstein, Bushnell, and Knittel 1998a,b). To date, however, there has not been a proposed merger or acquisition that would have a significant impact on the market structure in a restructured market environment.[15] Models of oligopoly competition have therefore been more appropriate for proceedings examining the granting of market-based rate authority to firms in restructured markets. Oligopoly models have not had any significant impact on such proceedings to date.

Cournot Models of Electricity Competition

The implementation of an oligopoly model involves making several important choices and assumptions, each of which can significantly impact the results. The interpretation of such models therefore requires at least an intuitive understanding of the implications of these modeling choices. Unfortunately, the more sophisticated models are often more difficult to extract such intuition from. This balance of complexity and interpretation is one of the critical trade-offs in applying oligopoly models to policy decisions.

One of the most fundamental choices to make in modeling electricity market competition is the way in which firms will compete with each other. Describing the form of competition involves defining the *strategy space* (i.e., the decision variables) from which firms can choose as well as an *equilibrium concept* that defines how firms determine which choices or strategies are the best ones for them.[16] The most basic strategy choices involve choosing either a single offer price for all one's output or a single output quantity to be sold at the market price. The former choice, price, is associated with Bertrand models of competition, and the second, quantity, is associated with Cournot models of competition.[17]

Cournot models have been widely adapted to electricity markets in the academic literature. They involve a set of firms deciding upon an output level for a given market period, based upon their knowledge of the output levels of all the other firms and assuming that the output levels of those other firms will not change. The Cournot-Nash equilibrium is the set of output levels where each firm is satisfied that its output level maximizes its profits, given the output levels of the other firms. For the most part, the application of Cournot models in electricity, as with other models, has been limited to theoretical or very stylized representations of markets. Schmalensee and Golub (1984) developed a large regional model of Cournot competition based upon actual unit-level cost data. Since restructuring in the United States was at that time on the distant horizon, the exercise was largely hypothetical. Borenstein and Bushnell (1999) modeled the proposed California market in great detail, utilizing plant-level data encompassing the western United States and Canada. The accuracy of that model in the California context is discussed in more detail in the following section. Cournot models have also been employed to simulate electricity markets in New Jersey (Borenstein, Bushnell, and Knittel 1998b), Scandinavia (Andersson and Bergman 1995), and Colombia (Garcia and Arbeláez, 2002).

Oligopoly Models and Delineation of Geographic Markets

It is widely recognized that transmission congestion contributes to market power problems by reducing the geographic scope of markets. However, it is also true that market power problems contribute to transmission congestion when strategic firms detect an advantage to withholding output, inducing congestion, and further reducing the scope of competition. Historically, when transmission congestion levels were considered at all in FERC proceedings, they were treated as exogenous states of nature. An important potential advantage of oligopoly models over concentration measures is their potential ability to predict the congestion that is caused by market power.

Modeling the impact of market power on congestion levels is a very difficult problem. Models differ on whether and how they allow for strategic firms to anticipate the impact of their decisions on congestion levels.[18] To date, I am not aware of studies that assess how well individual models have predicted specific congestion levels. While this is an important topic for future research, it is beyond the scope of the analysis described presently.

Evaluation of the Cournot Simulation Model

Despite their broad application to electricity markets in the academic literature, oligopoly models have met with substantial skepticism in the policy arena. For example, Frame and Joskow (1998) observed that they were "not aware of any significant empirical support for the Cournot model providing accurate predictions of prices in any market, let alone an electricity market." In the FERC proceedings on the use of computer models for merger review, many parties commented on the importance of benchmarking and testing of these models. However, the task of assessing the accuracy and potential usefulness of oligopoly models is complicated by the need to separate out the impacts of input assumptions from those of the modeling framework.

For example, the California market was modeled within the context of the wider western U.S. market by Borenstein and Bushnell (1999). In that paper, we estimated possible market outcomes for 2001 using 1996 vintage forecasts of such key factors as demand level, fuel prices, and hydro conditions. At the time that paper was written, even the eventual market structure in California was uncertain, as the process of plant divestitures had just begun.

To control for the impact of input assumptions, Bushnell (2003b) uses the actual California market data from Borenstein, Bushnell, and Wolak (2002; hereafter BBW) to simulate the Cournot outcomes for that market. In adapting the model of Borenstein and Bushnell (1999) to the available market data, several important modifications were made. In general, I attempted to adhere as closely as possible to the assumptions made in BBW. The details of these modeling assumptions are described in the appendix.

California Market Structure

Although much attention has been drawn to what the FERC has described as a dysfunctional California market structure and design, generation ownership in California is actually somewhat less concentrated than in New England, New York, Texas, or the Pennsylvania–New Jersey–Maryland market (PJM). Tables 6.1 and 6.2 summarize the ownership of generation in California in the summers of 1998 and 2000.

One crucial difference between California and the other restructured markets was the amount of generation owned by firms with no native load obligations. Much of the capacity in the other markets either remains owned by vertically integrated utilities or is committed to distribution companies through contracts that were imposed at the time of divestiture.[19] By the summer of 2000, almost all of the thermal generation plants in California had been divested to exempt wholesale generators (EWGs). No contractual obligations were included with those divestiture sales.

Tables 6.1 and 6.2 are therefore somewhat misleading. The two largest categories, Pacific Gas & Electric (PG&E) and "qualifying facility (QF) and other," represent supply either owned or contracted to regulated utilities. The owners of this capacity are not likely to have had an incentive to exercise market power to raise prices. This is the capacity represented in Borenstein and Bushnell (1999) as "price-taking" producers, who were expected to operate as long as the market price were greater than their operating costs. The capacity share of the largest EWG, AES, is in fact less than 10 percent of the capacity

Table 6.1. Generation ownership (MW) in California ISO: July 1998

	Fossil	Hydro	Nuke	Other	Total
AES	3,921				3,921
Calpine	487			621	1,108
Duke	2,639				2,639
Dynegy	1,635				1,635
PG&E	3,456	3,878	2,160	793	10,286
Reliant	3,698				3,698
SCE		1,164	2,150		3,314
SDG&E	1,988				1,988
QF & other	6,130	5,620		4,267	16,017
Total	23,953	10,662	4,310	5,680	44,605

Table 6.2. Generation ownership (MW) in California ISO: June 2000

	Fossil	Hydro	Nuke	Other	Total
AES	3,921				3,921
Calpine	487			621	1,108
Duke	3,343				3,343
Dynegy	2,871				2,871
PG&E	618	3,878	2,160	793	7,448
Reliant	3,698				3,698
SCE		1,164	2,150		3,314
Mirant	2,886				2,886
QF & other	6,130	5,620		4,267	16,017
Total	23,953	10,662	4,310	5,680	44,605

in the ISO. By the summer of 1999, the five largest EWGs jointly controlled roughly 17 GW of the 44.6 GW of capacity in the California market. Demand levels were such that at least some, and at times the bulk, of that 17 GW of capacity were needed to serve load. It was under those conditions that the five EWGs were able to exercise market power.

We can therefore think of modeling the strategic aspects of this market as a model of competing to serve this residual demand. By assuming that the five large EWGs follow Cournot strategies, I can calculate the expected Cournot-Nash price for each hour using the appropriate supply costs, demand levels, and import conditions. Imports into the ISO provide the price responsiveness of this residual demand. If prices are higher, imports increase and the residual demand declines.

Figure 6.1. CDFs of demand for August and September

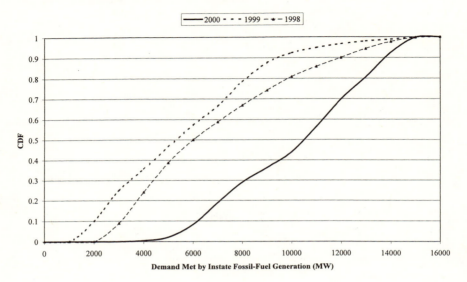

Figure 6.1, which is taken from BBW, illustrates the distribution of the demand that needed to be served by the 17 GW of capacity owned by the five Cournot firms over the summers of 1998, 1999, and 2000. Largely because of the reduction in import levels, the residual demand for this capacity was substantially higher in 2000 than in 1999.

Cournot Equilibrium Algorithm

Using the market data from BBW, I calculate a Cournot equilibrium for each hour of the summer of 2000. For each hour, I calculate the Cournot equilibrium iteratively. Using a grid-search method, the algorithm determines the profit-maximizing output for each Cournot supplier under the assumption that the production of the other Cournot suppliers is fixed. This is repeated for each Cournot firm: the first supplier sets output under the assumption that the other Cournot players will have no output, the second sets output assuming the first will maintain its output at the level that was calculated for it in the previous iteration, and so on. The process repeats, returning to each supplier with each resetting its output levels based upon the most recent output decisions of the others, until no supplier can profit from changing its output levels, given the output of the other Cournot suppliers. Thus, at the Cournot equilibrium, each firm is producing its profit-maximizing quantity given the quantities that are being produced by all other Cournot participants in the market.

At each iteration, each Cournot player faces a demand function equivalent to the market demand minus the inelastic supply from "fringe" producers from sources such as hydroelectric, nuclear, and other "must-take" production,[20] less the production quantities of all other Cournot players. In addition, market elasticity is provided by the presence of price-responsive imports. Therefore, although the market demand is initially assumed to be inelastic, imports provide an elasticity to the residual demand faced by the Cournot firms. More formally, every Cournot player i at time t faces demand

(1) $D_{it}(P) = D_t - Q_{mt} - Q_{hydro} - Q_{imp}(P) - \Sigma_{k \neq i} S_{kt}$

where D_t is the market demand in hour t, Q_{mt}, Q_{hydro}, and Q_{imp}, are, respectively, the production from must-take, hydro, and importing firms, and S_k is the production of Cournot firm k. More detail on the derivation of the import supply function is given in the appendix. The Cournot equilibrium is defined as the set of supply quantities, S_i, that maximize the profit of each Cournot producer given its demand function as expressed in equation (1).

Simulation Results

The results of these Cournot simulations for the summer of 2000 are summarized in table 6.3. As indicated in the "observations" column, not all hours were simulated, because the method for representing the price responsiveness of imports produced implausibly extreme demand elasticities for some hours in each month. The results from those hours are not included in these results. For the majority of hours where the calculation of import response produced reasonable estimates, the Cournot simulation does a pretty good job of recreating actual market outcomes. The estimates produced by the Cournot simulations, by way of contrast, are much closer to market outcomes than the counterfactual perfectly competitive price reported in the last column of table 6.3. Figures 6.2 through 6.5 illustrate a kernel regression of these same prices with respect to the residual load level for each summer month. Again, the Cournot simulation results do a reasonably good job of recreating the market outcomes. For the most part, the major deviations between the kernel fits of the California Power Exchange (PX) and Cournot prices appear where there were a few hours in which the Cournot solution reached the price cap at relatively low levels. This effect is largely driven by the slope of the import function. The Cournot spikes appear when the estimated slope of imports was greater than –5 MW/$.

Table 6.3. Cournot simulation and actual PX prices: Summer 2000

	Observations	Mean Cournot price ($/MWh)	Mean PX price ($/MWh)	Mean competitive price ($/MWh)
June	699	127.93	122.29	52.67
July	704	131.84	108.60	60.27
August	724	185.02	169.16	79.14
September	696	116.26	116.64	75.12

Figure 6.2. Actual and simulated prices, June 2000

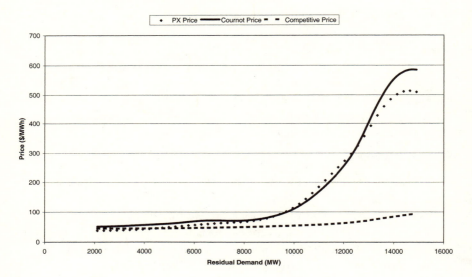

Impact of Further Divestiture

Given that the California market outcomes in 2000 resemble those produced by Cournot competition, we can employ the Cournot model to examine the potential impact of changes in the market structure. In the course of California's restructuring, some opportunities for a more competitive market structure were lost. For example, while the portfolio sales made during the spring of 1998 reduced the concentration substantially, some of the resulting portfolios were still quite substantial. Another lost opportunity was the divestiture of San Diego Gas & Electric's (SDG&E's) units. Ironically, concerns raised by antitrust authorities over the merger between Pacific Enterprises,

Figure 6.3. Actual and simulated prices, July 2000

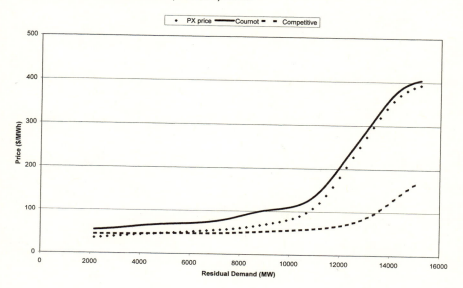

Figure 6.4. Actual and simulated prices, August 2000

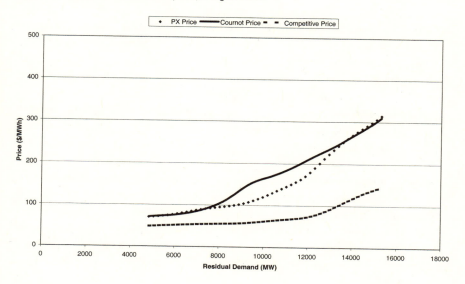

Figure 6.5. Actual and simulated prices, September 2000

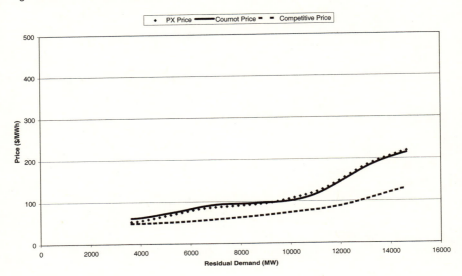

owner of Southern California Gas Co., and SDG&E initiated the sale of the SDG&E plants. The bulk of the capacity was sold to Dynegy, an existing player. The South Bay units were sold to the Port of San Diego but leased to Duke Energy, effectively increasing Duke's position in the market. Thus, concerns about the *vertical* merger between a gas company and SDG&E led to an increase in the *horizontal* concentration in the market.

I examine the question of the impact of market structure by modeling an alternative structure that, while less concentrated, is not altogether implausible given the way the divestiture process played out in California. I model the ownership pattern summarized in table 6.4. This assumes that the SDG&E units bought by Dynegy were instead sold to an unregulated new entrant and that the South Bay units were operated by the Port of San Diego independently as a strategic asset. I also reduce the AES and Reliant portfolios, distributing the large Alamitos and Ormond Beach units each to new entrants. Last, I separate the Moss Landing units from the remaining Duke portfolio. Table 6.4 also calculates the HHI for just this portion of California's capacity. Measured this way, the actual structure is "concentrated," while the new structure falls just above the "unconcentrated" range.

I utilize this new ownership structure to again simulate the summer

Table 6.4. Actual and hypothetical thermal ownership

	Actual		Counterfactual	
	MW	HHI	MW	HHI
AES	3,921	550	1,873	126
Dynegy	2,871	295	1,165	49
Duke	3,343	400	1,585	90
Mirant	2,886	298	2,886	298
Reliant	3,698	489	2,306	190
SDG&E units	n.a.	n.a.	1,407	71
Alamitos	n.a.	n.a.	2,048	150
Ormond	n.a.	n.a.	1,271	58
Moss	n.a.	n.a.	1,474	78
South Bay	n.a.	n.a.	704	18
Total	16,718	2,032	16,718	1,126

Note: n.a. = not applicable.

months of 2000 using the Cournot model. Table 6.5 lists the monthly average Cournot prices resulting from the current market structure and the hypothetical less concentrated one, along with the competitive price, for the summer of 2000. Although prices still remained considerably above competitive levels, the further divestitures lowered Cournot equilibrium prices by an average of about $31/MWh in these four months.

To gain further insight into the hypothetical benefits of less supply concentration, I calculated the aggregate costs of market power during this period, as well as the differential impact of the further divestiture. I employ the same calculation as in BBW. This calculation takes the difference between overall ISO demand and production from must-take resources that earned regulated, rather than market, prices. This difference represents the volume being purchased through the various short-term markets that operated in California during this time period. This volume is then multiplied by the market price. These results are summarized in table 6.6. The differential savings from the further divestiture total over $1.8 billion over this four-month period. This can be compared to the estimated $4.45 billion cost of market power for this period calculated from the Cournot equilibrium and the $4 billion cost of market power calculated from actual prices in BBW. Thus, to the extent the Cournot simulations are reliable estimators of market impacts, the hypothetical divestiture reduces the cost of market power by about 40 percent.

Table 6.5. Price impacts of divestiture (in $/MWh)

	Cournot	Divest to Cournot	Contract/divest to fringe price	Competitive price
June	127.93	98.40	88.95	52.67
July	131.84	102.09	89.99	60.27
August	185.02	144.18	126.63	79.14
September	116.26	91.30	78.74	75.12

Table 6.6. Market savings from further divestiture (in $millions)

	Total cost Cournot	Total cost divest to Cournot	Total cost savings
June	1,870	1,410	466
July	1,830	1,420	415
August	2,800	2,190	605
September	1,570	1,230	341
Total	8,070	6,250	1,827

The Impact of Contracts or Utility Ownership of Divested Units

The second column of table 6.5 reports the impact of further divestiture, assuming that the new owners acted as profit-maximizing Cournot firms. An alternative scenario to consider involves changing the incentives of the owners of this new set of divested units. Indeed, Bushnell, Mansur, and Saravia (2004) find that the extent of vertical arrangements (contracts and vertical integration) between generation and distribution utilities accounts for the most of the differences in the competitive performance of the California market and those in the eastern United States. I therefore examine the resulting market impact of having this second set of generation units acting as price-taking firms. That is to say, these units are assumed to operate as long as the market price exceeds the marginal costs of operation. Such a change in the objectives of these units' owners could have arisen from two alternative sets of actions: the retention of this generation by the regulated utilities (who found themselves to be net buyers in the market), or the commitment of these units to a long-term, dispatchable, contract. It is a rough approximation to describe the operation of either utility owned or contracted units as price taking, but this approximation better fits the incentives of such units' owners than does an assumption of profit-maximizing Cournot behavior.[21]

As the third column of table 6.5 indicates, market power is greatly reduced under an assumption that the newly divested units are operated as price takers, much more than when they were divested to Cournot firms.[22] Although the savings implied by such a result are seductive, one must consider the full implications of the assumptions that underlie it. Neither scenario, contracting or utility ownership, really represents an equilibrium situation, and both carry potentially substantial costs *outside* of the spot market. The cost neither of utility ownership nor, more important, of the long-term contracts is represented in this model. The contracts negotiated by the state of California were likely a major contributor to reducing market power in the spot market during the summer of 2001, but they were also notoriously expensive (see Wolak, chap. 3 in this volume). There is much theory to support the notion that the existence of a robust forward market, with contracts freely entered into by suppliers and load-serving entities, will produce more competitive outcomes than would be achieved through the spot market alone. However, I make no attempt here to calculate what the long-term equilibrium of such a forward-spot interaction would yield. These results only indicate that, given a certain exogenously specified level of contracting, spot market outcomes would be more competitive.

Impact of Demand Elasticity

Up to this point, the only source of elasticity in the residual demand function faced by the Cournot producers has been provided by price-responsive import quantities. End-use demand for electricity has been assumed to be perfectly inelastic, reflecting the fact that, outside of the San Diego region, retail rates were frozen during the time period studied. In order to examine the potential impact of price-responsive demand on the market power of producers, in this section I incorporate price-responsive demand into the model. I now represent system demand in the ISO as following a constant elasticity demand function, with an elasticity of $-.075$. This is somewhat lower than many estimates of the short-run elasticity of demand for electricity, but very few of the available studies have examined an environment in which prices change hourly.[23] Such a response could potentially be achieved by applying real-time pricing to all customers. To the extent that the underlying potential elasticity of large customers were greater than .075, this figure could also be achieved by applying real-time pricing to this more elastic subset of customers.[24]

Figure 6.6 illustrates the methodology for modeling demand. Whereas before the demand function was the linear function, D_1, demand in this sec-

Figure 6.6. Modeling rate increase and RTP

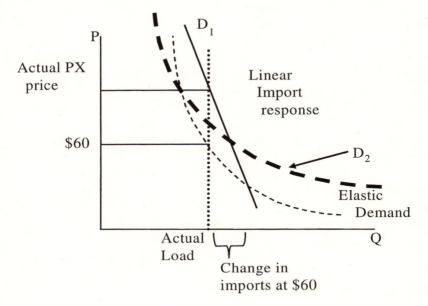

tion combines the change in imports (relative to the level observed at the actual PX price) with the change in end-use demand implied by the constant elasticity demand function. For each hour, this function is centered on the point of actual ISO load at a price of $60/MWh, roughly the energy component of end-use bills during that time. The resulting market demand is therefore D_2, the combination of the previously utilized linear demand function and the constant elasticity demand function.

Since all demand is assumed to be paying the current wholesale price, the changes introduced by this model therefore combine the effect of time-varying pricing with the effect of an overall increase in the average price. I attempt to separate out these two effects later by also modeling the impact of a rate increase that is applied evenly to all periods, assuming the same .075 elasticity. This latter model therefore shifts overall demand inward but does not change the slope of the demand function.

The results of these simulations are described in table 6.7. The impact of even a modest level of elasticity is substantial when it is applied to the entire system load on an hourly basis. The average wholesale price during this period is reduced from $144.32/MWh under the base Cournot simulation to $85.25/MWh. By contrast, the impact on wholesale prices of the same rate in-

Table 6.7. Price impacts from changes in retail rates (in $/MWh)

	Inelastic demand	Real-time pricing	Constant rate increase
June	127.93	72.47	122.26
July	131.84	79.04	124.23
August	185.02	107.98	175.15
September	116.26	80.66	107.21

Figure 6.7. Impact of rate increase versus real-time pricing, Summer 2000 (all months)

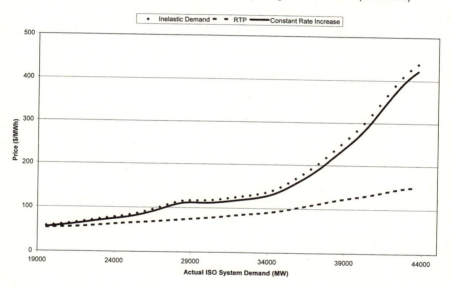

crease (to $85.25/MWh) is minimal when it is applied evenly to all periods. Figure 6.7 illustrates the relationship between the price impacts and the actual (i.e., inelastic) load. The conventional rate increase creates modest savings at high demand levels, but these savings pale in comparison to those achieved under real-time pricing. This highlights the fact that retail rate reform involves much more than simply passing on wholesale prices on a lagged basis. Although a rate increase during this period might have kept the California utilities financially viable and therefore eliminated the prospect of blackouts, it would not have had a substantial impact on the competitiveness of the market during this period.[25]

Conclusions

This paper has described the use of competitive assessments in implementing competition policy in the U.S. electricity industry. At the federal level, these policies have always been driven by the FERC. The FPA provides the FERC a powerful platform from which it can pursue its policy goals. The complex web of overlapping regulation and jurisdictional battles between the FERC and state regulators does constrain the Commission's ability to develop wholesale power markets in the manner it would prefer. The FERC has limited explicit powers to force structural changes, such as the development of price-responsive consumers and the reduction in supplier concentration. However, the preeminent role played by the FERC in the approval of electricity mergers and in the granting of market-based rate authority also gives it the ability to influence firms with both carrots and sticks.

In the past, these tools have been employed to encourage firms to undertake various reforms aimed at reducing vertical barriers to competition in the industry. The FERC's current proposals are consistent with this practice. The application of a potentially more restrictive market power hurdle for market-based rate authority, the SMA, has been restricted to firms that do not participate in ISO-supervised markets. This provides suppliers with additional incentive to join ISOs. The FERC's SMD proposals appear consistent with this trend. The threat of structural changes is being employed as a stick to encourage firms to submit to the regulation of their offer prices and other market power mitigation measures.

But is the carrot leading the mule in the right direction? The focus on ISOs and market power mitigation under SMD creates the danger of confusing ends and means. Competition policy in the United States has been predicated on the goal of creating a reasonably competitive environment. By contrast, current policies at the FERC have been increasingly focused on regulating behaviors and outcomes. Should a competitive assessment of market structure be used as the stick to implement pricing regulations, or should pricing regulations be used as the stick to encourage structural changes? The answer depends both on the consequences of the regulations and on the prospects for and benefits of structural change.

I examine this question in the context of the California market. By employing the oligopoly model first developed in Borenstein and Bushnell (1999), I study the ability of oligopoly simulations to recreate actual market outcomes. This gives some indication of the potential value of such models as screens for the impact of horizontal market power. I then utilize the oligopoly model to examine the impact of a hypothetical, less concentrated, California market structure. The results provide some fodder for both sides of the argument. The model indicates that additional divestiture of generation units would have yielded a savings of nearly $2 billion during the four summer months of 2000 in California. However, this constitutes less than half of the costs of market power from the current structure indicated by the oligopoly model and by empirical estimates using actual market outcomes. The savings from introducing real-time pricing into the market during this period are even more striking. Even a relatively modest elasticity of .075, when applied to the entire system demand through a dynamic pricing regime, reduces wholesale prices by 40 percent.

Clearly the gains are substantial, but are they enough to justify a reversal of emphasis away from mitigation measures and toward structural change? The fact that the simulations indicate that nontrivial levels of market power remain even under the structural changes examined gives cause for caution. However, the California market in 2000 is almost universally considered a worst-case scenario for electricity markets. Supply-side structural change, when combined with a robust forward market and large end users with dynamic prices, would go a long way toward obviating the need for most regulation of pricing behavior.

In weighing such changes, we must consider that the benefits likely far outweigh the costs. While the economies of scale of individual generation plants and of vertically integrated utilities have been extensively studied, there is little evidence about the potential efficiencies to be gleaned, for example, from owning a 6,000 MW portfolio as opposed to a 3,000 MW portfolio. Dynamic real-time pricing carries the potential for substantial efficiency improvement even if its impact on market power is ignored. The main impediment to such changes appears to be the fact that no institution has the clear mandate or jurisdiction to make them a reality. By virtue of its unique position in directing policies in wholesale markets, the FERC comes the closest. The results in this paper indicate that the FERC should reconsider its emphasis on pricing regulation and direct more of its focus to being an agent for structural change.

Appendix A

A Cournot Model of the California Electricity Market

In this appendix, I describe the model and assumptions used to generate the results of section 6.3. The model is described in more detail in Bushnell (2003a). The Cournot model utilized is based upon that of Borenstein and

Bushnell (1999). It uses an iterative global search algorithm to calculate the profit-maximizing best response output quantity for each firm. At each iteration, the optimal output level for a given firm is calculated, holding constant the output levels of the other strategic firms. The process iterates through each strategic firm and then repeats itself. A Cournot-Nash equilibrium is found when each firm, given the output levels of the other firms, does not change its output. The model of Borenstein and Bushnell was adjusted to incorporate the hourly market data from the California market. These data are drawn from BBW.

Market Demand

As in BBW, the Cournot simulation models competition for the residual demand served by fossil-fired generation plants located within the California ISO system. All of the divested generation plants fall into this category. This residual portion is equivalent to the total ISO system demand less the output from hydro and geothermal resources, as well as from must-take resources operating under regulatory or contractual arrangements. Supply from units in this latter category is assumed to be inelastic because the majority of the revenues earned by these plants were not tied to market prices. End-use demand is assumed to be inelastic.

Imports into the California ISO comprise the source of residual demand elasticity faced by the Cournot producers within the ISO. In BBW, the import elasticity is taken from the day-ahead adjustment bids of import schedules. Although these bids constitute a reasonable estimate of the overall responsiveness of imports to price changes in a given hour, it is not reasonable to expect that the depth of that import supply curve represents the overall availability of import capacity into the California ISO. This is because the day-ahead adjustment bids only represent offers into the day-ahead markets, while there were other venues for trades, most notably the ISO real-time market.

To integrate the import responsiveness from BBW into a Cournot simulation, I derive an hour-by-hour slope of the import demand curve from the measured change in import quantities and the change in price between the actual market outcomes and the counterfactual competitive outcome estimated in BBW.[26] I then derived a linear residual demand curve for each hour by applying that slope to a linear demand curve running through the observed actual market price and quantity.[27] The statistics on these import calculations are summarized below.

As table 6A.1 illustrates, taking the import slopes from the BBW calculation yields a few extremely small and large values. In fact, there were approx-

Table 6A.1. Import summary statistics

	Actual net imports	Slope (−ΔMW/Δ$)			
		Mean	Median	Min	Max
June	3,943	153.89	61.74	1.7E–13	2.9E+04
July	3,321	70.63	40.24	4.0E–14	2.7E+03
August	3,096	36.91	18.66	1.1E–12	1.8E+03
September	4,240	57.88	26.15	3.4E–04	2.2E+03

imately forty hours in which the BBW results implied a negative slope. These extreme results were all the result of extremely small changes in either price or import quantity (or both) in the BBW calculation for that hour. Since the calculated changes in price and import quantity are both the average of the results of 100 Monte Carlo iterations, aberrant values can result in individual hours in which the price change was small. As one would expect, these extreme slopes produced extreme values for both the Cournot and competitive prices. Since these are driven by the import slopes and not by the underlying model, I report only the results for hours when the calculated import slopes were between −1 and −1,000 MW/$. These account for 2,790 of the possible 2,928 hours in the study period. The main distinguishing feature of the dropped hours is that they were low-price, competitive hours. The mean PX price in the dropped hours was about $55/MWh (as opposed to $128/MWh for the full sample), and the mean estimate of the margin over the competitive price from BBW for those hours was less than $2/MWh (as opposed to $62/MWh for the full sample).

Thermal Generation

The marginal costs of thermal generation units are modeled exactly as they were in BBW. Unit average heat rates (Mbtu/kwh) are multiplied by appropriate fuel prices ($/Mbtu) that are updated daily for natural gas and monthly for petroleum-based fuels. Where appropriate, emission rates for nitrogen oxide (NOx) are multiplied by the monthly average price for NOx emissions credits.[28] Unit variable operating and maintenance expenses are the same as in BBW. The generation capacity of each unit is reduced according to its forced outage factor, effectively reducing the available capacity of each unit by the same level in each hour. This is in contrast to BBW, where unit availability was modeled using Monte Carlo simulation draws for each hour using the same respective forced outage factors for each unit.

***

References

Andersson, B., and L. Bergman. 1995. Market structure and the price of electricity: An ex ante analysis of deregulated Swedish markets. *The Energy Journal* 16 (2): 97–110.

Baldick, R., R. Grant, and E. Kahn. 2000. Linear supply function equilibrium: Generalizations, application, and limitations. POWER Working Paper no. PWP-078. Berkeley, CA: University of California Energy Institute.

Blumstein, C., L. S. Friedman, and R. J. Green. 2002. The history of electricity restructuring in California. *Journal of Industry Competition and Trade* 2 (1–2): 1–15.

Borenstein, S., and J. B. Bushnell. 1999. An empirical analysis of the potential for market power in a deregulated California electricity industry. *Journal of Industrial Economics* 47 (3): 285–323.

Borenstein, S., J. B. Bushnell, and C. R. Knittel. 1998a. Comments on the use of computer models for merger analysis in the electricity industry. FERC Docket no. PL98-6-000. Washington, DC: Federal Energy Regulatory Commission.

———. 1998b. Review of GPU's restructuring petition, final report. Appendix A, Docket no. EA97060396. Trenton, NJ: New Jersey Board of Public Utilities.

———. 1999. Market power in electricity markets: Beyond concentration measures. *The Energy Journal* 20 (4): 65–88.

Borenstein, S., J. B. Bushnell, and S. Stoft. 2000. The competitive effects of transmission capacity in a deregulated electricity industry. *RAND Journal of Economics* 31 (2): 294–325.

Borenstein, S., J. B. Bushnell, and F. Wolak. 2002. Measuring market inefficiencies in California's deregulated electricity industry. *American Economic Review* 92 (5): 1376–1405.

Breathitt, L. 2002. Concurring opinion: Standard market design and structure Notice of Proposed Rulemaking. FERC Docket no. RM01-12-000. Washington, DC: Federal Energy Regulatory Commission.

Bushnell, J. B. 2003a. Market structure and competition in electricity markets. University of California Energy Institute. Mimeograph.

———. 2003b. A mixed complementarity model of hydro-thermal competition in the Western U.S. *Operations Research* 51 (1): 80–94.

———. 2004. How accurate are oligopoly models of electricity markets? University of California Energy Institute. Mimeograph.

Bushnell, J. B., and E. Mansur. 2003. Consumption under noisy price signals: A study of electricity retail rates in San Diego. CSEM Working Paper no. 110. Berkeley, CA: University of California Energy Institute, Center for the Study of Energy Markets.

Bushnell, J. B., E. Mansur, and C. Saravia. 2004. Market structure and competition: A cross-market analysis of U.S. electricity restructuring. CSEM Working Paper no. 126. Berkeley, CA: University of California Energy Institute, Center for the Study of Energy Markets.

Cardell, J. B., C. C. Hitt, and W. W. Hogan. 1997. Market power and strategic interaction in electricity networks. *Resources and Energy Economics* 19:109–37.

Carlton, D., and J. Perloff. 1990. *Modern industrial organization.* Boston: Addison Wesley.

Day, C. J., B. F. Hobbs, and J.-S. Pang. 2002. Oligopolistic competition in power networks: A conjectured supply function approach. *IEEE Transactions Power Systems* 17 (3): 597–607.

Edison Electric Institute (EEI). 2002. Comments of the Edison Electric Institute and the Alliance of Energy Suppliers on order establishing refund effective date and proposing to revise market-based rate tariffs and authorizations. Docket no. EL01-118-000. Washington, DC: FERC.

Federal Energy Regulatory Commission (FERC). 1996. Order no. 592. Inquiry concerning the commission's merger policy under the Federal Power Act: Policy statement. Docket no. RM96-6-000. Washington, DC: FERC.

————. 1998a. AES Huntington Beach, LLC: Order accepting for filing proposed market-based rates and denying request for waiver of filing requirement. Docket no. ER98-2184-000. Washington, DC: FERC, April.

————. 1998b. Notice of request for written comments and intent to convene a technical conference: Inquiry concerning the commission's policy on the use of computer models in merger analysis. Docket no. PL98-6-000. Washington, DC: FERC.

————. 2000. Order directing remedies for California wholesale electricity markets. Docket no. EL00-95-000. Washington, DC: FERC, December.

————. 2001a. Market-based rate options paper. Washington, DC: FERC, September. Available at http://www.ferc.fed/us/calendar/commissionmeetings/discussion_papers/9-26-01/Public.pdf.

————. 2001b. Order directing sellers to provide refunds of excess amounts charged for certain electric energy sales during January 2001 or, alternatively, to provide further cost or other justification for such charges. Docket no. EL00-95-017. Washington, DC: FERC, March.

————. 2001c. Order establishing prospective mitigation and monitoring plan for the California wholesale electricity markets and establishing an investigation of public utility rates in wholesale Western energy markets. Docket no. EL00-95-012. Washington, DC: FERC, April.

————. 2001d. Order establishing refund effective date and proposing to revise market-based rate tariffs and authorizations. Docket no. EL01-118-000. Washington, DC: FERC, November.

————. 2001e. Order on triennial market power updates and announcing new, interim generation market power screen and mitigation policy. Docket no. ER96-2495-015. Washington, DC: FERC, November.

————. 2002. Remedying undue discrimination through open access tariff and standard electricity market design. Notice of Proposed Rulemaking. Docket no. RM01-12-000. Washington, DC: FERC, July.

————. 2003. Order amending market-based rate tariffs and authorizations. Docket nos. EL01-118-000 and EL01-118-001. Washington, DC: FERC, November.

Federal Trade Commission (FTC). 2002. Comments of the staff of the Bureau of Economics and the Office of the General Counsel of the Federal Trade Commission. FERC Docket no. EL01-118-000. Washington, DC: FERC, January 7.

Frame, R., and P. Joskow. 1998. Testimony in State of New Jersey Board of Public Utilities. Docket nos. EX94120585Y and EO97070463. Trenton, NJ.

Frankena, M. 2001. Geographic market delineation for electric utility mergers. *Antitrust Bulletin* 46 (2): 357–402.

Frankena, M., and B. Owen. 1994. *Electric utility mergers: Principles of anti-trust analysis.* Westport, CT: Praeger.

Garcia, A., and L. Arbeláez. 2002. Market power analysis for the Colombian electricity wholesale market. *Energy Economics* 24 (3): 217–29.

Green, R. 1996. Increasing competition in the British electricity spot market. *Journal of Industrial Economics* 44 (2): 205–16.

Green, R., and D. Newbery. 1992. Competition in the British electricity spot market. *Journal of Political Economy* 100 (5): 929–53.

Hieronymus, W. H. 2001. The SMA test: Critique and suggested changes. Docket no. PL02-8-000. Washington, DC: FERC.

Joskow, P. 1997. Restructuring, competition, and regulatory reform in the U.S. electricity industry sector. *Journal of Economic Perspectives* 11 (3): 119–38.

Joskow, P. 1999. Restructuring electric utilities: BG&E and PEPCO propose to merge. In *The antitrust revolution*, ed. J. E. Kwoka and L. J. White, 89–115. New York: Oxford University Press.

Joskow, P., and J. Tirole. 2000. Transmission rights and market power on electric power networks. *RAND Journal of Economics* 31 (3): 450–87.

Kahn, Alfred. 2002. Indicated generators' submission of statement of Alfred E. Kahn. FERC Docket no. EL01-118-000. Washington, DC: FERC, January 7.

Koch, C. 1996. Prepared supplemental direct testimony of Chad J. Koch. FERC Docket no. EC95-16-000. Washington, DC: Wisconsin Electric Power Company, Northern States Power Company, and Cenergy Inc.

Massey, William. 2000. Concurrence by Commissioner Massey re November 21, 2000 order concerning NSTAR's concerns regarding market power in a subregion of NEPOOL under ER00-3691. Docket no. ER00-3691-000. Washington, DC: FERC, November.

Morris, J. R. 2002. Supply margin assessment: FERC's new market power screen. *Economists Ink* 7 (2): 167–78.

Rosen, R. 1999. Direct testimony of Dr. Richard A. Rosen. FERC Docket no. EC97-56-000. Washington, DC: FERC. September 9. Western Resources, Inc. and Kansas City Power & Light Co.

Rudkevich, A., M. Duckworth, and R. Rosen. 1998. Modeling electricity pricing in a deregulated generation industry: The potential for oligopoly pricing in a poolco. *The Energy Journal* 19 (3): 19–48.

Schmalensee, R., and B. Golub. 1984. Estimating effective concentration in deregulated wholesale electricity markets. *RAND Journal of Economics* 15:12–26.

Schweppe, F., M. Caramanis, R. Tabors, and R. Bohn. 1988. *Spot pricing of electricity.* Boston: Kluwer Academic Publishers.

Sacramento Municipal Utility District, the State of Michigan, Michigan Public Service Commission, and the Vermont Department of Public Service. 2002. Supplemental comments. FERC Docket no. EL01-118-000. Washington, DC: FERC, March 22.

U.S. Department of Justice (DOJ). 1998. Comments of the U.S. Justice Department. Inquiry concerning commission's policy regarding the use of computer models in merger analysis. FERC Docket no. PL98-6-000. Washington, DC: FERC.

Williams Energy Marketing and Trading Co. 2002. Motion to intervene and comments of the Williams Energy Marketing & Trading Company. FERC Docket no. EL01-118-000. Washington, DC: FERC, January 7.

Wisconsin Electric Power Company and Putnam, Hayes & Bartlett (WEPCO/PHB). 1998. Joint comments on the use of computer models in merger analysis. FERC Docket no. PL98-6-000. Washington, DC: FERC.

Wolak, F. A. 2002. An empirical analysis of the impact of hedge contracts on bidding behavior in a competitive electricity market. *International Economic Journal* 14 (Summer): 1–40.

Notes

James Bushnell is research director at the University of California Energy Institute.

I wish to acknowledge the helpful comments of Severin Borenstein, James Griffin, Alvin Klevorick, Steve Puller, Frank Wolak, and participants at the Texas A&M Bush School Electricity Deregulation conference.

1. Joskow (1997) describes the evolution of the industry and its regulatory institutions.

2. Under section 206(a) of the FPA, if the FERC finds, after hearing, that rates are "unjust, unreasonable, unduly discriminatory, or preferential, the Commission shall determine the just and reasonable rate, charge, classification, rule, practice, regulation, or contract to be thereafter observed in force, and shall fix the same by order."

3. A recent bill introduced to Congress would take away the FERC's authority to review mergers.

4. While it reserves the right to pursue an independent policy, the U.S. Department of Jus-

tice antitrust division has traditionally allowed the FERC to play the lead role in the review of electric utility mergers. When the antitrust division has gotten involved in an electricity merger, it is usually as an interested party intervening in the FERC proceeding.

5. See FERC (1996), order 592. This chapter will focus on policies dating from the mid-1990s. See Frankena and Owen (1994) for a description of merger policies before this time.

6. Joskow (1999) describes the FERC's historical approach to merger analysis and the adoption of the 1996 policy statement in the context of the proposed merger of BG&E and PEPCO.

7. See the comments of the Edison Electric Institute (EEI; 1998) and Wisconsin Electric Power Company and Putnam, Hayes, & Bartlett (1998).

8. Several theoretical papers have examined this phenomenon. See Borenstein, Bushnell, and Stoft (2000), Cardell, Hitt, and Hogan (1997), and Joskow and Tirole (2000).

9. The HHI measures the sum of the squared market shares of all the suppliers in the market. The convention is to multiply the resulting sum by 10,000. Thus, for example, a market with four equal-sized producers would yield an HHI of $4 \cdot 0.25^2 \cdot 10,000 = 2,500$.

10. See for example, the 1998 order accepting market-based rates for AES facilities in California (FERC 1998).

11. For example, regulations exist in all of the ISO supervised markets to limit the offer prices of firms with 'local' market power conveyed upon them by transmission network constraints. In some circumstances, these constraints can bestow monopoly power on specific generation units or firms.

12. See Blumstein, Friedman, and Green (2002) for a full review of the California restructuring process.

13. The FERC order of March 9, 2001 (FERC 2001b), outlined a calculation that essentially set a maximum allowed offer price according to a formula that applied updated gas and emission cost indices.

14. The model is described in several filings in the case. See, for example, Koch (1996).

15. The proposed Western Resources–KCP&L merger as well as the merger between Ameren Corp. and Central Illinois Light Co. are both mergers between traditional vertically integrated regulated utilities.

16. For a general overview of basic oligopoly models, see Carlton and Perloff (1990).

17. The other equilibrium concept that is frequently applied to electricity markets allows firms to specify a full supply function (i.e., a function specifying different price-quantity combinations) of either a general or specific functional form. Supply function equilibrium models have been applied to the U.K. market by Green and Newbery (1992) and Green (1996). Supply function models are also used by Rudkeivich, Duckworth, and Rosen (1998) and Baldick, Grant, and Kahn (2000).

18. Borenstein, Bushnell, and Stoft (2000), and Borenstein, Bushnell, and Knittel (1998b) simulate the impact of market power on congestion in California and New Jersey, respectively. Day, Hobbs, and Pang (2002) simulate market power and congestion in the England and Wales market.

19. As the transition periods in those other markets expire, the incentive effects of vertical integration will change. Currently most of those companies are operating under retail price freezes similar to those imposed in California during its transition period. It is largely expected that once these rate freezes expire, distribution companies obligated to serve their retail customers will be allowed to pass on increases in wholesale electricity costs. At that point, the impact of retail obligations on mitigating the incentives of vertically integrated generation companies to raise prices will be removed.

20. See BBW for the details on the derivation of a residual demand function faced by strategic suppliers.

21. See Wolak (2002) for a description of the impact of long-term contracts on the incentives of generation unit owners.

22. In the simulation, this capacity was treated like the import capacity described in equation (1). The production from all these price-taking units at a given price was subtracted from the residual demand curve of the remaining Cournot firms.

23. Bushnell and Mansur (2003) find a reduction in consumption of around 7 percent in the San Diego region during a period in which rates roughly doubled, implying an elasticity of around .07. Although I assume here that elasticity does not vary by time of day, it should be noted that Bushnell and Mansur find a somewhat larger reduction in demand during peak afternoon hours.

24. See Borenstein (chap. 8 in this volume) for a detailed discussion of dynamic pricing regimes.

25. To the extent that the presence of financially solvent utilities would have limited the chaotic market conditions seen during the following winter of 2000–1, an earlier rate increase may have improved competitiveness somewhat during this latter period. See Wolak (2003) for a description of the California crisis during this time period.

26. As described in BBW, the market price used is the day-ahead unconstrained price from the PX. The market quantity is the residual demand served by thermal generation within the ISO and imports into the ISO.

27. I also tried applying a constant elasticity demand curve, but this produced extremely aberrant results for some hours. The aggregate import supply curve more closely resembles a linear function.

28. Generation units in the South Coast Air Quality Management District (SCQAMD) are subject to the RECLAIM emissions credit trading program for NOx emissions.

7

The Oversight of Restructured Electricity Markets

Alvin K. Klevorick

Introduction

To gain perspective on the oversight of restructured electricity markets in the United States, consider a hypothetical situation. Suppose that in the United States for a long time bread has been produced and distributed by a small set of vertically integrated firms. Suppose too that, because of this market structure, some years ago Congress passed the Federal Bread Act establishing the Federal Bread Commission, which it charged with assuring that the price of bread carried in interstate commerce was "just and reasonable." Recent academic studies of the bread industry have revealed that production technology, food-preservation methods, and expanded transportation possibilities seem to render it possible to have competition at various stages of the production and distribution of bread. The Commission, after holding appropriate hearings and receiving comments from interested parties, concludes that competition can work in the bread industry and can deliver the just and reasonable prices the Commission is to assure.

The Commission decides to deregulate the bread industry and to leave the bread market to the forces of competition. Perhaps to foster that development, the Commission requires some degree of unbundling and divestiture by the large integrated bread firms. In its order, the Commission explicitly states that, of course, all the firms in the newly developing bread market will be subject to the antitrust laws, and for good measure, the Commission will follow market developments with an eye to detecting violations of the antitrust statutes. Let's assume, however, that to avoid any interagency jurisdictional issues, the Commission would refer any such alleged violations to the Department of Justice or the Federal Trade Commission.

Would we find our hypothetical Federal Bread Commission remiss in not having established a detailed structure for monitoring the newly deregulated bread market? I think not. When we reflect on the demand side and the supply side of the bread market—in particular, the availability of substitutes for consumers, the technology for producing bread, the alternative means of transporting it, and the likely ease of entry by firms at all the different stages of the industry—we're not likely to see much to distinguish the new bread market from the many others that we leave to competitive forces subject to the antitrust laws.

Why Oversee Electricity Markets?

Why, then, would we expect to find market-monitoring plans and institutions included as part of the restructuring of the electricity industry, and why would it be desirable to have such an apparently regulatory structure? To begin, observe that the changes the Federal Energy Regulatory Commission (FERC) has wrought in the electricity industry are better characterized as a restructuring or a partial deregulation than as deregulation plain and simple. The FERC has allowed some jurisdictions to use market-based rates as a means to meet the "just and reasonable" standard for wholesale power prices—regulation by competition, if you will—but transmission rates in interstate commerce are still regulated by the FERC, and the progress to retail competition ranges widely across the states. Hence, unlike our hypothetical bread example, some regulatory oversight is a salient characteristic of the restructured electricity industry.

The narrower question, then, concerns why there needs to be any explicit regulation and monitoring of the wholesale power markets once the FERC deems it possible to achieve just and reasonable rates in a given area by using market-based rates. Why require the filing of market rules with the FERC, and why not simply rely on antitrust enforcement to yield the desirable outcomes?

The answers, unsurprisingly, rest with fundamental characteristics of the demand for and supply of electricity. First, at least in the short run, the demand for electricity is highly inelastic, and the way that regulators have historically set the prices for electricity has fostered the lack of any significant response of demand to price. Regulatory institutions and technological arrangements have resulted in very limited implementation of real-time pricing and energy flexibility of industrial investments. Hence, the restructuring of the electricity industry entails an effort to introduce markets in which one blade of Marshall's scissors hardly cuts at all.

Second, the supply to meet this inelastic load requirement must be provided subject to stringent physical laws wherein demand and supply must balance at each instant of time, storage is an extremely limited possibility, and the laws of nature cannot be denied. Furthermore, although there is some scope for flexibility by tweaking the transmission system, in the short—and even medium—run, the delivery of electricity is sharply constrained by the transmission network that is in place. In short, on both the demand and supply sides, the market for electricity seems a far cry from the run-of-the-mill well-functioning market we usually have in mind and that it seems, for example, a market for bread might reasonably resemble.

The novelty and distinctiveness of markets for electricity imply the need for specially designed rules to guide their functioning and computer software to implement those rules. In turn, this means that monitoring is required to assure that the software is performing as intended. Even more, market surveillance is needed to determine whether the market rules are producing the operations and performance that they were intended to yield. Such monitoring can detect market-design flaws and channel efforts for responding promptly and effectively, with rule modifications, when significant problems are identified.

Compare the situation facing our hypothetical Federal Bread Commission. Given the apparent similarities between the market for bread and the many already-functioning markets, the Commission could well believe that no special design or software is needed and that the bread market would evolve quite naturally like one of those cognate markets. Of course, the bread market might develop some new exchange of its own, in which case rules of the exchange would be needed and monitoring of those rules would be required. But, once again, the similarity between bread and so many other commodities for which such exchanges already exist would make the Bread Commission's problem many orders of magnitude simpler than the FERC's concerns about electricity markets.

The character of the demand for electricity also suggests that concerns about a market for wholesale power might go beyond those encompassed by the antitrust laws. Prosecution of violations of Section 1 of the Sherman Act—

the formation of contracts, combinations, or conspiracies in restraint of trade—would satisfactorily address instances of collusive behavior by market participants. But with demand so unresponsive to price, regulators might find actions brought under Section 2 of the Sherman Act insufficient for combating detrimental unilateral behavior.

Under Section 2 jurisprudence, proving a monopolization offense requires showing more than that the actor possessed monopoly power. The plaintiff also must demonstrate that the defendant attained or sustained that power by illegitimate means. For example, the canonical *Grinnell* test requires a showing of "(1) the possession of monopoly power in the relevant market and (2) the willful acquisition or maintenance of that power as distinguished from growth or development as a consequence of a superior product, business acumen, or historic accident" (*United States v. Grinnell*, 570–71).

This well-established approach to Section 2 cases faces two problems in the context of wholesale electricity markets. First, in assessing monopoly power, courts often look principally to evidence of market share, with the threshold usually being well above 50 percent. But when electrical load is pressing on engineering capacity for energy and the reserves required for reliability, sellers with much, much smaller market shares can effectively raise the price above the level that would result from price-taking behavior. Second, even if the trier of fact were to be sophisticated and, by examining the elasticity of demand facing a Section 2 defendant, ask directly about the ability of the firm to exercise market power, a problem remains. Suppose that a wholesale power seller recognizes the elasticity of its residual demand curve and sets its offer curve accordingly—specifically, in a way that diverges from its marginal cost curve (Cramton 2003; Wolak 2003, chap. 3 in this volume). How can we say that such a firm, which does nothing more than choose an offer curve to maximize profits in its market situation, illegitimately acquired or maintained its monopoly power? It seems implausible to characterize that firm's behavior in that way. Consequently, the monopolization prong of the Sherman Act could leave unchallenged the harmful effects of the exercise of monopoly power.

But regulators, consumers, and other market participants will be concerned about what is often termed market manipulation, wherein a player in the market attempts to move the market price in her or his favor and blunts effective price competition (Johnson and Hazen 2002, section 5.02). This behavior impairs the functioning of the market and closely resembles the exercise of monopoly power. To take action against such conduct in electricity markets will require more direct monitoring and remediation than could result from even very vigilant antitrust enforcement under Section 2.

Beyond *Ex Post* Regulation

Market monitoring directed at assessing overall market performance and the effectiveness of the market design has a character that is simultaneously distinctly ex post and prospective. It is not addressed to what is happening in the market here and now. The monitor examines past operations and performance, and if it detects any shortcoming, it proposes rule changes going forward. This is consistent with the approach that antitrust generally takes toward violations by market participants. The body of antitrust law sends signals to market players about appropriate conduct, about what is legal and what is illegal behavior. Detected violations of those rules are then penalized ex post, and an offending practice also might be enjoined or an offending structure might be dismantled.

The price inelasticity of demand in wholesale power markets might call, however, for responding to some market conditions and market-participant behavior before the market result is determined. The concern is with prices that are excessively high or price changes that are exceedingly large in that the levels or changes, respectively, do not accurately reflect scarcity conditions in the market but result from either previously undetected market design flaws or the exercise of market power, whether by one firm alone or by two or more colluding together. The worry is that without enough price responsiveness in demand to choke off the price increases of concern, there will be severe distributional impacts, inefficient production of the electricity to meet the load requirements, and a general undermining of confidence in the market. To be sure, if the price spike results because of market manipulation, an investigation and penalty after the fact could make the losers whole, but in the meanwhile considerable damage may have been done to the market itself and its ability efficiently to allocate wholesale power resources.

As a result, three different damage-control measures are used in the wholesale electricity markets that have been instituted in the last eight years (U.S. Department of Energy 2003, 48). One is a price cap that is imposed at the market level; for example, the price can never rise above \$1,000/MWh (ISO New England Inc. 2003, market rule 1, section 1.10.1A; New York Independent System Operator 2003, attachment F). The second device mitigates the offering price of an individual participant if the unconstrained offer crosses both a conduct threshold and a market-impact threshold (ISO New England Inc. 2003, market rule 1, appendix A, section 5; New York Independent System Operator 2003, attachment H). For example, the market monitor asks whether the seller's offer is \$W or X percent above a reference price, which is usually historically determined, for the seller, and whether the offer would have an effect of $Y or Z percent on the market price. The offer-mitigation aspects of different markets' monitoring programs use different methods for determining the level to which the seller's offering price is reduced. Finally, in "load pockets," where demand exceeds native generation and transmission constraints impede imports, units that are required to run for reliability purposes and would otherwise enjoy monopoly power are contractually committed to run for compensation equal to a markup—say, 10 percent—above some measure of cost (PJM Interconnection, L.L.C. 2003, schedule 1, section 6). This last damage-control measure closely resembles the regulatory arrangement the restructured market was to displace.

Observe that in one sense offer mitigation interferes less with the market's operation than does imposition of a price cap. With offer mitigation, the market still sets the price, albeit one under a process in which the bidding of one or more sellers is restrained. Of course, a market participant whose offer is mitigated will find that action intrusive indeed. That seller is unable to decide for itself the price at which it will offer its output to the market. But if the automatic-mitigation program is well applied, it should have no effect on truly competitive offers and should not impose a binding constraint on a workably competitive market. A price cap, on the other hand, fixes the market price and sets aside information from market participants about the terms on which they would offer to supply. The need for a damage-control price cap can be regarded as an indicator of the immaturity of the wholesale power markets that restructuring has produced.

As these markets develop through innovations that bring about more price-responsive demand, the reactions of buyers themselves will serve to choke off prices that are excessively high due to market-design flaws and general market power (Borenstein, chap. 8 in this volume). Although one may not be sanguine about the near-term prospects for successfully applying real-time or dynamic pricing on a substantial scale, in the long term demand response will need to play a major role in counteracting the price effects of sellers' exercising monopoly power in these markets. Even then, however, the offer-mitigation device might continue to serve the useful function of both deterring and nipping in the bud individual sellers' attempts to exercise market power. Finally, at least some offer-mitigation programs are not fully automatic; some discretion remains with the market monitor. A seller who "fails" both the conduct and the market-impact tests will be contacted by the monitor, and the seller can attempt to explain why the offering price is cost-justified. If the monitor is persuaded, the offer will not be mitigated.

Assessing Markets for Wholesale Power

The basically bright-line character of the automatic-mitigation programs employed in different markets raises the more general question of how to assess the degree of success of these newly developed wholesale power markets and how to use the results of such an assessment to design improved market rules and procedures. It seems natural to proceed in this inquiry the same way a good market-organization economist would approach the analysis of any market or industry. There is no "cookbook" for such a study, but there is a well-developed set of questions and tools—actually a continually developing set of tools—that can be brought to bear on the issue, all of which must take account of the specific features of wholesale electricity markets.

The specialist in industrial organization would look at the structure, conduct, and performance of these markets, and indeed these are precisely the elements of the studies of these markets that have been undertaken by the FERC staff, the independent system operators running these markets, individual market monitors, and independent academic analysts. The idea is to draw on as much information as possible, viewing the market from different perspectives, to achieve as complete a picture of the market as possible.

As with the study of any market, the specific character of the wholesale power market will render some tools and measures more helpful than others. For example, there is widespread agreement that because of the constraints imposed by the transmission system, the commonly used Herfindahl-Hirschman Index is less helpful in analyzing the structure of electricity markets than it is in examining the structure of others (Borenstein, Bushnell, and Knittel 1999: Borenstein, Bushnell, and Stoft 2000; Bushnell, chap. 6 in this volume). Alternatives, such as the residual supply index, that focus on how pivotal a particular supplier or a set of suppliers is will be more informative measures of the degree of concentration in the market and the threat that such concentration carries for the market's competitiveness. Another distinctive feature of the analysis of electricity markets requires that the analyst account for the way in which the transmission system creates "load pockets" and "generation pockets."

With regard to the conduct of market participants, economists analyzing the recently developed electricity markets are fortunate to have a potential treasure trove of bidding data. Detailed examination of the bids and offers of market participants is valuable in several ways. Aggregate bidding data can be used to examine whether there has been economic withholding at the market level. At the individual level, one might be looking for the development of particular bidding patterns or, in turn, sudden departures from rather stable patterns. Comparisons might be drawn between the offer curve for a unit and some estimated measure of the cost curve for such a unit based on its known physical characteristics (Bohn, Klevorick, and Stalon 1999). The results of such analyses, however, would provide the basis for further, focused inquiry—including communication with the party responsible for any such unit's offers—and not for drawing any direct conclusion about whether the supplier's behavior complies with market rules and policies. For example, in examining how the seller's offer curve compares with its marginal cost, the appropriate measure of the latter is the supplier's opportunity cost. Determining that opportunity cost requires going beyond an estimate of production cost estimated from a unit's physical characteristics. A comparison between the seller's offer curve and an estimate of its marginal production cost would be but a first, coarse screen. In short, the analysis of bidding patterns is a diagnostic tool, not a ground for immediate inference about individual market participants' conduct.

The possibility of physical withholding of capacity, by individual suppliers and in the aggregate, also should be considered when examining the conduct of market participants. There are data on maintenance downtime, unforced outages, and the like. Paul Joskow has suggested that generators should be required to have an established protocol for withdrawing units from service and that a senior person should be required to approve such withdrawals (FERC 2002b, 49–50). Following Joskow's suggestion would serve both to improve the quality of reports on developments that affect physical capacity and to discourage physical withholding of supply from the market.

The ultimate test of the restructured wholesale power markets is whether they yield an efficient allocation of resources. The methods that have been developed and applied in various benchmarking studies of the new electricity markets are excellently suited to the task of assessing the markets' performance (Borenstein, Bushnell, and Wolak 2002; Bushnell and Saravia 2002; Joskow and Kahn 2002; Wolfram 1999). The studies compare the actual price outcomes in the markets with the result that would emerge if suppliers followed price-taking behavior. Of course, these studies require assumptions and approximations that can be—and have been—challenged as the researchers performing them must accurately represent the system marginal cost of supply and take account of the idiosyncratic physical characteristics of particular types of generation. It is difficult, for example, to capture the nonconvexities in the system, start-up times, no-load costs, minimum running times, and ramp-rate constraints. Because such studies require many assumptions and approximations, the results of these analyses are best presented as a range or with some indication of their error bounds. But the benchmarking studies do provide a very good indication of how well the electricity markets match up against the price and quantity results that a set of price-taking competitive generators would produce.

While the benchmarking studies and the analyses of economic and physical withholding provide insights into the static efficiency of the new electricity markets, we are concerned as well with the dynamic efficiency of these institutions. Here a principal question is whether the prices emerging from these markets provide the appropriate signals to potential investors. This inquiry into the market-provided incentives for investment can be conducted by identifying areas in which generation is in short supply and then estimating whether the actual wholesale energy market prices, taken together with any other streams of revenue a new generator could anticipate—for example, from the supply of ancillary services—would make investment in the marginal type of generation financially worthwhile (Joskow, chap. 1 in this volume). If the market prices are not effectively signaling desirable investment opportunities and discouraging socially unwise ones, then other mechanisms will be required to promote efficient investment. For example, the FERC suggests that regions adopt some type of a resource adequacy requirement (FERC 2002a, 2003). In some regions, load-serving entities face installed-capacity requirements, which can be met through bilateral purchases or from supply provided in an auction, and in some areas the independent system operator and stakeholders are developing plans for new types of forward-capacity markets (ISO New England Inc. 2003, market rule 1, section 8).

In addressing the dynamic-efficiency, investment-incentives concern, the analysis will be taking account, of course, of the effects of any damage-control measures that operate in the market. The observed market prices might not be effectively indicating remunerative investment opportunities because a price cap or an automatic-mitigation program has put a lid on the price that suppliers can receive and has, rather than blunting the exercise of market power, limited the market price's ability to communicate scarcity conditions. Indeed, one argument that the FERC and others put forward for a resource adequacy requirement is the need to compensate for the investment effects of what are essentially false positives of market-price controls—occasions when the price is capped or mitigation imposed although, in fact, market power was not exercised.

This recommendation about resource adequacy serves to highlight the interdependence of the new wholesale power markets and the various regulatory instruments that are brought to bear on them, whether by the market operators or by state and federal regulators. In that regard, one must recognize that even if the market prices correctly point the way to socially optimal investments, investor concerns about the vicissitudes of required regulatory decisions—for example, those of state siting councils or environmental protection regulators—or the uncertainty of future regulatory interventions in the markets may deter those capital commitments.

Applying the Results of Market Evaluations

How should the results of this careful, multifaceted study of the structure, conduct, and performance of the new electricity markets be put to use? How, if at all, can policy implications be distilled from the findings of such studies? Any program of market monitoring—and market-power mitigation—must confront the major issue of how to determine that a market-power problem exists, whether it is due to the market rules or the market structure, or to the behavior of participants within that set of rules and that structure. And if there is such a problem, the market monitor needs to examine whether the expected benefits of coping with the problem exceed the expected costs of such action. Here the designer of a program of market monitoring and mitigation faces an important policy choice.

Economic analysis does not lend itself to the specification of sharp, bright-line criteria that enable an observer to say with definiteness that a market-power problem does or does not exist. For example, the conduct and market-impact thresholds that form part of several markets' automatic-mitigation programs do not follow directly from any economic calculus. They result, instead, from some rough balancing of the expected costs of false positives—declaring an offer problematic when it is not—and the expected costs of false negatives—failing to label appropriately a participant's offer that could be seriously detrimental to the market as a whole.

But it is precisely the kind of clarity in such bright-line rules that market participants seek so that they can assess in advance whether or not their behavior will fall within or outside the bounds of what is acceptable. The clarity of bright-line rules and certainty about the conditions that will trigger intervention create a more stable setting in which market participants can plan and make decisions, and hence they serve to promote confidence in the markets and their stability. That very same sharpness, though, can mean that those entrusted with market-surveillance responsibilities may either deter efficient behavior by some market participants or miss market-damaging behavior with detrimental long-run consequences.

We are replaying in the context of restructured electricity markets the long-standing debate in antitrust law about the relative merits of a per se approach or a more open-textured rule-of-reason approach to analyzing and remedying market problems. There is no easy answer, and at least until a substantial degree of price responsiveness of demand develops, we are going to have a diversified approach—a mix of bright-line rules and more open-ended analysis. The former will be employed to the extent that market monitors deem it necessary to be able to intervene before the market price is determined, while the latter rule-of-reason method will form the core of ex post monitoring, enforcement, and market redesign. I expect that as the wholesale power markets mature, the monitoring enterprise will come to rely more on the analogue of rule-of-reason analysis just as, over time, antitrust law has seen the shrinking of the domain in which per se rules predominate.

No matter which approach is taken, though, sellers whose offers are mitigated ex ante or parties that are subject to ex post penalties must have some legal recourse beyond the market monitor that mitigates or imposes the penalty. In the case of action by the market operator, the appeal would be to the FERC, while if the action was by the FERC itself, the recourse would be to a circuit court of appeals. This right of appeal would be most important under a rule-of-reason regime, since arguably that provides less advance notice than does a set of per se rules about what is legitimate behavior and what lies out of bounds.

The FERC and Decentralized Market Surveillance

Who should perform the market-monitoring function, and what should be the institutional structure of market surveillance? The ultimate regulatory authority and responsibility for the restructured electricity markets rest, of course, with the FERC, which therefore is the market monitor. To enhance its ability to perform that function, the FERC has, several years ago, established its Office of Market Oversight and Investigation. That office is still at an early stage of development of staff, knowledge base, and methods, but over time it will play an increasingly important role. The FERC, however, cannot carry out the market-monitoring function on its own and in a totally centralized way. It is implausible that the considerable variation in local conditions and the need for detailed understanding of particular markets would permit a single entity effectively to monitor a set of dispersed markets, especially from a distance. The Commission has recognized that reality in the market structures it has approved, in the standardized market design that it is in the process of proposing, and in the efforts of its Office of Market Oversight and Investigation to reach out and coordinate its activities with market monitors functioning at the regional level.

In essence, the FERC decentralizes and delegates part of its market-monitoring function to the entities that it authorizes to run the wholesale power markets. At the current time, these are independent system operators, which are responsible for operating both the wholesale markets and the bulk power systems in their regions. (In California, these functions originally were separated as the California Power Exchange ran the energy market.) If the FERC's final order on market standardization emerges in close to the form described in the Notice of Proposed Rule Making on Standard Market Design and in the subsequent White Paper on Wholesale Market Platform, the organizations carrying the dual responsibilities of running the markets and operating the bulk power system will be a set of regional transmission operators (RTOs) and independent system operators (ISOs). The latter simply will lack the scope of the former. Whatever their names—for ease of exposition, let's simplify and suppose all these entities will be RTOs—these organizations will be responsible for the efficiency of their markets and the reliability of their power systems, and they will be answerable to the FERC. In particular, they will be responsible for monitoring their markets, just as today's ISOs are. The ISOs and the RTOs should file regular reports to the FERC, inform the FERC of any short-term exigencies or irregularities, and have easy and effective channels of communication with the FERC's Office of Market Oversight and Investigation.

Charging a regional transmission organization with responsibility for the efficient operation of its markets carries with it important implications about the character of the RTO. Although the entity should be attentive to the concerns of all its stakeholders and willingly receive input from them, the RTO's charter responsibility should be to further the public interest of providing system reliability through efficient, competitive markets. Consequently, its board of directors should be fully independent and not a collection of stakeholders whose respective numbers are allocated among various sectors of interested parties. To assure that the board focuses on the fundamental goals of power-system reliability and power-market efficiency, and not on the financial interests of market participants, members of the board must have no financial stake in the board's decisions. Even any appearance of financial interest must be abjured. In contrast, a stakeholder board could lead to decisions that further the interests of a majority of stakeholders represented there but do not best serve the public interest. Furthermore, a stakeholder board, with something akin to proportional representation—however proportionality might be measured—provides a formula for gridlock in articulating goals, communicating core values, and creating incentives for management and staff. It also impedes action when rapid responses in market rules or system procedures are needed.

The formation of the initial board of the RTO should be guided by input from the various constituencies it serves—including consumers, generators, transmission owners, suppliers, governmentally owned power systems, and state regulators. But the process should have as its objective the selection of an independent board dedicated to providing efficient markets and a reliable power system and possessing in aggregate the diverse skills and competencies to do that. The goal is distinctly not to produce a board chosen to assure "appropriate" representation of the interests of major players in the market and the power system.

The rules for succession on the board should embody the same principles of independence and competence. Again, the voices and concerns of the diverse set of stakeholders about the board's performance and perceived needs should be heard in the selection process. The board should be accountable to all stakeholders, and to market participants in particular, for its actions, but the board should not be beholden to any particular set of stakeholders. The board's accountability would run to its having to explain, which it would need to do to the FERC in any event, how the RTO's decisions and actions further the public interest's twin goals of system reliability and market efficiency. The model is distinctly not one of a for-profit corporate board with market participants as the analogues of corporate shareholders whose "value" the board is to oversee management in maximizing. And the right to hold the board accountable does not carry with it, as would be the case in the for-profit corporate world, the right to select its members. Unless the selection procedures preserve the independence of the board, market stakeholders, and especially market participants, cannot have the confidence that the operation of the markets, and specifically the monitoring of the markets' performance, is being executed in a fair and objective way that serves the public interest.

It is legitimate to ask whether the independent board I describe is a pipe dream. Will it be possible to compose such a board, whose members will single-mindedly pursue the public interest in system reliability and market efficiency? Numerous case studies of the political economy of regulation and theories of the capture of regulatory bodies formed with similar public-interest charters must give one pause (Joskow and Rose 1989; Noll 1989). But experience with some existing ISO boards provides grounds for optimism, especially since, unlike the regulators in the traditional political economy stories, these board members will not be looking to their board positions as a principal source of their incomes. They will have continuing "day jobs," and the revolving door between regulatory bodies and the industries they regulate will not be operating here. Furthermore, these board members will accept their RTO positions with a clear understanding of the public-interest goals they are to pursue, and the board's performance will be judged by how well the RTO it oversees attains those objectives.

The Structure of the Local Market Monitor

What structure should be adopted to perform the decentralized market-monitoring function? Who should conduct the careful, wide-ranging assessment of the structure, conduct, and performance of the regional wholesale power market that I describe? And if the RTO adopts, with the FERC's approval, an automatic-mitigation program, what entity should administer it? Although ascertaining whether a firm's offers put it across the specified thresholds of such an automatic plan seems straightforward, these are just screens, and the local market monitor retains discretion about the appropriateness of a mitigation action. There is no algorithm for exercising such discretion, no substitute for good judgment based on a robust understanding of the monitored markets. Furthermore, the more general ongoing evaluation of the market cannot be reduced to the mechanical application of a set of specified tests, which could be easily embodied in a software package. As market monitors gain experience in their craft, new methods of analysis will emerge, and as the several market watchers share their learning with one another and with the FERC's Office of Market Oversight and Investigation, these analytical innovations will diffuse.

The structure of the local market monitor will matter, as will, to be sure, the quality of the people serving in that structure. Various alternatives have been proposed and tried; they include a market-monitoring unit within the organization responsible for the markets, an external unit, and some combination of the two. I believe that the two-pronged approach, with both an internal and an independent external market-monitoring unit, is to be preferred. The internal unit would be responsible for continuous, day-to-day monitoring and mitigation. The understanding would be that the internal monitor could consult as needed with the external monitor, with regard to both the detection of market anomalies and the imposition of offer-mitigation actions. The head of the internal market-monitoring unit would report directly, and on a regular basis, to the chief executive officer and the board of the RTO.

The external market monitor would be an independent market advisor or an independent market surveillance committee, which would report directly and simultaneously to the board of directors of the RTO and to the FERC. The independent external surveillance entity—whether an individual, a firm, or a committee—would provide the FERC and the RTO board with regular reports on the state of the markets and with immediate notification of any exigent problems that the external monitor may detect. Although for completeness I include the possibility that the external monitor might be an individual, I do not believe that is a realistic alternative; the task is simply too large for one person.

I envision the independent external monitor—in the acronym-happy spirit of the electricity industry, let's call it an IMSU (independent market surveillance unit)—as akin to a FERC field agent or FERC regional franchise. As such, the selection of the IMSU would require approval by the FERC, as would the terms of the agreement between the RTO and the IMSU. In particular, to assure the independence of the external market monitor, that contract ought to borrow a provision from auditing contracts—namely, if either party terminates the relationship, the IMSU by resigning or the RTO by canceling the agreement, each of the parties must immediately communicate the termination to the FERC and explain why it occurred.

Beyond providing analytical expertise, the independent external monitor will enhance confidence in the markets and provide assurance that parochial concerns of RTO management do not impede the detection and resolution of market problems. Both the internal market-monitoring unit and the external surveillance team must have access to all the data that they need for effective monitoring of the RTO's markets. The FERC must ensure that the regional transmission organization's market rules and the IMSU's contract with the RTO guarantee that all-encompassing access to data.

Assessing the Regional Transmission Organization's Performance

The management of the entity running the markets and the bulk power system, the RTO, is of course itself an actor in the restructured electricity markets. The independent board of directors of the RTO must provide its management and staff with performance incentives that reward efficient functioning of the markets as well as quick and effective responses to perceived market problems. Difficult as it may be to achieve, the nonprofit RTO needs to mimic with internal performance-based compensation structures and retention policies the discipline that the market for managers would provide to a private, for-profit firm with responsibility to shareholders. In monitoring the performance of the RTO's markets and the alacrity with which the RTO detects and implements necessary reforms, the external market-surveillance unit will be monitoring the RTO itself. And this is a very important function that the IMSU will serve for the FERC.

There is, however, another type of check that the FERC ought to want to have on the regional transmission organization, and indeed that the RTO ought to desire for itself. That is a performance audit that examines the RTO's operation of both the markets and the bulk power system to assess whether the RTO, through its staff and management, is following its own rules and procedures. If the audit identifies departures from those rules and procedures, then it should ascertain as well as possible the reasons for those deviations and their effects on the performance of the markets and the power system.

Such a performance audit is extremely valuable, indeed essential. But it is unlikely that an entity that has the analytical capacity with regard to markets that the IMSU must have will be adept as well at executing a performance audit. Hence, the FERC should assign this task elsewhere by requiring that the RTO's board commission a performance audit on a regular basis and that the FERC approve the choice of auditor. Then the auditor's report should be submitted both to the RTO's board of directors and to the FERC. The results of the performance audits ought to be made available to the public, especially to market participants, a step that can help to enhance the transparency of the markets and to build confidence in them.

Informal Market Monitoring and the Release of Market Information

Other interested parties, with no specific FERC-assigned responsibility, will also monitor the markets. These include the regulators, consumer advocates, and attorneys general of the states for which the regional transmission organization operates the wholesale power markets and the bulk power system. And, driven by financial self-interest, market participants themselves will monitor the performance of the markets and the RTO's operation of the power system. These informal monitors can direct concerns and complaints about market performance to the RTO, to the IMSU, or if need be, to the FERC itself, and they can provide a valuable set of alternative checks on the markets and suggestions for improvements in market rules and design.

To be effective, though, these state and private monitors need to have relevant information about the markets. This raises the important question of the optimal degree of information release. Consistent with the preservation of proprietary and confidential information, the FERC should encourage—perhaps direct—the earliest and maximal disclosure of information about bids and offers in the market that is compatible with the prevention of collusive behavior. Information about market conditions, including bids and offers by market participants, is a double-edged sword. Better information helps market participants to make better decisions about the allocation of their resources—recall that in the textbook model of perfect competition all agents are perfectly informed—but better information about the behavior of one's competitors also enables cooperation among participants that can be detrimental to the market. The FERC needs to balance the competing considerations and come to a decision about the character of the best achievable information-release policy.

The Centralization of Investigations

The responsibility for one aspect of market monitoring needs to stay centralized with the FERC or perhaps to be shared between the FERC and the Antitrust Division of the Department of Justice. That is the investigation of claims of market-power abuses and market manipulation. The RTO's market monitors—both the internal and the external one—can identify incidents or patterns of behavior that are of concern. And the RTO could develop, as some entities in the restructured electricity markets have, procedures and protocols for investigations. But the RTOs just will not have the staff or the legal capacity required to carry out major investigations. They will have difficulty extracting required information from reluctant parties, and the investigations will become protracted. In some cases, the result may be a negotiated settlement that is not sufficiently transparent to the market, which can lead to a very unfortunate undermining of the confidence in the market.

There are significant economies of scale in the pursuit of investigations of such offenses against the market, and the legal authority for compelling production of individuals and documents resides much more readily in the FERC and the Department of Justice than in a regional transmission organization. The RTO or its IMSU should refer to the FERC any market events or market-participant behavior that it deems a potential market-power or market-manipulation abuse. The FERC's Office of Market Oversight and Investigation should take control of the inquiry, perhaps in coordination with the Department of Justice, and draw upon the resources of the local monitors as necessary.

Conclusion

The wholesale electricity markets that have developed in the United States since the mid-1990s are a far cry from the pure laissez-faire paradigm. They are even quite different from the more common markets where agents' market behavior is bounded by only the antitrust laws. In contrast, the existing wholesale power markets are subject to intense monitoring and to various kinds of regulation by the entities that operate the markets and by the FERC. The same will be true of the new markets that the FERC's ongoing wholesale-market-platform initiative eventually will produce. Indeed, only the presence of these regulatory superimpositions provides any comfort that these new markets can yield the just and reasonable rates the Federal Power Act promises. Given the special characteristics of electricity, a "satisfactory" market structure, as represented by some measures of sellers' market shares and level of concentration, cannot suffice to assure that market-based rates will be just and reasonable.

The regulatory measures currently in place will be required at least until the demand side of these markets becomes adequately responsive to price. Even then there may be some value in retaining a damage-control price cap, albeit one probably much higher than those in effect today and set at a level more firmly based on estimates of the value of lost load (Cooke 2003). But until dynamic or real-time pricing of electricity becomes sufficiently widespread at the retail level that short-run wholesale demand is sufficiently price-elastic, these wholesale power markets will feature pervasive market monitoring and mitigation. Under the current approach, prices are deemed just and reasonable because of the *process*—market determination cum monitoring and mitigation—that produces them. These prices replace the rates that were formerly deemed just and reasonable because they were the *outcomes* of applying a set of administrative rules, which allowed the recovery of operating costs and a fair return on capital.

The putative benefits of competition in electricity markets are much the same as in other markets—the efficient production and allocation of the good or service and the appropriate incentives for innovation to improve production and distribution and to stimulate the provision of new services. Perfectly competitive—even fully workably competitive—electricity markets could be expected to deliver these benefits. The question in the current policy environment, and in the medium term at least, is whether today's restructured electricity markets with their regulatory overlay yield greater net benefits than the old administrative regulatory system did or than some improved version of it would bring. On that question the jury is still deliberating. The answer, though, will become more definitely affirmative as, and only as, the restructured wholesale power markets become more robust with substantial price-responsive demand facing off against price-responsive supply.

**

REFERENCES

Bohn, Roger E., Alvin K. Klevorick, and Charles G. Stalon. 1999. Second report on market issues in the California Power Exchange energy markets. Pasadena, CA: California Power Exchange, March 9.

Borenstein, Severin, James B. Bushnell, and Christopher R. Knittel. 1999. Market power in electricity markets: Beyond concentration measures. *The Energy Journal* 20 (4): 65–88.

Borenstein, Severin, James B. Bushnell, and Steven Stoft. 2000. The competitive effects of transmission capacity in a deregulated electricity industry. *RAND Journal of Economics* 31 (2): 294–325.

Borenstein, Severin, James B. Bushnell, and Frank A. Wolak. 2002. Measuring market inefficiencies in California's restructured wholesale electricity market. *American Economic Review* 92 (5): 1376–1405.

Bushnell, James, and Celeste Saravia. 2002. An empirical assessment of the competitiveness of the New England electricity market. CSEM Working Paper no. 101. Berkeley, CA: University of California Energy Institute, Center for the Study of Energy Markets. http://www.ucei.berkeley.edu/PDF/csemwp101.pdf.

Cooke, J. Alexander. 2003. The resource adequacy requirement in FERC's standard market design: Help for competition or a return to command and control? *Yale Journal on Regulation* 20 (2): 431–66.

Cramton, Peter. 2003. Report on competitive bidding behavior in uniform-price auction markets in the matter of San Diego Gas & Electric Company v. Sellers of Energy and Ancillary Services into markets operated by the California Independent System Operators Corporation and the California Power Exchange, investigation of practices of the California Independent System Operator and the California Power Exchange. FERC Docket nos. EL00-95-075 and EL00-98-063. Washington, DC: Federal Energy Regulatory Commission, March 20.

Federal Energy Regulatory Commission (FERC). 2002a. Remedying undue discrimination through open access transmission service and standard electricity market design. Notice of Proposed Rulemaking. FERC Docket no. RM01-12-000. Washington, DC: FERC, July 31.

———. 2002b. Staff conference on market monitoring, remedying undue discrimination through open-access transmission service and standard electricity market design. FERC Docket no. RM01-12-000. Washington, DC: FERC, October 2.

———. 2003. Wholesale power market platform, remedying undue discrimination through open-access transmission service and standard electricity market design. White paper. FERC Docket no. RM01-12-000. Washington, DC: FERC, April 28.

ISO New England Inc. 2003. Market rules and procedures. http://www.ISO-NE.com.

Johnson, Philip McBride, and Thomas Lee Hazen. 2002. *Commodities regulation.* 3rd ed. New York: Aspen Law & Business.

Joskow, Paul L., and Edward Kahn. 2002. A quantitative analysis of pricing behavior in California's wholesale electricity market during summer 2000. *The Energy Journal* 23 (4): 1–35.

Joskow, Paul L., and Nancy L. Rose. 1989. The effects of economic regulation. In *Handbook of industrial organization*, vol. 2, ed. Richard Schmalensee and Robert D. Willig, 1449–1506. Amsterdam: North-Holland.

New York Independent System Operator, Inc. 2003. ISO market administration and control area services tariff. http://www.NYISO.com.

Noll, Roger G. 1989. Economic perspectives on the politics of regulation. In *Handbook of industrial organization*, vol. 2, ed. Richard Schmalensee and Robert D. Willig, 1253–87. Amsterdam: North-Holland.

PJM Interconnection, L.L.C. 2003. Operating agreement of PJM interconnection, L.L.C. http://www.PJM.com.

United States v. Grinnell Corporation, 384 U.S. 563 (1966).

U.S. Department of Energy. 2003. Report to Congress: Impacts of the Federal Energy Regulatory Commission's proposal for standard market design. Washington, DC: U.S. Department of Energy, April 30.

Wolak, Frank A. 2003. Measuring unilateral market power in wholesale electricity markets: The California market, 1998–2000. *American Economic Review* 93 (2): 425–30.

Wolfram, Catherine D. 1999. Measuring duopoly power in the British electricity spot market. *American Economic Review* 89 (4): 805–26.

NOTES

Alvin K. Klevorick is the John Thomas Smith Professor of Law and professor of economics at Yale University.

I have served as a member of the Board of Directors of ISO New England since its inception, and I was the chair of the Market Monitoring Committee of the California Power Exchange from January 1998 through September 2000. In writing this paper I have drawn on my experience in both of these positions, but the views I express here are my own and do not necessarily reflect the positions of either of these organizations.

I am grateful for helpful comments on an earlier version that I received from the participants at the Bush Center Conference, the volume editors—Jim Griffin and Steve Puller—Stephen L. Diamond, Robert Ethier, Michael E. Levine, and Thomas Welch. I alone am responsible for any errors that remain.

8

Time-Varying Retail Electricity Prices: Theory and Practice

Severin Borenstein

Electricity is not economically storable, and production is subject to rigid short-term capacity constraints. Because demand is highly variable, this means there will be times when there is plenty of capacity, and the only incremental costs of producing electricity will be fuel and some operating and maintenance (O&M) costs. At other times, the capacity constraint will be binding, causing the incremental cost to increase greatly and wholesale market prices to rise. Supply constraints are even more likely if sellers are able to exercise market power, exacerbating the volatility of wholesale prices.

The result of this structure is that the wholesale price of electricity, reflecting the supply-demand interaction, varies constantly. In most markets, the wholesale price changes every half hour or hour. The end-use customer, however, sees the retail price, which typically is constant for months at a time. The retail price does not reflect the hour-by-hour variation in the underlying wholesale cost of electricity. A number of programs have been implemented or proposed to make the economic incentives of customers more accurately reflect the time-varying wholesale cost of electricity. Opponents have expressed concern that these programs expose customers to too much price volatility. Still, time-varying retail prices hold the key to mitigating price volatility in wholesale electricity spot markets.

In the first section of this paper, I present the theoretical argument in support of time-varying retail prices and explain the societal loss from using flat-rate retail pricing. Time-varying prices send more accurate signals about both the cost of consumption at any point in time and the value of building additional capacity. They also can play an important role in reducing the incentive of sellers to exercise market power. In the second section, I discuss the variety of programs used that implement time-varying retail prices and discuss their effectiveness in giving customers economically efficient incentives. In the third section, I focus primarily on real-time retail pricing (RTP) and examine a number of issues and complaints that frequently arise in implementation of RTP. I show that RTP need not subject customers to significant energy price risk through the use of forward contracts. The fourth section presents the results of some simulations of the effect that RTP would have in the long run on prices, consumption, and investment, which suggest that the benefits from RTP for large customers, at least, are likely to far exceed the costs. The fifth section concludes.

The Economic Efficiency of Time-Varying Retail Price

For most of the twentieth century, electricity was sold in regulated environments in which the retail price did not vary based on the time it was used. Customers faced a constant price for electricity regardless of the supply-demand balance in the grid. Discussions of changes to greater variation in retail price have usually focused on who, among customers, would win or lose from such a change. While the distributional impact among customers is certainly important, time-varying electricity prices are also very likely to affect the total cost of the electricity and, in the short run, the allocation of the cost between customers and deregulated producers. In this section, I examine the economic impact of moving to a system in which prices more accurately reflect the supply-demand balance.

Efficient Time-Varying Electricity Pricing

For illustration, I will assume that there are only two levels of demand, peak and off peak, as shown in figure 8.1, and that all producers have the same cost of production, *MC*, up to their capacity. I'll begin by illustrating how this market would operate if different prices were charged during peak and off-peak times and no producer were able to exercise market power. I return to the market power issue in the following.

Figure 8.1. Peak and off-peak price with fixed capacity

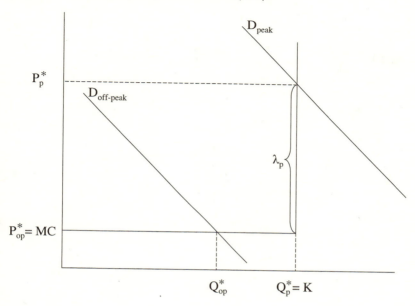

If the market were competitive and total installed capacity were K, the market supply curve would be flat at c out to K and then vertical. It is easy to see that the prices in the market would be P_p and P_{op}. If any producer tried to charge a price above P_{op} during off-peak periods, it would be unable to sell its power as there is idle capacity waiting to jump in if the price is above the producers' marginal cost. During peak times, no producer would be willing to sell at a price below P_p, because P_p clears the market (i.e., as there is no idle capacity, any producer can sell all of its output at that price, so it would have no incentive to charge less). If any producer tried to charge more than P_p, it would find that its unit sales would decline and it would be unable to earn enough on the power it sold to justify selling less than its full capacity, as it could at P_p. This follows from the assumption that no firm can profitably exercise market power.

Now consider the outcome if, due to either technological or legal constraints, the firms charged the same price for peak and off-peak demand. If the firms were still to break even overall, the price would lie somewhere between the peak and off-peak price from the previous example, a price we'll call $\bar{P}$. This is illustrated in figure 8.2. For the off-peak demand, this would raise the price and inefficiently discourage off-peak consumption, because the price would exceed the true marginal cost of production. Some consumption that would

Figure 8.2. Time-invariant pricing with variable demand

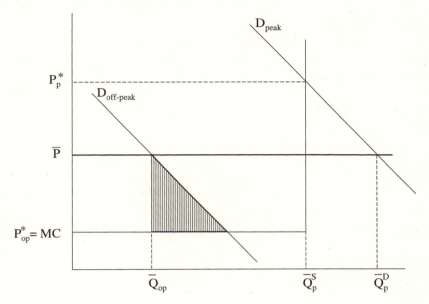

produce value greater than the incremental cost of production would not take place. This is illustrated by the vertically shaded "deadweight-loss" area.

A single-price restriction would result in a price for peak demand that is below P_p. This would increase the total quantity demanded above the current market capacity. Absent additional capacity, this would cause a shortage and would require some sort of rationing, using either economic incentives or some alternate approach. Putting aside, for the moment, the disruption of blackouts, such rationing doesn't even necessarily deliver power to the most valuable use. A use with a value just barely above $\overline{P}$ would be as likely to receive power as a use with a much higher value.[1]

In reality, of course, the excess demand at peak times is not allowed to cause blackouts. Instead, capacity is expanded to meet the high demand that results at peak times. The question then is whether this is a good use of resources. The answer is almost certainly no, as is explained in the next subsection.

Efficient Capacity Investment

To analyze the efficiency of capacity investment with and without time-varying prices, we return to figure 8.1 to illustrate capacity investment with time-varying prices. It is clear in this situation that additional capacity has no value for the off-peak period. Off-peak consumption does not even utilize all of the currently available capacity. Additional capacity does have value in the peak period because the marginal value of power to customers is greater than the marginal cost that would have to be expended after an additional unit of capacity was built. To be exact, the value of an additional unit of capacity is $P_p - MC$, which is λ_p in the illustration. λ_p is the peak-period shadow value of marginal capacity at the current level, K. The off-peak shadow value of marginal capacity is $\lambda_{op} = 0$.

The per-day (where a "day" includes one peak and one off-peak period) cost of one additional unit of capacity is the fixed operation and maintenance cost plus depreciation and the opportunity cost of the capital investment (i.e., the forgone interest on the funds used for this investment).[2] I will call this full fixed capacity cost r per unit of capacity per day. The efficient criterion for capacity choice is to expand capacity so long as the sum of the capacity shadow values for all periods is greater than the capacity cost, $\Sigma\lambda > r$, and to stop expanding capacity at the point that $\Sigma\lambda = r$. Note that we take the sum of the λs because the peak and off-peak operation are noncompeting uses of the same capacity.

Luckily, this is also the criterion that will determine the competitive level of capacity because each price-taking owner of capacity will receive λ_p above its operating costs in peak periods and λ_{op} above operating costs in off-peak periods. Thus, a firm will have an incentive to expand capacity so long as the sum of the λs is greater than the cost of expanding capacity.[3]

Now, let's return to the issue of capacity investment under a single-price retail system. At price $\bar{P}$, the off-peak demand is well below capacity, so the shadow value of capacity for off-peak demand remains zero. In order to meet the peak demand at $\bar{P}$, however, we have built additional capacity, ΔK. But it is not efficient to build that capacity: the net value of the additional power produced by the capacity is less than the cost of the capacity. To be concrete, building the extra ΔK of capacity creates deadweight loss equal to the shaded triangle in figure 8.3 because the net value of this additional capacity is less than the cost of holding the capacity, which is $r \cdot \Delta K$.

In the real world, this inefficiency shows up in the form of excess capacity that is underutilized but still must be built in order to accommodate the peak demand. The value customers get out of this capacity is not great enough to justify the capital investment. With time-varying pricing of electricity, this excess capacity is not necessary because higher prices at peak times encourage customers to consume less at those times, either by shifting peak consumption to off peak or by simply reducing consumption at peak times.

Figure 8.3. Excess capacity resulting from time-invariant pricing

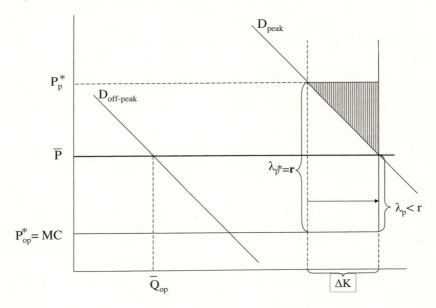

Time-Varying Prices and Market Power

Thus far, the analysis has considered only the case of a competitive whole-sale electricity market. When producers are able to exercise market power, however, the benefit of instituting time-varying prices is greater. In any market, a seller or group of sellers exercises market power by raising the price above the competitive level. The financial attractiveness of this action depends on the trade-off of higher prices on the quantity the firm still sells versus lost sales due to the increased price. It is clear that the payoff to exercising market power is greater if raising prices has a smaller impact on sales.

When the retail price of electricity does not vary over time, a wholesale seller's attempt to exercise market power and raise wholesale prices has no short-run impact on quantity as end-use customers do not see a change in the retail price they face. This makes it much more profitable for the wholesale seller to exercise market power. With time-varying prices that reflect changes in the wholesale price, an attempt to raise wholesale prices will impact retail prices and thus reduce the quantity of power that customers demand. This customer response reduces the profitability of raising wholesale prices and, thus, discourages the exercise of market power.

To be a bit more concrete, consider a hot summer day when the system is stretched to near its limit, and consider the incentives of a wholesale seller in the market that owns 5 percent of the system capacity. On such a day, the wholesale seller knows that if it withdraws 1 percent of the system capacity from production, it will have a significant effect on the wholesale price. If, however, the retail price also increased when the wholesale price rose, then customers would get a signal that they should scale back usage. The resulting reduction in demand means that the withdrawal of production capacity would have less impact on the wholesale price and, thus, would be less profitable for the seller. In contrast, if retail prices are not linked to the wholesale price level, then there is no demand response when the seller withdraws capacity, and the wholesale price is more likely to increase dramatically.

Without time-varying retail prices, the combination of supply-demand mismatches and the ability of sellers to exercise market power at peak times creates a relationship between price and system load that looks like a hockey stick laid on its side. Figure 8.4 shows a price/load scatterplot for California during June 2000 and a polynomial curve fitted to the points. The hockey-stick relationship is a fairly constant price over a wide range of outputs and then steeply upward-sloping price as demand grows closer to capacity. Time-varying prices would reduce the frequency and degree of price spikes during periods of high system load. Bushnell (chapter 6 in this volume) shows simulations of how much prices might decrease if firms exercising market power faced more responsive demand.

Time-Varying Prices in Practice

While the simple model presented in the previous section makes clear the value of time-varying prices that send accurate price signals, the actual details of implementation are, not surprisingly, more complex. In the model, there were only two time periods, and both demand and supply in each period were known with certainty. In reality, the supply-demand balance changes continuously, and there can be a great deal of uncertainty about supply and demand in advance of any given period. This raises the two fundamental issues in designing time-varying retail electricity prices:

1. *Granularity of Prices:* The frequency with which retail prices change within the day or week, and
2. *Timeliness of Prices:* the time lag between when a price is set and when it is actually effective.

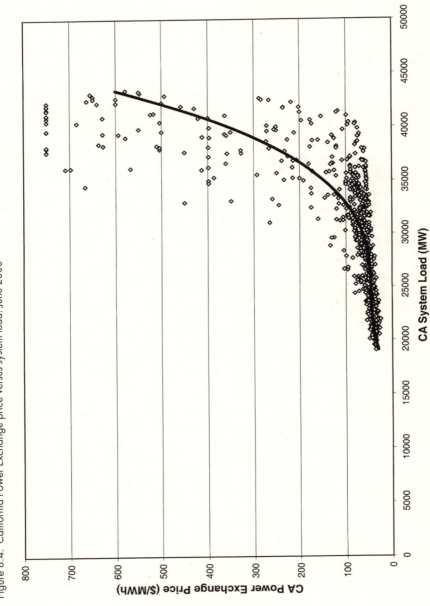

Figure 8.4. California Power Exchange price versus system load: June 2000

Flat retail rates are obviously at one extreme: no granularity—there is a single price for day and night, weekdays, and weekends—and price setting is not timely—the price is set months before some of the hours to which it is applied. At the opposite hypothetical extreme would be a real-time pricing program in which prices change every minute and are announced only at the minute in which they are applied. This hypothetical would be the ideal in terms of economic efficiency in the electricity market, but customers are likely to want more certainty about prices, an issue addressed in the following.

The granularity and timeliness issues in retail electricity pricing are distinct, but they are closely related and interact in somewhat subtle ways. The granularity of prices will affect the accuracy of price signals only to the extent that the *expected* cost of electricity differs across time intervals at the time the prices are set for those intervals. For instance, if prices were determined a month in advance, the value of having prices change every ten minutes rather than hourly would be negligible, because the *expected* costs for adjacent ten-minute periods barely differ one month ahead. In contrast, if prices were determined in real time, at the start of each ten-minute period, they would incorporate much more information about idiosyncratic supply or demand shocks. Thus, there is generally greater value of fine granularity in prices when price setting is more timely.

In debates over RTP, there is often a focus on granularity and the fact that prices change every hour in most cases. Timeliness is, in fact, at least as important. Hourly price changes would not be much of an improvement over just two or three daily price blocks per day if prices were set a month or more in advance. When timeliness is discussed as part of RTP, the issue is whether prices should be set a day ahead or an hour (or less) ahead. This choice turns out to have a large effect on the efficiency of RTP, as I discuss later.

A retail system in which prices are set in advance may at first seem to be the retail equivalent of the day-ahead and long-term contract transactions that take place in wholesale electricity markets, but there is a critical difference: the retail programs offer these prices as "requirements contracts," meaning that at the time of delivery the customer may choose to buy as much or as little as desired at the posted price.[4] If a wholesale electricity buyer purchases in advance, the purchase contract specifies both the price and the quantity. Deviations from that quantity in the wholesale buyer's actual consumption are then priced at the spot-market price in the hour in which they take place.

With this foundation, we can analyze the programs that have been designed for implementing time-varying retail prices. The possibilities range from slight augmentations on flat pricing to more radical change that would make retail electricity markets more closely resemble the wholesale electricity markets.[5]

Real-Time Pricing

Depending on one's view, either the most natural or the most extreme approach to time-varying prices is RTP of electricity. Real-time retail pricing describes a system that has a very high degree of both price granularity and price timeliness. This approach is consistent with most other industries that have highly volatile wholesale prices—such as fresh fish, produce, gasoline, or computer chips—where retail prices adjust very quickly to reflect changes in the wholesale price of the good. In most designs, retail electricity prices under RTP change hourly. For each hour, say 4–5 p.m. on June 21, the price may differ from the price at any other hour, such as 3–4 p.m. on June 21 or 4–5 p.m. on June 22.

Real-time retail prices are typically set either "day ahead" or "real time." In the day-ahead formulation, the retail provider announces all twenty-four hourly prices for a given day at one time on the prior day. In the real-time approach, the retail provider announces prices on a rolling basis, typically with the price for each hour determined between fifteen and ninety minutes prior to the beginning of that hour. In the largest RTP program in the United States, Georgia Power allows customers that sign up for RTP (all of its RTP customers are large industrial or commercial firms) to choose whether to be billed based on day-ahead or real-time announced prices. Most have chosen day-ahead.

In terms of economic incentives and efficiency, RTP using real-time announced prices offers the greatest value. The marginal incentives of consumers facing such prices most closely reflect the actual supply-demand situation in the market. Despite that attraction, most RTP implementations have used day-ahead announced prices for the hourly price that RTP customers pay. In all programs, these have been requirements contracts, so the customer can buy any quantity desired at that day-ahead price.

If RTP based on real-time announced prices is the "gold standard" in terms of economic efficiency, how much is being lost by instead using day-ahead prices as the basis for an RTP program? Part of answering that question is determining how much of the real-time price variation is captured in day-ahead prices. I've done this for two electricity markets that posted prices in both a day-ahead market and a real-time balancing market, California and the Pennsylvania, New Jersey, and Maryland market (PJM). On average, the day-ahead price captures 45–50 percent of the variation in the real-time balancing price over a year or longer period.[6]

That figure alone, however, does not answer the question. Imprecise retail pricing has economic consequences only if buyers would respond to the additional information offered by more precise pricing. For instance, if the only way that an industrial customer could respond to high prices is to cancel a shift of workers, and if this decision must be made a day in advance, then there would be no efficiency loss from basing RTP on day-ahead prices, even though those prices reflect the real-time supply-demand situation with some degree of noise. That is, one must ask not only how large the day-ahead forecast error is but also how much customers would alter their behavior if they received better information. Assuming, however, that there is some way for customers to respond, at least marginally, to changes in real-time RTP prices, retail prices that more closely reflect the real-time wholesale price will improve efficiency.

Whether based on a day-ahead or real-time wholesale price, RTP does not mean that customers must buy all of their power at the RTP price. Hedging— purchasing some power through a long-term contract before a period of system stress is evident—allows customers to stabilize their overall bill while still facing the RTP price for incremental consumption, as I discuss in detail later.

Time-of-Use (TOU) Pricing

While RTP has not been widely accepted or implemented, time-of-use (TOU) pricing has been used extensively in the United States for large industrial and commercial customers. Under TOU, the retail price varies in a preset way within certain blocks of time. For instance, a typical TOU pricing plan for weekdays during the summer charges 5.62¢ per kilowatt-hour (kWh) from 9:30 p.m. to 8:30 a.m., 10.29¢ per kWh for 8:30 a.m. to noon and 6 p.m. to 9:30 p.m., and 23.26¢ per kWh for noon to 6 p.m.[7] In most cases, the weekend and holiday rates are equal to the off-peak weekday rate. The rates for each time block (usually called peak, shoulder, and off peak) are adjusted infrequently, only two or three times per year in most cases. Price is the same at a given time of day (on a weekday) throughout the month or season for which the prices are set. Time-of-use retail pricing lacks both the granularity and the timeliness of RTP.

The lack of timeliness of TOU prices means that they cannot capture any of the shorter-term variation in supply-demand balance. In addition, TOU programs don't reflect *expected* wholesale market variation very well, due to the lack of price granularity. The standard three-block pricing format means that the 4–5 p.m. weekday price is the same as the noon–1 p.m. weekday price, because they are in the same block, despite the fact that the expected wholesale-market price is significantly different for these hours. Furthermore, because TOU programs typically reset prices for each block only two or three times per year, the same peak, off-peak, and shoulder prices may apply from May to October, even though the average demands and costs change in a quite predictable way during that time.

These attributes mean that TOU price variation will reflect little of the true variation in the wholesale market. Empirically, one can show this by looking at a given time period and asking how much of the wholesale price variation would be reflected in TOU prices, assuming that the TOU prices were set optimally to maximize their relationship to wholesale-market prices. For California, even setting TOU prices after the fact to reflect the actual average price in peak, shoulder, and off-peak periods, the TOU rates would have reflected only about 6–13 percent of the real-time wholesale price variation on average.[8] And these numbers assume that the agency setting the rates can forecast the average price in each period as accurately before the period as one can do after the fact, which is virtually impossible.

Put differently, TOU prices, while giving greater advance notice of prices and offering less price volatility, do quite poorly in reflecting variation in wholesale prices. As before, the cost of this loss of information will depend very much on how customers would react if they were given the finer information. For instance, if a factory can react to price changes only by making long-term adjustments, such as changing worker shift schedules that can be altered only semiannually, then the information in TOU prices may be as much as the factory can use. In that case, no price responsiveness is being sacrificed in using TOU prices instead of RTP. On the other hand, if the customer can make such adjustments more frequently, such as weekly or monthly, or can adjust quickly to idiosyncratic supply-demand information, such as by adjusting air conditioning settings and lighting when the system is strained, TOU rates won't yield such adjustments because they fail to signal the short-term variation in the supply-demand balance.

Technology plays a role in this trade-off. Until recently, the cost of TOU metering was substantially less than real-time metering and the ability to send real-time price information to customers was limited. Technology changes of the last decade have virtually eliminated these issues. Advances in technology also have enhanced and continue to enhance the customer's ability to respond to real-time price changes. Responding to frequent retail price changes does not now require human intervention. Instead, the real-time price is sent electronically to a computer that is programmed to respond. If the price goes above 15¢ per kWh, for instance, the computer might automatically reset air conditioning from 72 to 74 degrees. A computer could also automatically reset lighting and reschedule energy-intensive activities that are time adjustable, such as running a pool pump. Thus, historical measures of firms' abilities to respond to real-time price changes are likely to significantly understate the price responsiveness that technology and education will evoke in future years.

Augmenting TOU with Demand Charges

Because TOU rates don't capture the wholesale price variation within a time block, TOU pricing is often combined with a separate charge for peak usage. These "demand charges" are a price per kilowatt based on the customer's maximum usage (typically, during a fifteen-minute interval) during the billing period (usually a month), regardless of whether that usage occurs at a time when the system as a whole has a tight supply-demand balance. Most of the meters that register maximum usage for demand charge billing are not capable of storing information indicating the precise date and time at which that maximum usage occurred.[9]

Demand charges are a way to charge for a customer's peak usage, but the economic incentives that they establish are a very imperfect proxy for the real economic cost imposed on the system. First, demand charges are not synchronized to the usage on the system as a whole, so they charge as much for a peak usage that occurs at a lower demand time as at a higher demand time. In fact, this might not be as bad as it seems at first, because heating or air conditioning-driven demand peaks tend to be highly correlated across users within a region. More important, however, by charging only for the peak usage, demand charges don't give strong (or potentially any) incentive for a customer to conserve until usage is near the peak level for the period. If a very hot day occurs early in a billing period, the demand charge may give a customer little incentive to conserve after that.

The economics of demand charges made more sense under traditional utility regulation. The concept was to charge customers for their contribution to the need to build additional peaking capacity (though in practice this still suffered from the problem that the customer's peak consumption may not coincide with the overall peak consumption). Apart from the peak, charges varied little. This makes much less sense in a deregulated wholesale market where demand increases result in significant increases in wholesale price even before the system gets right up to its capacity.

In addition, demand charges make no adjustment for the supply side of the market. If an unusually high number of forced outages occurs on a moderately hot day, the system can be more strained than on a very hot day, even if the total system load is lower. Though wholesale prices vary systematically with system demand, many other factors cause wholesale prices to fluctuate throughout the month. Variations in supply availability (and the prices at which that supply is offered) can be as important as variations in demand in explaining fluctuating wholesale prices. Thus, although demand charges do enhance the ability of TOU pricing to reflect true economic costs of service, they still fall well short of RTP. The demand charge approach grew out of the technological metering limitations that existed many decades ago and is now obsolete.

Interruptible Demand Programs

The physical attributes of electricity systems imply that excess demand cannot be rationed using the standard nonprice mechanism: queuing. Instead, a systemwide excess demand can lead to a collapse of the entire grid, cutting off supply to all users. Thus, if for some reason economic incentives fail to equilibrate supply and demand for even a brief period, the system operator must have the ability to curtail usage by some customers. The response has been interruptible demand programs, which give the system operator the right to instruct the customer to cease consumption on very short notice. In return, the customer usually receives a reduction in its flat (or TOU) electricity rate, or it receives a periodic fixed payment.

Along the spectrum of time-varying price plans, interruptible electricity rates are nearly at the opposite end from RTP. These rates are constant nearly all of the time. When the system operator declares certain potential shortages, however, these customers are called upon to cease electricity consumption entirely. Despite the name, service to these customers is not actually physically interrupted in most cases. Rather, the price that they face increases dramatically. In one program in California, customers on interruptible rates were required during declared shortages either to stop consuming or to pay $9.00 per kWh for their continued consumption, a more than fortyfold increase. Thus, although these programs appear at first to be a departure from using a price system to allocate scarce electricity, in fact most programs are simply a crude form of RTP.

Seen in this light, interruptible programs are RTP with very blunt price changes: very poor granularity or timeliness unless a system emergency occurs, in which case the rate increases—for short periods and on short notice—so much that nearly all contracted customers choose to stop, or drastically reduce, consumption.[10] Interruptible programs offer a certain amount of insurance to customers, because they are told that they won't be called more than a pre-specified number of times during a year. As I discuss presently, however, price protection products can supplement RTP to offer at least as much insurance.

Critical Peak Pricing Programs

A recent innovation in time-varying pricing is critical peak pricing (CPP), which has some attributes of RTP and some of interruptible programs. The CPP programs usually start with a TOU rate structure, but then they add one more rate that applies to "critical" peak hours, which the utility can call on short notice.[11] While the TOU program has poor granularity and timeliness, as discussed previously, CPP allows a very high price to be called on very short notice, thereby improving both aspects of the rate structure. Thus, CPP is similar to interruptible programs except prices are not set so high as to cause most customers to reduce consumption to zero. In practice, interruptible programs are usually offered only to large customers, while CPP is envisioned to be used much more broadly.

Critical peak pricing programs typically limit the utility to call no more than 50 or 100 critical peak hours per year. Critical peak pricing is a clear improvement on TOU with demand charges, because the additional charges are based on consumption when the system is actually constrained rather than when the particular customer's demand peaks. Critical peak pricing has some of the advantages of RTP, because retail prices are allowed to vary with the wholesale market. Of course, CPP is much more constrained than RTP: the CPP peak price is set in advance and the number of hours in which it can apply is limited. A modification of the single-peak CPP is CPP with two callable peak retail prices, such as 50¢ or $1.00 per kWh so that the utility has more flexibility in the strength of the retail price incentives it can utilize.

CPP programs are the natural evolution of demand charges when more sophisticated metering is available. Charges increase at critical system peaks rather than at the individual customer's demand peak, which is much more consistent with the true costs of consumption. Critical peak pricing still has two economic weaknesses, though they may actually be strengths in terms of customer acceptance. First, the prices are limited and levels are preset for the critical peak periods; therefore, they can't be calibrated to move with the actual prices in the wholesale market. Second, the number of critical peak hours that can be called in a year is limited. As a result, the utility protects customers against seeing very high prices, even only on marginal purchases, for more than a fixed number of hours. As discussed in the following, RTP can be designed to offer much the same level of hedging, while still giving the customers strong incentives on the margin to conserve when the market is tight.

Real-Time Demand-Reduction Programs

While all of the pricing approaches discussed thus far charge customers time-varying prices, demand reduction programs (DRPs) pay a customer to reduce consumption at certain times. A customer signed up for a DRP is eligible to be contacted by the utility or system operator with an offer of payment in return for the customer reducing consumption.[12] These programs must first determine a baseline from which demand reduction can be measured. Once the baseline is set, the price offered for demand reduction determines the level of economic incentive to reduce demand when the system operator calls.

Much like CPP, and unlike TOU, real-time DRPs attempt to recognize the idiosyncratic daily and hourly variation in system stress and give customers incentives to respond. Demand reduction programs are activated by the system operator when grid conditions meet certain predetermined criteria that indicate that the supply-demand balance is likely to be very tight over some ensuing period of time. The operator then offers to pay participating customers to cut back their usage. In general, these programs are fairly blunt instruments; the system operator simply announces when the program is in effect. The price offered is usually predetermined and does not vary with the tightness of supply. In this way, DRPs might be thought of as just the mirror image of critical peak pricing and, like CPP, an improvement in both price granularity and timeliness compared to TOU pricing. Unfortunately, DRPs have a significant flaw that make them much less effective than CPP.

The fundamental weakness with DRPs is that there is no reliable baseline from which to pay for reduction.[13] With most goods, the natural baseline is zero: you start with none of the good and pay more as you consume more. Programs that pay for demand reduction generally set a baseline that comes from the past behavior of the customer. The baseline-setting process creates two serious problems.

First, if the program is voluntary, it will be joined disproportionately by the customers that already know they will have lower consumption relative to their assigned baseline. For instance, if the program uses last year's consumption as the baseline (perhaps with an adjustment for weather), the companies that have shrunk since last year will be the first to sign up. Their electricity consumption has fallen compared to the baseline for reasons having nothing to do with the program. The operator ends up paying for "conservation" that would have occurred anyway. Meanwhile, the companies that have grown rapidly since last year simply won't sign up.[14]

Second, if the baseline that is used can be affected by the customer, it will probably discourage conservation during times when the payments are not in effect. For instance, consider a plan that sets the baseline at the level of consumption the customer had on the previous day. Then on days when the payments are not in effect, customers would be foolish to conserve at all since that would just lower their baseline. Californians saw this effect in the 1970s with water rationing. Many users figured out that they were better off being profligate in normal-rainfall years so that they would have a higher baseline if a drought hit.

To overcome these problems, there could be a program that uses a baseline from an earlier period and is not voluntary. However, this would raise serious equity concerns. Shrinking companies would reap a windfall and expanding successful companies would be penalized.

Ultimately, real-time DRPs are very imperfect substitutes for critical peak pricing or RTP. They require the same metering technology as critical peak pricing and approximately the same level of information transmission from the system operator. Demand reduction programs limit the customer's liability by starting from a flat rate and reducing bills from there, but such bill protection can be done easily within a CPP or RTP program, as described in the next section. Unlike CPP or RTP, DRPs suffer significant problems and potential conflicts in setting baselines.[15]

Last, although DRPs are often favored as a positive reinforcement mechanism, all the money that is paid out in positive reinforcement has to come from somewhere. Paying for demand reduction is not a free lunch. It most likely comes from higher general rates than would be necessary to reach the same revenue requirement under CPP or RTP.[16]

Issues in Implementing Real-Time Pricing

I will now focus on real-time pricing in discussing four important issues in implementation: risk to customers and retailers, distributional impacts of adopting RTP, mandatory versus voluntary implementation, and the role of demand response in setting and meeting reserve requirements. Time-of-use pricing already exists and is used widely but does not give economic incentives that are particularly accurate, as discussed previously. Much of the discussion that follows applies to other time-varying retail price programs, including

CPP and pay-for-demand reduction. As discussed in the prior section, interruptible programs are extreme and extremely blunt versions of RTP; their usage would be minimized in a well-functioning electricity system.

Mitigating Customer Price Risk and Retailer Revenue Risk

For more than seventy-five years, customers of regulated electricity utilities were protected from price volatility by a regulatory system that permitted rates to change only very infrequently. Regulated utilities met their revenue requirements over the long run by adjusting rates monthly or annually, with regulatory approval. Because utilities produced most of the power that they delivered, the primary risk they faced was from fuel price changes. Even that risk was reduced over the last thirty years, actually shifted to customers, with the increasing use of automatic fuel adjustment clauses.

Now that more utilities (and other retail electricity providers) are net buyers of power, much of the utility retailer cost risk comes from volatility in the wholesale price of power. Under a simple RTP system the retailer transfers that risk to customers by setting a retail RTP price based on the wholesale-market price. If the retailer owns generation of its own or has other costs unrelated to wholesale power, however, it will still face risks in meeting its own revenue requirements. Thus, both potential customers and utility retailers have expressed concern about the risks that may accompany RTP.

There are a number of different models for mitigating customer price risk and retailer revenue risk under time-varying retail prices. They differ in two basic dimensions: (1) customers can actively participate in hedging of price risk or the retailer can carry out hedging on behalf of passive customers, and (2) other costs unrelated to power consumption (such as stranded investments, and transmission and distribution costs) can be incorporated through adjustments to time-varying retail power prices or through lump-sum mechanisms. Capital gains and losses from retailer hedging are among the costs (or gains) to be incorporated.

The historical flat retail electricity pricing represents the extremes in both of these dimensions. All retail price hedging is carried out by the utility, which offers only the very-hedged flat-price product, and customers are completely passive. The utility meets its revenue requirement completely through adjustment of the flat rate, which covers both fixed and variable costs. To the extent that the retailer hedges its wholesale (or fuel) price risk, the capital gains or losses associated with those sunk gains or losses are incorporated when the flat rate is changed. Likewise, TOU programs limit the customers' retail price risk by drastically reducing the volatility of retail prices, and they meet revenue targets by adjusting these rates gradually over time. Similarly, demand reduction programs limit customer risk by guaranteeing that the customer never faces a price above the posted tariff and underwrites the program with higher flat or TOU retail rates.

RTP with a Customer Baseline Load (CBL)

A number of RTP programs, including the largest U.S. program, operated by Georgia Power, limit customer price risk by assigning each customer on RTP a baseline consumption level that the customer is required to purchase at the regulated rate during each hour. The price the customer pays for its baseline consumption is usually the regulated TOU rate that the customer would otherwise face. Starting at the baseline, the customer then pays the real-time price for any consumption above its baseline level and receives a rebate based on the real-time price if its consumption falls below its baseline level. In financial terms, the baseline is just a forward contract for a quantity equal to the customers baseline level, that is, a hedge contract, which the customer has purchased at a price set by the regulatory process. Such programs are generally called two-part RTP programs with a CBL.[17] Under RTP with a CBL, customers are passive in the hedging activity, though Georgia Power offers additional hedging instruments that the customer can actively choose to purchase.

The CBL approach also creates a mechanism for covering costs that are not directly related to the incremental cost of energy without distorting the RTP price signal. By setting the CBL and the rate at which that energy is purchased, the utility (or regulatory agency) builds in a fixed charge for a fixed quantity of energy. That fixed charge can be used to cover costs (or give refunds) without distorting the incremental energy price. For instance, if the regulator decided that the utility was permitted to raise an additional $1 million to cover a stranded investment, an increase to the TOU rate would increase revenue earned from customers on RTP with a CBL by raising the cost of the baseline power. Importantly, it would not affect the price that the firm pays for power on the margin.

The California crisis, however, made clear a significant difficulty with the CBL approach. If the customer buys the baseline at a price that is not closely related to the expected market price, purchase of the baseline quantity amounts to either a subsidy or a tax depending on whether the regulated price is above or below the expected market price. That alone would create an equity issue, but in practice it also creates a significant influence and lobbying problem.

An RTP plan with a CBL was proposed in California during the spring of 2001. At that time, the real-time price was expected to be well above the regulated price at which customers would purchase their CBL. Once companies understood this (the plan was to be only for large customers), their focus turned almost entirely to lobbying for a high CBL for themselves.[18] Any RTP program with a CBL will include an implicit transfer payment to or from the customer so long as the regulated price differs from the expected real-time price. Thus, baselines set by any regulatory process will be subject to intense lobbying and related influence activities.

RTP with Build-Your-Own Baseline

There is a device similar to the CBL that can avoid the lobbying and influence problems: the forward contract that the CBL itself was meant to mimic. One way to think of this is as real-time pricing with a build-your-own (BYO) baseline. As the name suggests, customers take an active role in determining the extent to which they hedge price risk. Rather than being assigned a CBL for each hour of the year, the customer can purchase a baseline quantity (i.e., a forward contract) for each hour in order to hedge as much price risk as it wants. The key would be for the retailer to offer the baseline or forward contract for each hour at a price that equals the best forecast of that hour's future spot price. Georgia Power, one of the first users of the CBL, now offers such futures contracts for RTP customers that want more hedging than is provided by the CBL. They refer to these as price protection products. The advantage of this approach is that because the BYO baseline is purchased at a price that reflects the expected real-time price, unlike the CBL, it contains no subsidy or tax on average. It is simply a risk-hedging device. This approach also makes it easy for the retailer to offset the baseline it sells forward by purchasing power forward in the wholesale market at approximately the same price at which it sells power forward for the BYO baseline.

The BYO baseline allows customer to avoid purchasing most of their power at the real-time price. Yet, for incremental consumption decisions, the customer still faces the real-time price as its cost (or opportunity cost, as it can resell power it doesn't use from its BYO baseline), and thus has strong incentives to conserve at peak times. The BYO baseline cannot create a perfect hedge because the customer won't know in advance exactly what quantity it will want to consume in each hour. To the extent that customers want even more-stable electric bills than the BYO baseline would provide, other products, including call options, may develop in a private market. In fact, the BYO baseline itself could be provided by a private market. In reality, however, regulatory uncertainty at the beginning of an RTP program may make private parties reluctant to enter this retail hedging market, so it would probably make sense for the utility to be the first provider of such risk-hedging products.

One disadvantage of the BYO baseline in comparison to the CBL is that the BYO baseline cannot be used to cover sunk or fixed costs. The forward price offered must be very close to the expected real-time price when customers voluntarily choose how much baseline to purchase. The BYO baseline would have to be augmented with some other fee (or rebate) mechanism in order to assure that revenue requirements are met. The CBL implicitly creates such a fee mechanism by assigning each customer in the program a baseline level of consumption that is required to be purchased at a regulated price that is not tied to the expected spot price. An alternative is to use a fixed adder on the RTP price to cover sunk or fixed costs, as I discuss in the next subsection.

RTP with Retailer Hedging on Behalf of Customers

Even if customers are on a simple RTP plan without any baseline and retailers are buying most of their power in the wholesale market, retailers can still stabilize RTP customers' bills by hedging on their behalf and using the profit or loss from such hedging to offset power price fluctuations. In this approach customers are completely passive, putting all hedging decisions in the hands of the retailer. By purchasing some power on long-term contracts, the retailer hedges wholesale power costs. The question this creates is how the retailer can pass through the profit or loss from hedging in a way that minimizes price distortions.

Historically, utilities have hedged on behalf of their customers by generating most of their own power, but they have passed through the results of this hedging through occasional adjustments to flat retail rates, a process that creates distorted incentives to customers. In restructured markets, the practice has continued: by retaining ownership of generation, signing long-term power contracts, or buying generation inputs forward, retailers still hedge power prices. And they've still passed along the outcome of their hedging through occasional adjustment to a flat retail rate. Retailers, however, can hedge on behalf of RTP customers and can pass along the outcome from hedging without undermining the volatility of RTP prices by attaching a constant (over the billing period) adder or subtractor to the RTP price.

To see this, begin by assuming that the retailer engages in no hedging. It charges customers a fixed per-kWh transmission and distribution (T&D) charge plus the spot price of energy in each hour.[19] In this case, the customers' monthly bills, and retailer's revenues, would be as variable as the month-to-month variation in the weighted-average spot energy prices.

To attain the goal of monthly bill stability, the retailer would sign a long-term contract to buy some amount of power at a fixed price.[20] To fix ideas and keep the presentation simple, assume that the retailer signs a long-term contract at the same price for each hour. Such a contract will be at about the average spot price of the electricity that the parties anticipate over the life of the contract, but in any given month the contract price could be greater or less than the average spot price. If there are significant shifts in the market, the contract prices could end up being much cheaper or more expensive than the spot wholesale prices.

This contract can be considered a financial investment that is completely independent of the retailer's service to final customers. The critical point is that the retailer's return on this financial investment varies directly with the average spot price of energy, and that return can be applied to change the average level of customer bills. When viewed this way, it becomes clear that the long-term contract can be used to affect the average price level without dampening the price variation. The gains (when the average spot price is higher than the contract price) or losses (when the average spot price is lower than the contract price) from the long-term contract could be distributed to customers with a constant surcharge or discount on each kWh sold during that billing period.

The retailer would then charge the customer the spot price plus or minus an adjustment equal to the average return per-kWh from the long-term contract. Because the profit earned from holding the contract is greater when the spot price is higher, it would be used to offset the high *average* spot price, thus lowering the volatility of monthly electricity bills. If the retailer hedged nearly all of its expected load, then this offset would eliminate most variability in monthly bills. If the retailer hedged, say, 80 percent of the load, then about 80 percent of the variability in monthly bills would be eliminated. The actual price that the customer was charged in each hour, however, would still have the same volatility as the spot price. The critical point is that the gains or losses in any given hour from the forward contract need not and should not be collected in that particular hour. There is no economic argument for doing so, and doing so would greatly reduce the variability of retail prices and, thus, the economic incentive for conservation.

Figure 8.5 illustrates the effect that this approach would have had in California during June of 2000 if the retailer had been lucky enough to sign a long-term contract before prices increased. In this illustration, the retailer is assumed to have signed a contract for 80 percent of its load at 6¢ per kWh. In addition to energy charges, the retailer is assumed to assess a 4¢ per kWh charge for transmission and distribution. The T&D charge is added to all prices for ease of comparison. The three horizontal lines show the load-weighted average price a customer would pay (assuming it had the same load profile as the system as a whole) if the retailer were fully hedged (lowest line), if it were completely unhedged (highest line), and if it were 80 percent hedged (middle line).

Figure 8.5. Real-time pricing with monthly bill stability

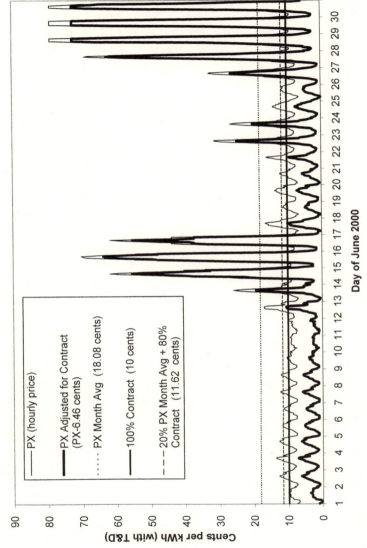

Note: Assumes contract at 6 cents/kWh. Price includes 4 cents/kWh T&D.

Of the two volatile lines, the higher shows the real-time price a customer would pay with no hedging, and the lower shows the price the customer would have paid if the retailer had combined real-time pricing with 80 percent hedging, in this case, purchased through long-term contracts. The load-weighted average of the higher line is 18.08¢, the same as the highest horizontal line. The load-weighted average of the lower line is 11.62¢, the same as the middle horizontal line.[21] This illustration demonstrates that under real-time pricing with long-term contracts, a customer could face the same volatility in prices as it would under RTP with no hedging. The only difference would be that the price curve would be shifted down by the "profits" from the long-term contract, which in this example are 6.46¢ per kWh. During the hours of extremely high spot prices, customers would face prices nearly as extreme, and would have a strong incentive to reduce consumption. Yet the average monthly prices (and monthly bills) the customer would face would be much less volatile than without hedging.[22]

Hedging by the retailer is particularly valuable in a regulated context where customers do not have the choice to hedge price risk themselves by signing private contracts with generators or other market participants. In a competitive retail market, retailers would probably not arbitrarily impose a level of hedging and retail price. Instead, they would offer to pass through the wholesale spot electricity price and would augment that offering with various price protection programs, such as a BYO baseline. The retailer would then hedge its wholesale price risk in a way to match the retail price hedging that its customers have chosen to purchase. In essence, the retailer would serve as a broker of risk-hedging services.

More generally, a fixed per-kWh adder or subtractor can always be used to attain any desired average retail price while maintaining the time variation in retail prices.[23] The issue of time variation in retail pricing can be completely decoupled from the issue of targeting a given average price or a given revenue requirement. Thus, the same approach can be used with BYO baseline to recover costs unrelated to wholesale power prices, including payments for stranded investments and T&D.

This is, of course, not the ideal way to change average bills, as it means that retail prices will not exactly reflect the wholesale market costs, creating deadweight loss. The economic ideal would be to pass through wholesale prices exactly in each hour and separately make lump-sum adjustments, unrelated to consumption during the month, in order to hit an average price target. The problem is that lump-sum adjustments, as illustrated by the CBL, raise significant equity issues and lobbying costs. Furthermore, the size of the deadweight loss from mispricing increases in proportion to the square of the mispricing. The adder or subtractor envisioned here would probably be quite small compared to the variation in wholesale prices. Thus, while it would create small mispricing in many hours, it would allow a system that prevents the large mispricing that occurs during peak hours absent RTP.

Distributional Impacts of Adopting RTP

Of great concern in discussions of RTP programs is which participants will be winners and which will be losers from adoption of such a change. A significant effect of RTP in the short run is to reduce the total payments to generators in the wholesale electricity market. This occurs because peak demands, when prices are very high (even if the wholesale market is competitive), are reduced. In the long run, this means fewer new power plants need to be built and their costs need not be borne by customers. It is important to note these effects can benefit all customers, those on RTP and those who are not. Furthermore, if the wholesale market is not completely competitive, RTP reduces the ability of sellers to exercise market power, which further reduces wholesale prices and, again, benefits all customers whether or not they are on RTP. By creating real-time demand elasticity, RTP also lessens the likelihood of system shortages and the potential for customer interruptions or rolling blackouts.

Among customers on RTP, the benefits vary depending on when a customer consumes power. Customers with a relatively flat consumption profile—whose consumption has less hour-to-hour and day-to-day variance than others on RTP—will see the greatest benefits. Because their consumption does not peak as much as the aggregate demand at high-demand times, they will be buying a smaller share of their power at the most expensive times. As a result, their average price per kWh will be lower than for customers with more "peaky" demand.

Customers with more "peaky" demand, who do not respond to the higher retail prices that will occur when supply is tight, will consume a disproportionate share of their power at the more expensive times. These customers will face a higher average price per kWh than will customers with a flatter demand profile. In California, the peak demands occur on hot summer days and are driven primarily by air conditioning. There are no completely reliable rules, but customers that use power disproportionately for air conditioning (or for heating in areas that peak in the winter) generally have more "peaky" demand that is greatest at the time when electricity is more expensive. Customers that use power disproportionately for other uses (lighting, industrial production, machinery) generally have flatter demand profiles.

Customers with "peaky" demands might end up paying more than under flat rates, but it is quite possible that they would not. While they would pay high prices at peak times, the overall efficiency of the system would improve and there would be less idle capacity that all customers must pay for in the long run. The average price would decline with RTP, but these customers would consume a disproportionate share of their power at higher-price times, so it is hard to know for sure whether their bills would increase or decrease. Certainly, to the extent that they can respond to high prices by conserving or shifting demand, their bills would be more likely to decrease.

Many industrial customers that run twenty-four hours a day, seven days a week have expressed concern about RTP because they say that they cannot reduce their demand or shift usage. Customers that run 24/7, however, tend to have flatter demand profiles than the system as a whole. Thus, although they would have to buy power at higher prices during system peaks under RTP, they would buy a smaller share of their power at these times than would other users. Their overall power bills would decline.

The reason for this is that the system is driven not by one customer's ability to conserve but by the ability of users in aggregate to lower demand at peak times, thereby reducing wholesale electricity prices and reducing the risk of rolling blackouts. If a certain customer cannot conserve at all without suffering major economic losses, then RTP offers enormous benefits, because it reduces the chance of rolling blackouts, which are especially costly to such customers, and it reduces the wholesale price of electricity at peak time because other users reduce their demand.

In nearly all areas where RTP is being considered or has been implemented, it has not been offered to small commercial or residential customers. It certainly makes sense to start with large customers, because the cost of metering them is trivial compared to the potential efficiency gains. But it should be recognized that customers who remain on flat-rate service are imposing demands at peak times that they are not paying for. In the following section, I discuss a strategy for avoiding cross-subsidies between RTP and flat-rate customers.

On the other hand, some industrial customers have suggested that if they switch to RTP they should be rewarded because their behavior benefits other consumers at peak times. While that is true in the short run, it is only at the expense of producers. The price reduction at peak times is a transfer from producers to consumers, not a net benefit to society. The overall saving to society from a RTP customer reducing its consumption by 1 kWh is no more than the price of that kWh.[24] In the long run, Borenstein and Holland (forthcoming) and Borenstein (2004) show that the net externality of a customer switching to RTP can be positive or negative. If prices are set appropriately for both RTP and flat-rate customers, as I describe in the next section, then being an RTP customer is its own reward and most likely would not require further subsidy. The proper policy is to end implicit subsidies in flat-rate retail pricing, not to create offsetting subsidies for customers on RTP.[25]

Mandatory versus Voluntary Implementation

A question that arises frequently in discussions of RTP is whether it will be mandatory or voluntary for a given class of customers. As virtually all consideration of RTP has been only for large customers, the class of customers for whom RTP might be mandatory is those large customers. In practice, nearly all of the programs in the United States are voluntary.

It is important to remember that a mandatory RTP program does not mean that customers need to be exposed to the full risk of the spot electricity market because hedging by the retailer or by the customer can greatly reduce the price risk associated with RTP. A more accurate description would be a "default" RTP program: customers by default pay the real-time price, but they can sign forward contracts that mitigate the volatility in costs they would face if they purchased all of their power at the spot price.

Still, many market participants argue that if any RTP program is instituted it should be done on a voluntary basis. While a voluntary program is attractive in many ways, it also raises difficult equity and efficiency issues that don't arise if RTP is the default.

The customers that would sign up for a voluntary RTP program would be those that have a more attractive load profile—either flatter than most or actually peaking at times when the system demand is low—or those that *would have* a more attractive profile once they responded to real-time prices. These customers would get lower bills if they paid the wholesale price of the power they used under RTP rather than the average wholesale price of the power that all customers use. In large part, a voluntary program would identify the customers who have been subsidizing other users that consume more at peak times.

This, however, creates a problem for the retailer. In order to avoid a revenue shortfall, either it must charge a higher average price to those that don't sign up for RTP than to those that do or it must place an adder on the RTP price so that the RTP group as a whole faces the same average price as non-participants.[26] A lower average price for RTP participants would be consistent with the cost of serving this group, but it would very likely raise difficult political issues. Rather than being seen as an end to a historical cross-subsidy, it would likely be portrayed as a new subsidy to RTP customers.

On the other hand, an adder to RTP prices that equalizes the average RTP price and the average non-RTP price would undermine the incentives to join the program. If the average per-kWh price for RTP customers is the same as for non-RTP customers, then some—probably about half—of the customers on RTP are paying a higher average per-kWh price on RTP than they would if they switched to the non-RTP rate. Those customers would be better off switching to the flat rate. As they did, this would reduce the average per-kWh rate among those remaining on RTP. In order to equalize prices between RTP and non-RTP customers, the retailer would have to raise the RTP adder. Once it did so, a new set of RTP customers would find they were paying a higher average price than they would on a flat rate. They would then be better off switching to the flat rate. This RTP death spiral would continue until only the customer with the most attractive load profile is left on RTP and the adder is set so that this customer is just indifferent between staying on RTP and switching to a flat rate.

An alternative to the RTP death spiral would be to institute RTP on a voluntary basis but to charge each group, RTP and flat-rate, an average price equal to the average cost of serving that group.[27] That is, this would be a no-cross-subsidy implementation of a voluntary RTP program.

When first offered, the RTP plan would primarily attract customers with the most attractive load profiles. But once these customers switched to the RTP plan, the average cost of serving customers that remained in the flat-rate plan would rise. This would make the flat-rate plan less attractive relative to RTP and would cause more customers to switch. Those that would now want to switch would be a selection of customers remaining in the flat-rate plan that have relatively more attractive load profiles. Again, the switching would cause the average cost of serving flat-rate customers to rise and thus would increase the price charged to them, making the flat-rate plan even less attractive. While this approach might not cause a complete unraveling of the flat rate, it would almost surely attract significant business and result in a higher average price for those that remain on flat rate than for those that move to RTP.

Again, it could still lower the price charged to both groups compared to no RTP because the incentive to consume less at peak times would reduce overall peak demand and wholesale prices. It is worth pointing out that the no-cross-subsidy implementation of a voluntary RTP plan might also be achieved without a regulatory process. Retail choice is likely to have this effect if it is implemented in a way that does not offer a subsidized default utility rate. Customers that are cheaper to serve will abandon the flat-rate utility service in order to get the lower prices associated with their more-attractive load profiles. As they do, if the remaining utility customers are not subsidized, their flat-rate price will rise above the average price paid by customers who have moved to a competitive retailer offering RTP.

Implementation of retail choice thus far, however, has generally offered customers remaining with the utility a fixed price independent of the costs of serving these customers. This has set up two types of incentives. First, it has reduced the attraction of moving to a competitive retailer, because as some customers have moved, the price to the remaining customers has not been affected, in contrast to the no-cross-subsidy implementation I've just described.[28] Second, it has created incentives for customers to jump back and forth between competitive suppliers and the fixed-price utility offering. When wholesale prices in California jumped in summer 2000, competitive retailers raised their prices to reflect that increase. The result was that many customers returned to the fixed-price utility rates, which were then being heavily subsidized. When wholesale prices fell in summer 2001, many of the same customers jumped back to competitive retailers.

Successful implementation of RTP does not depend on making it compulsory for any group. It can be implemented on a voluntary basis if it is done with a commitment of no cross-subsidy between RTP and flat-rate customers. In fact, such an approach would be likely to create its own momentum as low-cost customers abandon the flat rate and increase the wedge between the average prices paid by RTP and flat-rate customers. This would be the result of retail competition if prices to customers that remained on the utility's flat-rate plan were reset to reflect the cost of procuring power for those customers. In practice, however, a voluntary program is usually implemented with price, or subsidy, protection for customers that choose not to switch. This dampens the economic incentive to switch to RTP. The problem is greatly exacerbated if the flat-rate customers are also given a fixed rate that doesn't change when average prices in the wholesale market change, as occurred in California during the summer of 2000.

Using Demand to Meet Reserve Requirements: Economics Meets Engineering

Administrators of nearly all restructured electricity markets, and of many that are still fully regulated, have suggested that demand response to time-varying retail prices could be used to help meet reserve requirements. The Federal Energy Regulatory Commission (FERC) has endorsed this concept in its draft standard market design. Implementation of this approach, however, exposes a conflict between the economic analysis of electricity markets and the operating procedures that electrical engineers use in operating the grid. The grid operator wants to have resources that it knows with near certainty it can call on to increase supply or reduce demand.[29] Grid operators tend to be resistant to the idea of equilibrating supply and demand by increasing the price in a spot electricity market and hoping that demand in aggregate will respond.

The grid operators' concerns are understandable because any supply-demand imbalance that lasts even a split second can be catastrophic. They are less attracted to the idea of balancing supply and demand through price adjustments that yield small-quantity changes from thousands of customers, because none of those customers precommits to make a specific change under specific conditions. Rather, the responses to price changes are probabilistic, and the reliability of the aggregate response is due only to the law of large numbers applied to many independent buyers. To be concrete, if demand is exceeding supply and adjustment is supposed to occur through a price mechanism, a grid operator has no one to call to assure that demand response occurs.

It is for this reason that grid operators tend to be much more supportive of interruptible demand and contracts for prespecified demand reduction than they are of critical peak or real-time pricing as a method for balancing supply and demand. Grid operators, however, can be satisfied while still allowing price response to play a major role in supply-demand balancing. Interruptible and demand reduction contracts will still have roles to play as backup mechanisms. Given the engineering realities of electricity systems, the system operator has to have some ability to cut off customers when the system is nearly overloaded and normal market processes either have failed or cannot respond quickly enough. It makes much more economic sense to establish priorities for such situations in advance and compensate those who volunteer for curtailment, rather than choosing customers or areas randomly, as was done in California during early 2001.

Still, it is important to recognize that reducing demand through customer interruption or large prespecified demand reductions is likely to take a much larger economic toll than is time-varying retail prices: forcing 100 customers to reduce consumption by 100 percent will be much more costly than inducing 10,000 customers to each reduce consumption by 1 percent, on average. Grid operators have long recognized that it isn't practical to enter into thousands of contracts for small demand reductions or to call each customer to ask for reduction, but the price mechanism is the tool that can achieve that outcome without formal contracting. If market processes are allowed to operate effectively, interruptible programs and demand reduction contracts will be an absolute last-ditch mechanism that will hardly ever be used.

Currently, reserve requirements are established based on forecasts of system peak demands that do not take into account demands response to price changes. Implicitly, demand is assumed to be completely price inelastic, and system reserve requirements are set to be some percentage, usually between 10 percent and 20 percent, above the forecast system peak. Contracts for demand interruption or reduction fit easily into that paradigm. Incorporating the price responsiveness of demand under RTP or CPP requires a change in the paradigm. It overstates the effect of RTP to say that no reserves are needed once RTP is implemented, but it understates the impact to say that RTP would simply reduce the system peak so the same reserve requirement should be applied to a somewhat lower peak forecast. Time-varying retail price demand will mean not only that the system peak will be lower but also that the necessary percentage reserve level will be reduced, because an unexpected system shortage will be addressable in part through the response to price increases. When it is first implemented in a system, the reliability of price response will be unproven, so the operator will rely very little on it to meet reserve requirements. Over time, however, the response will be more reliably forecast, and price responsiveness will be able to take on an increasing role in assuring system reliability. Although it will never fully replace other forms of reserves, price-responsive demand will eventually cut the necessary reserve levels substantially.

The Long-Run Impact of Real-Time Pricing

It is clear from the previous section that conversion to real-time pricing of electricity would require changes both in the technology of metering and billing and in the financial transactions associated with electricity consumption. It is important to examine the benefits of RTP to determine whether they justify the costs. To do so, I have simulated a competitive electricity market in the long run with plausible demand elasticities, load shapes, and production technologies, assuming free entry and exit of generation.[30] These simulations are not intended to be a precise reflection of any particular market but are intended to illustrate with plausible parameters the magnitude of impacts that RTP would have.

The first difficulty in such simulation of the impact of RTP is that it is dependent on the demand response that the price fluctuation will elicit. Estimation of electricity demand elasticity has a long record, but the experiments that have been used as the basis for estimation have significantly constrained inference about how an RTP program would change behavior.

Most of the estimates that exist are based on pilot programs that were run by utilities in the 1970s and 1980s. Two factors make these programs and the resulting econometric studies inapplicable to forecasts of the impact of RTP. First, most of the programs were pilot studies of residential TOU pricing, not RTP. Those that were RTP-like programs mostly used blunt price changes (more like critical peak pricing). Second, and more important, the response to RTP is largely dependent on the technology available for automated response. Few customers would find it worthwhile to manually adjust most electricity usage in response to real-time price fluctuations. The technology for automated response has improved drastically since the 1980s and continues to improve at a very rapid rate. Thus, to get a reasonable sense of the possibilities for demand response, we must look to recent studies, though even these probably understate the elasticity that will result as technology continues to improve.

The two most relevant programs for estimating elasticity of demand to real-time price variation are in the United Kingdom and Georgia. Patrick and Wolak (1997) studied the response of industrial customers to real-time price variation in the United Kingdom during 1991–95. Braithwait and O'Sheasy (2002) studied the response of industrial customers on Georgia Power's RTP program that has been in existence since 1993. Unfortunately, even these recent studies give a wide range of elasticities, from −0.001 to −0.25 in Patrick and Wolak and from −0.01 to −0.28 in Braithwait and O'Sheasy. I use two figures in the simulations I present: −0.075 to represent price response in the shorter run, and −0.15 to represent price response in the longer run. The short-run response might be less elastic than −0.075, and the long-run response might be more elastic than −0.15, especially as the technology for automated response improves, but this will at least give an idea of the possible effects within a plausible range of elasticities.

The second important input to the simulation is a system load profile. I take the load profile of the California ISO system for the two-year period November 1998 to October 2000. While this is not perfectly representative, the first year of the period was moderately low demand and the second year was moderately high demand, so it does give a broad representation.[31]

The third type of inputs necessary to carry out such a simulation is the production technologies available. I assume that there are three technologies: a baseload technology (high fixed capacity cost, low variable cost) with approximately the cost properties of coal plants; a mid-merit technology (medium fixed capacity cost, medium variable cost) similar in costs to combined-cycle gas turbines; and a peaker technology (low fixed capacity cost, high variable cost) that reflects costs of a combustion turbine generating plant. Table 8.1 presents the exact cost assumptions used for each technology. I would not suggest that these are the best forecasts of costs for these tech-

Table 8.1. Generation costs assumed in long-run RTP simulations

Generation type	Annual fixed cost	Variable cost	Efficient use of capacity
Baseload	$155,000/MW	$15/MWh	operated > 4,000 hrs/year
Mid-merit	$75,000/MW	$35/MWh	operated < 4,000 and > 1,000 hrs/year
Peaker	$50,000/MW	$60/MWh	operated < 1,000 hrs/year

nologies, but they are in a plausible range. More important, the qualitative results are robust to a wide variety of assumptions about the exact costs, as discussed in Borenstein (2004).

To carry out the simulation, I first calculated the flat-rate tariff that would be required to cover the costs of the least-cost production of the assumed load duration curve, where least-cost production was defined by the range of hours a plant is used per year, as shown in table 8.1. I assumed that the load duration curve taken from California would be the actual quantities demanded at this flat rate, $79.13 per MWh (or 7.913¢/kWh). This yielded the top row in both tables 8.2 and 8.3. Note that because demand is inelastic in this case, capacity payments are required in order for firms to cover their costs. The flat-rate tariff is set at a level that produces enough revenue to cover those capacity payments as well as operating costs.[32]

I then calculated competitive generation equilibria for each hour assuming that demand would be equal to its level in the assumed load profile if price were equal to $79.13/MWh but that it would change according to the assumed (constant) elasticity for higher or lower prices. Generators earn scarcity rents when the wholesale market clears above their marginal cost, and these scarcity rents provide efficient investment incentives for each production technology.[33] The lower rows in tables 8.2 and 8.3 provide the resulting changes from the flat-rate base case in capacity of each generation type, costs, quantity consumed, and consumer surplus.

Tables 8.2 and 8.3 reveal a number of effects of RTP. Table 8.2 illustrates that RTP would likely raise the use of baseload technology slightly and greatly reduce the use of peaker technology.[34] Even a very slight elasticity of demand, –0.025, reduces the need for installed capacity by more than 10 percent. The shorter-run elasticity I posit of –0.075 would reduce the need for capacity by about 19 percent, and the longer-run elasticity of –0.15 would reduce it by about 26 percent.

In this simulation, firms are assumed to be perfectly competitive, exactly covering their full costs (including a normal return on investment) in the long

Table 8.2 Long-run effect of RTP compared to flat-rate tariff: Capacity changes

	Base capacity (MW)	Mid-merit capacity (MW)	Peaker capacity (MW)	Total capacity (MW)
Flat-rate tariff	27,491	5,472	12,912	45,875
Real-time pricing Elasticity				
−0.025	27,631	5,257	7,798	40,686
−0.050	27,772	5,036	5,709	38,517
−0.075	27,912	4,822	4,281	37,015
−0.100	28,052	4,613	3,156	35,812
−0.150	28,331	4,188	1,446	33,965

Table 8.3 Long-run effect of RTP compared to flat-rate tariff: Annual changes in cost and consumer surplus

	Total energy (MWh)			Total energy bill
Flat-rate tariff	236,796,579			$9,265,850,141
	Change in total energy (MWh)	Change in total energy bill	Change in consumer surplus	Δ CS/ flat-rate energy bill
Real-time pricing Elasticity				
−0.025	+800,441	−$259,997,701	+$233,825,698	+2.52%
−0.050	+1,462,755	−$377,627,882	+$335,913,373	+3.63%
−0.075	+2,097,715	−$463,153,781	+$409,994,816	+4.42%
−0.100	+2,723,226	−$534,312,079	+$472,647,808	+5.10%
−0.150	+3,968,346	−$650,109,447	+$578,088,940	+6.24%

run. Thus, the only change in surplus in the long run is for consumers. The "Change in Consumer Surplus" column of table 8.3 shows the increase in annual consumer surplus, and the adjoining column shows this change as a percentage of the customer's annual energy bills prior to the introduction of RTP. Thus, for instance, introducing RTP in a market in which market demand exhibits an elasticity of −0.075 increases consumer surplus by about $410 million per year, or 4.42 percent of the pre-RTP energy bill.

In reality, RTP is unlikely to be introduced to an entire system simultaneously. Rather, it is likely that the largest customers would move to RTP first. In California, the state paid to have RTP meters installed for the largest 20,000 customers in the state, who together comprise nearly one-third of the state's demand. Assuming that the customers moving to RTP have about the same load profile as the system as a whole, moving one-third of customers to RTP can be approximated by examining a case with demand elasticity equal to one-third of the actual demand elasticity.[35] Examining the row in table 8.3 with demand elasticity of –0.025, therefore, gives an idea of the effect of putting one-third of load on RTP when all demand has a price elasticity of –0.075.

Comparing the –0.025 elasticity row with the –0.075 elasticity row, it is immediately apparent that putting one-third of load on RTP attains much more than half the benefit one would get from putting all of the load on RTP. In fact, the first third on RTP creates a consumer surplus increase of about $234 million per year; the second third (from the –0.05 elasticity row) increases that figure by $102 million per year, and the last third adds $74 million in annual consumer surplus. This demonstrates the effect that many researchers have recognized, that there are diminishing returns to moving additional customers to RTP.[36]

At the same time, there are increasing costs of putting greater percentages of the load on RTP, because metering the largest users is cheapest per MWh. The costs of implementing RTP are difficult to pin down, because technology is constantly improving and because the costs may be greater or less than the direct metering costs. When California put RTP meters in the 20,000 largest customers that represent nearly one-third of load, it cost about $35 million. Some argue that the actual costs are greater than this, because utilities must create and install new software for billing and metering. Others argue that the utilities will actually save more than the costs of metering through reduced labor, because the new meters can be read remotely, without an on-site visit. In any case, recognizing that the RTP metering and other setup costs are one-time, or at least recur over decades, and the consumer surplus gains in table 8.2 are *annual*, it is clear that RTP for the largest customers easily passes a cost-benefit test, even when overall demand is thought to be fairly insensitive to price.

The results of these simulations are less conclusive on the net gain from metering the remaining customers in a California-like system. The annual benefit from going from one-third to all load is estimated to be about $176 million per year. Doing this would require installing about ten million new meters in California. Some private companies have said they could install and operate the meters for a monthly charge of $1–2 per meter. That would put the annual benefits in the same range as the annual costs. The other costs and benefits might then determine the outcome. How much would actually be saved on meter reading? How much additional cost would there be in billing operations, recognizing that systems would have already been put in place for having the largest customers on RTP?

The assumption of a –0.075 overall demand elasticity is probably reasonable in the shorter run, but it is likely to be too low in the longer run, both because technology will improve over time and because customers will, with experience, become more savvy about how they can respond to higher and lower prices. The simulations assuming an overall demand elasticity of −0.15 may be more reasonable for the longer run, although I must emphasize that these figures are only intended to be in a plausible range, not precise estimates of how much demand response would actually occur.

With an overall elasticity of −0.15, putting one-third of the load on RTP can be approximated by the −0.05 elasticity row. The effects are larger than in the shorter-run case, but the additional impact from doubling the elasticity is only a 44 percent gain in the effect on consumer surplus from putting one-third of the load on RTP. The greater elasticity does mean greater gains from RTP, but the incremental gains from greater elasticity are declining.

Although these illustrations are useful in giving an idea of the potential gains from RTP, they don't take into account all aspects of electricity markets. First, there is no consideration of operating reserves. Including reserves would almost certainly move the analysis more strongly in support of RTP, which would decrease system peak loads; so, using standard proportional reserve rules, it would reduce the amount of reserve capacity needed and the payments for that capacity. More important, RTP would increase the responsiveness of demand to system stress and thus would reduce the level of reserves needed for any given level of demand.

The simulations also have assumed that all generation is completely reliable and have ignored outages. Outages would simply change generation costs if they occurred in equal proportions in all hours, but in reality they occur stochastically. Because significant quantities of capacity can randomly and simultaneously become unavailable, the variation in supply-demand balance is more volatile than would be inferred from looking at load variation alone. Greater volatility increases the value of RTP.

Lastly, the simulations also have ignored market power issues, instead assuming that free entry would bring a completely competitive market over the longer run. As Bushnell (chap. 6 in this volume) points out, price-responsive demand reduces sellers' ability to exercise market power. Reducing the exercise of market power not only reduces the large wealth transfers that it can engender but also reduces the inefficient investment, allocation of production across plants, and consumption choices that result from market power. Including market power effects would almost certainly bolster the case for RTP.

Conclusion

It is clear that time-varying retail electricity prices can significantly help to reduce system production or procurement costs, as well as helping to meet operating capacity reserve requirements. Many approaches to implementing this idea are in practice, some of which are more widespread than others. The most attractive approach from an economic viewpoint, RTP, has faced two important impediments. The first, which is technological, has greatly diminished in the last decade.[37] The second, concern over price volatility, can be addressed effectively with hedging instruments or price protection plans, as has been demonstrated here.

When we recognize that these impediments have been overcome, RTP is clearly the right policy for medium to large customers. For small customers, including residential consumers, metering costs and concerns about financial complexity might suggest a simpler approach. Some of the alternatives, particularly CPP, accomplish some of what RTP offers, while others, like TOU pricing, are a much smaller step toward improving the efficiency of electricity systems.

For more than seventy-five years, electricity planning has been based on meeting a peak demand that has been assumed to be price insensitive. The payoff for greater demand-side price responsiveness is reduced reliance on generation capacity that is operated only to meet occasional demand peaks. The failure to incorporate demand flexibility has imposed unnecessary generating plants, production costs, and environmental harm on society. An electricity system that permits adjustments on both the supply and demand side will improve efficiency, reduce costs, and benefit the environment.

***

References

Borenstein, Severin. 2000. Understanding competitive pricing and market power in wholesale electricity markets. *The Electricity Journal* 13 (6): 49–57.

———. 2001. The trouble with electricity markets and California's electricity restructuring disaster. Program on Workable Energy Regulation Working Paper no. PWP-081. Berkeley, CA: University of California, September. http://www.ucei.org/PDF/pwp081r1.pdf.

———. 2004. The long-run effects of real-time pricing. Center for the Study of Energy Markets Working Paper no. 133. Berkeley, CA: University of California Energy Institute, June. http://www.ucei.berkeley.edu/PDF/csemwp133.pdf.

Borenstein, Severin, and Stephen P. Holland. 2004. On the efficiency of competitive electricity markets with time-invariant retail pricing. *RAND Journal of Economics*, forthcoming.

Borenstein, Severin, Michael Jaske, and Arthur Rosenfeld. 2002. Dynamic pricing, advanced metering, and demand response in electricity markets. Study sponsored by The Hewlitt Foundation and The Energy Foundation. Center for the Study of Energy Markets Working Paper no. 105. Berkeley, CA: University of California Energy Institute, October. http://www.ef.org/documents/DynamicPricing.pdf.

Braithwait, Steven D., and Kelly Eakin. 2002. The role of demand response in electric power market design. Study by Lauritis R. Christensen prepared for Edison Electric Institute. Washington, DC: October. http://www.eei.org/industry_issues/retail_services_and_delivery/wise_energy_use/demand_response/demandresponserole.pdf.

Braithwait, Steven D., and Michael O'Sheasy. 2002. RTP customer demand response: Empirical evidence on how much can you expect. In *Electricity pricing in transition*, ed. A. Faruqui and K. Eakin, 181–90. Boston: Kluwer Academic.

Faruqui, Ahmad, and Stephen S. George. 2002. The value of dynamic pricing in mass markets. *The Electricity Journal* 15 (6): 2–86.

Faruqui, Ahmad, Joe Hughes, and Melanie Mauldin. 2002. Real-time pricing in California: R&D issues and needs. Report prepared by the Electric Power Research Institute (EPRI) for the California Energy Commission, February.

Faruqui, Ahmad, and Melanie Mauldin. 2002. The barriers to real-time pricing: Separating fact from fiction. *Public Utilities Fortnightly* 15 (4): 30–41.

Hirst, Eric. 2002a. Barriers to price-responsive demand. Prepared for Edison Electric Institute. Washington, DC: June. http://www.ehirst.com/PDF/PRDBarriers.pdf.

———. 2002b. The financial and physical insurance benefits of price-responsive demand. *The Electricity Journal* 15 (4): 66–73.

Patrick, Robert H., and Frank A. Wolak. 1997. Estimating the customer-level demand for electricity under real-time market prices. Stanford University, Department of Economics. Working Paper. ftp://zia.stanford.edu/pub/papers/rtppap.pdf.

Ruff, Larry E. 2002a. Demand response: Reality versus resource. *The Electricity Journal* 15 (December): 10–24.

———. 2002b. Economic principles of demand response in electricity. Prepared for Edison Electric Institute. Washington, DC: October. http://www.eei.org/industry_issues/retail_services_and_delivery/wise_energy_use/demand_response/economicprinciples.pdf.

NOTES

Severin Borenstein is E.T. Grether Professor of Business and Public Policy at the Haas School of Business, University of California, Berkeley. He is also director of the University of California Energy Institute and a research associate of the National Bureau of Economic Research. Steve Braithwait, Jim Bushnell, Ahmad Faruqui, Jim Griffin, Stephen Holland, Michael Jaske, Jennifer Kaiser, Karen Notsund, Steve Puller, Art Rosenfeld, Larry Ruff, Celeste Saravia, Frank Wolak, and Catherine Wolfram provided valuable comments. Jennifer Kaiser contributed excellent research assistance. An earlier version of this paper appeared as part of Borenstein, Jaske and Rosenfeld (2002). Financial support from The Hewlitt Foundation and the Energy Foundation is gratefully acknowledged.

1. When this occurred in natural gas markets in the 1970s, rationing was enforced in some areas by grandfathering all who already had gas service and requiring a queue for new hookups.

2. I assume here that capacity can be adjusted in very small increments, although the general conclusions hold even if investments are fairly lumpy.

3. Borenstein and Holland (2004) discusses in detail the efficiency of competitive equilibrium in this market and the social loss when some customers are charged flat rates.

4. Thus, the advance prices that retail sellers offer under these systems are not the equivalent of selling forward in a wholesale market but rather are the equivalent of buyers' holding infinite-quantity call options, though with the provision that the buyer cannot resell the commodity.

5. Braithwait and Eakin (2002) and Braithwait and O'Sheasy (2002) give overviews of the empirical evidence on the effectiveness of time-varying prices in eliciting demand response.

6. This comparison is not exactly the one we would like, because real-time RTP prices are still announced slightly in advance, while the balancing market prices are determined during the actual period in which they are effective and are announced ex post. Thus, some of the 50–55 percent that is not captured by day-ahead prices still wouldn't be captured by "real-time" RTP prices.

7. This is Pacific Gas & Electric's summer 2002 commercial TOU rate.

8. This number results from a regression, covering April 1998 to October 2000, of the hourly real-time wholesale price on dummy variables for each of the TOU periods (with observations weighted by quantity demanded, so the resulting TOU rates would exactly meet the retailers' revenue requirements), where the coefficients on the TOU periods are allowed to differ in each summer/winter period. Comparing the explained sum of squares of such a regression to the explained sum of squares of a regression with just a single dummy for each summer/winter period gives the additional price variation captured by using the TOU periods rather than using a single constant price in each period. This difference as a share of price variations was 6 percent in northern California and 13 percent in southern California. The comparable figure in PJM for the same period is 6 percent.

9. Customers that have TOU meters usually face on-peak and off-peak demand charges, with the on-peak maximum usage carrying a much higher price. Within the peak price TOU period (e.g., noon–6 p.m. on weekdays), however, the meters do not indicate at what time or day the maximum usage occurred.

10. There is another widespread view that many interruptible customers believed when they signed up that they were simply getting a price break and would never actually be called on to stop usage. Statements by these customers during the California electricity crisis of 2000–2001 reinforced this view.

11. See Faruqui and George (2002) for a more detailed analysis of CPP.

12. In practice, either the utility makes a standard offer to all customers on the program or customers are asked to bid prices at which they would be willing to reduce their consumption.

13. See Ruff (2002b) for further discussion of baseline-setting problems.

14. This phenomenon, known as "adverse selection," is a major concern in insurance markets, because high-risk individuals are more likely to buy insurance than are low-risk people.

15. Borenstein (2001) and Ruff (2002a) point out another problem with payments made under demand reduction programs. Many people argue that payments should be equal to the wholesale price, because the retailer saves this much by not buying the last kWh. But this overcompensates the customer, because the customer is also saving the retail price it would otherwise have to pay (and that the retailer does not receive if the customer reduces consumption). If the wholesale price is 30¢/kWh and the retail price is 8¢, then the appropriate payment for demand reduction would be 22¢/kWh, not 30¢/kWh.

16. The rates might still be lower than under flat pricing because the reduced demand might lower the wholesale market price sufficiently to more than cover the cost of payments for demand reduction. Nonetheless, the revenue requirement implies that overall average rates will not be lower with demand reduction programs than with CPP.

17. See Faruqui, Hughes, and Mauldin (2002) and Faruqui and Mauldin (2002) for more discussion of two-part RTP programs.

18. Although the California economy was clearly entering a recession and the dot-com economy was declining, many companies still claimed that they were growing at phenomenal rates and therefore needed a CBL well above their past usage.

19. The spot price here could refer to a day-ahead price or a spot imbalance energy price.

20. In fact, the contract just has to have less variance than the spot price. It could, for instance, have a fuel adjustment clause.

21. This illustration, in which the long-term contract price is below the average spot price, is not meant to suggest that forward prices are systematically cheaper than spot prices. On average, the forward contract price will be about equal to the expected spot price during the life of the contract. Although it does not occur in this illustration, it is possible that this formula could result in negative prices in certain hours. This outcome could be easily avoided, however, with a small modification. A minimum price, say 1¢ per kWh, could be set, and any resulting excess revenue could then be redistributed evenly among all other hours.

22. This illustration slightly overstates the monthly bill stability that could be achieved through 80 percent hedging because it assumes that the hedged quantity is 80 percent of the actual demand in each hour. The contract (or contracts) would quite likely hedge a larger quantity during periods when demand is anticipated to be high, but the variation would probably not match exactly the actual variation in consumption that occurs. Since price will be highest in periods when the quantity exceeds anticipated levels, the protection from the hedging contract would be slightly less than if it matched the actual consumption pattern exactly.

23. To be clear, the average price discussed here is the average over all customers on RTP, not a guaranteed average price for any one specific customer.

24. If the market is not competitive, then price is above the marginal cost of producing that unit and even the market price is giving too great an incentive to reduce consumption, leading to the standard deadweight loss outcome.

25. Ruff (2002a) makes a similar point about subsidizing demand reduction programs. Hirst (2002b) discusses the size of the cost premium from flat-rate service.

26. It is quite possible that voluntary RTP would lower the cost of serving both groups, compared to no RTP, by reducing wholesale prices. Nonetheless, given any set of wholesale prices, the non-RTP participants will almost certainly be more costly to serve (on an average cost per kWh basis) than the RTP participants.

27. I abstract here from other costs, including T&D charges and the adders necessary to cover financial losses from the retailers' long-term contracts or other stranded investments, all of which would be added to the charges of both groups. It is best to think of this approach as applying only to large industrial and commercial customers, all of whom could be fitted with real-time meters at relatively low cost.

28. By some, this has been called an attempt to prevent "cherry picking" that would drive up the cost to other customers. By others, this has been called an attempt to preserve the historical cross-subsidy.

29. Although many interruptible customers cannot actually be physically interrupted, as discussed earlier, the programs usually involve a small number of large customers, so it is feasible for the system operator to contact each by phone to see how they will respond to the call for demand reduction (and the extremely high retail price that accompanies the call).

30. I present an overview of the simulations and results here. For details, see Borenstein (2004).

31. I compress this two-year data set into one year by assuming that each load datum represents thirty minutes rather than one hour.

32. Here and throughout, the retail tariff is also assumed to include $40/MWh for T&D.

33. See Borenstein (2000) for a numerical example of this.

34. Borenstein and Holland (2004) show that it is theoretically possible for capacity to increase or decrease with the introduction of RTP. These simulations demonstrate that, for these reasonable parameters, the actual effect is a large decrease in capacity.

35. This is only an approximation, but it is accurate to within a few percentage points for looking at the response to price changes over the relevant range.

36. The increase in consumer surplus accrues to both customers on RTP and remaining flat-rate customers, although it goes disproportionately to customers on RTP. See Borenstein (2004).

37. See Michael Jaske's section of Borenstein, Jaske, and Rosenfeld (2002). Also, see Hirst (2002a) for a general discussion of the technological and bureaucratic barriers to RTP.

9

Transmission Market Design

William W. Hogan

Introduction

Transmission policy stands at the center of electricity market design. The special complexities of electric power transmission require nothing less than a paradigm shift in order to support a restructured competitive electricity market. The change in perspective is captured in the seeming oxymoron of "coordination for competition." Unlike other commodities markets, successful electricity markets require new institutional infrastructure with a visible hand to support competition. Given a coordinated spot market with consistent pricing, most decisions can be left to market participants. Building on this spot market design, it is possible to create new forms of property rights and allow private responses to price incentives to drive most operating and investment decisions.

Reliance on market participants to make most or all investment decisions for generation and demand alternatives seems both natural and much like other normal markets. Extending this policy to the realm of transmission investments is less obviously easy and may in some cases be problematic. The result has been a growing controversy about the relative roles of merchant and regulated transmission investment, and about the implied proper policy for the transmission investment part of the overall electricity market design.

The purpose here is to summarize the main developments that build on a coordinated spot market and point to the use of market incentives to facilitate transmission investment. The focus is on a line of argument that points to a critical choice that must be made for transmission investment policy, drawing a line between merchant and regulated investment. The choice could reverberate throughout the rest of electricity market design. With the right choice, merchant transmission investment could play a significant but not exclusive role in efficient transmission expansion. With the wrong choice, the unintended consequences could undermine the whole foundation of electricity market restructuring.

Standard Market Design

In their prescient discussion of the potential of markets for power, Joskow and Schmalensee pointed to a central unresolved problem:

> The practice of ignoring the critical functions played by the transmission system in many discussions of deregulation almost certainly leads to incorrect conclusions about the optimal structure of an electric power system. (Joskow and Schmalensee 1983, 63)

The struggle to address the critical functions of the transmission system has been a central theme of the subsequent turmoil in electricity restructuring (Hogan 2002a). The names keep changing, but the same issues recur in defining the institutional requirements of an electricity market.

The core elements of the Federal Energy Regulatory Commission's (FERC) standard market design (SMD) Notice of Proposed Rule Making (NOPR; FERC 2002c) target the essential requirements for a competitive electricity market (Chandley and Hogan 2002, 56). The twin principles of open access and nondiscrimination require fundamental change in the rules and organization of the electricity system. When coupled with the objective of achieving an economically efficient electricity system, these principles lead inexorably to the requirements for a standard market design. Standardization is important for the obvious effect of reducing "seams" issues between regions and markets. Less obviously, but even more importantly, certain critical market activities require standardization in order to support efficient operation with open access and nondiscrimination in an electricity market.

The market cannot solve the problem of market design. The FERC provides an accurate description of the problems inherent in the large externalities of transmission usage and a sound solution in the application of the necessary coordination in support of a market. In each region, an independent transmission provider (ITP) must administer a single tariff and operate the transmission system to support certain essential services. The critical centerpiece of the design is a coordinated spot market for energy and ancillary services. This spot market employs the framework of a bid-based, security-constrained, economic dispatch with locational marginal pricing (LMP). The framework includes bilateral contracts with a transmission usage charge for each transaction based on the difference of the locational prices at the points of input and withdrawal.

This centerpiece of the SMD framework, shown in figure 9.1, builds on the analysis found in the FERC's previous orders on regional transmission organizations (RTOs) and supports additional features such as financial transmission rights and license plate transmission access charges. A good design for the spot market can facilitate long-term bilateral contracting or support market participants' self-supplying to meet their own loads, arrangements that could constitute the bulk of energy transactions. Given the incentives from locational pricing, there is a natural market stimulus to sustain generation and demand-side investments. In addition, the creation of financial transmission rights provides further opportunities and incentives for market participants to undertake transmission expansion.

At great expense, the United States has gone through an extended period of experimentation with designs for market institutions for the electricity system. There have been notable successes, as in the Eastern independent system operators (ISOs),[1] as well as notable failures (Hogan, 2002a). These experiments have been punctuated by major decisions by the FERC that advanced the development of an open-access regime and efficient electricity markets. However, faced with sharply conflicting views across the industry, the FERC's vision had not previously been sufficiently complete or clear.

The notable failures in electricity markets brought the nation to a crossroads in electricity restructuring, with some voices urging a halt or retreat out of fear that the failures will be replicated elsewhere. Learning from these failures is essential, but turning back would be the wrong lesson, and standing still is not tenable. However the names may change as the debate continues, in the end the FERC must move forward with the core elements of SMD. The nature of the electricity system requires an ITP's visible hand to coordinate the markets and assure reliability.

By now, the costly experiments have made plain that certain fundamentals are necessary for a successful electricity market. These are the elements at the core of the SMD framework, and the elements often absent in the failed ex-

Figure 9.1. The SMD NOPR contains a consistent framework

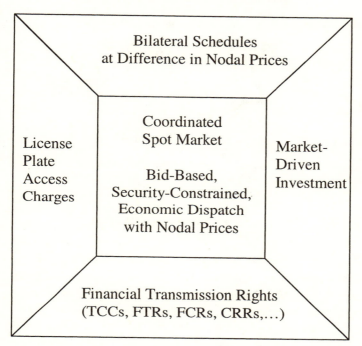

periments. An independent entity operating with the protocols of a coordinated real-time spot market with consistent locational pricing to reflect the actual limitations of energy availability and transmission constraints is first among these necessary elements. This by itself is not sufficient for a successful energy market. But we know from both theory and experience that it is necessary.

This core market design includes financial transmission rights as a central element in protecting economic uses of the existing grid and providing a foundation for transmission investment.

Financial Transmission Rights

Given the core elements of the SMD structure, the natural definition of transmission rights is financial and closely related to the net revenues collected by the system operator in the balancing and short-term transmission market. In

Figure 9.2. Transmission capacity.

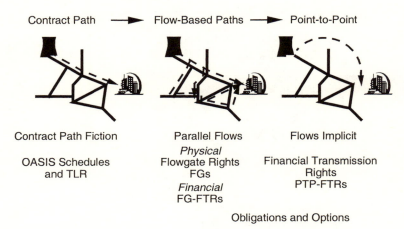

Contract Path $\longrightarrow$ Flow-Based Paths $\longrightarrow$ Point-to-Point

Contract Path Fiction   Parallel Flows   Flows Implicit
                               Physical
OASIS Schedules   Flowgate Rights   Financial Transmission
and TLR   FGs   Rights
                               Financial   PTP-FTRs
                               FG-FTRs

                        Obligations and Options

the presence of electrical losses and congestion, the revenues collected under an LMP model would be greater than the payments to participants. This net revenue is sometimes referred to as the merchandising surplus, congestion rent, or similar terms. More precisely, under the framework of bid-based, security-constrained, economic dispatch the net revenue difference is simply the inframarginal rent on losses and transmission constraints. This source of revenue is critical in designing and understanding the nature of financial transmission rights (FTRs).[2]

There has been a great deal of debate about the nature of transmission rights, starting with the fictional contract path and ending with FTRs. The stages of this discussion are shown in figure 9.2. It is to be hoped that the SMD NOPR marks the conclusion of that costly and sometimes confused conversation. In its most turbulent stages, there were many attempts to argue that transmission rights should be defined as "physical," meaning that somehow the actual flow of power would be constrained by the rights acquired, and schedulers would have to match the schedules and rights. The hope was that these physical rights would provide the mechanism of coordination rather than the coordinated spot market of the system operator. In the real system, this would be simply unworkable. Hence, other common proposals have been to socialize some or all transmission congestion costs in order to make it possible to ignore the real network and define simple transmission rights divorced from reality. Inevitably, the socialization of costs would create perverse incentives in a market. It took a while, but at least for the moment these ideas appear to have fallen of their own weight (Hogan 2000; Ruff 2001).

As the debate moved beyond these unworkable physical models, there was an extended discussion about the nature of different financial transmission rights. Here too we find more than a little confusion lingering in the conversation. Although the details can be important, particularly when dealing with losses and unbalanced rights, for the present discussion it is possible to reduce the choices to the elements of a simple two-by-two matrix. A cursory summary of a much more extensive analysis of FTRs provides the backdrop for a discussion of the rules for transmission investment (Hogan 2002b).

The starting point is the bid-based, security-constrained, economic dispatch problem:

$$\underset{d,g,y,u \in U}{\text{Max}} \; B(d) - C(g)$$

s.t.

(1) $y = d - g,$

$L(y, u) + i^t y = 0,$

$K(y, u) \leq 0.$

Here the vector $\mathbf{y} = d - g$ is the net load at each location, the difference of demand and generation. The variables in U represent various controls used by the system operator. The objective is the bid-based net benefit function as the difference in the bid benefit for demand and the bid cost for generation. The constraints balance actual losses L and net load $i^t - y$. The (many) contingency limits define the security constraints in K. The constraints are a complex function of transmission flows and other factors.[3] The corresponding multipliers or shadow prices for the constraints would be (p, λ, η) for net loads, reference bus energy, and transmission constraints, respectively.

With the optimal solution (d^*, g^*, y^*, u^*) and the associated shadow prices, we have the vector of location prices $\mathbf{p}$ as

(2) $\mathbf{p}' = \nabla B(d^*) = \nabla C(g^*) = \lambda i^t + \lambda \nabla L_y(y^*, u^*) + \eta' \nabla \tilde{K}_y(y^*, u^*).$

Therefore, locational prices equal the marginal benefit of demand, which equals the marginal cost of generation, which in turn equals the reference price of energy plus the marginal cost of losses and congestion.

Using this terminology, the alternatives for financial transmission rights consist of four types, as shown in figure 9.3. The column dimensions refer to point-to-point (PTP) and flowgate definitions. The row dimensions refer to

Figure 9.3. Financial transmission rights

	Point-to-Point	Flowgate
Obligations	$P_{Destination} - P_{Source}$ Demonstrated in PJM, New York	$\sum_k \eta_k f_{fk}^f,$ $\eta_k = shadow\ price,$ $f_{fk}^f \begin{matrix}\geq 0 \\ \leq 0\end{matrix}, the\ flowgate\ amount.$ Too complicated to use?
Options	$\max\left(0, P_{Destination} - P_{Source}\right)$ More complicated to evaluate simultaneous feasibility.	$\sum_k \eta_k f_{fk}^o,$ $\eta_k = shadow\ price,$ $f_{fk}^o \geq 0,\quad the\ flowgate\ amount.$ Too complicated to use?

obligations and options. Consider first the PTP obligation. Here the FTR for 1 MW applies to a source and a destination, and the holder of the right receives a payment equal to the difference in the prices in the coordinated spot market. The obligation feature refers to the possibility that the payment may be negative. Whether positive or negative, the PTP obligation is a perfect hedge when matched with an actual power flow. The flow is charged at the difference in the locational prices, and the FTR pays out the same difference in the prices. If the set of PTP obligations is simultaneously feasible, then there is revenue adequacy in the sense that under mild regularity conditions the net revenues from the actual coordinated spot market would always be sufficient to cover the net payments under the FTRs.[4]

Importantly, the PTP definition says nothing about the actual path of the power flow. The definition is the same whether the source and destination are connected by a single line or a complex network. As discussed presently, the PTP obligation is inherently simple to implement, and it has been the initial form of FTRs in the successful markets of New York and Pennsylvania, New Jersey, and Maryland (PJM), and is part of the new system in New England.[5]

For loads wishing to hedge purchase contracts with generators, the PTP obligation would be enough. However, for speculators who do not have such a hedging interest, the possibility of negative payments when price is higher at the source than at the destination creates an expressed interest in defining PTP options. In short, an option involves only a positive payment on the FTR, but if prices reverse there is no obligation to pay.

The PTP option is usually the first idea that comes to mind in defining FTRs. It would be natural to wonder why this has not been the first choice in successful markets.[6] Although it is workable in principle, on closer inspection there are problems with the PTP option. For example, PTP obligations easily reconfigure to support a system of trading hubs, whereas PTP options are inherently point-to-point and difficult to reconfigure. For similar reasons, it is easy to decide on a simultaneously feasible allocation of PTP obligations but much more difficult to decide if a collective allocation of PTP options would be revenue adequate. And by construction the option excludes the effects of counterflow that relieves constraints in the network, so fewer options than obligations would be feasible. Given these complications, the first choice for implementation by the PJM, New York, and New England ISOs has been PTP obligations.

Motivated by the attempts to develop physical rights, the flowgate idea can be explained in terms of the pricing in equation (2). Ignoring losses, we see from the definition of locational prices that the difference in prices between locations consists of a particular aggregation of the shadow prices times the gradients of the transmission constraints. In other words,

(3) $p'\delta = p_{\text{Destination}} - p_{\text{Source}} = \eta' \nabla K_y(y^*, u^*)\delta,$
$\delta' = (0 \ldots +1 \quad 0 \ldots 0 \quad -1 \ldots 0).$

Hence, we could decompose the difference in congestion prices into two parts: the amount of impact in the constraints $\nabla K_y(y^*, u^*)\delta$, sometimes known as the shift factors, and the shadow prices of the constraints in η. The idea would be to define a flowgate amount equal to some ex ante amount f and then to pay the holder of the right according to the shadow prices on the flowgates.

In most discussions of flowgates, there is a tendency to think of the flowgate as a transmission line or collection of lines, and the flowgate right is the amount of power that flows over that line. However, in the more sophisticated formulations, each constraint defines a flowgate, and the flowgate right is just the amount of that constraint (O'Neill et al. 2002). If the amount of the flowgate right matches the implied flow of a PTP transaction for 1 MW, then

(4) $\mathbf{f} = \nabla K_y(y^*, u^*)\delta,$
$p_{\text{Destination}} - p_{\text{Source}} = \eta' \mathbf{f}.$

Under these conditions, the flowgate right would also provide an exact hedge for the PTP schedule. However, notice that some of the elements of the vector **f** may be negative. Even though the shadow prices would be nonnegative, the payments could be negative just as with the PTP obligations. Hence, flowgate rights that are positive or negative for a given constraint would be essentially obligations.

The obvious alternative for flowgate obligations would be to select only the positive value for a particular constraint. Then, with the nonnegative shadow prices, the flowgate would be an option in the sense that payments would never be negative. Of course, we can see that, like the PTP option formulation of an FTR, the flowgate option would then not provide a perfect hedge for a PTP transaction.

The consistent formulation of the flowgate rights would define each constraint as a flowgate, but there would be no requirement to match to $\nabla K_y(y^*, u^*)\delta$ or select all the elements of **f**. The design would leave it to the market participants to decide on how much of a right to purchase and on which flowgates.

These flexible features are necessary since in all but the most trivial cases it would be virtually impossible to determine ex ante the shift factors that would apply in the actual dispatch at any time in the future. Further, the dimensionality of the shift factors can be enormous. The illustrative examples used in policy discussions always refer to a handful of flowgates, which seems manageable. However, in the complete formulation for a real system, the number of flowgates could easily reach hundreds of thousands, reflecting the combinatorial problem of many constraints, with every constraint different in every monitored contingency. Ex post, the actual dispatch would find relatively few of these constraints actually limiting; otherwise it would be impossible to solve the dispatch problem. But ex ante we do not know which of the few constraints would be limiting, and the full dimensionality of the constraints would come into play for long-term rights.

Early optimism that the number of possible binding constraints would be small and easy to identify in advance has faded but not disappeared. Hence, market participants might be able to choose only a few flowgate rights and provide an adequate, albeit less than perfect, hedge for transmission schedules. But in this case, the consensus has become that the unhedged portion of congestion costs would be just that—unhedged. There would be no socialization of congestion charges.[7]

An attraction of the flowgate approach is the ability to trade rights in different flowgates without having to limit transactions to the given configuration of PTP options or obligations. However, an inherent cost of this attractive flexibility would be the need to anticipate how the actual system would operate on the day and acquire a very large and changing number of flowgate rights in order to hedge a single point-to-point transaction.

There are other details that arise in defining the rights. However, it is possible to develop a common framework that is general enough to incorporate all these definitions of FTR formulations. This suggests using all four types at the same time (Hogan 2002b). An advantage of this approach is that the market, not the market designers, could choose whatever combination provided the best package of rights for their own transactions. Other things being equal, the do-everything design would be a dominant solution. However, other things are never equal. It would not be very expensive to set up the tariffs and systems to accommodate all four types of FTRs, but it would not be free. And it is not yet clear that it is practical to solve the associated auction or allocation problem for all four rights without imposing substantial limits on the eligible flowgates. Regulators should be cautious about creating expectations about the viability of the do-everything strategy.

Given the simplicity and success with PTP obligations, another market design strategy emerges. Start with what we know works, take no action that precludes an expanded definition up to the do-everything approach, and implement the design expansions as resources, experience, and market demand dictate.

Happily, this common-sense approach is exactly the policy offered by the FERC in the SMD NOPR. Starting with financial congestion hedges, the design strategy is summarized this way:

> We propose that Congestion Revenue Rights be made available first in the form of receipt point-to-delivery point *obligation rights*, which we propose to mandate now, and later in the form of receipt point-to-delivery point *option rights* and *flowgate rights*. (FERC 2002c, 134, emphasis in original)

This strategy is commendable. It takes the lead on what is most urgent but remains agnostic about how far to go. It may be that once market participants become familiar with PTP obligations, options will not be much in demand. Or both PTP obligations and options would be needed and would solve all the problems, with flowgates failing to produce sufficient market interest. Or it might be that everything would have its place, and the flowgate approach could move into a workable implementation without socialization of costs or creation of perverse incentives. Everyone can have a view on how far we might go, but that does not need to be decided at the beginning. About all that seems clear is that the PTP obligations would be part of the package, as this

FTR type provides the only workable method to provide a perfect hedge on a simple energy transaction.

These FTRs in their various forms have other important properties not widely understood. Although further details are described elsewhere, three features of PTP obligations deserve mention in that they appear frequently to be misconstrued.

First, configuring PTP obligations is relatively simple. It has been asserted that such an allocation would require

> a process in which a set of all feasible (i.e., consistent with the transmission network) *physical* combinations of bilateral contracts between injection and receipt points is first calculated. The process of defining the feasible set must be conducted by the SO [system operator] by performing a large set of simulations of the use of the network under various supply and demand conditions and contingencies (e.g., line outages) using load flow models. The process envisioned for defining the feasible set appears to be purely physical in the sense that the SO does not rely on prices or other valuation procedures to define the set of feasible rights. (Joskow and Tirole 2003, 40, emphasis in original)

This would be an onerous task were it required. However, it is not. The misconception may flow from the long history of utilities attempting to assign physical rights that were to apply for long periods of time. In order to guarantee the physical rights, it was necessary to do just as described, and the simulation wars were endless because it was always possible to find some pattern of possible future demand and a contingency where the new rights would be infeasible.[8] By contrast, a great simplification of the PTP obligation as a financial right is that in order to check feasibility of any particular set of awards, the simulation is reduced to a check of a contingency-constrained load flow, for which software is readily available. Furthermore, the PTP awards are made regularly through an auction process that uses a characterization of the constraints, not an enumeration of the feasible set. Hence, allocating PTP obligations through an auction does not require anything much more than the same calculations as in a regular economic dispatch, a familiar and well-understood problem. This auction software is in regular use for just this purpose in PJM and New York.

Second, revenue adequacy does not depend strictly on maintaining feasibility of the FTRs for every short-term configuration of the grid and load pattern. For example, shift factors can change under different operating conditions. One analysis described this feature of PTP FTRs in accommodating changes in shift factors as "[shift factor] insurance." There was an assertion that "the cost to other market participants or to the ISO of fulfilling the obligations inherent in this insurance could be very large, and might have a substantial impact on the ISO's uplift charge in later years" (Chao et al. 2000, 40). This conjecture may flow from an assumption that changes in shift factors would necessarily make the FTRs infeasible, thereby exposing the system operator to some inappropriate financial risk. To be sure, investment in the grid as well as changed operating conditions could have a significant effect on shift factors. But this need not affect revenue adequacy.

The explanation for grid investment appears presently. As for grid operations with any given topology of the grid, changing the control settings for phase angle regulators or switching lines in or out need not create any financial exposure despite the resulting change in shift factors. In particular, to ensure revenue adequacy under market equilibrium it is sufficient that the FTRs be feasible for some value of the transmission parameters that are under the control of the system operator, $\hat{u} \in U$. It is not necessary that the FTRs would be feasible at the current optimal setting of the transmission parameters, u^*. Hence, the FTRs might not be feasible at the current settings required in the economic dispatch solution, but as long as they would still be feasible with some possible control settings, there would be revenue adequacy. In addition, infeasibility of the FTRs is a necessary but not sufficient condition for violation of revenue adequacy. In other words, almost by definition, revenue inadequacy of the FTRs requires both that there is no available transmission control parameter setting that would make the FTRs feasible and that the FTRs would provide a preferred schedule at the current prices. This is possible but unlikely without the unexpected loss of a major facility. Revenue adequacy is not always guaranteed, but the conditions for revenue adequacy are not as brittle as often assumed.

Changes in grid conditions that could lead to the revenue inadequacy of FTRs must be limited to those conditions that are outside the control of the system operator (such as lines falling down) that the system operator otherwise would reverse in order to accommodate the preferred FTR schedule. Such events do occur, but these do not describe all or even the most important conditions that result in changed distribution factors. The actual determination of who bears the risk in the case of such revenue inadequacy is different in different implementations and could be connected to the discussion of incentives for the transmission owner responsible for line maintenance (Hogan 1999, 24–25).

A third misconception is related to the effect of contingency constraints.[9] In a representative instance, a discussion of an example illustrating the effects of transmission line outages in a network asserts that

> Whether it is an efficient investment will depend on the benefit of the link during contingencies like these (and others when it is valuable), the costs of the link during conditions when it is not "needed" and leads to an inefficient dispatch, and the cost of the investment. It is clear that noncontingent transmission rights cannot be defined properly to capture the varying valuations of a transmission investment under the many contingencies that characterize real electric power networks and provide the right incentives to support efficient investments. Only contingent rights provide the proper incentives. (Joskow and Tirole 2003, 49)

This comment and its accompanying examples appear to imply that a constraint induced by a lost transmission line applies only when the line is actually lost. However, this is not the way security-constrained dispatch operates. A principal reason that networks contain highly meshed systems is to preserve reliability in the case of contingent events. The events themselves do not happen very often. However, when the contingencies do occur the power flow redistributes automatically as long as there are loops or parallel paths. The adjustment is so quick that it is generally not possible to redispatch the system. Hence, to keep the lights on, before the contingency occurs the dispatch must be set so that if the contingency occurred the resulting power flows would still be feasible. This is the essence of "n – 1" contingency-constrained dispatch. If one out of the "n" facilities is lost, the constraints would still be met. Therefore, the contingency of a line's being out always applies as a constraint in the dispatch, even though the line may seldom be out.

The definition of FTRs already accounts for this contingency effect, as does the security-constrained economic dispatch. This is the main reason that there are hundreds of thousands of constraints in K. The FTR simultaneous feasibility test means precisely that the FTRs would still be feasible in the event of any of the possible contingencies. Of course, in the relatively small percentage of time that the contingency actually occurs, either the dispatch ignores other contingencies for a brief period until the line can be restored or the FTRs may be infeasible. Dealing with these occasions is an important issue, but it is secondary compared to the problems of the normal contingency-constrained dispatch. Most of the time is spent and most of the congestion cost appears during normal operation of the security-constrained dispatch and the many contingency constraints. And for these purposes the FTRs already recognize and accommodate the effects of the monitored contingencies.[10]

The effect and intent of the FTRs is to create a property right that makes electricity more like other markets. It is not possible to craft physical rights that achieve this objective. But with the essential coordinated spot market in place, the FTRs provide the economic instrument equivalent to a perfectly tradable physical right. These FTRs could play a prominent role in the market design for transmission investment.

Transmission Investment

The motivation for developing FTRs addressed the need for long-term rights that would be compatible with the short-term electricity market (Hogan 1992). In addition to providing hedges for the users of the existing network, these FTRs can play a role in the design of transmission markets to include market-driven investment in the transmission system.

Citing the work of the U.S. Department of Energy (2002), the FERC has been concerned with a need for more transmission investment and pursuing the design of a market for transmission investments in conjunction with the SMD.

> The recent DOE [Department of Energy] National Grid Study documented the problems resulting from recent under-investment in transmission infrastructure and identified a number of causes. Among the causes were the lack of regional planning and coordination of transmission needs and siting issues. (FERC, 2002c, 187)

The subject of transmission expansion is important and recognized as a complex problem in electricity restructuring throughout the world (Woolf 2003). In some special cases, such as for England and Wales, there is a single transmission monopoly over the whole grid, and this special feature allows market designs that are interesting but may not travel well (Léautier 2001; Vogelsang, 2001). In the United States, multiple transmission owners, independent transmission providers, and strong interactions among these entities in the same grid limit any application of a simple monopoly approach.

With publication of the SMD NOPR, the FERC launched a vigorous discussion of alternative models for transmission investment. To (over-) simplify for the moment, it is useful to think of this discussion as centering on the optimal mix of two approaches. At one end of the spectrum we have merchant transmission investment, which might be defined in the minimalist sense as market participants' making transmission investments in response to market incentives. The merchant transmission investment would be voluntary. The investment cost would not be included in rate base or other mandatory

charges. The benefits for the merchant investor would include an award of incremental FTRs created by the investment.[11] At the other end of the spectrum
would be regulated investment. This would be much like traditional transmission investment, with cost recovery through mandatory charges subject to
regulatory approval. Under the FERC plan, this would include an evaluation
to identify the beneficiaries for cost assignment. This latter type of "participant funding" is important, but it is not the main concern of the present discussion (FERC 2002c, 110).

Hybrid Model

The SMD NOPR began the conversation, and the immediate reaction
was all over the map. At one end of the spectrum, there was an assertion that
the FERC's approach

> seems to be based on the assumption that we can rely primarily on "private ini-
> tiative" to bring forth needed transmission capacity and views "market driven"
> decisions as the "fundamental mechanism" to provide efficient levels of trans-
> mission investment. Thus it appears that the Commission has in mind a regime
> in which the bulk of future transmission investment will be realized by "mer-
> chant transmission projects" that would be supported financially through con-
> gestion revenues. (Joskow 2003, 6)

At the other end was the reaction of potential merchant transmission investors that the evolving FERC rules would in fact foreclose any significant
merchant transmission investment (TransÉnergieUS 2003, 2).

An alternative reading would be that the FERC was more agnostic about
an investment model that was still a work in progress. Clearly the FERC intended to include merchant transmission investment that would be motivated
by LMP prices and the opportunity to acquire incremental FTRs (FERC
2002c, 194). But this is far from a commitment to rely solely or primarily on
merchant investments. For example, from the SMD NOPR:

> The Commission proposes a pricing policy and process for recovering the costs
> of new transmission investment so as to develop the infrastructure needed to
> support competitive markets. The policy builds on the price signals provided
> by the proposed spot market design. However, there are cases where LMP
> price signals alone will not encourage all beneficial transmission investments.
> Therefore, we propose to require market participants to participate in a re-

gional process to identify the most efficient and effective means to maintain reliability and eliminate critical transmission constraints. (FERC 2002c, 8)

This could be read as a policy with a fundamental mechanism that is market driven in responding to price signals made transparent by the core features
of the SMD but that is neither dependent on merchant investment to provide
all transmission investment nor seeking to have most investments handled as
regulated cost of service projects. The distinction is between (1) using the
price and FTR information to identify transmission investment opportunities
and (2) relying solely on market initiatives to make the investment. This interpretation is further reinforced by many other parts of the SMD NOPR. For
instance:

> After Standard Market Design is fully implemented, . . . [t]here will still remain
> a significant need for a regional planning process to supplement private
> "ground up" investment decisions. The regional planning process is intended
> to supplement these private investment decisions, not supplant them. The re-
> gional planning process must provide a review of all proposed projects to assess
> whether the project would create loop flow issues that must be resolved on a re-
> gional basis. In addition, because of the externalities involved, there may be no
> private investment sponsor for some projects that would benefit the region.
> (FERC 2002c, 191–192)

Hence, one reading of the SMD NOPR is that locational prices provide
the signals, but the benefits of reduced congestion and FTRs may not be sufficient to support investment in all cases.[12] The goal is to define a workable
hybrid model that could accommodate both merchant and regulated transmission investment.

This is an important but difficult strategy. As is generally acknowledged,
"[m]ixing regulated and unregulated activities that are (effectively) in competition with one another is always a very challenging problem" (Joskow and
Tirole 2003, 13). If there is to be a hybrid model, a principal task would be
to draw a line that would mark the boundary between merchant and regulated
investment. Perhaps the most urgent expression of this challenge can be
found in a paper by the National Grid that raises a series of questions that it
sees as "weighty and complex issues."[13] The complex issues require careful and
explicit attention, and they are not likely to be addressed well in a series of
piecemeal decisions. A quite real danger is that seemingly innocuous early decisions might have implications that reach further than the FERC intended in
the narrow context.

Merchant Transmission Challenges

There are many challenges in designing a market to include merchant transmission investment. "Complete reliance on market incentives for transmission investment would be unlikely as a practical matter and is subject to a number of theoretical challenges" (Hogan 1999, 21). The intent here is not to discuss or dispose of all the difficulties, many of which have been discussed elsewhere (Woolf 2003; Hunt 2002). Rather, the intention is to highlight the most important problems and consider what these imply about any line to be drawn between merchant and regulated transmission investment.

An initial task is to put the problem in the context in terms of the criteria for evaluating market design components. An operating assumption here is that there is a trade-off between imperfect markets and imperfect regulation. At present, there is no first-best solution available at either extreme to guarantee perfect economic efficiency in transmission investments. This should affect the form of argument. It should not be sufficient to reject a design feature simply because under some conditions this design element alone would not produce the most efficient solution. Uniformly applied, this one-handed comparison would reject all proposals, including the status quo. Rather, the hybrid approach looks to a portfolio of methods that can work concurrently with tolerable friction in addressing most investment opportunities.

Typically expansive lists of the challenges to merchant transmission investment include distinct classes of problems (Joskow and Tirole 2003): problems that have been solved; problems that apply in any market, or at least any regulated market; problems that pertain especially to transmission but are of second-order importance; and problems that are significant and possibly insurmountable for merchant investment alone.

As discussed earlier, examples of (substantially) solved problems include characterizing auctions for FTRs, dealing with changing shift factors, and accommodating contingency conditions that appear in security-constrained dispatch. Another example is the preservation of the feasibility of existing FTRs in the presence of transmission investment that changes the configuration of the grid. In practice and in theory, an elegant and simple set of expansion rules merely defines the incremental FTRs, including counterflow, to guarantee feasibility by construction (Hogan 1999, 28). Existing rights would be unaffected, perhaps through the device of having expansion FTRs include an FTR obligation in the reverse direction that nets out with an existing FTR.

Examples of problems that apply to any market would include the distortions from efficiency that arise through information asymmetries and agency problems. The SMD—with its reliance on independent transmission providers, separate independent transmission companies, and decentralized market participants, all operating in a highly interconnected and interdependent grid—is rife with these conditions. For example, it remains to be seen how to maintain incentives in the long run for good performance by the system operator. As important as these problems may be, it is not clear how they would alter the line between merchant and regulated transmission investment. They are not the focus of discussion here. Rather, a goal in thinking about design of transmission markets is that transmission could become more like these other markets, where we have only imperfect solutions even absent the special complications of electricity transmission. It would be real progress if these were the problems of major concern.

Problems that apply to transmission but are of second-order importance would include the contingent nature of transmission capacity as a function of temperature, wind speed, thunderstorms, solar magnetic disturbances, and so on. These random conditions can affect transmission capacity, but their impact is typically small and transitory compared to the potential of contingency constraints and changing load patterns. Further, it is not clear how or if these facts could provide much guidance on how to draw a line between merchant and regulated transmission investment.

The most prominent examples of problems that are significant and possibly insurmountable for merchant investment arise from economies of scale and scope. In the presence of such effects, investment in transmission expansion might both expand transmission capacity and have a material effect on market prices. The investment might be economic because the savings in total operating costs could be more than the investment cost, but the resulting value of the FTRs at the new locational prices would not be greater than the investment cost (Joskow and Tirole 2003, 21–23). By contrast, if the transmission investments could be made in small increments relative to the size of the market as a whole, they should have a minimal effect on market prices. In this case of no or small returns to scale, acquisition of the financial transmission rights could provide the right market incentive. Prices after the modular expansion would not be materially different than before, even though there would be an increase in capacity and throughput. The FTRs would provide the hedge against transmission prices, and for the investor the arbitrage opportunity in the spot market would be sufficient to justify the investment. But with significant returns to scale, prices might change substantially and for everyone, and everyone would wait for somebody else to make the investment. With everyone waiting for the free ride, the investment would never come. This could be important, and it could be the central issue in drawing a line between merchant and regulated transmission investment.

Slippery Slopes

The need to draw a line between merchant and regulated transmission investment is fundamental, and its importance goes well beyond the matter of transmission. Failure could strike at the core of the SMD and electricity-restructuring policy. More than is usual, here everything is connected to everything else.

The commonsense problem is that transmission investment does not occur in a vacuum. The choice is not between transmission or nothing: typically, investment in transmission is one alternative among many. In addition to transmission coupled with distant generation, there is local generation or demand-side investment. Both of the latter investments could reconfigure, reduce, or eliminate the supposed need for a transmission investment. In the case of a merchant investment, investors would make the investment choices and take the business risk that alternatives might later alter the value of the investment.

In the case of regulated investment, it is regulators that would make the choice and typically the customer that would take the bulk of the risk flowing from the regulators' choice. It follows, therefore, that the regulator will be under pressure to be explicit about these trade-offs and investment risks.

This will present the regulator with a slippery slope problem (Hogan 2001, 10–11; Shanker 2003). By definition, regulated investment shifts the risks and provides cost recovery mechanisms not available to the merchant investor. Absent a bright line between merchant and regulated transmission investment, there will be enormous and justifiable pressure on the regulator to consider the alternatives and to put them on the same playing field of reduced risk and mandatory collection through rate base or similar regulated mechanisms. Soon the intended modest domain of planning for and funding regulated transmission expansion would expand to include integrated resource planning and funding for competing generation and demand-side investments.

Absent a demarcation between merchant and regulated investments, there is no logical or principled stopping point down this slippery slope. The end point would be with all investment in transmission, generation, and demand defaulting to regulated investment with mandatory charges levied outside the market mechanism in order to provide subsidies or guarantee revenue collection. Therefore, a poor design for transmission investment is a threat to the entire premise of the SMD. The end state could be a recreation of the central regulatory decision problems that motivated electricity restructuring in the first place. But now the central regulator would be the FERC and its hand-maidens at the ITPs, replacing the old utilities and their state regulators.

This concern for bad market design leading down the slippery slope cannot be easily dismissed. The logic is compelling, and it has already happened in the context of California (Hogan 2002a). Although the California proposals were swept away first by the FERC's revulsion at "fundamental flaws" in the original California market design and then by the implosion of the California crisis, California was well along in developing just such a central procurement process that would provide ratepayer-funded cost recovery for generation and demand investments that were alternatives to transmission investment (CAISO 1999). Further, the SMD NOPR appears to propose exactly this type of integrated resource procurement process (FERC 2002c, 193). The terse discussion in the NOPR does not play out the implications of a single sentence (in paragraph 348), but such a mandate would have far-reaching implications. Once we socialize costs for some erstwhile market decisions, more follow, and market choices are replaced as formalized integrated resource development soon appears again on the agenda of the regulator.[14]

A Portfolio of Merchant and Regulated Projects

The FERC's principal tool for coordinating the portfolio of transmission investments is through the planning protocol required of every RTO. However, as this plan moves from guidance to prescription, more than good engineering analysis would be required. To avoid the problem of the slippery slope, any electricity market design needs an economic rule to distinguish merchant from regulated investment. The conversation took several new turns with the release of the SMD NOPR.

Before the SMD NOPR, virtually all the action on this front was in the design of the New York market and the rules of the New York ISO (NYISO). The New York system for merchant transmission investment was launched at the beginning of 1999 and was much in keeping with the eventual outline of the SMD NOPR. The core features of the coordinated spot market and FTRs provide the market setting. Transmission expansion by merchant investors would result in the award of long-term FTRs, but without any guarantee of transmission investment cost recovery (NYISO 2003b, especially para. 19.4–19.5). There was a process for deciding on reliability, as opposed to economic, transmission expansion.[15]

The subsequent work at the NYISO has gone much further in dealing with the practical steps for supporting merchant investment and awarding incremental FTRs (Pope 2002). This itself is a difficult problem in the context of long-term awards for expansions without a complete set of long-term FTRs for the existing grid. Similar problems arise in trying to use the FTRs to create incentives for better maintenance, as envisioned in the SMD NOPR (Hogan 2002c). However, the transmission market design model is well advanced in New York.

Notably, driven in part by history and by its unique status as a single state entity, the NYISO tariff deferred to the state regulator the bulk of the process for deciding on traditional regulated transmission investments. The role of the NYISO is primarily that of the information producer, conducting studies and evaluations of proposed expansions. But, most important, the NYISO does not have the authority to mandate regulated investment for reasons of economics alone.

The NYISO tariff supports merchant transmission investment and allows for regulated transmission investment on the initiative of the transmission owners and with the approval of the New York Public Service Commission. However, the NYISO tariff does not envision a process for requiring transmission owners to make regulated investments for economic purposes. Nor does the NYISO tariff consider mandating regulated investments in demand or generation alternatives to transmission. In its comments on the SMD NOPR, the NYISO expressed reservations about imposing such mandates and recreating "integrated resource planning" in the guise of a transmission expansion protocol (New York Independent System Operator 2003, 8).

Development of rules for merchant transmission investment has taken longer in PJM, and the process has gone further in the direction of pushing the ISO to play a central decision role in mandating regulated transmission investment. The basic outlines of these developments flow from a few key directions from the FERC and responses by PJM. These have produced substantial debate among PJM stakeholders and would have profound effects on the "complex issues" that could affect all markets under the SMD.

Initially, PJM was inclined toward an approach similar to the New York model. However, the FERC directed that

> the planning process should also focus on identifying projects that expand trading opportunities, better integrate the grid, and alleviate congestion that may enhance generator market power. The PJM ISO planning process appears to be driven more by the particular needs of TOs [transmission operators] in serving their traditional retail customers than in fostering competitive markets.

Consequently, we will require PJM . . . to specify an RTO planning process
that gives full consideration to all market perspectives and identifies expansions
that are critically needed to support competition as well as reliability needs.
(FERC 2002a, 29)

There may have been some ambiguity about the degree to which the
FERC's charge "to support competition" implied also mandating regulated
investments for economic purposes. This ambiguity was resolved in a subsequent FERC order that clearly indicates that "to support competition" means
investment for economic purposes (FERC 2002b, 9). In the concern for
showing progress on transmission investment, therefore, these FERC directives have pushed PJM from the role of information provider toward the
precipice of the slippery slope of mandating regulated transmission investments for economic purposes, with no demarcation as yet to prevent slipping
into the role of full-blown integrated resource planning and procurement.

The unintended consequence is a system of rules that if implemented could
virtually eliminate merchant transmission investment incentives and require
central procurement of generation and demand alternatives. As envisioned in
its filing with the FERC in response to these directives, PJM proposed a procedure with an initial screen that would identify "unhedgeable" congestion
(PJM LLC 2003, 5–6). Although the term was not formally defined, the expectation and intent were that this category would cover all electricity demand
that did not have direct access to inexpensive generation either locally or at a
distance coupled with existing FTRs. In effect, therefore, this category would
include virtually every transmission expansion that could possibly be of interest to anybody. This would be a screen, but it would only screen out that load
that already had FTRs or low-cost local generation sources.

For this "unhedgeable at a low price" congestion, the second step would
be to perform a cost-benefit study to see if a transmission investment would
be economic in the sense that the reduced congestion cost would be greater
than the cost of the investment. For the unhedgeable congestion that passes
the economic benefit test, the proposal envisions a one-year period during
which competitive merchant transmission or other investments could be
made to remove the unhedgeable congestion. If at the end of the year no market solutions have been forthcoming, PJM would require the transmission up-
grade as a regulated investment by one or more of the existing transmission
owners (PJM LLC 2003, 6–9).

The PJM proposal includes language expressing its intent that "PJM's
planning process thus will allow for competition among all possible alterna-

tive solutions for transmission congestion, including generation, merchant transmission and demand response measures" (PJM LLC 2003, 6). However, it is hard to see how this could be true once implemented. In essence, the proposal would confront all the potential beneficiaries of the transmission investment with the following choice: invest now and pay all the cost yourself, or wait a year and have much the same benefits with the costs rolled in with transmission access charges for everyone in the region. As Roy Shanker has noted, unless there is a very good match in identifying the beneficiaries and assigning the costs under the principle of participant funding, it is difficult to see how the choice would be other than to wait. At best, if the investment had no impact on prices but only expanded transmission capacity, the value of transmission rights would be unaffected at the margin and most customers would just be indifferent. This could produce a narrow or vanishing field for merchant transmission investment.

The PJM proposal does not mention the possibility that the ISO might also have to mandate generation or demand investments as an alternative to transmission expansion, and socialize the cost of these investments accordingly. But under the circumstances, it is not hard to see this as the next step down the slippery slope. In addition, the PJM plan and the SMD NOPR avoid the question of what should happen when the market has a different view of the value of transmission expansion. The default proposed is the same central planning default as under the old model of utility regulation. The central planner will be forced to proceed while spending other people's money (the customers'). We would not have the advantage intended for electricity restructuring that investments would be dominated by choices made when participants were spending their own money.

Apparently the unintended consequence of the pressure from the FERC would be to drive the investment process away from market solutions. There might be better and more open information in prices and the values of FTRs flowing from the core of the SMD design, but the investment process would be progressively driven to central control and funding through a new broad regulatory process evolving under the rubric of transmission expansion. Like New York, PJM and everyone else should be asking the FERC to reconsider before they slide much further down this particularly slippery slope.

A Line between Merchant and Regulated Investment

The logic driving the FERC is understandable. But the resulting direction of policy on merchant transmission could undermine most of what the FERC is trying to accomplish in the SMD. Something else is needed.

A critical task, it seems, would be to modify the rule for drawing the line between merchant and regulated investment. A modest proposal is to leverage the principal problem for merchant transmission investment into a solution. In particular, as discussed earlier, transmission investments that would produce large and pervasive changes in market prices present particularly severe problems for merchant investment. Pervasive change in prices would apply to many beneficiaries, so it would be hard for the market to prevent free riding. And large changes in prices would make the ex post value of incremental FTRs much lower at the margin, so low that the FTRs alone would not be sufficient to support the investment. In these cases, only large coalitions would be able to justify a merchant transmission investment, and these coalitions would be difficult to assemble. The alternative then would be to turn to a regulated investment that, in effect, compels participation in the coalition.

A necessary but not sufficient condition for this large and pervasive impact on market prices is that the investment is inherently large and lumpy. Not all lumpy investments are big enough to make a big impact on the market, but anything that is lumpy and makes a big impact on the market would be difficult to organize as a merchant investment. This argument then suggests a decision rule that would draw a line between merchant and regulated transmission investment (Chandley and Hogan 2002, 56). Regulated transmission investment would be limited to those cases where the investment is inherently large relative to the size of the relevant market and inherently lumpy in the sense that the only reasonable implementation would be as a single project like a tunnel under a river. Further, "large" would be defined as large enough to have an impact on market prices such that the ex post value of incremental FTRs and other explicit transmission products could not justify the investment. Everything else would be left to the market.

In evaluating regulated transmission investments, this rule would still be subject to the inevitable pressure to consider generation and demand alternatives that would compete with the regulated investment. However, the same rule would apply to these investments as well. The only generation and demand alternatives that would be included as a mandate and funded through regulated collection mechanisms would be those that were also both inherently large and inherently lumpy. Since relatively few such generation and demand investments would have this characteristic, the line would demarcate the difference between merchant and regulated investments and prevent a slide back into centralized integrated resource procurement. This rule would also recognize that the large network externalities that apply to transmission and frustrate market-driven transmission investments do not generally apply to generation and demand-side investments.

Even though many individually small investments in generation and demand could aggregate to compete with a large lumpy transmission investment, there would be no need to include these in the regulated system. For if it were true that small generation and demand investments would be economic, then there would be no market failure and no need to mandate the investment. The benefits would be easy to capture, and prices would provide the needed incentive. The same would apply for small-scale transmission investments that would not have a major effect on market prices. In the event that the small investments were not being made, the presumption would be that they were simply not economic, with the market coming to a different conclusion than the cost-benefit analysis of the ISO. In that case, the ISO rules would respect the market's judgment.

This decision rule would be similar in spirit to the PJM proposal to limit attention to "unhedgeable" congestion but would draw a line that would not require the ISO to make judgments about the price that would define the difference between hedgeable and unhedgeable congestion. It would also be in keeping with the spirit of the NYISO and others to avoid as much as possible any requirement to mandate economic investments in generation and demand. The only exceptions that would require a regulatory mandate would be those cases that have an inherent logic of the same type as large, lumpy transmission expansions.

Applying this rule would require someone to define the criteria and execute the evaluations to determine the effects on market prices and make a judgment about when these are large and the investments lumpy. Although not trivial, this would seem a smaller task than the requirement to do a cost-benefit analysis of the investment (Australian Competition and Consumer Commission 2003; Mountain and Swier 2003). The information required would be a subset of the cost-benefit study already envisioned. The details would matter, but making this judgment call seems an easier task for the ISO than taking on the much harder problem of selecting virtually all investments in a central planning function.

Drawing this line between merchant and regulated investment would be about as clean and clear as could be expected for any principled approach based on the broader market design. Merchant investment could proceed as PJM intends with "competition among all possible alternative solutions." Regulated investment would be mandated under the special conditions that appear most important in creating market failures that would foreclose a market solution. To be sure, there would be a middle ground where "it would be difficult to distinguish between a project that was simply uneconomic and which the market had rightly rejected and a project that was needed, but the market had failed to profit from the opportunity to build it" (Woolf 2003, 251). By construction, this circumstance would imply that no market failure had been identified, only that the market and the ISO disagreed about the market evaluation. Then the burden of proof would lean against these investments as part of the trade-off needed to maintain a market at all.

Other Challenges

Drawing a line to demarcate a workable boundary between merchant and regulated transmission investment is the most important challenge. However, there are others that should occupy the continuing debate. How best to provide incentives for good maintenance? How should we handle investments for reliability, voltage support, or other services not explicitly priced in the market? What limitations, if any, should apply to affiliates of regulated transmission companies that want to make merchant investments? What expansion obligations should accompany merchant investments? Who should have access to acquire the rights for "embedded" upgrades of the existing network, and at what cost? What should be done with merchant projects that later apply for regulatory treatment? What performance-based incentives should be crafted for operation of the existing grid?

These topics and more could be considered with some deliberation, because they do not strike at the core of the SMD. However, the problem of the slippery slope is more urgent.

Conclusion

It should come as no surprise that regulation of a mixed system is harder than being fully in charge of everything. The challenge for regulators is to design rules that set the right incentives and that mesh well within a coherent design. The SMD NOPR achieves a great deal in this regard. However, vigilance is required to guard against seemingly good ideas that would produce bad outcomes. The argument here is that the FERC's early guidance on transmission expansion policy presents such a case. The proposed solution outlined in the present paper draws a line between merchant and regulated investment that would support the FERC's goals and reinforce rather than undermine the SMD.

Appendix

National Grid USA Questions on Merchant and Regulated Transmission

In the context of an application by Conjunction for a proposed merchant transmission investment in New York, National Grid USA raised a series of questions that arise in considering the relative roles of merchant and regulated transmission investment:

> Below is a partial listing of the myriad complex issues raised in those proceedings by National Grid, other parties and the Commission itself and also likely to be raised by Conjunction's proposed merchant transmission line:
>
> - What role, if any, should merchant transmission have in meeting the Commission's overarching goal of satisfying the critical needs for investments to expand the integrated transmission system to ensure a robust transmission grid to support competitive wholesale electricity markets? How does the Commission plan to resolve the real-world issues raised by TransGrid based on the Australian experience with merchant transmission regarding (a) the amount of investment merchant transmission can be expected to attract; (b) the impact that it will have on investment in regulated transmission; and (c) other operational and planning concerns about the coexistence of merchant transmission and regulated transmission within the same transmission grid?
> - Should the regional planning process encompass both reliability and economic upgrades to the transmission grid, since the two are largely indistinguishable, and if so, how should merchant transmission projects be folded into that process and/or the generator interconnection queue?
> - What type of "transmission rights" (physical or financial) does Conjunction intend to sell at negotiated rates? If they are physical rights over the proposed controllable HVDC [high voltage direct current] line, which they appear to be, can they be integrated with minimal disruption into a financially based market design such as the one employed by NYISO and contemplated under SMD?
> - What regulatory precautions are needed to ensure that merchant transmission providers such as Conjunction follow through on their commitment to assume all market risks for their projects and do not later attempt (a) to shift such risks onto customers of regulated transmission; (b) to exchange their merchant status for a regulated utility status; (c) to block needed transmission upgrade projects that may tend to undermine the value of the

transmission rights sold by the merchant provider; or (d) assert market power?

- What responsibility should Conjunction bear for the cost of upgrades to the existing transmission grid that are necessary to ensure the safe and reliable interconnection of Conjunction's proposed merchant transmission line?

These weighty and complex issues are only tangentially related to Conjunction's request for authority to sell transmission rights at negotiated rates, and National Grid certainly does not expect that the Commission would resolve these issues in the present case. To the contrary, the Commission should resolve these issues in the pending rulemaking proceedings where they first arose and where the national debate has produced an extensive record on which to base such a decision. (National Grid USA 2003, 4–5)

***

References

Australian Competition and Consumer Commission. 2003. Discussion paper: Review of the regulatory test. Camberra: ACCC.

California Independent System Operator (CAISO). 1999. Tariff proposed Amendment 24 docket no. ER00-866-000 (revised long-term grid planning). December 21. Folsom, CA: CAISO.

Chandley, J. D., and W. W. Hogan. 2002. Initial comments on the standard market design NOPR. FERC Docket no. RM01-12-000. Washington, DC: Federal Energy Regulatory Commission.

Chao, H., S. Peck, S. Oren, and R. Wilson. 2000. Flow-based transmission rights and congestion management. *Electricity Journal* 13:38–58.

Federal Energy Regulatory Commission (FERC). 2002a. Order granting PJM RTO status, granting in part and denying in part requests for rehearing, accepting and directing compliance filing, and denying motion for stay. Docket nos. RT01-2-001 and RT01-2-002. Washington, DC: FERC, December 20.

———. 2002b. PJM: Order provisionally granting RTO status. Docket no. RT01-2-000. Washington, D.C.: FERC, July 10.

———. 2002c. Remedying undue discrimination through open access transmission service and standard electricity market design. Notice of Proposed Rulemaking. Washington, DC: FERC, July 31.

Hogan, W. W. 1992. Contract networks for electric power transmission. *Journal of Regulatory Economics* 4:211–42.

———. 1999. Market-based transmission investments and competitive electricity markets. Harvard University, Center for Business and Government. Working Paper.

———. 2000. Flowgate rights and wrongs. Harvard University, Center for Business and Government. Working Paper.

————. 2001. The slippery slope of socialization. *Public Utilities Fortnightly* 139:10–11.

————. 2002a. Electricity restructuring: Reforms of reforms. *Journal of Regulatory Economics* 21 (1): 103–32.

————. 2002b. Financial transmission right formulations. Harvard University, Center for Business and Government. Working Paper.

————. 2002c. Financial transmission right incentives: Applications beyond hedging. Presentation at Harvard Electricity Policy Group. 3 April, Atlanta, GA.

Hunt, S. 2002. *Making competition work in electricity*. New York: Wiley.

Joskow, P. 2003. Comments: Remedying undue discrimination through open access transmission service and standard electricity market design. FERC Docket no. RM01-12-000. Washington, DC: Federal Energy Regulatory Commission, January 10.

Joskow, P., and R. Schmalensee. 1983. *Markets for power: An analysis of electric utility deregulation.* Cambridge: MIT Press.

Joskow, P., and J. Tirole. 2003. Merchant transmission investment. MIT Center for Energy and Environmental Policy Research. Working Paper.

Léautier, T. 2001. Regulation of an electric power transmission company. *The Energy Journal* 21 (4): 61–92.

Mountain, B., and G. Swier. 2003. Entrepreneurial interconnectors and transmission planning in Australia. *The Electricity Journal* 16:66–76.

National Grid USA. 2003. Motion to intervene and comments of National Grid USA. Conjunction, L.L.C., Federal Energy Regulatory Commission, Docket no. ER03-452-000. Washington, DC: Federal Energy Regulatory Commission, February 18.

New York Independent System Operator (NYISO). 2003a. FERC Electric Tariff. March 13, 2003.

————. 2003b. Additional comments: Remedying undue distribution through open access transmission service and standard electricity market design. Federal Energy Regulatory Commission, Docket No. RM01-12-000, January 10, 2003.

O'Neill, R. P., U. Helman, B. F. Hobbs, W. R. Stewart, and M. H. Rothkopf. 2002. A joint energy and transmission rights auction: Proposal and properties. Washington, DC: Federal Energy Regulatory Commission. Working Paper.

PJM LLC. 2003. Transmittal letter. Docket no. RT01-2-00-. March 20, 2003. Washington, DC: FERC.

Pope, S. L. 2002. TCC awards for transmission expansions. LECG Working Paper. Cambridge, MA: LECG.

Ruff, L. E. 2001. Flowgates, contingency-constrained dispatch, and transmission rights. *Electricity Journal* 14 (1): 34–55.

Shanker, R. 2003. Drawing the line for transmission investment. Harvard Electricity Policy Group Presentation. April 7.

TransÉnergieUS. 2003. Market-based transmission and open access under SMD. Presentation to FERC Staff. Washington, DC: Federal Energy Regulatory Commission.

U.S. Department of Energy. 2002. *National transmission grid study*. Washington, DC: U.S. DOE.

Vogelsang, I. 2001. Price regulation for independent transmission companies. *Journal of Regulatory Economics* 20 (2): 141–65.

Woolf, F. 2003. *Global transmission expansion: Recipes for success*. Tulsa, OK: Penn Well.

NOTES

William W. Hogan is the Lucius N. Littauer Professor of Public Policy and Administration, John F. Kennedy School of Government, Harvard University, and director of LECG, LLC.

This paper draws on work for the Harvard Electricity Policy Group and the Harvard-Japan Project on Energy and the Environment. Joseph Bowring, John Chandley, Art Desell, Scott

Harvey, Pete Landrieu, Laura Manz, Andrew Ott, Susan Pope, Jose Rotger, and Roy Shanker provided helpful comments.

1. The ITP is the new name for the ISO or the RTO. There are differences in meanings, but here we treat the terms as interchangeable.

2. The many FERC orders and market designs have produced a proliferation of terms for essentially the same ideas. In the case of financial transmission rights, which might include the effect of losses, we have a generic name. These are very similar to congestion revenue rights (CRR) and transmission congestion contracts (TCC). For most purposes here, the terms are interchangeable.

3. For simplicity of exposition, the constraints treat only net loads. Some constraints may have separate effects for load and generation. This would lead to different prices for load and generation at the same location, but that is not important for the present discussion.

4. There could be excess revenues, reflecting constraints not binding in the allocation of FTRs. This is not critical to the discussion here.

5. The new market design largely consistent with the SMD NOPR began operation in New England on March 1, 2003.

6. A form of option has been implemented without much success, as in California.

7. The same principle should apply to marginal losses, which the flowgate model does not address.

8. The first development of PTP obligations arose in an attempt to solve this problem.

9. A contingency refers to the possible loss of a major line or other facility in the system.

10. Besides actual outages, other factors ranging from temperature to magnetic disturbances from the sun can influence transmission capacity. Again, these are real effects but not as significant as outage contingency constraints.

11. Other rights might accompany transmission expansions. This is particularly the case for designs that include installed capacity (ICAP) markets or their equivalent. Here we exclude consideration of these ICAP markets. Either the ICAP markets will persist and will have to be integrated with the analysis here, or ICAP markets will wither and the present analysis of an energy-only market will suffice.

12. Transmission investment would produce other benefits than FTRs, so support through the ex post value of FTRs is not strictly necessary.

13. See the appendix for details of the National Grid's questions.

14. The reader will notice that the same logic applies to any intervention that socializes costs while competing with market forces.

15. This distinction between reliability and economics presents another problematic topic separate from the focus of the present discussion.

10

Ensuring Generation Adequacy in Competitive Electricity Markets

Shmuel S. Oren

Introduction

The reliability of electricity supply has been one of the overriding concerns guiding the restructuring of the electric power industry. The slogan "keeping the lights on" has been the principal motivation for many technical and economic constraints imposed on market designs. The term *supply reliability* encompasses, however, a mix of system attributes that have diverse economic and technical implications under alternative market structures. The National Electric Reliability Council (NERC) defines reliability as "the degree to which the performance of the elements of the technical system results in power being delivered to consumers within accepted standards and in the amount desired" (Hirst, Kirby, and Hadly 1999). Imbedded within this definition is the notion of the "obligation to serve," which is arguably out of step with the notion of a deregulated industry with competitive supply. In fact, the concept of reliability as defined by NERC encompasses two attributes of the electricity system: *security*, which describes the ability of the system to withstand disturbances (contingencies) and *adequacy*, which represents the ability of the system to meet the aggregate power and energy requirement of all consumers at all times.

The notion of system security identifies short-term operational aspects of the system that are characterized through contingency analysis and dynamic stability assessments. Security is provided by means of protection devices and operation standards and procedures that include security constrained dispatch and the requirement for so-called ancillary services such as voltage support, regulation (AGC) capacity, spinning reserves, black start capability, and so on. The notion of adequacy, on the other hand, represents the systems ability to meet demand on a longer time-scale basis, considering the inherent fluctuation and uncertainty in demand and supply, the nonstorability of power, and the long lead time for capacity expansion. Generation adequacy has been traditionally measured in terms of the amounts of planning and operable reserves in the system and the corresponding loss-of-load probabilities (LOLP) that served as criteria for planning and investment decisions.

From a technical perspective, security and adequacy are clearly closely related as a system with abundance of reserve capacity provides more flexibility in handling unforeseen disturbances. However, while a system with limited planning reserves may experience shortages, it can still be operated in a secure manner, while a system with ample reserve can be operated insecurely.

All the restructured electricity systems around the world recognize the need for centralized provision and control of ancillary services that are procured by the system operator either through an auction-based market or through long-term contracts with generators. In some cases, market participants are allowed to self-provide certain ancillary services, but the quantities are dictated by the system operator who is also the provider of last resort for these services. With respect to long-term reserves, however, there is considerable diversity in reliance on market-based approaches, and the debate over which is the correct way of ensuring generation adequacy is still raging. In California, for instance, where the initial market design relied on a pure market solution for provision of generation adequacy, the capacity shortages experienced in 2001 have prompted a proposal for an available capacity requirement (ACAP) to be imposed on load-serving entities (LSEs). Discussions concerning the appropriate form of regulatory intervention in generation adequacy assurance are also taking place in Texas where currently generation reserves are plentiful, but the California experience raises concern for the future. The Federal Energy Regulatory Commission's (FERC) Notice of Proposed Rule Making on standard market design (SMD; FERC 2002a) also recognized the need for LSEs to insure the supply of power to their customers through adequate contracted provision of capacity reserves. However, the most recent FERC white paper articulating a vision for a wholesale-market platform (FERC 2003) has backed off from imposing minimum requirements for reserve margins and has recognized the States' jurisdiction over resource adequacy decisions.

From an economic point of view, security and adequacy are quite distinct in the sense that the former is a *public good* while the latter can potentially be treated as a *private good*. Security is a systemwide phenomenon with inherent externality and free-ridership problems. For instance, it is not possible to exclude customers who refuse to pay for spinning reserves from enjoying the benefits of a secure system. Hence, like in the case of other public goods, such as fire protection or military defense, security must be centrally managed and funded through some mandatory charges or self-provision rules. The resources for such central provision, however, can be procured competitively through ancillary service markets, long-term contracts, or other procurement mechanisms. Adequacy provision, on the other hand, as will be explained later, amounts to no more than insurance against shortages, which in a competitive environment with no barriers to entry translate into temporary price hikes. Such insurance can, at least in principle, be treated as a private good by allowing customers to choose the level of protection they desire. Empowering such customer choice is a fundamental goal of electricity deregulation, but achieving this goal is hindered by several obstacles:

• *Technological barriers:* Enabling customer choice of generation adequacy requires deployment of metering control and communication technology that will allow differential curtailment of load when prices exceed a preselected level or will allow direct customer response to real-time prices. While the rapid decline in the cost of information technologies is promising the economic justification for direct customer load control for low-end consumption levels is still questionable.

• *Political barriers:* Empowering customers to make their own tradeoff between service availability and cost requires that customers be exposed to real-time prices. Customers should have a default fixed-price service in the same way that homeowners can obtain fixed mortgage rates, but such options should be assessed a fair market risk premium. Unfortunately, electricity tariffs are riddled with politically motivated cross-subsidies that distort direct assignment of costs, and most public utility commissions are reluctant to embrace real-time pricing.

• *Market imperfections:* The unique characteristics of electricity and the lack of demand response expose the electricity market to potential market power abuse. The severe economic and political consequences of extreme prices that could result from such abuse (as seen in California) have persuaded regulators to introduce price caps and various automatic market mitigation measures. Unfortunately, such measures tend to suppress legitimate scarcity rents that are essential for a healthy investment environment. Paul Joskow's chapter in this book contains empirical evidence regarding scarcity rents reflected by the energy prices in New England. These figures clearly demonstrate that energy prices alone fail to provide an appropriate capacity cost recovery mechanism that is needed in order to provide an incentive for adequate generation capacity investment.

• *Operations paradigm:* Systems operators around the country continue to operate the system under the traditional "obligation to serve" paradigm. For example, while rotating outages are considered acceptable when reserve levels drop below a certain level (stage 3 alert), high prices (e.g., $1950 per MWh in California during fall of 2001 or $990 per MWh in Texas on February 25, 2003) are not considered an acceptable reason for involuntary load curtailment. Treating generation adequacy as a private good requires a paradigm shift in system operation from an "obligation to serve" to "obligation to serve at a price." In an environment in which the system operations are guided by "obligation to serve at a price," the concept of LOLP is not well defined unless a distinction is made between probability of lost load due to system collapse versus lost load due to inadequate supply. It is a prerogative of consumers and producers to decide what the appropriate level of price insurance they wish to procure is and how much they are willing to pay for it as long as they are able to bear the consequences of their decisions without affecting others. In the remainder of this discussion we will only focus on adequacy provision.

The traditional approach to ensuring generation adequacy in vertically integrated utilities was to build planning reserves based on load forecasts, LOLP calculation, and estimates of the value of lost load (VOLL). The cost of the extra capacity was assigned to customers as a rate uplift. More elaborate schemes attempted to allocate the cost of capacity according to time of use so that peak consumption bears a larger portion of that cost. In an ideal competitive market where prices of energy vary continuously to reflect the equilibrium between supply and demand at each moment, payment to inframarginal generators (above marginal cost) should cover their capacity cost. The question is whether market forces are indeed sufficient to provide generation adequacy given the realities of electricity markets. If market forces alone are not sufficient, as many believe, then what is the extent and form of regulatory intervention that might be needed as a transitional or a permanent measure? The primary objectives of such intervention must be to insure adequate supply of energy with minimal distortion of energy prices and investment incentives.

Generation Adequacy in Energy-Only Markets

Energy-only electricity markets have been adopted in the original (defunct) California design, in Nordpool, and the Australian Victoria pool. Generators in such markets bid only energy prices and, in the absence of constraints, all bids below the market-clearing price in each hour get dispatched and paid the market-clearing price. The primary income sources for recovery of capacity cost is the difference between the market-clearing price and the generators' marginal costs. When ancillary services are procured separately by the system operator, as in California and the Electric Reliability Council of Texas (ERCOT), generators can earn additional revenue by selling ancillary services, such as regulation and spinning reserve capacity, through short-term ancillary service markets or long-term contracts.

Economic theory tells us that in a long-term equilibrium of energy-only markets, the optimal capacity stock is such that scarcity payments to the marginal generators when demand exceeds supply will exactly cover the capacity cost of these generators and will provide the correct incentives for demand-side mitigation of the shortage (i.e., the scarcity rent will induce sufficient demand response so that available supply can meet the remaining load). Furthermore, in equilibrium the optimal generation mix (where generators are characterized by their fixed and variable cost) will be such that the operating profit of each generator type will exactly cover its capacity costs. This optimal equilibrium mix is achieved through exit of plants that do not cover their cost and entry of plants whose cost structure will yield them operating profits that exceed their capacity costs. Figure 10.1 illustrates the scarcity rent embedded in the energy price and the corresponding demand reduction (relative to the demand at marginal cost pricing) in a long-term equilibrium. A shortage of capacity will increase scarcity rents, producing profits in excess of what is needed to cover the amortized capacity cost. Such profits will attract generation expansion. On the other hand, excess generation capacity will eliminate scarcity rents, driving prices to marginal cost. When this occurs, generators on the margin (like generator 5 in figure 10.1) will not be able to cover their investment cost. Unless such generators receive extra revenues through some form of capacity payments, this will result in early retirement or mothballing of plants that will reduce capacity and drive prices back to their long-term equilibrium level. Unfortunately, a capacity payment that will make generator 5 content with selling its energy at marginal cost will also attract generator 6 to enter the market and will eliminate the incentive for demand response, resulting in overexpansion at increased social and consumer cost.

Figure 10.1. Optimal capacity and energy prices in long-term equilibrium

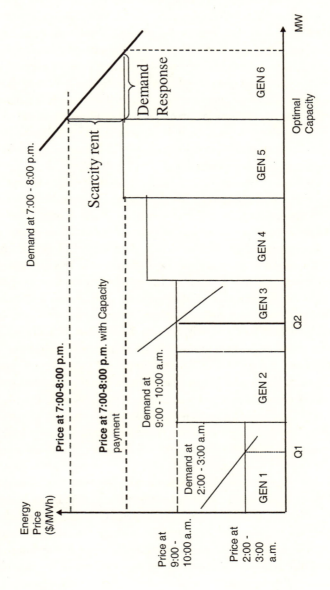

The critical role of electricity in the economy and the political ramifications of widespread electricity shortages have prompted many regulators around the world to take steps above and beyond reliance on market forces in order to ensure generation adequacy. In theory, allowing the prices of energy to reflect short-run supply and demand equilibrium will create market signals and provide adequate financing for proper capacity expansion. However, many regulators have been concerned that energy prices occurring in the various restructured systems are not sufficiently high to cover generators' capacity costs and to prompt adequate investment. The prevalence of regulatory intervention to suppress energy prices even when they reflect legitimate scarcity rents justifies the concern that, indeed, generators would not be able to cover their fixed costs through energy sales alone. Indeed such concern is supported by empirical evidence presented in Paul Joskow's paper in this volume regarding the scarcity rents embedded in the New England energy prices.

Reliance on energy prices to cover capacity costs through scarcity rents draws many legitimate counterarguments. Nonstorability of electricity, demand and supply uncertainty, inelastic demand, and the steepness of the supply curve at its high end all contribute to high-price volatility when reserve margins are low. While some temporary high prices reflect legitimate economic signals that are needed in order to attract investment, they are politically unacceptable, especially as it is impossible to differentiate between legitimate scarcity rents and high prices resulting from market power abuse, or from strategies such as "hockey stick" bidding that exploit the inelastic demand and flawed market rules. Furthermore, even if high prices do reflect legitimate scarcity rents that induce investment, sustained levels of scarcity rents while new capacity is being built will result in unacceptable transfer of wealth from consumers to producers. Such concerns have prompted the impositions of price caps and market mitigation procedures that arguably "throw out the baby with the bath water" by suppressing legitimate scarcity price signals.

One could argue that the adverse effects of price volatility would be mitigated in a well-functioning market by forward contracting and other risk management practices. This is indeed true; however, the realities of electricity markets suggest that vertical disintegration in many restructured electricity markets and the reregulation of some segments (e.g., the retail market) has resulted in improper distribution of risk along the electricity supply chain. This misallocation of risk results in improper risk management, as was the case in California. Consequently, some regulatory intervention, at least on a temporary basis, might be needed in order to achieve socially efficient risk management. Such regulatory intervention, however, requires caution as measures taken to ensure generation adequacy may have the effect of suppressing energy prices due to excess capacity or perverse incentives so that the necessity of such measures becomes self-perpetuating. This has clearly been the case in Argentina, for instance, where a large capacity payment paid on the basis of generated energy induces generators to bid below marginal cost so as to increase production and capacity payment revenues. In Peru, on the other hand, where bidding below marginal cost is severely restricted, generous capacity payments have resulted in a large amount of excess capacity and, arguably, inefficient entry.

The Origins of Capacity Payments

Ensuring generation adequacy through capacity payments has been implemented in the United Kingdom (before the new trading arrangements [NETA]), Spain, and several Latin American countries. Generators in such systems are given a per MW payment based on their availability (whether they get dispatched or not) or based on generated energy as an adder to the energy-market-clearing price. The capacity payments are collected from customers as a prorated uplift similar to other uplift charges, such as transmission charge. In some cases, such as in Spain, capacity payments are indistinguishable from stranded investment compensation, which are viewed as an additional source of revenue for the generators that is needed in addition to the competitive energy revenues in order to guarantee their profitability.

The concept of capacity payment is rooted in the theory of peak-load pricing, whose application in the context of electric power was pioneered by Boiteux (1960). According to this theory, generation of electricity requires two factors of production, capacity and energy, where the amount of energy that can be produced in any given time period is constrained by the available capacity. Consider a simple case of two consumption periods: peak and off peak, with two respective deterministic demand functions, and assume that the same fixed capacity is available in both periods. According to the basic theory, energy is priced at marginal cost in both periods, and a capacity payment that would recover the fixed capacity cost is imposed on the peak-period energy users. The optimal capacity will be such that the incremental cost of a capacity unit equals the shadow price on the capacity constraint that is active during the peak. That shadow price reflects the incremental value of unserved load as measured by willingness to pay net of marginal energy cost. It is important to realize that the preceding approach to pricing has evolved in the context of a regulated monopoly, whose primary objectives have been to recover cost and encourage consumption.

Subsequent developments of peak-load pricing theory focused on two important aspects of electricity supply: uncertainty and technology mix (see Chao 1983 for a general treatment of these two aspects). The effect of uncertainty leads to redefining the basic ingredients of electricity service as energy and reliability where reliability is manifested by LOLP calculation as a function of available capacity relative to load. The distinction between peak and off peak then becomes a matter of degree. This perspective rationalizes levying a time-varying capacity charge on all consumption and the payment to generation capacity that is not utilized for production of energy on the ground that such capacity provides added reliability. The capacity adders employed in the U.K. system to augment energy prices and compensate available nondispatched capacity are based on the preceding perspective.

Another perspective motivating capacity payments focuses on cost recovery in a system with optimal technology mix serving a load profile characterized by a load-duration curve. In the following we adopt a deterministic interpretation of the load-duration curve. However, a similar argument can be developed by interpreting the load-duration curve as a cumulative probability distribution on load level and using average availability in determining the technology mix. Consider a set of generation technologies characterized by a fixed and variable cost per capacity increment (the variable cost defined with respect to load factor). The lower envelope of the different cost functions creates a nonlinear technology mix cost curve per capacity unit as function of operating duration. That curve can be interpreted as the system's cost of serving any horizontal load slice under the load-duration curve, as illustrated on the left-hand side of figure 10.2.

This interpretation is the basis for Wright tariffs that price load slices nonlinearly based on load factor. In a system with coincident peaks, pricing each load slice according to the load-slice nonlinear cost curve will exactly recover the total cost of generation. Furthermore, that nonlinear function coincides with the technology specific cost function in the relevant duration interval. Hence, compensating generators based on the load-slice nonlinear cost curve is equivalent to paying generators their technology specific capacity and energy costs.

An alternative approach illustrated on the right-hand side of figure 10.2 is to price consumption and compensate generation of energy at each point in time at the corresponding marginal energy cost, that is, the variable cost of the most expansive energy dispatched at that time. As we can see from figure 10.2, the sum $\sum_{i=1}^{3} C_i \cdot T_i$ of marginal costs times the duration during which they are applied produces the same payment as the variable portion of the nonlinear duration-based cost function. Thus if each generator is paid the uniform

Figure 10.2. Recovery of generation cost through marginal cost and capacity payments

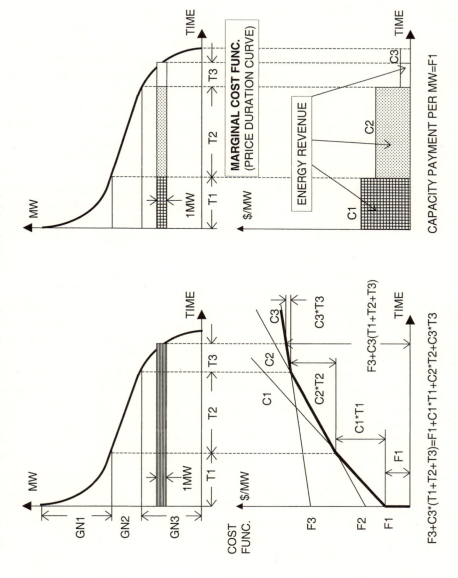

system marginal cost for their energy at each point in time, they end up with a shortfall in the amount of F_1, the fixed cost of the peaking technology, per each unit of capacity.

The preceding argument rationalizes awarding generators a uniform capacity payment based on the fixed cost of the peaking technology (typically combustion turbines [CTs]) to supplement energy revenues based on marginal cost. Under optimal capacity planning the marginal cost of incremental capacity equals the marginal cost of unserved load, which can be approximated by the marginal VOLL times the probability or fraction of time that load must be curtailed due to insufficient capacity. Hence, two alternative methods for capacity payment calculation (which are, in theory, equivalent under optimal capacity configuration) are to base the payment on the cost of peaking technology (e.g., CT) construction or to use the expected value of unserved load estimated by the product VOLL × LOLP.

The need for a capacity payment to make up for generation cost recovery shortfall can be eliminated by introducing into the technology stack demand curtailment as an equivalent supply technology with zero fixed cost and marginal cost equal to VOLL. The supply curve describing cost per capacity unit as function of operating duration for the augmented technology stack starts continuously through the origin with a slope of VOLL. Hence, if we set a spot price so as to equal to the marginal cost in each duration interval, the spot price during the period where demand is curtailed should be set to VOLL as illustrated in figure 10.3. Paying generators that spot price during supply scarcity periods will provide them with the same income as capacity payment. There is, however, an important difference between the two alternative forms of compensation. Capacity payments set to the value of peaking technology capacity cost fully compensates such technology even if it is idle and consequently may induce excess capacity. On the other hand, paying the VOLL for energy produced during scarcity periods only compensates generators that can sell their power at that price and will hence avoid the incentive for overinvestment. Furthermore, capacity payments are usually paid to generators whereas curtailed load can only avoid the peak technology marginal cost of energy. On the other hand, when the capacity cost is collected by generators in the form of a scarcity spot price, the curtailed load avoids the full VOLL payment and hence such an approach provides an incentive for demand-side participation in shortage mitigation.

Setting the spot price at VOLL during a curtailment period is a proxy to demand-side bidding where true values of lost load would be manifested. Thus VOLL attempts to represent an average of the value of lost-load distribution. With demand-side bidding, the full distribution (rather than a

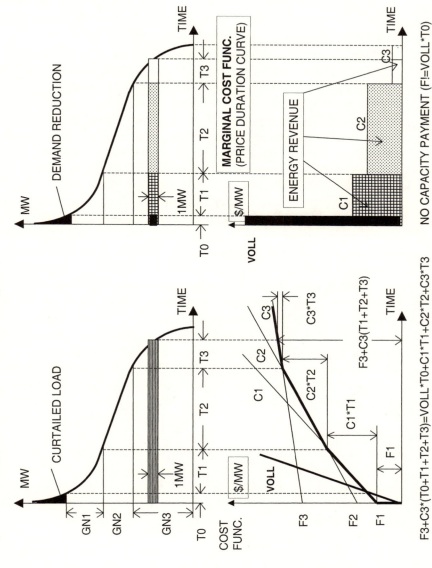

Figure 10.3. Adding demand curtailment to the technology stack

uniform approximation set to VOLL) is included in the supply stack. This could be depicted by replacing the straight line representing curtailment on the bottom left of figure 10.3 with a concave curve whose average slope equals VOLL. The resulting spot prices during curtailment periods will at times go below the VOLL level, and consequently more demand-side displacement of peak generation capacity will occur.

In the absence of demand-side bidding it is often the case that involuntary curtailments are averted by the system operator through dispatch of reserves whose energy is priced based on their marginal operating cost. Such practices give rise to an important practical question: what should be considered as a curtailment period during which the price is raised to VOLL? If the right amount of reserves were procured, such deployment of reserves impacts security and that impact should be reflected in the price of energy. The use of reserves to mitigate energy shortages at prices reflecting the incremental energy costs of the reserves amounts to a subsidy between security and adequacy. This is analogous to using the army to mitigate labor shortages and charging the employers variable hourly incremental cost for the soldiers' time. A pricing scheme that would reflect the scarcity that led to deployment of reserves should augment the energy price during such periods with some prorated portion of the reserve capacity payments (of the ancillary service market) that would have otherwise been levied on all customers as an uplift. Intuitively that adder should increase gradually as more reserves procured for security purposes are being deployed to meet energy shortages and price of energy plus the adder should approach the VOLL when involuntary load curtailments are invoked.

A rigorous determination of how to set the real-time spot price when reserves are being deployed would require a model that assesses the effect of such deployment on system security.[1]

Planning Reserve Obligations and Capacity Markets

The eastern pools in the United States, including Pennsylvania, New Jersey, Maryland (PJM), the New York Power Pool (NYPP), and New England ensure generation adequacy by imposing an installed capacity obligation on LSEs. Specifically, the LSEs are required to have or to contract with generators for a prescribed level of reserve capacity above their peak load within a certain time frame. The specific forms of the reserve requirement and the time frame over which such obligations are determined varies among systems and are still undergoing revisions. New England, for instance, had at some

Figure 10.4. Characteristic shape of supply and demand functions for capacity

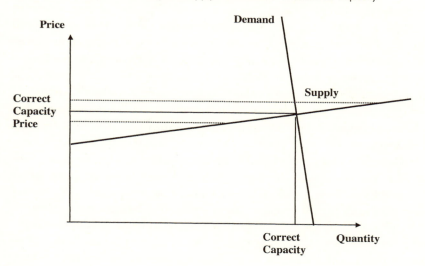

point separate requirements for installed capacity specified with respect to the annual peak and separate requirements for operable capacity specified relative to the monthly peak. Formal or informal capacity markets that allow trading of capacity obligations among the LSEs have accompanied installed capacity (ICAP) obligations. The basic motivation for the ICAP requirements is similar to the argument in favor of capacity payments. The capacity markets prompted by the obligation provide generators with the opportunity to collect extra revenue for their unutilized reserve generation capacity and provide incentives for the building of reserves beyond the reserves that meet the short-term needs for ancillary services.

One could argue that if we consider generation capacity as a separate product that is needed in order to provide reliable electricity service, then the supply of that product can be controlled either through prices in the form of capacity payments or through quantity control in the form of capacity obligation. The case for quantity control can be supported by the classic prices versus quantities argument depicted in figure 10.4. The basic argument is that the demand function for capacity is nearly vertical while the supply function is flat. Thus a small error in price will result in a large error in quantity so that direct quantity control is more accurate.[2] Furthermore, from an engineering and system reliability perspective, the ICAP obligation insures "iron in the ground," which is not always the case with capacity payments.

The calculation of either planning reserve requirements or capacity payments is typically based on engineering models of LOLP and on estimates of the VOLL. The LOLP calculations take into consideration the quantity and mix of the available capacity in relation to the forecasted load and the probabilities of forced outages. In the original U.K. design capacity, payments were directly computed as the product of LOLP × (VOLL – system marginal energy price) and updated each half hour. In systems with mandated planning reserves, the prescribed reserve requirements are based on a threshold criterion on the expected cost of lost load given by the product of LOLP and VOLL net of energy cost.

The reliance of capacity payments and capacity requirements on engineering-based calculation has been criticized repeatedly on the grounds that the VOLL used in these calculations is administratively set and has no market base. The usual remedy proposed, for instance, by Chuang and Wu (2000) is to employ VOLL figures based on demand-side bidding. Further criticisms by Graves, Hanser, and Earl (1998) and by Hirst, Kirby, and Hadly (1999) point to the fact that the LOLP calculations often employ simplistic models of probabilistic failure (e.g., Poison arrivals) and do not account for more-complex phenomena such as the incentives of operators to keep plants running during peak-price periods. Both the arbitrariness in the VOLL and the approximate nature of the LOLP calculation are likely to result in a mismatch between energy-market prices and capacity values set directly or via a capacity market induced by capacity obligations. Furthermore, as the U.K. experience taught us, the predictability of calculated capacity payments can lead to gaming and manipulation of the payments.

One of the basic problems with capacity markets is their disconnection from energy markets. The fundamental relationship between capacity and energy prices in a long-run equilibrium is such that the expected social cost of unserved energy as reflected by the energy-only market prices should equal the marginal cost of incremental capacity. However, the separate capacity markets created for trading reserve capacity requirement set through engineering-based methods may produce prices that are not in equilibrium with the energy-market prices. For instance, overestimating the expected cost of lost load would create artificially inflated demand for capacity and result in high capacity prices, which in turn will lead to overcapacity that results in suppressed energy prices and socially inefficient production and consumption. Similarly, capacity payments based on such calculations would tend to suppress energy prices to or below marginal cost, resulting in excess consumption and excess generation capacity. The disconnection between capacity and energy markets is also manifested by the fact that installed capacity contracts

Figure 10.5. ICAP market daily and monthly price trends at PJM

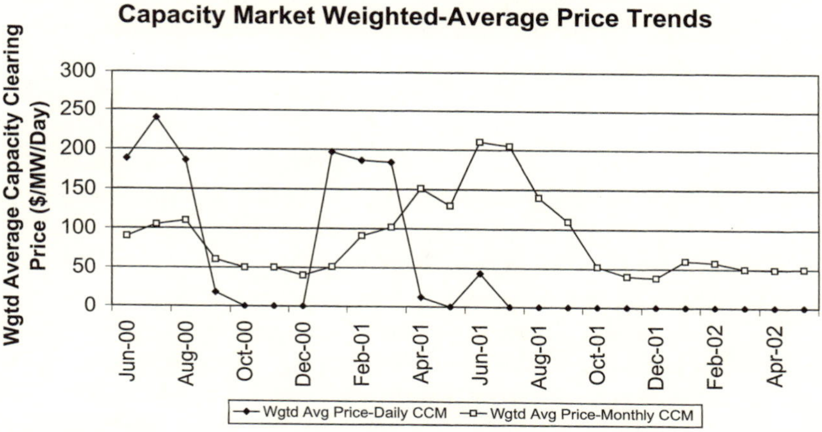

Source: FERC 2002b.

typically have no performance obligation requiring the capacity to be bid or to provide energy at some specified price.

Another difficulty with capacity markets relates to the time step associated with the traded obligation, which is typically a month. Within this time frame both the supply and demand function for ICAP are vertical (i.e., inelastic) resulting in prices that are either very low (when supply exceeds demand) or very high (when there is a capacity shortage). Response to ICAP demand through generation planning and investment require longer-term obligations. In New England, for instance, the ICAP market has cleared at zero price for a long time period that eventually led to the recent implementation of a forward reserve market championed by Mario DePhillis.[3] At PJM the high volatility and eventual collapse of the daily capacity market led to the development of a more sustainable monthly capacity market, as shown in figure 10.5, and to a proposal for a seasonal capacity obligation (FERC 2002b).

In a market reform proposal filed with the FERC, the California ISO has proposed a new type of capacity obligation that tries to address some of the shortcomings of ICAP. The proposed approach is similar to the ICAP requirement in the sense that a capacity obligation is imposed on LSEs as a percentage of their forecasted monthly peak load. However, the capacity product is defined as available capacity (ACAP), which must be offered in the day-ahead energy market. The ACAP product will be of various durations and can be provided either through generation capacity or physical load management. The ACAP obligations do not have, however, a specified energy price ceiling, which currently is by default the regional price cap mandated by the FERC. That price cap, however, is subject to change.[4] Uncertainty in the price cap makes the pricing of long-term ACAP contracts difficult.

Revisiting the Role of Capacity Payment and Generation Adequacy

Theoretical rationale and practical experience suggest that energy-only markets with spot prices that are allowed to reflect scarcity rents will generate sufficient income to allow capacity cost recovery by generators. Hence from a supply adequacy point of view a well-functioning energy-only market can provide the correct incentives for generation adequacy. Yet there may be good reasons for some form of capacity payment and even for regulatory intervention to ensure generation adequacy. Legitimate concerns for failure of the energy markets to reflect scarcity rents or failure of the capital market to produce proper levels of investment in response to such rents may justify some intervention. In some cases regulatory intervention in adequacy assurance is needed to compensate for regulatory interference in the energy market.

   The supply resource stack of electricity generation in systems with significant amounts of thermal generation exhibits an inherently steep rise in cost around the capacity limit. This phenomenon combined with the typically low short-term elasticity of electricity demand tends to produce high price volatility in fully competitive energy spot markets. Spot markets that clear on an hourly or half-hourly basis tend to average out some of the volatility, but even in such markets it may be politically infeasible to allow the energy spot prices to fully reflect scarcity rents. Consequently, energy prices are often suppressed through regulatory intervention (price caps and market mitigation) and by the market design, which in turn creates revenue deficiency for the generator that may cause insufficient investment in generation capacity. Often the threat of regulatory interference to curb scarcity rents is sufficient to inhibit capital formation and raise the capital cost for investment in generation capacity. Such interference is due to misperceptions and difficulties in distinguishing between market power abuse and legitimate scarcity rents. Thus, capacity payments or capacity obligations that stimulate capacity markets are largely viewed as remedial measures needed to offset suppression of energy prices and to ensure generation adequacy.

   A useful perspective in addressing the generation adequacy problem is to view the regulatory intervention as a form of insurance against price volatility. Rather than considering the intervention as a reaction to the failure of the energy spot prices to properly reflect scarcity rents, one may regard the regulatory intervention as a proactive measure in the form of a mandatory hedge or insurance that will assure that prices stay within a socially acceptable range. Such an insurance-based view recognizes the private good nature of generation adequacy. It lays the foundation for introducing customer choice in selecting the appropriate level of price protection and for establishing a relation between the capacity payment awarded to a generator and the responsibility that such payment entails. For instance, rather than setting a uniform capacity obligation or payment whose cost is evenly distributed among consumers, LSEs, direct access customers, and generators may be able to select their desired level of exposure to price risk and pay or receive an appropriate premium. Thus, generators receiving a capacity payment will guarantee the availability of their capacity to produce energy at a prespecified strike price so the capacity payment is interpreted as premium for a call option on that capacity. The higher the payment the lower the strike price and vice versa. In an ideal market where LSEs are free to choose the level of price insurance they want to acquire, the strike prices and corresponding capacity payments will emerge spontaneously as market-based risk premia driven by the risk management preferences of the market players. However, as we explain in the following, there are good reasons for regulatory intervention at least as a transitory measure to insure that the public is protected against excessive price or shortage risk.

Some Caveats and Impediments to Market-Based Provision of Generation Adequacy

An important concern that is often voiced in countries where there is no well-developed institutional infrastructure that can enforce the financial liability of corporations is that LSEs or generators may assume more risk than they could handle reliably. So, for instance, hydrogenerators may oversell their water in the present market and not be able to meet their generation adequacy obligations for which they collected capacity payments through premiums on private contracts. Likewise, LSEs left to their own devices may not hedge their supply sufficiently in order to reduce their capacity payments and may go out of business or default on their obligation to their customers if the spot prices for electricity skyrocket due to supply shortages. We cannot ignore the reality that U.S. bankruptcy laws provide a de facto hedge to LSEs, which may result in assumption of imprudent risk. This is not just a theoretical possibility;

indeed, the chapter eleven filing by the Pacific Gas and Electric Company (PG&E) during the California crisis and the more recent bankruptcy filing by a Texas retail energy provider during the February 2003 ice storm suggest that, either due to regulation flaws or by choice, LSEs do not always manage risk in ways that are socially optimal or provide adequate protection to their customers.

It is common for commercial entities involved in underwriting risk, such as banks, savings and loans, and insurance companies, to be subject to some form of regulation that will protect the customers from default. Likewise, in the case of electricity it may be necessary to set some minimum contracting or hedging level on LSEs. The premium payment for meeting such requirements through contracting with generators will produce the capacity payments that generators need in order to insure the stable income stream for financing adequate generation investment. In exchange for a stable source of income, the generators will forgo some of the opportunity to collect high scarcity rents. However, there is no need for a one-size-fits-all approach that awards a uniform capacity payment to all generators and imposes a uniform capacity charge on all the loads. A market-based approach, which allows parties to trade energy price risk and investment risk through different contractual arrangements, can achieve better efficiency in risk sharing and investment. Regulatory intervention can then be limited to enforcement of minimal hedging requirements and oversight of commercial liability standards and adherence to contractual arrangements.

A system of capacity payments that is linked to assumption of energy price risk can also address the problem of over- or undercompensation of generators based on simulated market conditions. In Colombia, for instance, capacity payments to generators are based on simulation results of hydro scarcity and the forecasted need for dispatch of thermal plants under such scarcity conditions. Generators that are not "dispatched" by the simulation are not entitled to capacity payments although they may still be dispatched in reality, whereas a generator that received the capacity payment may be unavailable.

Another problem that may arise in a market-based capacity payment system concerns possible failure of the capital market to provide long-term financing for generation investments at rates that commensurate with the associated risk. Such market failure may arise since supply contracts that will provide the equivalent capacity payments as option premiums are typically of short duration (no longer than five years), whereas generation investment requires fifteen to thirty years of financing. The practice of securitizing long-term investment by rolling over short-term contracts is prevalent in many industries (e.g., using short-term savings to finance thirty-year mortgages).

However, lack of experience with commodity trading in the electricity industry and the perceived regulatory intervention risk (especially in developing countries) may raise the cost of capital to levels that will reduce investment below the efficient adequacy level. Capacity payments are often viewed as a means of income stabilization that would enable generators to obtain financing for adequate investment level. If this indeed was the concern that capacity payments address, a more appropriate mechanism would be some form of loan guarantees by the regulator. Because regulatory intervention is one of the key risk factors concerning investors in this business, government-backed loan guarantees may inspire confidence in the regulator's commitment to uphold free market principles.

Capacity Payments as Call Option Premiums

A call option is a financial instrument that gives its holder the right to purchase the underlying commodity at an agreed-upon strike price. A system where the capacity payments represent a call option would require generators that receive capacity payments to be available to produce energy at the strike price or purchase it and provide it at that price. On the other hand, generators that did not receive capacity payments should be allowed to collect whatever prices the market will bear.[5] The short term inelasticity of demand and steep supply curve may necessitate the setting of a price cap at an administratively chosen VOLL. That cap value will then serve as both, a penalty for unmet availability obligation and as a cap on the scarcity rents collected by generators who did not receive capacity payments. Further extension of this approach would allow generators to select among different levels of capacity payment in exchange for being available to provide energy at corresponding strike-price levels or buyout of their obligation at VOLL.

Viewing capacity payments as premium for call options at corresponding strike prices requires the specification of contract duration. Locking in the capacity payment for a longer duration has the effect of averaging out price volatility, thus providing the security of a stable income stream for the generator and stable energy prices for the consumers. However, the argument for diversity of choices in strike prices also applies to diversity of choice in contract terms. As contracts get shorter, the corresponding option premium constituting the capacity payment becomes more volatile and starts to behave as a spot market for capacity. At the limit the capacity payment becomes an energy adder, which is indistinguishable from energy payments for dispatched generators or from ancillary services payments to generators providing spinning reserves. Ideally the capacity adder should be rolled into the energy bids and reflected in the hourly or half-hourly energy-market clearing prices.

When a subsequent ancillary service market exists as in California, equilibrium between the energy and ancillary service market dictates that energy bids are raised by the opportunity cost of selling capacity in the ancillary service market. Hence, the market-clearing price for reserves is a good estimate of the capacity component contained in the market-clearing prices for energy. In the old U.K. system, that equilibrium condition was enforced administratively by calculating a capacity adder based on the product LOLP × (VOLL – SMP), which is paid to dispatched generators on the top of the system marginal energy price (SMP) and to nondispatched generators that declare availability. Excess availability will depress the capacity adder, but all the available capacity receives that payment regardless of the price that they bid for energy. An option-premium-based calculation of the capacity adder would adjust the capacity adder according to the energy price bid by the generator. Thus dispatched generators would receive an option premium based on the hourly SMP serving as strike price, while generators whose bids exceeded the SMP should be paid a call-option premium according to their energy bid serving as strike price.

A Straw Proposal for Provision of Generation Adequacy through Hedging Obligations

Under this scheme, at the beginning of each month LSEs are required to hold verifiable hedges in the form of forward contracts and/or call options, totaling at least some predetermined percentage (say 112 percent) of their next month's forecasted peak load.[6] Qualifying hedges must have at least two years' duration with no less than one year of remaining life, whereas the strike prices for the call options should be at or below a maximum level set by the regulator (e.g., price cap). The requirement for long-duration hedges is needed in order to attract participation by new entrants who can offer capacity beyond the existing stock and hedge their investment by selling long-term forward contracts or call options. One of the major shortcomings of the existing ICAP markets is the short duration of the ICAP obligations, which prevents any meaningful response by investors to high ICAP prices. Hedging obligations imposed on LSEs may be multitiered with respect to the strike prices, creating an effective demand function for planning reserves. For example, an LSE may be required to hold 104 percent (of forecasted monthly peak load) in forward contracts and call options having strike prices not to exceed $400/MWh, another 4 percent with strike prices at or below \$600/MWh, and 4 percent with a strike price at or below \$1,000/MWh. Hedging obligations can be met by a portfolio of contracts with generators and curtailable load resources. A limited amount of financial self-provision (backed by rigorous credit worthiness requirements) may be allowed. Under such self-provision, the LSE will be obligated to absorb the difference between the market price and the strike price without being able to pass it to its customers. The determination of strike prices and the quantities of hedges at each price enables the regulator to shape the price volatility in the market. Such control is a delicate task that needs to balance the proper short-term price signal with public risk-management objectives.

Call options may be procured by the LSE through bilateral contracts with generators or load, they can be self-provided by LSE controlled resources (or through a financial security as described previously), or they can be procured through a voluntary auction hosted by the ISO. In order to reduce the exposure to generators providing the call options and consequently reduce the call-option prices, the strike price of the call option may be indexed to fuel cost. Alternatively, the call options may be defined on the "spark spread."[7] When call options are exercised, the counterparty is obligated to provide the contracted power at the strike price or be liable for the difference between the market-clearing price and the strike price times the called quantity. The proposed ACAP in California may be viewed as call-option obligations with a strike price that equals to the price cap (which is currently rather low). The problem with the ACAP is that the strike price is not explicitly stated, and therefore long-term ACAP contracts are viewed as too risky on the supply side and consequently too expensive from the demand perspective.

The provision of supply adequacy through hedging obligations captures several important features. First of all, this approach focuses on mitigation of price volatility as a primary objective rather than on "steel in the ground," which is only one of the possible market responses to anticipated supply shortages. The ability of the LSEs to meet their hedging obligations through alternative means will discipline the capacity supply and maintain equilibrium between investment in new generation, demand response, and risk management. Specifying the hedging obligation in terms of long-term instruments facilitates investment response. Investors in new generation can raise capital by issuing the long-term obligations, which can be subsequently traded among the LSEs in secondary markets. Facilitating the market for such long-term hedging obligation enables reserve generation capacity to secure a stable income stream in exchange for a tangible commitment to sell energy at reasonable prices when needed. Because the LSE obligations may be adjusted monthly to reflect fluctuations in forecasted peak demand, a secondary market for call options should emerge (similar to the ICAP markets) that will enable the trading of call options among the LSEs who may wish to adjust their positions.

The prices of the option will fluctuate from day to day to reflect demand for the call options. However, the generators underwriting the options are not exposed to these fluctuations. Short-term price fluctuations of long-term call options are analogous to the daily fluctuations in long-term treasury bond prices. The treasury that issued the bonds is immune to such fluctuations unless it issues new bonds or recalls existing ones. As the market matures, individual hedging obligations may be relaxed if the market as a whole proves to be properly hedged in the aggregate.

Centralized Procurement

One of the major objections raised by LSEs against long-term hedging requirements concerns the discrepancy between the length of the required hedging contracts and the LSE's business-planning horizon. LSE peak-load forecasts vary from month to month due to seasonal effects. Retail competition that exists to various degrees in deregulated electricity systems adds uncertainty and variability to the LSE's peak load upon which the hedging obligation is based. Consequently, many LSEs raised objections to having to carry two- to three-year hedges based on an amount that may vary from month to month. While secondary markets for hedges would allow LSEs to adjust their positions each month, the price volatility in such markets increases LSEs risk and their cost of doing business and may arguably suppress retail competition. A solution that will address the preceding problem without shortening the duration of the hedging contracts is to treat the hedging obligation as another ancillary service, allowing self-provision through bilateral contracts, with the ISO being the provider of last resort. Under such a scheme all hedging contracts, whether self-provided or centrally procured by the ISO through a periodic auction, will meet the criteria outlined in the previous section. However, the cost of the centrally procured hedges will be assigned to the LSEs that meet their obligation through the ISO on a monthly basis.[8]

The primary objective of the regulated hedging obligation and centrally procured hedges is to create a backstop mechanism for ensuring generation adequacy by providing a cash-flow stream to reserve generation capacity that is not capable of recovering its costs due to suppression of scarcity rents. The danger in instituting such a mechanism, however, is that it may interfere with the contract market and be perceived by some LSEs as an alternative to prudent risk-management practices. Long-term (three years) call options with fairly high strike prices (say 50 percent of the bid cap) will serve the generation adequacy objective while minimizing interference in the contract market. A high strike price will deter LSEs from leaning on the centrally procured hedges as a substitute to bilateral forward contracting and will reduce the exposure of the ISO underwriting the centralized procurement. It is important, however, to maintain sufficient headroom between the strike price of the hedging obligations and the bid cap imposed on generators. For instance, if the strike price is set to the currently prevailing bid cap of $1,000/MWh, then that will become a de facto cap for all the generation capacity that sold call options, but the cap should be raised (or eliminated) for generation capacity that is not bound by call options. The headroom between the bid cap and the strike price effectively creates a two-tier bid cap: a high "damage control" cap and a lower "compensated" cap. This differentiation plays an important role in encouraging demand response and in performance enforcement as discussed in the following.

It is expected that a significant portion of the hedging obligation imposed on LSEs will be self-provided through bilateral contracts that the LSE enter into as part of their regular risk management. The self-provided hedges can be backed by verifiable physical supply and resources or by verifiable demand-response commitment. Alternatively, the financial effect of self-provision can be replicated through bilateral financial contracts for differences (relative to the ISO prices) between the LSEs and any willing counterparty, which may or may not cover its position by selling long-term hedging contracts in the ISO procurement auction.

One of the central issues in implementing the preceding scheme is the intertemporal allocation of the procurement cost incurred by the ISO to the LSEs relying on the central procurement for meeting their hedging obligations. It is intuitively clear that reserve margins that are based on an annual peak-load level are more valuable (as a hedge against high prices) during high-demand periods when shortages are more likely. Consequently, load operating during high-demand periods should bear a larger share of the reserve costs. In a decentralized market for hedges, as described in the previous section, LSEs will seek to reduce their holdings of call options during low-load months, resulting in reduced prices. Likewise, during high-load months, LSEs needing to meet their increased hedging obligations will cause a rise in the market prices for call options. When long-term call options are centrally procured and their cost is allocated to load on a monthly basis, the intertemporal price fluctuations reflecting the supply and demand for the hedges must be computed. A reasonable allocation scheme would spread the cost of hedges over time in proportion to the LOLP, which is a function of the reserve margins relative to the load level (produced by standard engineering calculations). Alternatively, the allocation can be based on the probability that spot prices will exceed a given strike price.

Another issue that must be addressed under the central procurement approach concerns the penalties that should be imposed for nonperformance by a hedge provider. In other words, if a generator or curtailable load contracted under a call option fail to deliver energy when called, how should they be penalized? At the minimum, such a resource should be liable for the difference between the market price and the strike price. However, if the strike price is close to a price cap on energy, such a penalty may not be severe enough as it does not reflect the difference between the VOLL and the price cap. A more severe penalty that is based on estimated VOLL or forfeiture of capacity payment for several months might be more appropriate as a deterrent to nonperformance. Under a two-tiered bid cap, as discussed previously, nonperforming generators who are bound by a call option should be liable for the difference between the bid cap and the strike price for the undelivered energy. In addition, nonperformance penalties may include forfeiture of the capacity payment for the month during which the nonperformance event occurred.

Summary

The role of capacity payments in ensuring adequacy of supply can be fulfilled by risk-management approaches and hedging instruments that permit diverse choices and promote demand-side participation. The market should determine the value of capacity as a hedge for price risk. If capacity payments are intended to correct failures of capital markets, then regulatory intervention should address directly the availability and cost of long-term financing for capacity expansion secured by short-term contracts (e.g., through loan guarantees) and focus on promoting market confidence and rules that facilitate liquid markets for energy futures and other risk-management instruments.

When energy markets are not sufficiently developed to provide correct market signals for generation investment, setting capacity requirements with secondary markets that enable trading of capacity reserves is the preferred approach. It is more likely to produce correct market signals for investment than administratively set capacity payments that are likely to distort energy prices and result in overinvestment.

A more market-friendly approach that will guide markets toward prudent risk-management practices is to impose hedging requirements on LSEs. Such hedging obligations can be met through bilateral trading or through centralized procurement of long-term hedges. The cost of these centrally procured hedges is then allocated to the LSEs based on monthly forecasted peak load and some intertemporal allocation rule that reflects seasonal variations in the insurance value of the procured hedges. Under such a scheme, incumbent generators and new entrants can secure capacity payments in the form of a premium for a long-term call option that they sell with a mandated strike price. The LSEs, on the other hand, will face a monthly pro rata cost of the call options. Since such a scheme solves the credit-risk problem that may be faced by some LSEs if they attempted to meet their hedging obligation through bilateral contracts, it is likely to reduce the cost of meeting such obligations.

***

REFERENCES

Boiteux, Marcel P. 1960. Peak load pricing. *Journal of Business* 33:157–79.
Chao, Hung Po. 1983. Peak load pricing and capacity planning with demand and supply uncertainty. *Bell Journal of Economics* 14:179–90.
Chuang, Angela, and Felix Wu. 2000. Capacity payments and pricing of reliability in competitive generation markets. Paper presented at the 33rd Hawaii International System Science Conference. January, Maui, Hawaii.
Federal Energy Regulatory Commission (FERC). 2002a. Notice of Proposed Rule Making. Docket no. RM01-12-000. Washington, DC: FERC, July 31.
———. 2002b. Report of PJM Interconnection, LLC, re: supporting seasonal capacity commitment structure. Docket no. EL01-63-001. Washington, DC: FERC, May 31.
———. 2003. Wholesale power market platform. White Paper. Washington, DC: FERC, April 28.
Graves, Frank, Philip Hanser, and Robert Earl. 1998. The death and resurrection of electric capacity pricing. Brattle Group working paper. Cambridge, MA: The Brattle Group, October.
Hirst, Eric, Brendan Kirby, and Stan Hadly. 1999. Generation and transmission adequacy in a restructured U.S. electricity industry. Report to the Edison Electric Institute. Washington, DC: March.
Ruff, Larry. 1999. Capacity payment, security of supply, and stranded costs. Presentation to the National Spanish Electricity System Commission. June 7, Madrid.
Vazquez, Carlos, Michel River, and Ignacio Perez Arriaga. 2002. A market approach to long-term security of supply. *IEEE Transactions on Power Systems* 17 (2): 349–57.
Teknecon Energy Risk Advisors. 2001. A revised framework for the capacity change, *minimos operativos*, and rationing rules. World Bank Colombian Electricity Project final report, vol. 3. February 28, Austin, Texas.

NOTES

Shmuel S. Oren is a professor at the University of California, Berkeley, in the Department of Industrial Engineering and Operations Research (IEOR).

1. Ruff (1999) argued that the capacity adder in the old (pre-NETA) U.K. system was designed to accomplish this objective. In the United Kingdom there was no separate procurement of reserves by the system operator; rather, all the capacity that was bid and not dispatched was regarded as reserves. The extent to which the load use of reserves impacts security was reflected by the LOLP calculation, which determined the capacity adder to the spot price.

2. This argument and the illustration of figure 10.4 are due to Larry Ruff.

3. According to a personal e-mail communication from Mario DePhillis (December 24, 2003), the new forward reserve market in New England is functioning well and most recently cleared at $4,495 $/MW-Month.

4. The price cap in the west was raised by the FERC from $90/MWh to $250/MWh in September 2002 and is likely to be increased eventually to $1000/MWh, which emerges as a national bid cap standard.

5. Capacity payments based on call-option premiums have been proposed for the Columbian electricity system in a report by Teknecon Energy Risk Advisors (2001). A similar approach developed independently for the Columbian market is reported in a recent paper by Vazquez, River, and Perez Arriaga (2002).

6. The 112 percent figure was proposed by the FERC as a minimum in the SMD Notice of Proposed Rule Making (NOPR; FERC 2002a). However, the SMD NOPR recognizes that state regulators wishing to protect customers against shortages or price spikes may wish to increase the proposed percentage.

7. Spark spread-electricity price-heat rate adjusted fuel price.

8. Central procurement of long-term call options (by ERCOT) on behalf of the LSEs was proposed by Reliant Co. at a workshop on generation adequacy provision held by the Public Utility Commission of Texas.

11

Perspectives from Policymakers

Pat Wood III, Thomas R. Kuhn, and Joe Barton

Remarks by Pat Wood III

I appreciate this opportunity to provide my views about how to foster healthy and well-functioning wholesale electricity markets for the benefit of customers and the national economy. Competition is so firmly implanted in wholesale power markets that national policy discussions center on *how* to make competition work rather than *whether* competition is the right policy choice. Wholesale power markets have generally worked very well, but there have been some glaring exceptions that highlight the structural challenges that must be addressed. The agency I chair plays an important role in making sure competition works as intended, to provide reliable service at just and reasonable rates to customers. The FERC's current agenda aims to address the structural challenges in wholesale power markets through vigilant oversight, balanced rules, and sufficient infrastructure.

Is "deregulation" worth reexamining? That depends on whether there is even a choice to be made. At the state level there is a choice of whether to fundamentally alter the "regulatory compact" through which retail suppliers accept an obligation to serve in return for recovery of prudently incurred costs. That is an important and difficult question that many states are examining, as we did as in Texas when I chaired the Public Utilities Commission. *Wholesale service*, on the other hand, is not premised on a statutory obligation to serve, but instead is based primarily on voluntary contractual obligations.[1] Wholesale customers, which are typically utilities or municipal and cooperative systems, made "build" versus "buy" decisions while suppliers could choose to sell or not sell. These buyers and sellers have always come together voluntarily to negotiate service through contractual agreements. Rates, terms, and conditions of service were determined largely by these negotiations. Legislative and regulatory decisions have addressed ways to promote competition and modified regulatory roles for a market environment but, unlike state initiatives, have not required an older paradigm based upon an obligation to serve to be undone.

The challenge lies, then, in answering the deceptively simple question of how to make wholesale power markets work well.

Wholesale Competition Benefits Customers

Wholesale markets are an important source of value for end users and an important engine of economic growth. They have generally performed well. Markets have placed strong incentives on suppliers to invest and operate efficiently. Investors and suppliers have a much greater ability to control these costs than do captive customers. This ability combined with high-powered market incentives gets the full attention of management, which knows someone better will take their place if they do not perform. Electric competition is the means to the same ends that were achieved in the successful deregulation of the natural gas market: billions of dollars in annual benefits and reliable service for American customers. According to the Department of Energy, wholesale power markets are already saving customers $13 billion per year.

Many harder-to-quantify benefits come from placing investment risk on investors. Most of the dollars coming out of customers' wallets go into generation investment. Stranded costs incurred under the old system were all placed on captive customers. During the 1970s, generation investments led to rate increases of 100 percent for industrial customers and 37 percent for residential customers in real dollars. As a result of our national policy to rely on markets, investors now bear the risk for the quantity, timing, and location of generation investments. This is the first economic downturn where the stranded costs of excess capacity have not resulted in increased rates for captive customers. The same is true for construction cost overruns. Uneconomic investment can still happen from time to time, but it happens a lot less when investors pay for them, and they no longer show up in customers' rates.

Many unquantifiable benefits also come from innovations in generation and transmission technology. Combined cycle and other generation technologies have brought production efficiencies that are one-third greater than earlier technologies. These efficiencies reduce pollution and reduce bills. While technologies would have improved with or without competition, the rapid technological developments coincided with the laws and regulations of the early 1990s, reducing barriers to entry and expanding competitive opportunities.

Competition has also increased operating efficiency. The availability of generating units in well-functioning restructured markets increases. In the Mid-Atlantic and New York, availability has increased approximately 5 percent due to competitive pressures. On a national scale this would be like getting $15 billion of capacity built for free to serve customers.

The proof is in the prices, which are down since restructuring began. Wholesale power prices in most regions are very low now (relative to rising fuel input costs), due in large part to competition and significant generation capacity development.

Independent monitoring reports generally confirm that prices have been competitive and efficient. Well-designed markets have benefited from significant generation and transmission investment because the market platforms provide investors with clear rules and predictable rates and rewards for their investments.

Competitive Performance Requires a Competitive Structure

It would be naive to expect that competition could naturally spring up everywhere from a historically monopolistic industry. The "invisible hand" cannot take over immediately and do the job alone. We have seen instances where some customers were very poorly served by markets when they were not properly managed with balanced rules, sufficient infrastructure, and vigilant oversight.

Wholesale markets are scarred by the experience of California. Whatever one's view of the causes—extreme weather conditions, lack of adequate resources and infrastructure, lack of long-term contracting, lack of retail price incentives to conserve, market power and manipulation, or delayed federal and state response—the harm to customers was unacceptable.

Other regions have suffered from much less-visible insufficient competition. In areas without large regional transmission organizations (RTOs), artificial "seams" between the many islands of the grid hinder customers' supply choices. The absence of markets in balancing energy, at the minimum, makes long-term contracting difficult. There are tollgates along each transmission path road that slow down electron traffic.

Transmission service is arbitrarily curtailed without providing customers any reasonable ability to find the cheapest redispatch option to preserve their service. New technology and new entrants have limited market penetration due to grid access barriers. Small customers and utilities and competitive suppliers are all disadvantaged because they have no spot market to sell into or buy out of every hour that they have an excess or shortage of power. There is no platform to support demand-side participation in the market without an independent grid operator and transparent prices. New generation has been poorly located in regions that do not provide locational price signals and do not allocate transmission costs and transmission property rights on a fair basis. And despite a crying need for new infrastructure, little new transmission backbone has been built in the country.

The problems with electricity markets result from underlying structural features of the industry and the failure of redesigns of markets to address these features. Many areas, including California, have not appreciated the public good/free-rider attributes of system reliability, which leads to undersupply unless addressed by demand response or generation reserves. The California wholesale design also distorted the locational values of electricity, which encourages inefficient behavior and creates opportunities for manipulation. Many areas have had minimal demand-side participation, which increases price volatility and increases opportunities for manipulation. Some regions simply have too few sellers to allow for competitive outcomes. These are all features of supply and demand that must be addressed by public policy to make markets actually work for customers.

Policy Intervention Should Fix Only What *Is* Broke

The structure of supply and demand for electricity provide many exceptions to the textbook ideal of perfect competition. Noncompetitive structure invites noncompetitive conduct and performance. Intervention should be focused on remedying the structural features of the market that prevent competitive outcomes. Intervention that exceeds the structural need will interfere with the natural forces of supply and demand and harm customers in the long run. The goal should be to identify structural infirmities, design surgical transitional responses in the short term, and work to create more competitive structures in the long run. This trajectory is being seen in the more mature power markets.

In textbook "perfect competition," there are many buyers and sellers, perfect information, no transactions costs, and no externalities or free riders. Of course, no market in existence fully meets these ideal criteria. But they provide the benchmark to gauge the need for policy intervention. Taking each attribute in turn, we can put the FERC's regulatory policy in the appropriate economic policy context.

Many Buyers and Sellers

Transmission market power is the most obvious structural feature that prevents competitive outcomes. In many areas the transmission grid operator is affiliated with competitors in the generation market. Such companies have vertical market power—an incentive and ability to operate the upstream service (transmission scheduling and operation) for the benefit of its downstream (generation) business interests. The Commission has relied upon "behavioral" regulation through its open-access rules and standards of conduct to address this underlying structural problem. However, as is generally the case, these behavioral rules are far inferior to corrections of the underlying structural root causes.

Structural separation of the regulated transmission and competitive supply sectors of the industry solves the problem best, which is why the Commission is proposing to require membership in an RTO or an independent system operator (ISO).

Transmission, as a monopoly, also requires regulation to ensure sufficient infrastructure at reasonable prices. The FERC requires RTOs and ISOs to have a planning process to identify system expansions and fairly allocate costs to reliably and economically serve load. More-developed markets rely more on market price signals to direct timing and location of such expansions.

Generation market power is also an exception to the condition of "many buyers and sellers." At many times and places on the electric grid, suppliers can find themselves in a "pivotal" position such that their generating units must run to support the reliability of the grid. This can happen in small isolated "load pockets" where a unit must be running to support local voltage constraints. Or it can occur across a multistate region where at least part of demand must be met by some of a given seller's output. In either case, the "pivotal supplier" has market power; it has the ability to "name its price." To address this structural infirmity, the Commission relies on up-front spot-market bidding rules for entities that have market power.

Price-responsive demand is a structural feature of electricity markets that must be addressed. Customers must have an opportunity to state their true valuation of energy and be able to refuse to purchase above their stated valuation. This issue is primarily in the domain of state commissions that have jurisdiction over retail sales. However, because of its importance in overall market design, the FERC is playing a supporting role to encourage a more competitive demand-responsive market in the future.

Perfect Information

Market participants must know the value of services in order to guide their investment, operation, and consumption decisions. Prices are the communication vehicle to broadcast these values. Competition is fairest when all parties receive the same quality of information, including large and small participants and potential new entrants. In much of the country, transactions occur only through private negotiated contracts with limited price discovery for third parties. In areas of the country with RTOs or ISOs, far more information is available because of the transparent spot markets. These markets provide not only real-time energy value, but they are so disaggregated that they provide the information for each location on the grid every five minutes. The FERC encourages the expansion of such transparent spot markets. The FERC has also required price reporting for bilateral market transactions through the Electronic Quarterly Reports available on the FERC website (www.ferc.gov). The FERC is also working to facilitate better price formation for natural gas markets through improvements to the price indices that are used by so many market participants.

Transactions Costs

The electric grid must be in complete supply-demand balance at every moment. While textbook market operations achieve balance through the independent actions of many autonomous buyers and sellers, transactions costs prevent the electric industry from operating without a central administrator. This entity, which is the equivalent of the air traffic controller in the airline industry, ensures real-time balance of supply and demand while scheduling all requested and feasible schedules. The RTOs and ISOs have taken control of short-term reliability in order to more efficiently achieve this real-time balance. For longer-term transactions, the costs of such transactions are lower and there is less of a need for central administration.

Externalities

Electric power epitomizes the externality problem. Power flow on a network flows across multiple "paths" according to the laws of physics, such that transactions can disrupt each other. Property rights, a necessary feature of all markets, are difficult to define and protect. In areas without an RTO or ISO, grid efficiency is poor because of the need to reserve extra capacity to protect existing rights. With an RTO or ISO, the grid can be used to its full capacity because physical reservations are not needed to provide customers with physical and financial protections of their property rights.

Free Riders

Certain structural features of the electric power system create a free-rider problem. Metering and control systems do not coincide with individual customers closely enough for system operators to administer customer-specific curtailments. Customers can "lean on the grid," or take power that they did not pay to create to the detriment of those who did invest and produce long-term supply. The result of the free-rider problem is an incentive to undersupply. Interestingly, in the past this incentive was counterbalanced by retail cost-of-service regulation that encouraged *over*investment (the Averch-Johnson effect). In competitive regions, the free-rider problem typically has been addressed through tradable resource adequacy obligations. Other, more market-based incentives may address this issue successfully, but they have been difficult to develop.

Markets Require a Policy Platform

Twenty years ago, with the publication of *Markets for Power*, Paul Joskow and Richard Schmalensee advocated neither a completely free market nor a fully regulated industry, but a mixture of regulation and competition. They wrote: "Successfully managing a system that mixes competition and regulation is complex and requires that regulatory institutions, industry structures, and arenas of competition be designed carefully to complement one another." The authors knew then that electric supply, demand, and the transmission grid could only work on an effective market platform. The lack of storage, free flow across state and company boundaries, and the need for a central grid operator to maintain instantaneous reliability are permanent structural features of electric power systems everywhere that must be accounted for.

John McMillan's recent book *Reinventing the Bazaar: A Natural History of Markets* describes the evolution of markets from the nontransparent bazaars of Marrakesh to stock exchanges to eBay. He concludes:

> Markets do what they are supposed to do, only if they are well structured. Any
> successful economy has an array of devices and procedures to enable markets
> to work smoothly. A workable platform has five elements: information flows
> smoothly; property rights are protected; people can be trusted to live up to their
> promises; side effects on third parties are curtailed; and competition is fostered.

In electricity, it is impossible to achieve any one of these goals without a coherent set of rules.

A Proven Platform Will Make Competition Work

An extensive and public review of the structural features of the electric power market has resulted in a wide consensus around a set of appropriate policy responses. The FERC has recently stated that certain elements need to be in place in all regions of the country to support well-functioning markets. These include

1. *Regional independent grid operation:* Independent operators remove vertical market power from the grid operation function, provide and protect transmission property rights, reduce transactions costs of scheduling service through a one-stop service for the region, and reduce "seams" from small transmission islands.

2. *Regional transmission planning process:* A transparent regional planning process provides infrastructure that the market would not provide by itself, to provide systemwide benefits and capture the economies of scale in grid facilities.

3. *Fair cost allocation for existing and new transmission:* The benefits of regional planning can only be captured if the investments can be paid for and such cost allocation decisions can be made on a timely basis, thus requiring up-front clarity on who will pay for what, particularly the key distinction of whether a given transmission investment will be paid for out of regulated rates or not.

4. *Market monitoring and market power mitigation:* To address the times and places where the generation market structure does not support competitive outcomes, up-front market power mitigation rules provide circuit breakers to automatically keep bids competitive without distorting long-run incentives. Market monitoring at all times will provide an early warning system protection against market power or market design flaws.

5. *Spot markets to meet customers' real-time energy needs:* Spot markets create market transparency and reduce structural barriers to entry for new entrants, particularly for intermittent resources but also for all other market participants who inevitably need to trade in the spot market to resolve imbalances.

6. *Transparency and efficiency in congestion management:* This feature, usually implemented through locational marginal pricing (LMP), ensures that the costs of grid congestion are borne by those who cause it. A market-based method reduces the transactions costs in the current system of having to find the lowest-cost generator to resolve a constraint. It also provides valuable market

information to all participants on a fair basis regarding the locational value of energy.

7. *Firm transmission rights (FTRs):* Tradable FTRs provide property rights to transmission that can be protected and efficiently allocated.

8. *Resource adequacy:* This requirement addresses the undersupply problem with public goods through incentives or direct requirements to have timely and sufficient generation or demand response.

A platform designed with these core features serves customers better over the long run than any other platform. Experience in the United States and abroad confirms that.

Conclusion

We know from natural gas and other industries that balanced competition brings benefits to customers. We know from power market experience that the above wholesale power market platform is required to make competition work for customers. The platform provides a strong customer protection plan. The platform provides regulatory certainty and clarity so that market participants can move forward with business decisions. The wholesale power market platform carefully provides the policy intervention and support that is required for efficient wholesale power markets right now, and no more. It facilitates efficient, decentralized decision making about operations and investment. The wholesale power market platform will bring benefits to customers in the form of reliable, reasonably priced electricity. And, perhaps, most important for the nation's economic future, it provides a foundation for technological innovation in the years and decades to come.

Remarks by Thomas R. Kuhn

It is a privilege to appear on a panel with the key leaders who are shaping America's energy policy.

I want to take a minute to thank Congressman Barton for his years of hard work in trying to get the rules of the energy business right. He has been tireless in his work on energy issues, and I am honored to be here with him tonight.

I would also like to thank Chairman Wood for his Herculean efforts to improve the function of the wholesale energy marketplace. We have been working very closely with the chairman and his staff to develop a market design that can bring greater stability to the marketplace and advance the growth of wholesale competition.

And, of course, thank you to Erle Nye. Erle Nye is the immediate past chairman of Edison Electric Institute (EEI) and has been a key figure in shaping this industry for years. His leadership is the kind of leadership that our companies are showing all across the country. And I appreciate his deep level of service to the electric industry in Texas and in those other forty-nine states.

All of us have been working for years to get policies on energy right. The business and political landscapes are always hard to navigate, but this year is an exception—it is even harder than usual to predict where things are going.

Today, as it did throughout the last century, the shareholder-owned electric utility industry meets the nation's energy needs in the face of wide-ranging challenges. But today is perhaps the industry's most challenging time. We face sagging investor confidence in an economic downturn, at the very time the country needs to spur investment in new generation and transmission—and at the very time electric markets are struggling toward standardization and many are questioning the role and nature of competition in those markets.

Among the industry's shareholders—in Congress, the Federal Energy Regulatory Commission (FERC), the Securities and Exchange Commission (SEC), the state commissions, Wall Street, the Environmental Protection Agency, the Department of Energy, and society in general—the debates rage as to how to address those issues. Still, as Thomas Edison said, "restlessness and discontent are the first necessities of progress."

Electricity is truly the lifeblood of our economy. You probably do not realize it, but since 1980 electricity consumption has increased 72 percent. In the next ten years, our economy will require more than 100 new gigawatts (GW) of capacity. In order to ensure affordable and reliable electricity, support a recovering economy, and enhance national security, the country needs several things.

First, it needs policies that encourage new generation and take advantage of its many fuel resources. To meet projected demand, the new generation portfolio requires the flexibility of many resources. No one fuel can balance all our energy and environmental needs. Fuel diversity helps ensure reliability, efficiency, and self-sufficiency, benefiting both the economy and our national security. We need energy and environmental policies that enable the use of coal, nuclear, natural gas, and hydro and other renewables for electric generation.

The president's National Strategy and the comprehensive energy legislation being considered by Congress would address many of these generation issues. And they have broad support from both sides on the aisle. Another example of the kind of legislation we need is outlined in President Bush's Clear

Skies Initiative. These efforts will help to give the industry the level of certainty it needs to attract capital and be able to meet the nation's energy needs.

Second, our nation needs policies to encourage investment in transmission and expand a constrained system. Originally built for intrastate power delivery, the transmission grid has become a "superhighway" for interstate transactions. In the second quarter of 2002, transmission congestion was almost three times the level experienced during the same period in 1999.

Several policy changes can help us to expand the system to meet the nation's demands. The industry needs financial and tax incentives to build and maintain the transmission grid. Right now, transmission owners have longer depreciation rates for tax purposes than other energy providers and face stiff tax consequences if they sell or spin off transmission facilities. Only Congress can change this.

The siting of transmission lines by federal agencies should be streamlined. In cases where traditional siting approaches do not solve regional needs, Congress should give the FERC backstop authority. For its part, the FERC should give transmission owners the clear signal that they have the right of first refusal for the construction of new transmission capacity.

Third, we need a standard set of rules governing power markets on a regional basis that will provide for a more-robust wholesale electricity market. Well-functioning wholesale markets go hand in hand with transmission investment. The FERC's recent standard market design (SMD) Notice of Proposed Rulemaking has the goal of improving the operation of wholesale markets for the benefit of participants and consumers—and EEI supports major elements of it.

There are, however, significant regional differences in matters such as the extent of retail competition, generation reserves, past organization and uses of the grid, the role of various fuel sources such as hydro, and the extent of the development of competitive markets that affect the potential economic benefits of wholesale regional markets to ultimate customers that have caused SMD to be extremely controversial in many quarters. We are working very closely with Chairman Wood and the FERC to get this crucial piece of the puzzle right.

Fourth, Congress needs to address outdated laws that are inconsistent with a competitive wholesale market. A prime example of this is the Public Utility Holding Company Act (PUHCA). Formed in response to abuses by large holding companies in the 1920s, PUHCA now actually hinders investment, discourages new market entrants, complicates new business models, and works against well-functioning, competitive energy markets—it is poorly suited to today's national companies that operate in regional competitive markets. The Bush administration, as well as previous administrations, the SEC, and many others, have called for its repeal for years.

The Public Utility Regulatory Policy Act (PURPA) needs reform, as well. The PURPA's mandatory purchase obligation is inconsistent with the nature of competition and instead has cost electricity consumers billions of dollars by requiring utilities to lock into long-term power contracts at above-market prices.

In addition, the FERC must have authority to include nonjurisdictional utilities, including government and cooperatively owned systems in its oversight. This is essential to realizing the goal of a workable, nationwide, competitive wholesale market.

Perhaps most importantly, the industry needs to boost the confidence of the investment community. We are aggressively addressing key financial matters, working closely with the Financial Accounting Standards Board, the SEC, and other agencies as they focus on critical accounting standards, disclosure policies, and governance matters, including implementation of the Sarbanes-Oxley Act.

We promote enhanced voluntary financial disclosure from companies and welcome the proposal by chief risk officers of a new set of best practices for merchant energy activities. These guidelines are designed to provide more transparent and comparable financial information about the business and accounting practices of electric power companies, particularly how much risk investors face. By the same token, we are working to ensure that proprietary and competitive information is protected.

Congress can also help by passing President Bush's economic stimulus package that includes an end to the double taxation of dividends. Our industry pays out more in dividends than any other, and this adjustment would be a major boost to Wall Street's confidence in our industry.

As Congress pursues energy legislation, the FERC wrestles with the SMD, and we address investor concerns, this year will be critical for the industry. We are committed to working with legislators and regulators to ensure that public policies enable us to provide adequate electricity infrastructure for the nation and attract the investment capital necessary to accomplish this mission.

I really do believe in Thomas Edison's statement. "Restlessness and discontent" may be challenges, but they signal progress—indeed, they are necessities. This is the time to turn those challenges into opportunities. The ability to meet growth needs, to make markets work, and to restore investor confidence demand it. We can see the light at the end of the tunnel. And it's being powered by our industry.

Remarks by Joe Barton

The question of where electricity deregulation "goes from here" is a very timely question. It is one that the U.S. Congress, the Federal Energy Regulatory Commission (FERC), and the electricity industry are all trying to answer right now.

Just two days ago, the House Energy and Commerce Committee completed consideration of comprehensive energy legislation, including many electricity reforms. Our bill should move to the House floor next week. We will then await action from the Senate, and I know the Senate Energy and Natural Resources Committee is working hard to write its own bill for a future markup. Meanwhile, FERC Chairman Wood continues to revise his proposal for standardizing market design. As panel members and many in the audience know, Chairman Wood's proposal has created many after effects that have shaken our legislative process.

Lessons from Our Experience with Wholesale Competition

While we work on the legislative and regulatory processes to finish, events like these offer a good opportunity to stop and evaluate the big picture.

First, deregulating wholesale power markets has been a success for consumers as well as for the industry's efficiency and innovation. Competitive power production is a robust market today, and utilities that are transmission dependent have many more opportunities to purchase power than under the old scheme of only vertically integrated utilities. According to the Energy Information Administration, wholesale power prices declined by 23 percent from 1985 to 2000. Even when one takes into account the volatile price increases of 2001, the decline from 1985 is still 12 percent. Put another way, consumers' bills have been reduced by $13 billion on an annual basis. We must as a nation find ways to further this competition, because our economic competitiveness, national security, and way of life depend upon abundant, reliable, and affordable energy, including electricity.

Second, it remains clear that wholesale competition will only succeed to the extent that transmission markets allow it. Transmission growth has not kept pace with electricity demand. Our current transmission infrastructure was never built for the purpose of moving large quantities of power across long distances. It simply cannot perform this function in an efficient manner until we supplement with new transmission facilities and technologies. Where transmission congestion exists, the benefits of wholesale deregulation are reduced, in some cases drastically. The Department of Energy's (DOE) National Transmission Grid Study in 2002 identified twenty-one eastern and fifteen western paths congested more than 10 percent of the year. Around one-third of all transmission paths are congested at some point this year.

Third, our nation's electricity industry may be the best in the world, but it is hurting today. The shareholder-owned electric utility sector lost $78.3 billion in market capitalization between December 2000 and December 2002, a 23.9 percent drop over two years. The independent power-producing sector fared even worse, with several merchant power companies losing more than 90 percent of their market capitalization. At the same time, many credit ratings have plummeted as rating agencies seek to understand this complex sector. This double pain of stock prices and credit ratings has crippled the ability of generators to invest in new generation and transmission.

Where to Go from Here?

Today, there is tremendous uncertainty about this industry's future, and that itself holds this industry back. At a recent Energy and Air Quality Subcommittee hearing on electricity, Department of Energy Deputy Secretary Kyle McSlarrow put it well:

> Developments in the electricity industry in recent years have brought the industry to a crossroads. While the move to competitive markets has fostered enormous benefits, some serious problems have given rise to a significant policy debate, especially over the past two years. We have three basic policy choices:
>
> - First, go back to comprehensive rate regulation for wholesale power sales. Have the FERC set regulated rates for each jurisdictional utility. Abandon reliance on market forces and competition as the underpinning of federal electricity policy.
> - Second, maintain the status quo. Defer making decisions on major policy issues. Continue to straddle the fence.
> - And third, complete the transition to effective competition in wholesale power markets.
>
> Going back to comprehensive rate regulation is not really an option. Too much has happened, and too much has changed. The process of change introduced into electricity markets by past federal and state policies is probably irreversible.

House Electricity Legislation

Legislation before the House today will put our nation on a forward path toward better electricity markets. It should further the transition to more-effective markets. Its goals can generally be described as in the following: Legislation before the House today will put our nation on a forward path toward better electricity markets. It should further the transition to more effective markets. Its goals can generally be described as

1. Increasing transmission capacity
2. Improving transmission operation
3. Furthering wholesale competition

I would like to outline the goals of the legislation and the major elements that pursue those goals.

Increase Transmission Capacity

Our Transmission Infrastructure Improvement Rulemaking would promote needed investment in transmission by requiring a FERC rulemaking on the question of whether the FERC should grant further incentive rates for the construction of new transmission to alleviate congestion. I am pleased that the FERC has recently established a policy of incentive rates for participation in regional transmission organizations (RTOs) for voluntary divestiture of transmission assets to an independent company.

Our Siting of Interstate Electrical Transmission Facilities section expedites the construction of critical transmission lines identified by the DOE. For such lines, persons may obtain a permit from the FERC and exercise eminent domain if, after one year, a state is unable or refuses to site the line. We also try to improve the process across federal land. The DOE is designated as the lead agency for coordinating federal review and permitting processes, including establishing deadlines, coordination with states and tribes, and consolidating environmental reviews into a single record to serve as the basis for decisions. If a federal agency denies an application or fails to comply with a time frame established by the DOE, an applicant or state may appeal to the DOE to review the denial and/or take action within ninety days.

Improve Operation of Transmission

The Open Access Transmission By Certain Utilities provision would improve the flow of interstate power among utilities and regions and harmonize regulation of interstate transmission by granting the FERC partial jurisdiction over the interstate transmission of currently nonregulated utilities (municipally owned utilities, rural electric cooperatives, and federal utilities).

Our RTOs section explicitly authorizes the federal utilities (Tennessee Valley Authority, Bonneville Power Administration, and the other power marketing administrations) to participate in RTOs. It also expresses the sense of Congress that all transmission owners should be members of RTOs. Full participation in RTOs is critical to transmission markets.

We also have a reliability section in which the FERC is authorized to certify an electric reliability organization such as the North American Reliability Council (NERC) with the ability to develop, implement, and enforce reliability standards for the bulk-power system.

Furthering Wholesale Competition

We repeal the Public Utility Holding Company Act of 1935, while providing for federal and state access to certain books and records, which should end many restrictions on investment in the utility sector. We allow prospective relief from the PURPA mandatory purchase obligation under certain conditions. We direct the FERC to establish rules improving transparency in wholesale electric power markets. We prohibit round-trip trades of electric power with intent to distort prices. And we increase and expand criminal and civil penalties for violations of the Federal Power Act.

We make refunds for sales above "just and reasonable" rates effective back to the date of complaint. And we provide that all spot-market sales of wholesale power, including those by municipally owned utilities and cooperatives, are subject to FERC-ordered refunds for sales above just and reasonable rates. Finally, we provide that the FERC, before abrogating certain contacts in the future, must meet a public interest standard, unless the contract expressly provides for a different standard.

Finally, we require the DOE to study the concept of "economic dispatch" and report to Congress on any legislative recommendations. Using economic dispatch and including independent generation in dispatch procedures should help retail consumers enjoy lower rates by making sure that independent generation is purchased when it is the most economic and efficient option.

Legislative Attempts to Respond to the FERC Process

No legislator can pass his or her perfect plan. To get the votes of col-
leagues and win on the floor of the House or Senate, one must deal with those
who have different designs on legislation. We will need to resolve include how
Members from regions opposing the FERC's standard market design (SMD)
proposal wish to use the legislative process to impact the regulatory process.

Reflecting that reality, the House bill now includes a federal statutory protection of transmission capacity for "native load." We would require the
FERC to ensure that utilities serving electricity consumers are entitled to use
their transmission facilities or firm transmission rights to meet certain service
obligations and certain contractual obligations. We grandfathered five RTOs
and ISOs that have already dealt with this issue or are dealing with it now. This
provision and its exemptions will be an important part of our process to watch
going forward. We must be careful to not go overboard and restrict needed
transmission capacity from the market when not necessary.

Also, some will want to prohibit the FERC from exercising jurisdiction
that it probably has today but has never exercised. As many of you know, the
same transmission lines simultaneously carry electrons regulated by the
FERC and electrons regulated by the states. In states that have not "unbundled" the transmission component from a retail sale, the state regulates that
transmission even if the power has come in from out of state. The FERC has
proposed to exercise jurisdiction over all transmission in its SMD proposal.
Some members of Congress would like to prohibit that from happening. I expect this question will be front and center during the Senate Energy Committee's consideration of electricity policy. This is a complex issue that has
sympathies on both sides. We must not get it wrong.

Conclusion

We cannot put the wholesale competition genie back in the bottle. Nor
should we. The impact upon consumers has been dramatic. Certainly, the experience of flawed state plans, tight transmission markets, and insufficient
supply of power in the West has made electricity competition look bad. But
the answer is to move forward toward better competition. Congress can do its
part by focusing on transmission capacity, operation of transmission, and removal of barriers to competition. Hopefully, "where we go from here" is toward a seamless national grid of the twenty-first century that can further our
economy and make us all proud.

***

REFERENCES

Joskow, Paul L., and Richard Schmalensee. 1983. *Markets for power: An analysis of electric utility deregulation*, 212. Cambridge, MA: MIT Press.
McMillan, John. 2002. *Reinventing the bazaar: A natural history of markets*, ix. New York: WW Norton & Co.

NOTES

Pat Wood III is chairman of the U.S. Federal Energy Regulatory Commission; Robert Gramlich assisted in the preparation of his paper. Thomas R. Kuhn is president of Edison Electric Institute. Joe Barton is a congressman.

1. "Unlike state statutes granting utilities their franchises, there is no express obligation to serve wholesale customers under the Federal Power Act." Construction Work in Progress, Order No. 474, III FERC Stats. & Regs. ¶ 30,751 at 30,718 (1987). See also Promoting Wholesale Competition Through Open Access Nondiscriminatory Transmission Services by Public Utilities and Recovery of Stranded Costs by Public Utilities and Transmitting Utilities, FERC Stats. & Regs. ¶ 32,514 at 33,101 (1995).

Conclusion

Final Thoughts

James M. Griffin and Steven L. Puller

After reading the previous policymakers remarks, it seems clear that while electricity policy may proceed unevenly with fits and starts, it will continue in the direction of greater deregulation. The problem facing policymakers is which of the various paths marked "To Deregulation" should be followed. The alternative paths are numerous. Many paths contain large potholes and some are dead ends. Policy is often crafted in an economic vacuum, but it is never crafted in a political vacuum. The stakes are enormous, the issues complex, and the eventual outcome uncertain. The goal is to design wholesale and retail markets that send the proper price signals on the value of adding new generation and transmission assets. The road toward that goal has important warning signs. What warning signs do the economists have to offer in choosing among the various paths marked "To Deregulation"?

The first road sign should warn that electricity has unique characteristics different from other successfully deregulated industries, such as natural gas production, airlines, and long-distance phone service. Therefore, standard prescriptions for deregulation simply don't apply. Unlike most goods, electricity cannot be stored in buffer inventories, so supply must equal demand at every instance. The combination of lack of storage and low-demand elasticity make for a market where a single firm can wield substantial market power during periods of high demand. As a result, typical measures of industry concentration used in antitrust are not good indicators of the potential for market power. "Deregulation" does not involve simply removing the existing regulatory infrastructure. Other regulatory institutions must be in place, and some market oversight is still required. In fact, many electricity economists eschew the term electricity *deregulation*, preferring instead "electricity *restructuring*." Creating a competitive and efficient market is by no means a hands-off process.

Fortunately, several market design options can significantly mitigate this problem. First, if generators sell power in both long-term forward contract markets and in spot electricity auctions, the prices on average are likely to be lower than if all power were sold in the spot market. The importance of contracts should not be understated. Recent research suggests that a first-order determinant of prices is the amount of contracts that generators face. "Contracts" is a general concept that incorporates any mechanism by which a generator is obligated to sell some portion of its capacity at a price that is independent of the spot price. Contracts can take several forms including bilateral sales, the obligation to serve incumbent load at regulated prices, or a policy which grants market-based rate authority contingent on generators signing long-term contracts at prices near long-run marginal cost. Second, if a substantial portion of consumers face the real-time price of electricity, they will have incentives to reduce consumption during price spikes. The additional demand elasticity can substantially reduce prices during peak-demand periods and help alleviate the problem of market power.

The second road sign warns that electricity restructuring must assure adequate reserve capacity to meet peaks in demand or unanticipated plant outages. By its very nature, reserve capacity is seldom used, so to recoup the investment costs during these periods, prices occasionally may have to rise to high levels. If market monitors and policymakers are unable to distinguish whether high prices reflect scarcity rents or the exercise of market power, price caps or bid mitigation practices may dull signals to invest in new generation capacity. Therefore, despite the fact that energy markets theoretically can provide the proper signals for investment, additional markets for reserve capacity may be required.

The final warning sign should address the question of how new transmission decisions should be made. Most analysts believe there is some role for regulated transmission investment and some role for merchant transmission. There is, however, substantial debate on where the line should be drawn. It is difficult to imagine significant upgrades to the grid that do not involve substantial externalities between generation and transmission. Currently, many incumbent generators own their own transmission lines and right-of-ways. Their incentives to alleviate congestion may well be minimal. As a result, private and social incentives to invest are unlikely to be aligned, requiring regulators to be major players in future transmission investment decisions.

Author Index

Subject Index

ACAP. *See* Available capacity (ACAP)

Adequacy, 388, 389–90

Aggregate bidding data, 303–4

Ancillary services markets, ERCOT and, 205

Antitrust policies, U.S., 258, 301

Automated mitigation procedures (AMPs), 272

Available capacity (ACAP), 403–4

Averch-Johnson effect, 236, 238, 249, 421

Balancing and Settlement Code, 129

Balancing energy market, ERCOT and, 193–94

Behavior rules, 270–72

Benchmarking studies, of electricity markets, 304–5

Benefits, of wholesale competition, 416–17

Bertrand models of competition, 274

Bidding data, aggregate, 303–4

Bilateral contracts, 52–53

Bilateral energy markets, 191–93

Blackouts, 6

Boston Edison Company, 228

British Coal, 122–23

British Energy, 101, 134

British Gas, 100, 114, 120

British Telecommunications (BT), 100

Build-your-own (BYO) baseline, real-time pricing with, 336–37

California: Cournot model of electricity market in, 289–90; electrical market structure in, 276–78; fundamental enabler of supplier market power in, 166–69; impact of contracts or utility ownership of divested units in, 284–85; impact of demand elasticity in, 285–87; impact of further divestiture in, 280–84; long-term generating capacity and, 73; market features of, enabling unilateral market power, 152–54; retail prices in, 91

California electricity crisis (2000–2001), 22, 32, 147–54; events leading up to, 154–58; FERC and, 269–70; FERC's response to, in summer and autumn of 2000, 162–65; FERC's response to evidence of substantial market power in, 165–66; introduced, 145–47; lessons learned from, 174–78; overview of, 158–62; recommended changes in FERC's regulatory oversight of wholesale market in, 178–80; regulatory dispute that led to, 169–71; restructuring initiatives and, 251; solution to, 171–74

439